DELL DIAMOND

Published in hardback	November 1998
Reprinted	December 1998
	and August 2001
First published in paperback	April 2004

Published by
HAGIOLOGY PUBLISHING
170 Westbury Road
Bristol BS9 3AH

ISBN 0-9534474-4-8

Designed and typeset by Perry Associates, Bristol
Printed and bound in Great Britain by The Bath Press

DELL DIAMOND

Ted Bates's 66 seasons with The Saints

DAVID BULL

in association with
SOUTHAMPTON FOOTBALL CLUB

&
Southern Daily Echo

This paperback edition
is dedicated to the memory of
Edric Thornton Bates MBE
3 May 1918 – 26 November 2003

TED BATES.

The cover photograph was taken at The Dell by Mike Atkelsky, for Southampton FC, on 30 December 2000, when it was announced that Ted Bates had been appointed MBE in the New Year's Honours list.

The back-cover photograph was taken by *The Southern Daily Echo* on the 60th anniversary of Ted Bates's arrival at The Dell. He is seen presenting the *Player of the Year* award to Egil Østenstäd.

DAVID BULL saw his first game at The Dell in 1948 but soon left his native Salisbury to become in turn a Camberley teenager, an Exeter student and a university teacher in Exeter, Manchester and Bristol. Qualified as a barrister in 1990, for the sole purpose of chairing tribunals (initially Social Security, though now mainly Disability, appeals) in his early retirement – which he does as an occasional time-out from working on histories of Southampton FC. Having written for the Saints Matchday Programme – in three spells since 1981 – and for three Southampton fanzines, he edited two collections of fans' memories (1992 and 1994), as fund-raisers for the Child Poverty Action Group, in which he has long been an activist. Helped to launch Hagiology Publishing in 1998, with the original publication of *Dell Diamond,* since when he has contributed editorially to three further Hagiology titles (as listed on the inside back-cover) and edited Matthew Le Tissier's Testimonial Programme – all of which has caused the repeated postponement of his biography of Terry Paine.

Contents

Ted Bates

Address by Rupert Lowe, Southampton FC Chairman, at the funeral of Ted Bates, 9 December 2003.

The year 2003 has seen two gatherings of the family of Southampton Football Club. Firstly on 17 May at the Millennium Stadium for the FA Cup Final and, secondly, today to say goodbye to Ted Bates. There is a tangible element of sadness to both, but I firmly believe that we should treat the two events as celebrations. Leaving behind 17 May, I want to say a few words on behalf of the Club to celebrate, rather than mourn, Ted and the 66 wonderful years' service that he gave to our Club.

I was privileged to know Ted for seven years, during which time I came to understand his immense contribution to laying the foundations for what the Club has become today. He never lost his ability to judge a player with incisive accuracy, whether it was in a first team game or while watching the Reserves at Marchwood. He could summarise a game or a player in one simple sentence and a polite enquiry as to how much we had paid for a player indicated that it may well have been too much. At the other end of the scale, Ted equally epitomised the family values which prevail at our Club when he habitually carried out the role of Father Christmas at the annual children's Christmas party, dressed in an ill-fitting red suit with a cotton-wool beard. His eyes always twinkled and the children inevitably enjoyed themselves.

I believe the foundations laid by Ted from which our success has flowed are based upon three overriding principles:

Service: Ted's 66 years as player, manager, director and President stand out as a monument in the game and as an example to everyone within the game. It is proof that true success is not founded on a short-term 'flash in the pan' but requires unselfish, and often unappreciated, dedication over a long period of time.

Loyalty: Modern football is lucky to have any number of participants who have made a life-time contribution to the game. However, only very few clubs are privileged enough to have someone like Ted who has given a lifetime to just one club.

Integrity: Even football's greatest friend would not pretend that the bedrock of our game is integrity. Today's game is sadly hall-marked by financial mismanagement, and worse, in direct contrast to the manner in which Ted conducted himself over his lifetime in football. The position of the game's curator of honesty and decency is now vacant.

I would like to thank Mary and all of Ted's family for allowing him to make 66 years of his life available to the Club. No one should underestimate the love and support necessary from a family in such a demanding and intrusive industry as football. Ted's achievements reflect well on them.

In the early days of my career at The Dell, much of our business was conducted beneath a photograph captioned 'Ted Bates showing poise, posture and balance'. It is thanks to David Bull, our Club Historian, that so much is now known of Ted's unique and successful career.

There are two short passages I would like to share with you, both of which have relevance to Ted's eminent career. The first is from *The Prophet* by Kahlil Gibran on 'giving' – which reminds me of Ted, a 'true giver':

> *Then said a rich man, 'Speak to us of Giving'.*
> *And he answered: you give but little when you give of your possessions.*
> *It is when you give of yourself that you truly give.*
> *For what are your possessions but things you keep and guard for fear you may need them tomorrow?*
> *And tomorrow, what shall tomorrow bring to the over-prudent dog burying bones in the trackless sand as he follows the pilgrims to the holy city?*
> *And what is fear of need but need itself?*
> *Is not dread of thirst when your well is full, thirst that is unquenchable?*
> *There are those who give little of the much which they have – and they give it for recognition and their hidden desire makes their gifts unwholesome.*
> *And there are those who have little and give it all.*
> *These are the believers in life and the bounty of life, and their coffer is never empty.*
> *There are those who give with joy, and that joy is their reward.*
> *And there are those who give with pain, and that pain is their baptism.*
> *And there are those who give and know not pain in giving, nor do they seek joy, nor give with mindfulness of virtue;*
> *They give as in yonder valley the myrtle breathes its fragrance into space.*
> *Through the hands of such as these God speaks, and from behind their eyes He smiles upon the earth.*

The second is some wise counsel from the great Winston Churchill:

> *Let us build wisely,*
> *let us build surely, let us build faithfully,*
> *let us build for the years that are to come, and so establish here below*
> *what we hope to find above – a house of many mansions,*
> *where there shall be room for all.*

Goodbye Ted and thank you for everything that you have done for Southampton Football Club.

Foreword

by Terry Paine MBE

They tell me I played 778 games for Ted Bates – and that's not counting summer jaunts and all the other 'unofficial' fixtures.

Playing for the same manager from March 1957 to November 1973 gave me plenty of insights into the many attributes and idiosyncrasies of Ted – as a manager and a person. So I was delighted to learn that a Saints' fan was putting together the story of Ted's first 60 seasons at The Dell and feel privileged to be asked to contribute this foreword.

You could call it a 'fairy tale', the way Ted took us, from the Third Division to Europe – except that it was commitment and hard work that got him there.

He did it with a youth policy that brought an unusually high number of players through to a professional career – 12 from one Youth team cohort, including John Sydenham and myself.

He did it with a shrewdness in the transfer market that often bordered on daylight robbery. 'Been up to your Dick Turpin tricks again?', I'd ask him.

It is so appropriate that he is now President of the Club that he built. What he's done for Southampton FC, starting on next to no money, is equal to what Matt Busby, Bill Nicholson and Bill Shankly did at their clubs.

And he did it with his feet firmly on the ground. Never more so than the night we 'won' promotion to Division One – *provided* we could avoid losing our final game by six goals. Raising his glass to me, Ted said 'Terry, I'm drinking champagne but I'm not celebrating'.

Well, it's about time you did celebrate, Ted. You've plenty to celebrate in your 60-odd seasons with the Saints and I'm thrilled that this foreword position makes me the first to raise my glass to you and say …

'*Well done!*' and '*Congratulations!*'

Preface

'We're not up here for fun, you know'.

That one-liner by Ted Bates, when I accosted him one Friday evening in
Manchester in the late 1960s, had been the sum of our acquaintance – until
April 1995, when I sat with him in the Dell carpark, where he'd played so
many games of head-tennis, discussing how I might go about recording the
story of his first 60 seasons with the Saints.

Having noticed that his 60th anniversary would be due on 3 May
1997, I had long been muttering to friends on the journey from Bristol to
home games that somebody should write a book about it. And I'd rather
fancy being that somebody.

The encouragement of my most regular companions on the A36 –
Dave Adlem and Barrie Bedford – was not, I'm afraid, convincing. Their
memories went back a long way – Barrie had even seen Ted Bates play –
and I suspected there might be a few other over 50s who'd want to read
about Ted Bates's loyal stint at The Dell. But would younger fans give a
damn about a man who had finished an undistinguished playing career in
1952 and whose management feats, from 1955 to 1973, were rather less
well-known than those of his successor?

It was going to a game with Alan Tonge, a mere twenty-something who
was editing the Southampton fanzine, *Red Stripe,* that made up my mind.
Alan persuaded me to be less defensive. As I recall – research of this kind
makes you very wary of memory loss, I can tell you – his reaction was along
the lines of we're all familiar enough with the record of Ted Bates to know
that his story is a 60-year history of the Saints; that's a story that would
appeal to fans of all ages; it would best be written, though, by a fan whose
own memories went back over a lot more of those 60 seasons than his did;
so, if anybody was going to do it, I should. Flattery will get you a lift home
to Bristol.

I hope this is the kind of book Alan had in mind – in two respects.

First, I hope it manages to be fairly biographical about Ted Bates –
which is why my interviewees included his sisters, Betty McTaggart and
Alice Webber – *and* something of a history of the Club during his 60
seasons there. The two approaches are distinguishable if, say, you're writing
a biography of somebody who's played for three clubs and managed as
many again. With Ted Bates, though, the two blur – which is why, of
course, I wanted to research and write this story in the first place. What I

felt I was trying to do, ultimately, was to write about 'The Life and Times of Ted Bates' – which, as I recall from watching *Mastermind* – means that I am justified in putting one person's career into a context in such a way that, sometimes, the context itself becomes the story.

Either way, the story was always going to be front-loaded. Even if Ted's involvement after 1973 is so much greater than I had imagined, Chapter 26 was bound to be something of a gallop through the last 25 years, using only snippets from some interesting discussions of what has happened to the Club in the 1990s.

Never mind! Gary Chalk and Duncan Holley are working on a major tome that will collate and update their two invaluable reference books on Southampton FC – *Saints: a complete record* and *The Alphabet of the Saints* – and they have asked me to bring to it the volume of surplus material that I have acquired.

Secondly, in respect of an outcome worthy of the man from *Red Stripe,* I hope this book will indeed be acceptable across generations of Saints' supporters. I was so encouraged, in this regard, when Ted Bates was announced to the crowd at The Dell, on 3 May 1997, and came out to make the *Player of the Year* award on his *Dell Diamond Day* – a moment captured on the back cover.

~

The ovation that he received underlined what I had been learning during a most privileged journey of discovery: Ted Bates was a much more esteemed figure – among fans and footballers – than I had ever imagined. I'd wanted to write a book about the magnitude of his achievement, but had been finding out about the magnitude of the man.

It is, I guess, the lot of the unwary biographer to discover that his or her hero suffers from closer inspection. My mystery tour has taken me in the opposite direction, forever running into expressions of admiration and affection. I was repeatedly told that Ted had never said a bad word against anybody. And his former secretary, Barbara Oakshott, could not countenance that I would hear a bad word against him. I did, though. And I appreciate that I might have heard a few more from one or two of those who would not speak to me.

Characteristically, though, Ted was pleased to hear of criticisms emerging. The last thing this honest man wanted was a whitewashing eulogy. Even so, I wondered about repeating the tittle-tattle discussed in Chapter 7 (and to which I return briefly in Chapter 14). These tales seemed to me, and to the majority of those friends with whom I shared a draft, to address two aspects of how football folklore develops: irrational explanations are bound to be advanced for one player being preferred, in the first team, to another – the moreso, perhaps, before football became a 14-a-side game; and fans who've never really expected (well, I haven't) to know the half of what goes on in the dressing room always had a way – before journalists began to invent the stories – of making do with the most unlikely gossip.

Ted's strong feelings on such national journalists are vented in Chapter 21. I had no idea that this affable man had strong feelings on anything as we sat in the carpark three-and-a-half years ago, although his enthusiasm was instantly apparent – often coming across with more chuckling than I would have expected from that sombre fellow, shuffling along in a none-too-fashionable raincoat towards the Midland Hotel in Manchester, to assure me that his lads were not up there for fun.

~

I owe our meeting in the carpark – and much else – to the good services of the Club's Commercial Manager, John O'Sullivan, who had taken to the project, put it to the Board for approval and introduced me to Ted. That was to be the first of many meetings, over the next three-and-a-half years, at Ted's Chandlers Ford home, amid his heaps of memorabilia. Mary was invariably there to check Ted's stories and to tell me many of her own – having been Assistant Secretary at The Dell from 1945 to 1958, she has plenty of those.

In the meantime, I've talked to a lot of people Ted had played with or managed, or who might otherwise have a view on Ted Bates and his 60 seasons. I am grateful to all of those interviewees listed on the back cover. They include a few fans whose memories go back even further than mine. But they do not include the likes of Ken Griffin, Tom Kelly, Herbie Taylor and Richard Walker, to whom my enquiries have introduced me and with whom I've reminisced often, without ever getting out the cassette-recorder.

Apart from half-a-dozen listed contributors, whom I met incidentally and interrogated about particular games, most of the interviews were recorded by appointment – usually in the interviewee's home, except when I was asked to come to a hotel, café, golf club or workplace; or unless I arranged a rendezvous at The Dell or nearby (in a living room kindly provided by Roy and Sheila Beazley, Ruth and Nick Martin or Peggy and Monty Worlock). Three interviews were recorded over the 'phone and three on cassettes sent from overseas. One person – Terry Paine – came to me (and stayed seven hours, bless him) while Ron and Chris Davies kindly invited me to overnight with them in Florida.

The project needed lots of other overnights. I am grateful to my friends in the north – Flo and Tony Brady; Geoff and Annie Fimister; Norman and Barbara Hull, Graham Thompson and Brenda Toward – and to Mike and Maureen Stavrinides, my sister, in Fleet; to Peter Dunning and Maureen

Dunn in Devon; and to Joanne Rhone in Atlanta, for keeping me out of hotels. I was fortunate to have access to two bolt-holes: the London flat of my partner, Margaret; and a cottage in Brockenhurst, which Aidan Hamilton was keeping warm for me, while he wrote his book on Charles Miller (see Chapter 8) and kindly translated Brazilian newspapers for that chapter.

Although I never needed a bed in Southampton, I gladly exploited the drop-in facilities of Tessa Davies and Roly Smith and of Dave Juson, for refreshments. Dave kindly transcribed several interviews, a laborious task with which Norman Hull also helped, read draft chapters and was hugely supportive all-round.

~

Early in my enquiries, Dave wrote a fanzine article, commenting on the ways in which half-a-dozen of us with an interest in Southampton's history were sharing information. He liked to call us *hagiographers*. When I looked it up, I found this meant 'writers of saints' lives'. But I decided I preferred *hagiologists* – 'writers of saints' legends'. In September 1998, he and I met, in order to formalise this sharing arrangement, with Norman Gannaway and the two most important hagiologists of all, Gary Chalk and Duncan Holley, the Official Historians and Statisticians to Southampton FC. The outcome was Hagiology Publishing, a collective committed to producing accurate publications about the Club's history.

Accuracy is a scarce commodity in this field. Interviewing people about events long gone will produce a lot of inaccurate recall. With the two Chalk and Holley bibles always to hand, though, I was able, even as we talked, to correct many of the false memories: 'No, I'm sorry, you couldn't have blasted the winning goal in that game. You'd been out of the side for two months'.

Even so, I still recorded lots of erroneous information. I hope I have been able to correct most, if not all, of it – with the help of other reference books acknowledged at the end of this book and thanks to the checks run for me not only by Gary and Duncan, but by Dave Adlem, Mike Swain, Norman Gannaway, Tom Kelly, Mike Davage, Dick Middleton, Leigh Edwards and Ray Spiller. And I am indebted to two librarians for access and assistance: David Barber at the Football Association and Peter Ashton at the *Southern Daily Echo*.

And then there were the Board Minutes. The enthusiastic support of Guy Askham, the then Chairman, manifested itself in several ways, one of which was permission to see these Minutes – up until 1978, when Ted joined the Board. Access to the Minute Books was provided by Brian Truscott, who helped in several other ways; Malcolm (Woggy) Taylor, an all-round facilitator who found me a desk near the photo-copier; and by Cynthia Dowsett and Barry Fox.

The several people I interviewed at the Club are included in the alphabetical list on the back cover, but I want especially to thank John Mortimore, who took the trouble to ring some elusive people and introduce my mission. Otherwise, my principal sources of contacts were Gary Chalk, Duncan Holley and Roy Beazley – supplemented, here and there, by Bob Britten, Perry McMillan, Jean Thomasson, the Sunderland Supporters Association and a few others at The Dell.

I was also helped to find interviewees and/or generate subscribers by the willingness of Graham Hiley, Ian Henderson, Lee Peck and Rachel Read to publicise the book in their respective local outlets and by the co-operation and forbearance of John Hughes, Kim Lawford and Nikki Saunders as I kept using the Saints Matchday Programme to those ends. I am grateful to Rupert Lowe for suggesting that I attend his meeting with supporters, to talk about the book, and to Perry McMillan for inviting me, as a consequence, to address a SISA meeting.

~

It was always such a pleasure, when I rang to crave an interview, to be told that the man I was speaking to would do anything to be part of a tribute to Ted. Only four declined to participate. Don Roper and John Hoskins weren't interested. John Flood and Fred Kemp felt it would not be worth my while. Both David Webb and Steve Williams were willing to come aboard – but somehow we could never arrange an interview.

I do not intend to rehearse here the names of those to whom I spoke – unless I've forgotten somebody, they're all on the back cover. This story is both by them and about them. They *are* The Life and Times of Ted Bates. I am indebted to them for their time and consideration – and for their trust in permitting me to extract bits and pieces from transcripts that most of them had not vetted. My selection, from over 2,000 pages of transcripts, became less systematic, as deadlines loomed, than it might have been and I will have neglected a few gems. I apologise both to the story-tellers and to readers for such omissions.

I owe an extra round of thanks to all those interviewees who loaned me cuttings and photos:

Paul Bennett, Bill Bushby, Betty Channon, John Christie, Brian Clifton, Alf Creecy, George Curtis, Stan Cutting, Ron (Tudor) Davies, Frank Dudley, Bill Ellerington, Bryn Elliott, Tony Godfrey, Ernie Hayter, Winifred Kirkman, Wes Maughan, Doug McGibbon, Betty McTaggart, Ted Meech, Terry Paine, Pat Parker, Gerald Penn Barrow, Ron Reynolds, Albie Roles, Cyril Smith, Charlie Wayman, Alice Webber, Eric Webber, Steve White, Ken Wimshurst and Peggy Worlock.

The use of these sources presents two problems, one of citation, the other of acknowledgment. First, footballers and their families have an almost universal habit, it seems, of sticking cuttings into scrapbooks in a way that conceals both the date and the name of the newspaper. The former can invariably be deduced by reference to the *Complete Record,* but I'm afraid I'm not familiar with which reporter used to write for whom. I've coped, in the text, in a number of ways and only hope that I haven't used 'X told his readers that...' too often for your liking. Most of the match reports cited are from the *Echo* – a title I have used to refer both to the Saturday *Football Echo* (as I've never learned to stop calling it) and a weekday copy of the *Southern Daily Echo.* I have not reminded the reader, at every turn, that reporters in the *Echo* used to have names like Argus, Commentator and Observer.

Secondly, the copyright of photographs in players' personal collections is not always apparent. I could identify 40-odd of those I have used as being *Echo* originals and I am grateful for permission to reproduce these. Any history of the local football team is bound to be massively dependent upon photographs taken by the local newspaper and the *Echo* has been an unstinting support, in this regard, to the hagiologising achievements of Chalk and Holley. This source has afforded some excellent originals for the first half of this book and I hope that a subsequent tailing off, in the illustrations, will not be too disappointing for you.

Several of the later illustrations are from the Club's holdings – mostly taken by Mike Atkelsky, who has kindly allowed their reproduction – or from the private collections of friends mentioned elsewhere in this preface. The photo' of the 'special' train, in Chapter 17, is by Michael Mensing. The excerpt, in the same chapter, from an article by John Arlott, is used with the permission of Mrs Pat Arlott and the trustees of the estate of John Arlott deceased. If I have otherwise used copyright material without permission, I would be pleased to hear from the holder of the copyright.

Don Osmond kindly allowed me to use any of the OZ cartoons in the two scrapbooks of them that Dave Juson had loaned me. Ron Davies has not only permitted the reproduction of a couple of his drawings, but volunteered to create the expressive original of Ted Bates that appears as a frontispiece and again on page 321. I feel so privileged to have this beautiful illustration by Ron up front – where else? – followed by a foreword from his astounding supplier, Terry Paine.

I had imagined I'd use Ron's illustration on the cover – until the design of the book was taken over by Robert Walster. Sally Miller and he showed me how I should be going about hagiology publishing and pointed me, with Robert's beautifully re-worked cover [substituted for this edition], to

Perry Associates, who cheerfully took on the task of assembling my text and illustrations in what I consider to be a most elegant way. I hope you agree.

The idea for the layout comes from the style adopted by Polar Publishing. I had hoped, at one stage, to publish this book with Polar and am grateful to Julian Baskcomb for his encouragement to that end. But switching to our own self-publishing collective gave me more editorial freedom and a greater flexibility about deadlines.

~

Having obtained control over my deadlines, I then put myself under pressure when I fixed the date, with Paul Bennett – who has put so much effort into arranging it – for a meet-the-player launch. But, you might well ask, shouldn't this book have come out in 1997, anyhow? That was the original idea, but I would have needed to start a lot sooner and to give up my dayjob a lot earlier. And, then, having taken early retirement in December 1996 and started to increase the rate of interviewing, I should not have accepted a four-month position at East Carolina University for the autumn of 1997. That said, I am grateful to Gary Lowe and all of those at ECU who gave me the space – in the form of a not-too-demanding schedule and a quiet apartment – to sit and transcribe of an evening. As ever, the makers of American TV guaranteed that, once a riveting World Series was over, I would have absolutely no distractions from them. I also drove some 10,000 miles, across the USA, in fulfilment of my residual responsibilities at the University of Bristol – with diversions to meet David Chadwick, Eric Martin and, as I say, Ron Davies.

A great opportunity to listen, in my Buick, to recordings of all those interviews I'd conducted in the UK. But it all meant that I would need to hurry, upon returning to England, to finish interviewing, transcribing, reading Minutes and the rest – and then write the thing – in 1998.

Playing catch-up has involved me in putting pressure on other people in more ways than I can adequately acknowledge here. Harold Williams, Rebecca Coats and Barrie Bedford all performed clerical chores to improve the momentum. In the final stages, I have made unfair demands on Mark Perry, a consummate professional who could not have achieved his perfectionist standards of book design without working ridiculous hours to meet my deadline at the printers.

Margaret Coats, my partner, has been forced to tolerate a lot more for a lot longer, as the materials for the book spread across three storeys of our home and as the summer of 1998 came and went with the scheduled holiday cancelled and barely a moment of shared leisure.

I'm led to understand that football managers are used to such a life. Bert Head told me that it's not a job for a married man. How grateful we

Saints' fans must be, then, that Mary Bates put up with all of Ted's player-hunting in Scotland, with being abandoned on holiday while he completed a transfer in the area and the rest.

I am privileged to have had so much time with Ted and Mary over the past three years. They have been helpful and supportive beyond all reasonable expectations. If the two of them enabled me to understand so much more about the team I've supported for a few weeks short of 50 years, Mary also helped me to understand my previous meeting with Ted – it's no wonder, with her incessant sense of fun, that he didn't need to have any in Manchester.

David Bull   Bristol, October 1998

Preface to the paperback edition: Ted Bates died on 26 November 2003. Within days, I was being asked to re-supply shops with *Dell Diamond* and, when I explained that the third printing had sold out the week before, I was told I should re-print. Initially unimpressed by that suggestion, I thought again as the enquiries kept coming in the build-up to Christmas, including a call from one of Ted's managerial successors, keen to buy his father a copy.

Ours not to reason why he'd never thought of such a gift in the previous five years: what is it about a man's death that heightens interest in his life? The question is rhetorical. But might the answer be a paperback? That had never been an option, hitherto, for the Sales team at the club: there was a continuing need, they reckoned, for a hardback on the shelves of the Saints Stores, alongside Hagiology Publishing's two paperbacks: *Match of the Millennium* and *Full-Time at The Dell*. But now we had a new hardback – massively so in the form of *In That Number* – so we agreed that we should now go for a paperback version, with a new final chapter, charting and commemorating Ted's final years.

I imposed one condition: Ted's family would have to agree. When I duly visited Mary Bates, she welcomed the idea. So did older daughter Jo, who was present, and we began to discuss what family photos we might use. Provided younger daughter Jackie had no objection, we were on our way. She didn't and I returned to interview Mary, with assists from Jo. I also recorded interviews with Chairman Rupert Lowe (who also kindly agreed to the reproduction of his funeral address) and Vice-Chairman Brian Hunt, plus Bill Ellerington and John Mortimore. And I have checked pertinent facts and developments with Brendon Batson, Ivan Golac, Ian Gordon, Chris Newman and Terry Paine.

I am grateful to them all and to those who have supplied photographs, as credited below at page 333. Duncan Holley kindly processed these photos for reproduction and Mark Perry assembled them, as ever, in the text.

David Bull   March 2004

Chapter 1

Dell Boy

On Monday 3 May 1937, Tom Parker, the Southampton manager, was a man in a hurry.

The 1936-37 season had finished two days earlier and the side that he had come to manage in March had narrowly escaped relegation from the Second Division. So he had a close season overhaul to be getting on with. By the time the next season kicked off in August, Southampton would have 11 new professionals on their books.

The initial consignment arrived that first Monday in May, when Mr Parker completed three signings at nil cost. These included two Norfolk-born youngsters who had signed for him at Norwich, but who had been released and allowed to follow him to The Dell. Stan Cutting, a 22 year-old wing-half, had been interesting Chelsea. His younger companion, an inside-forward, had been watched by Arsenal. Edric Thornton Bates. Known to his family as 'Eddie' – as he is to this day to his sisters – he was increasingly known as 'Ted' in the game. Such nuances were lost on the *Southern Daily Echo* (hereinafter the *Echo*), which announced him as 'Edward' when he signed for the Saints on 3 May 1937. That was, coincidentally, Eddie's 19th birthday.

Stan and Eddie roomed together in Mrs Penny's lodgings at 32 Thornbury Avenue, off Howard Road. Locals, and those of us who drive in from the west of a match day and park in this vicinity, will not need telling that this part of Shirley is a very short walk from The Dell. But who among us could tell anybody what Southampton was like, overall, in the 1930s? The first stop on J.B. Priestley's *English Journey* of 1933, this south coast port had 'recently opened the largest graving dock in the world' …

> *The town was making money. At first I felt like a man who had walked into a fairy tale of commerce. The people … all seemed well-fed, decently clothed, cheerful, almost gay.*
>
> *… Not a bad town, this … here was a town that had not let the universal depression master it and that was contriving to enjoy its unique situation, between forest and heath and deep blue water, a lovely bay window upon the wide world. It was not bad at all.*

If the depression had generally escaped the town, it was hanging heavily over its local football team. Southampton Football Club was in a financial mess.

Mr Parker reported on the players who had not yet resigned and remarked that H.R. Conner had since been placed on the Open to Transfer List at £500.

He reported that he had signed A. Day, Welsh International, from Millwall (S. Cutting, wing half) and E. Bates, inside forward, from Norwich.

He explained the dire need of another centre forward in the eventuality of J. Dunne not resigning, it was agreed to obtain the transfer of W. Dunn, from Brentford, and that the Chairman and Secretary should obtain the best terms for payment.

Mr Parker reported his inability to sign Mc Carthy

MR. TOM PARKER, the Saints' manager, has started his close season signings. He tells me that he has signed three new players, Alfred Day, Stanley Cutting, and Edward Bates.

Cutting and Bates are young players who were with Mr. Parker when he was at Norwich. Cutting, a Norfolk County player, has played well in the Norwich City Reserve side as an amateur, and Chelsea had become very interested in him. He stands 5ft. 9in. and weighs 11st. 7lb. He is a right-half.

Bates, an inside-forward, from Thetford, Norfolk, is the son of Bates, the former Glamorgan County cricketer. He celebrated his 19th birthday to-day. Arsenal had been watching him, but Mr. Parker stepped in first. Bates has built up his game well for a youngster, and has useful physique —5ft. 9in. in height, 10st. 7lb.

Birthday Beginning: Eddie Bates (whom the local *Echo* was determined to call 'Edward') signs for the Saints on his 19th birthday – 3 May 1937 – as formally noted in the Board Minutes of 6 May.

So much so that, in June 1936, the Board asked the manager, George Kay, either to give, or to accept, three months' notice. 'The reasons for dispensing with his services', the Chairman stressed, were 'financial'.

George Kay, who had captained West Ham United in the famous 'White Horse' Cup Final of 1923, had come to manage Southampton in May 1931. He had no money to spend – not even when he sold his young stars. Ted Drake fetched a fee of £6,000 in 1934 – of which £250 was left when the bills had been paid. With no prospects of buying players, he introduced the club's first 'nursery' side. It was coached by Bert Shelley, who had retired in 1932 after 12 years as a first-team player at The Dell, in which he had created an appearance record (which Tommy Traynor would break in 1964) of 448 games. Promoted to first-team coach and trainer in 1935, he was very much part of the directors' plans for restructuring.

But when Mr Kay promptly secured a position as manager of Liverpool, he scuppered those plans by taking Shelley with him to Anfield. While this pair was heading for success – Liverpool would win the First Division in 1947 and reach the Cup Final in 1950 – the Southampton directors had to find a new managerial structure. The team captain, John McIlwaine, would coach the first and second teams, while the Secretary, George Goss, would assume the other managerial duties. It was nine months before they appointed a more appropriate successor to Mr Kay although the title of Secretary-Manager would remain. There were said to be 120 applicants but only three were interviewed. These included two active managers: Percy Smith of Bristol Rovers; and the unanimous choice of the Board, Tom Parker of Norwich City.

Right-back Parker had played 275 times for his native Southampton between 1919 and 1926 and once for England. Like Shelley, he was in Southampton's losing semi-final side of 1925, when he scored an own-goal and missed a penalty in the 2-0 defeat by Sheffield United. In 1927, though, when the Saints and Shelley again went out in the semi-final – this time to Arsenal – Parker was on the winning side, having left The Dell for Highbury in the meantime. And he was twice back at Wembley as Arsenal's captain – in 1930 as a winner and in 1932 as a victim of Newcastle's famous 'over-the-line' goal. He retired in 1933 to become manager of Norwich City, who won promotion to Division II in his first season at The Nest.

~

Tom Parker had been responsible for taking the teenage Bates to Norwich, that 'grand, higgledy-piggledy, sensible old place', where Priestley's journey through a depressed England had ended. Norfolk's county town is some 30 miles from the market town of Thetford where Eddie had been born on 3 May 1918, the eldest child – Betty was to follow in 1920 and Alice in 1928 – of William Ederick ('Eddie') Bates and his wife, Florence Eva (née Taylor). Eva, as she was known, had two brothers and a sister, all living in Thetford, with or near their parents.

To listen to the three children of Mr and Mrs W.E. Bates describing their parents' First World War courtship and marriage is like listening to a reprise of Thomas Hardy's *Far From The Madding Crowd*, with Eva, the ingenuous country girl, being overwhelmed by a dashing young sergeant, a sophisticate who had stopped by in 1917.

Sgt Bates of the Royal Engineers had stopped by from the trenches. For First World War soldiers recuperating from the Front, one of the rest camps was at Elveden, near Thetford. This well-travelled man was more than just a soldier, though. He had been a professional footballer – two games at centre-forward for Bolton Wanderers in Division I in 1906-07 and a further 15, mostly as a full-back, over the next two seasons for Leeds City in Division II. And, now 33, he was still a professional cricketer. Having failed to win a regular place with his native Yorkshire, during 1907-13, he had joined Glamorgan, then still a Minor County, in 1914.

W.E. Bates of Glamorgan: This all-round sportsman was celebrated in cigarette cards, not only as a cricketer in the Wills's 1928 series (with spellings that differ from those recorded by the family) but also, it is alleged, in an earlier Spiro Valleri set of 'Noted Fooballers' (so rare that individual cards are catalogued at £250 each).

DELL DIAMOND

His father had been rather more successful with Yorkshire: Billy Bates is among those players who have scored a century and taken 10 wickets in a match (against Derbyshire at Leeds in 1886) and 'would have been the greatest all-rounder of his time', according to W.G. Grace, 'if his fielding had matched his batting and bowling'. It was only that 'lack of certainty in his catching', *Wisden* insists, 'that prevented him being chosen in this country to play for England against Australia'.

Billy Bates of Yorkshire and England:
'The greatest all-round player of his time' – if you overlooked his fielding.

Bates with the Urn:
A record-making all-round feat, by Billy Bates in Melbourne in 1883, helped Ivo Bligh's team to come home with the Ashes – with the name 'Bates' suitably central in the inscription on the urn:

When Ivo goes back with the urn, the urn
Studds, Steel, Read, Tylecote return, return
The welkin will ring loud,
The great crowd will feel proud,
Seeing Barlow and Bates with the urn, the urn
And the rest coming home with the urn.

Such shortcomings in the field mattered not, it seems, when England were down under: Billy Bates won all 15 of his England caps in five successive tours of Australia from 1882 to 1887 – with a batting average of 27.33 and 50 wickets at 16.42 apiece. He even took nine catches. His repeated selection to tour Australia brought especial pleasure – we're told in *The Complete Who's Who of Test Cricketers* – to the King of the Sandwich Islands, who habitually required this 'fine vocalist' to sing 'The Bonny Yorkshire Lass'. His cricketing career was prematurely ended by an accident in the nets at Melbourne in 1887, but not before his name had been inscribed on The Ashes urn, with which the touring side of 1882-83 returned. The second Melbourne Test of that series has become known as 'Billy Bates's match' – for reasons captured by David Frith in his records of *England versus Australia:*

The Yorkshireman, coming in at the fall of the seventh wicket at 199 [in England's innings of 294], dominated a stand of 188 ... Then, coming on as England's fifth bowler, he ... proceeded to decimate Australia. The crescendo of Bates's success came as he bowled McDonnell, caught-and-bowled Giffen next ball, then bluffed Bonnor out for the hat-trick ... In the follow-on ... Bates's slow-medium roundarm bowling, breaking appreciably from the off, was again too much for the home batsmen. His 14 wickets linked with a half-century is a unique distinction in a Test match against Australia. For his hat-trick, admirers presented him with £31 and a tall hat made of silver.

But, then, you'd have known Billy Bates was the first Englishman to take a Test hat-trick, if you were following carefully, in the summer of 1995, when the BBC flashed onto your screen the short list of his successors that Dominic Cork has just joined.

Alice, who'd enjoyed seeing that TV roll of honour headed by the grandfather she never knew – Billy Bates had died, aged 44, in 1900 – sadly recalls the doomed marriage of her mother to a father she barely knew:

I don't think they were terribly suited. My Mum was very much the country girl. She didn't really want to move away or travel ... My father was a more sophisticated man. He travelled a lot ... I suppose, in the war, six months [recuperation in Norfolk], he was going back in the trenches and they might not see each other again – the sort of thing you get in war-time. I don't think young people at that stage ever think ahead to the future.

It was a future that did not require Eva to follow her husband once peace and cricket were resumed. This 'very home-loving person' was not 'cut out', Betty feels, 'to be the wife of a professional cricketer' – a professional cricketer who would travel the country, returning only periodically during the summer, to his family in Norfolk. His son recalls him arriving once in an open-top Morris Cowley – 'nobody had cars in those days' – but none of his children can remember his being there very much, even in the winter, save that his rare visits were devoted to the local golf course.

In 1921, Glamorgan became a first class county. The best season for W.E. Bates, their opening batsman, was 1927, when – at the age of 43 – he set a record aggregate for his adopted county of 1,575 runs, at an average of 45.00, including a century in each innings against Essex at Leyton and an undefeated double century against Worcester at Kidderminster. His family eventually followed him to Glamorgan. But not the whole family. Betty was 'the little parcel who was left behind' in Thetford with her grandparents, while 11 year-old Eddie and baby Alice moved with their mother to Cardiff.

DELL DIAMOND

Begging Betty's absence, this was, for her brother, the only time that they ever 'lived as a family'. The arrangement was short-lived, though long enough for young Eddie to represent Cardiff Schools at football and to watch his father at Cardiff Arms Park, where Glamorgan then played, and at Swansea:

> He used to take me to watch games whenever he could ... I used to like to watch him play cricket ... Quite a good bat. Aggressive player – he used to get runs. A nice slow, left-arm bowler. I watched him quite a lot when I lived in Cardiff ... That was when I got really interested in cricket ... I think if I'd had a chance, then I'd have had a go at cricket, too, because I used to love cricket. And he could have coached me, spent a lot more time with me if he'd had a chance, I think. He never had enough time for me. He was always involved. Cricket was his world. He was a real, old-fashioned cricketer. I never really got that close to him. If I had, I'd have been a professional cricketer.

So there! The son who missed out on a cricketing career would spurn further opportunities when he was 30 and thereabouts – as we shall see. Meanwhile, back in Cardiff, his parents' 'up and down' relationship was coming to an end. Eva returned, with Alice and Eddie, to Thetford. After a while, she was off again, to Victoria Grove, Stoke Newington, to stay with her sister Alice, whose husband, Will, had also been at the rest camp.

Eddie went with her. His father stopped by and he went to watch him at Lord's and The Oval. And he saw his first game of professional football at Highbury: 'Alex James was playing and he's always been a sort of *hero* of mine'. Then it was back to Thetford, to the privations of life without their father, who was gone for ever, never to see his family again – having retired in 1931, he held various coaching positions in Ireland and died in Belfast in 1957. Betty finds it 'incredible', to this day, that he could have had 'three children and not really worry what became of them'. Alice and she both recall how Eddie and they managed without the male breadwinner, thanks to the hard work of their mother and the presence of their grandparents. According to Alice, their mother

> always said that if she hadn't had good parents, she could never have left my father. My grandfather was a bricklayer and he had regular employment in those days – which was quite something. He had some pretty rotten jobs but he had steady employment ... Mum worked at St Barnabas Hospital on the outskirts of the town. It had been the old workhouse ... She worked there in the laundry, to begin with, and then eventually she went into nursing. She nursed for many years. Not as a qualified nurse – they called them auxiliaries.

She'd got plenty of courage, had my Mum. Basically, we were her concern ... She just worked for us and looked after us. And that was her whole world. When I look back, I think 'Gosh! She was a young woman then and she didn't have any life of her own, really'. It was just going to work, coming home, going to work the next day, and all the pleasure she got was from us. We meant an awful lot to her.

Second Class: Eddie is fourth from the left, in the third row from the front, at Thetford Infants.

Country Cousins: The three Bates children, on the River Ouse, with their London cousins. In the 2-4 formation, Alice is to the fore, with Betty front right and Eddie back right.

First Born: Sgt W.E. (Eddie) Bates with Eva and Eddie junior.

So it is that the three Bates children can look back on a 'very happy' childhood: 'We had good times', Alice recalls. 'We had to make our own pleasures, which were mostly down by the river. Looking back, the summers were always sunny – long, hot summer days. I'm sure they weren't, but I can't remember the rain ... We used to spend hours down by the river'.

Betty has similar memories of idyllic summers, 'swimming and playing cricket, picnics and things like that', summers when the three of them entertained their three cousins from Stoke Newington. And the teenage Eddie fished in the River Ouse from his grandfather's punt – often at night for eels, which meant fishing needn't compete with day-time sports:

DELL DIAMOND

Opposite our house – where I lived in St Nicholas Street – there was a couple of big wooden doors … I used to get out there quite a lot, kicking up against the doors, two-footed … We used to go down by the River Ouse – only about 10 minutes' walk. I used to get friendly with the boy who'd got the best ball and we used to get down there. And we used to play up the Green at Brandon Road. And then, as I was getting into my teenage years, I used to play cricket.

Apart from caddying at the golf club on Sundays and helping out in the fields, it seems to have been mostly play for young Eddie, at the expense of his studies at Thetford Elementary School: 'All my schooldays were football, cricket, sport – more so than lessons … When I look back, I could have spent a lot more time on my lessons than on the football pitch. When I look back on it, I would have done that'.

At 14 he left school – his mother 'wanted the money. It was only ten bob a week then' – to become an errand boy at a grocer's shop: *Palmer's Stores* at the bottom of the road. His half-day was Thursday, a fact reflected in the unforgettable name of the local shopworkers' football team, Thetford Thursday, run by his boss at *Palmer's*, for which he was playing at 15.

~

Eddie's big break came on Saturday 5 October 1935. Norwich were away to Southampton, but Tom Parker wasn't there. As the *Eastern Daily Press* mysteriously put it, 'Mr Parker's absence was regretted by his old friends as the City manager was engaged elsewhere'. He was, by all accounts, in Thetford, watching Norfolk Juniors play Hertfordshire. When he first arrived in Norwich in 1933, Tom Parker was looked after by 'Bertie' Cowles, the longstanding Secretary of the Norfolk FA, and became a regular guest at the Cowles family home in Unthank Road. Naturally, Mr Cowles travelled to Thetford to see that county game and, for some reason, the Norwich City manager appears to have gone with him.

Who could have interested the Norwich manager so much that he let the first team go to Southampton without him, while he went to Thetford? We do know that it wasn't Eddie Bates, who had not been selected by Norfolk. But the away side arrived a player or two short – reports vary as to the number. 'Fetch Eddie Bates' went up the cry and the lad from Thetford Thursday made his county debut *against* his home county. It was a smart move. The visitors won 7-2. The *Eastern Daily Press* paid tribute to the 'brilliant'

visiting forwards, with 'the wings and Bates, the borrowed Thetford Thursday XI player, being the most outstanding', while another report concluded on an individual note: 'Bates ran through on his own and with a fine drive registered the 7th for Herts'.

Mr Parker took an instant fancy to the errand boy who was standing-in for Hertfordshire:

> *I had to go up to Norwich for a trial and Tom Parker put me in with the first team playing the Reserves on a Tuesday morning ... I must have done well [in] the trial with them, because he then wanted me to go on the ground staff.*
>
> *So next thing we know, he's got in touch with my mother to come down and see me. We met at the manager of Thetford Town Football Club's house – I'd had a few games for Thetford ... His name was Allison. My mother wanted him to [supervise the signing of apprentice forms on 17 October] because she was on her own. She didn't know what to do ... Of course, I couldn't get away quick enough. I was dead keen to play football ... My mother wasn't too happy about it because she preferred to have me at home ... I went up to Norwich on the ground staff. I used to travel up, early on, from Thetford to Norwich every day, 30 miles in the train. But, after a while, Tom Parker said 'That's too much for you, coming up and back. You'll have to come up in digs'. Well, that upset my mother even more, then. So I said 'I've got to go up – to carry on with it'. So up I go to Norwich in digs with Mrs Spall, a nice old dear. And I went in with a Norwich player called Harry Proctor, who was an established first team player and a good bloke to go with: he had all the good ideas of football – he wasn't a drinker – and he sort of kept his eye on me ... He eventually became trainer of Norwich.*

Norwich City had just left The Nest for Carrow Road. Eddie appeared often in the 'A' team during that 1935-36 season and was selected for Norfolk Juniors. The following season, he had a few games with the 'A' team that won the Norfolk and Suffolk League championship, but was a regular member of the Reserve side that finished runners-up in the Southern League.

That Norwich City Reserves team of 1936-37 makes for interesting inspection. Half the team had played for Southampton or Lymington and/or were on their way to one or both of those clubs. Ben Burley, an itinerant Yorkshireman, had had a couple of games for the Saints in 1934, his one season at The Dell. And to supplement his local finds – the likes of Thetford's Eddie Bates and Sheringham's Stan Cutting – Mr Parker had a scout in the Southampton area in the form of Jim Angell. Well known to generations of Saints' fans for his Woolston building firm that advertised both in the programme and on a substantial stretch of the stand, J.W. Angell had made three appearances for the Club in 1906. Upon Tom Parker's return to The Dell, Jim Angell would manage the Saints 'A' team.

It was he who picked up full-back George Woodford in 1934 and goalkeeper Ernie Hayter in 1936 – both from Lymington. He also took Harry Lanham to Norwich in 1936, when the former captain of England schoolboys was released by the

```
┌─────────────────────────────────────────────┐
│            PLAN OF THE FIELD.                 │
│ NORWICH CITY RES. (Yellow & Green Shirts, Black Knickers) │
│            Saturday, Sept. 19th, 1936.        │
│                      1                        │
│                  L. HAYTER                    │
│                    Goal                       │
│         2                        3            │
│      WOODFORD                 WORTON          │
│      Right Back              Left Back         │
│     4            5                     6       │
│  S. W. CUTTING      REILLY         LOCHHEAD    │
│   Right Half      Centre Half      Left Half   │
│   7         8         9        10        11    │
│ G. A. EDRICH  BATES  CASSIDY  MADDEN  WARNES   │
│ Outside Right Inside Right Centre Inside Left Outside Left │
│                      O                        │
│   12        13        14       15        16    │
│  WATSON    REEVE    ROOKE   QUAYELL   LIDDLE   │
│ Outside Left Inside Left Centre Inside Right Outside Right │
│         17              18            19       │
│      LEVINE          DAVIES       TELLING      │
│      Left Half      Centre Half    Right Half  │
│              20              21                │
│           RUMBOLD          MURRAY             │
│           Left Back        Right Back          │
│                     22                        │
│                   BRIGGS                      │
│                    Goal                       │
│ CRYSTAL PALACE RES. (Red Shirts, Blue Sleeves)  K.O. 3.30 │
└─────────────────────────────────────────────┘
```

The Norwich-Southampton/Parker-Angell Connections: Hayter, Woodford, Cutting and Bates played for Norwich City Reserves in 1936-37, when Eddie was partnered by Geoff Edrich of the Norfolk cricketing dynasty.

Saints. He presumably had a part in the arrival, that same year, of Eric Webber – like Hayter an unsuccessful Portsmouth trialist. And perhaps the recruitment of Maskell from the Isle of Wight was his doing, too. While Maskell remained, the others soon returned south, Lanham and Webber without ever making the City's reserve side. Hayter came back, after only a few weeks, when his father was dying, and resumed his career with Lymington. He had previously rejected part-time terms at The Dell because he calculated that he couldn't afford, on the money he was offered, to travel from Brockenhurst to train. He recalls a training regime at Norwich, which included the sight of Tom Parker using his weight in a practice match to flatten the 18 year-old Bates, who was not releasing the ball soon enough for Parker's liking. 'He probably wanted to teach me a lesson', the willing pupil reflects.

Hayter never did sign for the Saints. Lanham would rejoin them in 1941 but be restricted to a few war-time games, while Webber would make his debut in 1939 and, of course, become a fixture of the early postwar years. Meanwhile, Woodford would follow Cutting and Bates to Southampton in that summer of 1937 but manage only seven games before he, too, rejoined Lymington. George Ansell, an Oxford Blue who had had a few games for Norwich City's first team, also came to The Dell at this time but left before the new season started. He merits a mention here by way of an introduction to the Kimbolton School connection. Ansell was a master at this Bedfordshire school, where Tom Parker coached and where his sons were scholars. Norwich City's annual fixture at the school would sometimes be filled by the Saints, whose promotion in 1966 would benefit, we shall see, from a continuing association with an Old Boy.

Dell Boy

Completing the exodus from Norwich Reserves to The Dell, there was Jack Scott, at Norwich as a centre-half since 1931. An all-round sportsman, he had played rugby league for Featherstone Rovers and had chanced his arm at boxing and all-in wrestling. He now joined Southampton as player-coach for the 'A' side and as part of a training team headed by Horace Cope, the Norwich trainer who had often partnered Tom Parker at full-back for Arsenal. Scott's registration as a player would be needed just once by the first team – on 27 December 1937 at Swansea, when he turned out at No.9. And this for a team that had acquired *two* centre-forwards – Dunn and Gaughran – in that revolutionary summer of 1937.

Billy Dunn had started well enough, scoring in the opening game at Norwich, a 4-3 defeat by the club from which Mr Parker had acquired three players, a player-coach, a trainer and – not mentioned so far – assistant secretary, Bert Bush. But Dunn soon gave way to Benny Gaughran, whose goal-scoring quickly attracted the attention of, and a £1000 fee from, Sunderland. So much for Tom Parker's reconstruction plans. By Christmas Day, the No.9 shirt had passed to Ray Parkin, a sometime Arsenal team-mate of his who had arrived in September. And, by the end of that season, it had been worn by no fewer than six players.

That was hardly a perfect set-up in which to introduce – alongside Jack Scott at the Vetch Field – a 19 year-old at No.8. Edric Thornton Bates was making his debut for Southampton.

Debut Day: Eddie Bates (left) competes for the ball at the Vetch Field on 27 December 1937.

Norwich City 1936-37: The numbered characters are **1** Eddie Bates **2** Tom Parker **3** Harry Proctor, who 'kept an eye' on Eddie at Mrs Spall's digs **4** the itinerant Ben Burley **5** the mysterious Maskell of the Isle of Wight **6** Harry Lanham, who would return to The Dell in 1941; and five men who joined the Parker exodus, with Bates, to the Dell – **7** Stan Cutting **8** George Woodford **9** Jack Scott **10** Horace Cope and **11** Assistant Secretary Bush

Southampton 1937-38: The size of the Norwich City contingent arriving at the Dell is indicated by the first seven numbers: **1** Cutting **2** Woodford **3** Cope **4** Scott **5** Bush **6** Parker and **7** Bates. Among the names that will feature most prominently, in later chapters, you can see goalkeepers **8** Stansbridge and **9** Warhurst; other players **10** Sillett **11** Affleck **12** Bevis **13** Holt and **14** Osman; and directors **15** Corbett **16** Cosgrove **17** Jukes and **18** Sarjanston.

Chapter 2

In That Number

'There was a splendid holiday crowd at the Vetch Field', wrote 'Rolande', the local reporter, to watch a 'fast', but goalless, game.

The visitors' 19 year-old debutant was returning to the adopted Land of his Father. He had watched him play at the St Helen's ground nearby. Now, on his Football League baptism for the man who had discovered him, Eddie was playing alongside another of his Norwich mentors. Jack Scott was somebody he 'respected'. The same went for Horace Cope, while Tom Parker was himself a huge influence: 'He would keep an eye on me because he knew my situation … I got a lot of my early grounding in football from him. He was a very honest, straightforward bloke'.

And by taking him from Norwich, where Eddie felt 'they weren't too keen' on him, Tom Parker had given his protegé a significant injection of self-belief: 'I knew that he'd give me a chance. If he wanted me to go with him, he believed in me'. He knew, though, that he had to be prepared to learn from many more of those around him: 'You see, football's really very self-educational: if you want to learn, you mix with all the types you can in football … You can be pig-headed and not listen or learn, but the *amazing* thing about football is that you do meet such different people'.

On the other hand, there were those he should not mix with. He recognised that, as a young arrival, he was 'vulnerable and you've got to know that in football there are two ways you can go – the right way and the wrong way. And if you get mixed up with the wrong people, before you know where you are, you're going the wrong way – doing everything you shouldn't do after you've finished football time'.

POINTS SHARED IN FAST GAME AT VETCH FIELD

SWANSEA TOWN 0, SOUTHAMPTON 0

By ROLANDE.

THERE was a splendid holiday crowd at the Vetch Field for the second meeting of Swansea Town and Southampton, and when the game had started many hundreds of people were still pouring into the ground.

Southampton made changes, Scott being in place of injured Parkin, at centre forward, while Bates, son of the old Glamorgan cricketer, was at inside-right.

Swansea's new forwards, Beresford and Vernon, made their initial appearance before a home crowd.

SWANSEA TOWN.—Moore ; Lawrence, Emmanuel (T.) ; Warner, Leyland, Simons ; Foreman, Beresford, Vernon, Lang, Millington.

SOUTHAMPTON. — Warhurst; Sillett, Roberts ; King, Afflick, Hill ; Devis, Bates, Scott, Osman. Long.

Referee ; Mr. J. M. Wiltshire, Sher-

DELL DIAMOND

He was fortunate, in that regard, to be in digs with 'a sensible bloke' like Stan Cutting. But were there some of these 'wrong people' to get mixed up with at The Dell in 1937?

They're always about … But you've got to make sure that you don't do anything, anything you feel will take away your preparation for the game. I didn't have too much to play with. I wasn't that strong. I had to develop physically, so I had to work hard at that … Jack Scott and Horace Cope wanted me to do well. I didn't want to let them down, but it's always a danger in any club where you're a youngster, because you're very vulnerable. You've got to be strong-minded. I wanted to be a professional footballer and I wanted to get on at it. If you're half-hearted about it and you try to make excuses – this, that and the other – you're going to fall by the wayside … I was 19 and I was still a long way from being established in the game … So you have to keep working at it, so you feel you're getting better, even though you get disappointments. I mean, the manager wants to drop you, he talks to you, he talks about how you live, what you're doing. There's a lot more care, now, given to youngsters, when they're between, say, 16 and 19. At 19, you're getting over it, but if you're not in the team, you're not getting anywhere, are you?

Initially, Eddie was not in the team. When Tom Parker took the first team to Norwich for that opening day defeat, Eddie was at inside-right for the Reserves against Bristol City at The Dell. His right-wing partner was another summer signing – Billy Bevis, a Warsash youngster who had not made it with Portsmouth.

But Bevis was very soon in the first team – more or less to stay. The game at Swansea re-united this young pair, who began to excite reporters. The *Echo*, still hooked on the idea that he was 'Edward', paid tribute to this 'young wing – one of the youngest in Second Division football'. This wing was to remain intact for another dozen games that season, starting with Eddie's home debut, on New Year's Day, when George Woodford was also making his first appearance for the Saints. The visitors – who writes these scripts? – were Norwich City. That gave the man from the Norwich Pink 'Un the chance to report on the progress of what he called 'the Norwich "colony"'. While Bates and Woodford were playing against the team they'd left in the summer, Cutting was at Ashton Gate with the Reserves, while Jack Scott, just four days after his one first team game, was at Netley with the 'A' team.

Bevis and Bates again caught the eye in the Saints' 3-1 win. The *Daily Express* reporter felt that they 'formed a perfect right-wing and played match-winning football', while Tom Parker told the *Echo* that he was 'delighted with their play'. If 'Bevis was the "star" forward of the match' for the *Echo,* his wing-mate shared his 'confidence to hold the ball and beat an opponent, and the intelligence not to keep the ball too long … If these two young players go on in this way many clubs will envy the Saints their right wing'. An especially prescient reporter, who considered the 'partnership … on the Southampton right wing was one of the brightest features of the game', suggested that 'Bates … looks as though he has come to stay'.

Novice's Cup: Eddie Bates leaves Southampton to play in his first FA Cup-tie, a 3-1 defeat by Nottingham Forest.

(left to right): Sillett, Mr Sarjanston, Holt, Cope (trainer), Bates, Dunn, Warhurst.

Eddie's first FA Cup tie – a Third Round game at the City Ground – followed. The Saints went out 3-1 but Dunn owed his goal to 'the speedy Bates' and the right-wing partnership again caused a stir. In the last home game of the season, against promotion contenders, Sheffield United, Eddie scored the first of his 65 League goals for the Saints. One report described it as an 'exceptionally good effort'. The *Echo,* which was by now calling him 'Eddy' (complete with the inverted commas that it used for any diminutive), considered it 'a very neat goal' and felt that he had 'played a fine game all through, getting into position, pushing the ball here and there, making the work of colleagues around him easier all the time'.

This reporter went on to reveal that he had put to Horace Cope his anxiety that Bates was yet to score. The trainer had told him not to worry: once he had 'a little more experience', Eddie would 'be walking the ball into the net.' The man from the *Echo* found the trainer's case proven that afternoon: 'the way [Bates] dodged a path through the Sheffield defenders did look remarkably like "walking" the ball into the net – though it was a mighty brisk walk'.

The scorer's recall is more modest: he was 'on the spot at the right time – nothing spectacular'.

Then it was home to Thetford for the summer. Betty was by now working, but Alice can remember her big brother's summer recess, three months in which he would 'spend a lot of time fishing'. And he would open the batting for Thetford Town – at the Recreation Ground where Tom Parker had discovered him. The summer of 1939 was an especially successful one for the club, with Eddie Bates in fine form. On 1 July, in a game at Newmarket, he was on 98, with 11 fours under his belt, when the captain declared: 'incredible, that was!' Two weeks later, in a big home win over Attleborough, he scored only 25 of Thetford's 169. But he then took 7 for 13 in six overs to help dismiss the visitors for 56.

CRICKET.

NEWMARKET v. THETFORD.
Played at Newmarket on Saturday, a draw resulting. Thetford batted first and declared with their score at 157 for 4 wickets, mainly due to E. Bates, whose 98 not out included 11 fours. When stumps were drawn Newmarket had scored 81 for 4 wickets. Scores:

Thetford
J. H. Taylor, b Puddicombe 1
E. Bates, not out 98
C. W. Holmes, b Puddicombe 6
C. H. Watson c and b Claydon 4
E. Boyce, b Fuller 21
F. Crump, not out 27
Extras ....

(for 4 wkts. dec.) 157
W. Mutum, R. H. Nudds, G. Garrod, W. Pyne and D. Campbell did not bat.

Newmarket
R. J. Waugh, b Bates 4
E. Canning, not out 28
F. T. Day, c Bates b Taylor 0
F. C. Puddicombe, c Boyce b Taylor 0
G. R. Hopkinson, b Mutum 21
T. Hayward, not out 1
Extras 27

(for 4 wkts.) 81
A. F. Fuller, H. Stokes, G. Wedgewood, A Claydon and G. Heasman did not bat.

His cricket season was always truncated, of course, for him to report back to The Dell – an annual wrench for Eva, which, as Alice recalls, her brother sought to avoid: 'Whenever he was going back, he used to say to us "*Don't* let Mum come to the station to see me off", because there were always tears and he used to hate that. Poor Mum, she couldn't stop herself from crying'. The up-side for Eva was her share of Eddie's summer wages, the 'grand sum', as Alice recalls, of about £5 a week:

> *But, by golly, it was really a* lot *in those days. And I'll tell you something else about Eddie: when he left home and went away, he always used to send money home to my Mum, every week. He used to send her a pound. That doesn't sound a lot now; but, believe you me, it used to help out a lot in those days. He did that right up to the time he got married. Children did that kind of thing in those days … He was always a good boy, as my Mum used to say.*

This good boy made good progress in his first two seasons at The Dell, as Tom Parker tried to blend his new signings, young and old, with his limited inheritance. The line-up for Eddie's first game on 27 December 1937 reflects the partial impact of the revolution that the new manager had executed during the close season.

Apart from the three signings already mentioned – Bates, Bevis and Scott – the newcomers were centre-half Dave Affleck from Clapton Orient;

goalkeeper Sam Warhurst from Bradford City; and Frank Hill from Blackpool, a Scottish international wing-half who had played in the three Championship-winning Arsenal sides of 1932-33-34-35 – not to mention that famous cup-tie at Walsall.

But there was more continuity than observers of Mr Parker's busy summer of 1937 might have anticipated. Full-backs, Albert Roberts and Charlie Sillett – whose son Peter would play with Ted Bates in 1951-52 – had been at The Dell since 1929 and 1931, respectively, while the left-wing pair of Henry Long and Harry Osman went back to 1933 and 1935. And half-back Cyril King had been there since 1932.

In that 1937-38 season, Frank Hill became the captain and a new stimulant to Eddie Bates: 'He was always niggling me, keeping me working – running'. Neither the captain nor the newcomer played a big part the next season, however. The likes of Hill and Parkin had given the side, Bates felt, 'a little bit of a lift, but we were always, well, struggling a little bit'. Mr Parker's reshaped side eventually struggled to a goal aggregate of 55-77, remarkably similar to the previous season's 53-77, even if those extra two goals were worth an additional five points and a climb to 15th position.

The supporters seemed to be pleased with this measure of improvement. On the evening of 31 March 1938, the *Echo* reporter joined a crowd of nearly 2,000 packed into Southampton's Coliseum and heard Mr Parker received with shouts of 'Well played, Tom'. The theme of the evening was how to raise more money. An unpaid debt to the Supporters' Club of £2,200 – which had been used to pay the previous summer's wages – was acknowledged and a Shilling Fund launched with 200 shillings from the Mayor, Cllr G.E.H. Prince, a Southampton Director.

The Saints' Chairman, Mr J.R. Sarjantson, stressed the Club's financial contribution to Southampton and wondered if 'the tradesmen of the town realise what a successful team means to them' and whether they could appreciate their debt to the club, which fortnightly brought 'close on 20,000 people streaming into the town'. Yet this lesson in the economics of ground location – the like of which Lawrie McMenemy would take up four decades later – was perhaps overshadowed by the efforts of Canon R.B. Jolly, Rector of St Mary's, to put 'the most memorable public meeting in the history of the Saints' (as the *Echo* had it) into a European perspective. He wished

the Dictators in Europe could see this meeting tonight … if Europe played with footballs more they would play with bombs less (applause). In supporting football we are supporting peace. If Europe would learn to play the game, and learn to pass the ball, and not dribble it at their own feet all the time, it would lead to peace.

DELL DIAMOND

It would be another 18 months before Southampton would give up peace-time football and prepare to be bombed. Meanwhile, Mr Parker wasted little time in spending his extra shillings. During the 1938 close season, he signed another nine professionals, including six forwards.

Yet it was mainly Arthur Holt, who'd been at The Dell since 1932, who confined Eddie Bates to 14 first team appearances in 1938-39. In what was to be the final season of a career terminated by war, Holt captained the side in the absence of Hill and passed the 200-mark for his one and only professional club. One of two players blamed implicitly for a 6-1 defeat at Chesterfield in December, he was stood down for Bates. But, when the Saints lost that home game 3-1 to Blackburn, Eddie was back in the Reserves for a while. At least that meant missing a 4-1 defeat at Chelmsford, in the Third Round of the FA Cup.

Since their stirring Cup runs of 1925 and 1927, Southampton had only once survived this opening round. But this humiliation by a side lying 20th in the Southern League was something else – something meriting an entry, as derived from the *Essex Chronicle,* in Geoff Tibballs's *FA Cup Giant Killers*. It would appear that the scoreline flattered the visitors, as the home side reaped the benefit of preparing for the game in the brine baths at Southend – literally rubbing the salt in for Mr Parker, who had wanted to take his players to Clacton-on-Sea for a week before the game, for 'special training'. But the Board 'considered this unnecessary in view of the financial position' and decided to forgo such an expense until the next round. It was to be January 1946, however, before the Saints would play in any round of the FA Cup.

~

While Bates was in and out in 1938-39, nobody played more games than Bevis. Their celebrated right-wing partnership, which came together only a dozen times that season, enjoyed a solid run in the spring of 1939, when one or the other of them scored in five consecutive games. Billy's five goals in that spell included a hat-trick at the Vetch Field. Eddie's two – his only goals of the season – came in a 2-1 defeat at Maine Road, where he 'fully justified his promotion to the inside-right position and was throughout a hard and clever worker', and in a 3-2 setback at Bradford, where his goal 'crowned a wholehearted display by [an] enthusiastic worker'.

Their last game together, that season, a 4-0 home defeat by Luton, was the second of Stan Cutting's three games for the Saints before he left for Exeter City. As we have seen, his Thornbury Avenue room-mate had spent much of that season in the Reserves with him. That had enabled them to try out a move, straight from the kick-off, which they had plotted in their room. On 7 January 1939, when Queen's Park Rangers Reserves came to The Dell, the ploy brought about a goal. When QPR took the lead, Doug

McGibbon duly kicked off – a tap to Eddie Bates, who swung the ball wide to the left-wing, where left-half Cyril King met it and hit it back, on the diagonal, into the middle, ahead of 'home players on the "hunt"', as the *Echo* put it. Right-half Stan Cutting got there ahead of the pack to score 'with a capital shot'.

Centre-forward McGibbon was a young addition to all those other forwards Mr Parker had signed during the close season. He had been playing cricket, in that summer of 1938, for his works team, Air Service Training, against a side that included Tom Parker and 'one or two other Southampton players'. He'd taken the opportunity to ask for a trial at The Dell, had scored four goals in it and had begun to bang them in for the 'A' team, starting with hat-tricks against Lymington in successive games – which was no way to treat Ernie Hayter, back in Lymington's goal after his brief spell at Norwich.

The *Echo* greeted the arrival of this new hope who had 'football in his blood': his father, Charlie, had had one impressive goal-scoring season for the Saints in 1909-10. Doug was promoted to the Reserves for the rest of the season – until he made his first-team debut on the last day of that 1938-39 campaign, a 2-0 defeat at Plymouth. He cannot recall anything of that game against QPR Reserves, but refuses to believe that any team-mate could have been ahead of him when King crossed. Seven seasons later, Bates and he would often repeat the move and he would eventually score a record-breaking goal from it. And a month after that, he would accidentally miss – famously, as it transpired – a cup-tie at Loftus Road.

More of those two games later. Let's just note, for the moment, that that visit to Loftus Road, on 30 January 1946, would be the first official outing for the Bevis-Bates wing since that 4-0 defeat by Luton on 7 April 1939.

The Dictators of Europe and their bombs were to blame.

Three-Game Wonders
Tom Parker (left) welcomes his close season signings of 1939, whose new season will last but three
games before War wipes out League football for seven seasons. The three signings are (from the right)
Higham (shaking hands), Dodgin and Bradley. Bates can be seen between Dodgin and Bradley.

Chapter 3

What did you do in the War, Eddie?

The Dell was busy on the morning of Sunday 3 September 1939.

Whether you'd been injured on the Saturday and had a date on the treatment table or whether you were hoping to see your name on the teamsheet for the visit, the next day, to White Hart Lane, then you had a reason to be at the ground that Sunday morning. Doug McGibbon, Eric Webber and Jack Bradley all remember being there. McGibbon had made his debut, you may recall, on the final day of the 1938-39 season. Webber had made his first appearance at Blackburn three weeks earlier. A 6ft 1ins defender who would be called a 'centre-back' nowadays, Eric had survived an unsuccessful trial at Fratton Park and a fleeting visit to Norwich (as noted in Chapter 1) and signed professional for the Saints just before his debut.

McGibbon had good reason to think he was due another chance in the first team. He had scored a hat-trick, in the practice match, when the 'Whites' beat the 'Stripes' 4-3 and had scored in both of the Reserves' games so far. On the other hand, two of Mr Parker's 1938 signings, Briggs and Tomlinson – the leading scorers in 1938-39 – had shared the Stripes' three goals, but had managed only one League goal between them in the three games to date. Bradley, one of three forwards acquired in the 1939 close season – along with Higham from Middlesbrough and Perrett from Huddersfield – found himself on the wing for the Stripes. The *Echo* had announced him, upon arrival from Chelsea, as a 'left-wing forward', capable of playing at either inside-left or outside-left. He insists that he 'was *always* a Number 10' – but he was at No.11 for the Reserves in its opening games of 1939-40 and had scored at Southend on the Saturday.

Mr Parker's other new signings included a threat to Webber's aspirations: 30 year-old Bill Dodgin had arrived from Clapton Orient. Such, then, was the competition for places at The Dell as the town of Southampton prepared for the likelihood of war. On the night of 10 August, the local Air-Raid Precautions (ARP) Services, which had staged the country's first-ever 'black-out' exercise the previous summer, participated in the first national black-out operation and air defence exercise. The ARP reported a 'most successful' experiment and concluded that the service was 'undoubtedly on the fringe of a first-class war organisation'. But the football show must go on. Two days later, 2,908 turned out to see the practice match. Then, on 19 August, the side that had gone 12 seasons with only one Cup win to their name entertained the FA Cup-holders in a Football League 'Jubilee' friendly. Portsmouth rubbed it in by parading their trophy and let the home fans experience what it felt like – literally, if you were standing down at the front – as the Cup was taken round the ground. The Saints' players also had a feel. Tom Emanuel, for one, was 'really thrilled' to have the Cup in his hands.

Thou Shalt Not Covet Thy Neighbour's Cup
Fans at the 'Jubilee' Friendly, in which the Saints entertained Pompey in August 1939, touch the FA Cup, which Portsmouth had just won and would 'hold' for seven years.

Pompey's superiority extended even to the numbers on their shirts. This was the first season in which numbers were to be worn and 'Commentator' could not help noticing, for the *Echo*, that the visitors' numbers were more 'prominent'. And then, showing their supremacy where it mattered, Pompey won the game 3-0 with ten of the players who had beaten Wolves 4-1 at Wembley. The missing man was the captain, Jimmy Guthrie, who had been badly injured in a close season car accident.

⌒

After the practice match, in which Bates was 'a conspicuous success', the *Echo* predicted that he might be 'hard to keep out of the [first] eleven'. But not that hard. He was dropped after the opener, a 3-1 defeat at Newport. This game found him not paired with Bevis but 'combining well', the *Echo* felt, at inside-left to Perrett. That trip to Wales, on 26 August, coincided with a premature recall, from their holidays, of Southampton's teachers and schoolchildren, in readiness for a rehearsal of the town's evacuation scheme. On Wednesday 30 August, the docks became a closed area to all except those on business there and the *Queen Mary* left for New York and a five-and-a-half year absence from her home port. And the Saints lost again – 3-1 to Swansea at The Dell.

On Friday 1 September, the real black-out and evacuation began. And the *Echo* reflected that Europe was slipping 'down into the abyss with scarcely a chance now of that descent being arrested'. On the Saturday, as the evacuation continued, some London matches were postponed until the evening, so as not to clash with the special traffic arrangements for evacuating the capital. Southampton's visitors had quite the opposite concern: setting a dismal scene for his *Echo* readers, 'Commentator' revealed, in his match report, that Bury had been 'anxious' that the match start and finish on time, so as to assure their train connections. He continued in his paper's Friday mood: 'the effect of the international situation could be clearly seen', he suggested, in the spaces around the ground, where only 5,103 fans had assembled.

The Saints won at last – 3-0. But that was that. And the three games counted for nothing. They were to be expunged from appearance records. The teamsheet that the players had come to check, on Sunday 3 September, was rendered redundant as the assembled players listened, on a wireless at The Dell, to a broadcast by Mr Neville Chamberlain, the Prime Minister. The nation was at war with Germany. The Spurs players were likewise tuned in at White Hart Lane – as Ronnie Burgess has recalled in his autobiography.

One of the Saints' players who had not reported in that morning was full-back Tom Emanuel. Having turned out for Swansea on the occasion of Bates's debut, he had joined the Saints nine months later, becoming a first-team regular in 1938-39. He was at home, that Sunday morning, with his wife of two months. The next day they left Southampton to live with her parents in Swansea.

That's how quickly decisions about future residence and employment were being taken on Monday 4 September. The Southampton Board met at 2.30 pm and received Mr Parker's report on who was left at The Dell. Most of the training and ground staff had been stood off already. Three would remain, along with the Assistant Secretary, to clear up. All four would be gone by the end of the week. The manager himself was offered £3 a week,

Numbers Up: In preparation for the first season in which shirts were to be numbered, Doug McGibbon displays his No.8 in the practice match. Supported by Eddie Bates (left), who was 'a conspicuous success', he takes on Dave Affleck in the stripes.

if he would 'pay an occasional visit to The Dell, answer all correspondence, and keep in touch with all concerned'. At the follow-up meeting on the Saturday, Tom Parker accepted that offer, 'until such time as the Club shall resume playing or his existing Contract become expired' and undertook to handle all correspondence from his home in Chandlers Ford.

Which left only the players to be found employment. The manager and the chairman met them on the morning of 4 September. Mr Parker told the Board that he had explained to them that 'it would be in their interests to obtain a situation as soon as possible'. There was, Ted Bates recalls, no mention of military service:

> *Tom Parker didn't want us to go in. He said 'Look! Don't go in the Forces. The war won't last long and then you'll be able to get on with your football again'. So right, that was what I tried to do and my main object was wanting to get on with the football. So I stayed and he put several players, including me, in the Police War Reserve, to keep us in the area, in Southampton.*

The prospect of enlistment had in fact been raised as early as April when Mr Parker had read the Board a letter from the FA, requesting that the attention of players and staff be drawn to the prospects of National Service. And he had further reported, on 3 August, that a few players, including Bevis and McGibbon, had applied for 'delayed service'. But the service facing a considerable number of Southampton players was with the police. And for the majority of these it meant giving up professional football to become a full-time officer in the Southampton Borough Police Force. In fact, two players with first team experience – John Summers, a winger displaced by Billy Bevis, and Norman Chalk, one of Dave Affleck's deputies – had recently taken that route. They were now joined by full-back, Doug Henderson – transferred to Bristol City in the 1939 close season, he hurried home – and several others, straight from The Dell. These included three regular first-teamers – Affleck, Tomlinson and Brophy – and Tom Carnaby, another Affleck stand-in during 1938-39, each of whom initially joined the Police War Reserve but who promptly decided to throw in their permanent lot with the Borough force. 'It was a secure job', Norman Chalk explains, 'plus a pension. I suppose you could bluntly say they either joined the police force or went in the Army'. Four Saints Reserves – keeper Fright and forwards Clifton, Lock and Moore – also found their way to the permanent force, making a whole eleven of ex-Saints for the Borough Police team.

Sam Warhurst, too, had a short spell with the War Reserve, before he moved to Cunliffe-Owen, to keep goal in the Hampshire War League. Eddie Bates and Jack Bradley would stay with the War Reserve a little longer. For managers wanting to keep their players at hand, this was an obvious form of war-time employment. According to Ron Burgess, no fewer than 11 Spurs' players enrolled in it on Monday 4 September, the day on which they had been expecting to entertain the Saints. Across London, at Loftus Road, Alec Stock was also being sworn into the police – although he quickly tired of walking the streets, requiring the householders of Notting Hill to observe the black-out, and joined the Army. How Tom Parker's protegé wishes he had ignored the manager's forecast and done the same!

What did you do in the War, Eddie?

The duties of the Southampton War Reserve extended beyond the city's streets to the waterfront, to the docks and factories that were to be prime targets for the *Luftwaffe*. Jack Bradley recalls spells of guarding the Shell-Mex Oil Installation at Hamble and the Pirelli-General works in Woolston. Eddie Bates was also stationed at Woolston, working shifts on guard at the Supermarine works, where the *Spitfire* was being built.

~

The guardsmen shifts of Bates and Bradley left them free to turn out regularly for the Saints, who, after five friendlies against near-neighbours, restarted 'league' football on 21 October. The Football League South was geographically limited – to Hampshire, Sussex and London. In that first season, everybody had 36 fixtures. The War Cup South was a knock-out over two legs. In keeping with their Cup record of the previous 12 seasons, the Saints would fall at the first hurdle to Bristol Rovers.

Bradley, who missed only four of those 38 games, was top scorer with 21 goals; while Bates, who played in all but six of them, was the second highest on 14. In contrast, Affleck, Tomlinson and Brophy, each of whom had played in one or more of those three null and void fixtures, would return for only a war-time game or two for the Saints. They were now police officers and were generally expected to play their football for a formidable Police side. The departure of Affleck and two of his deputies opened the way for Eric Webber who became the only ever-present player in Southampton's first season at war.

Apart from the home-bound Emanuel, others who promptly left the area included Higham and Parkin. At its meeting of 5 October – by which time it had temporarily moved its meetings to the Norwich Union's High Street offices and back again – the Board recorded requests by these two players to guest for Chorley FC and Holiday Sports. After five games, Bevis was in the Navy. And Doug McGibbon was too busy in the Air Training Service to manage as many as half the games.

But then, conversely, there were the *guests*. One of the first to arrive was John Harris of Wolves, who had come to live in Swindon, where his father had recently become manager of Swindon Town, a club that completed a season in the South West division of the war-time League but then packed up for the duration. Harris was to miss only one game that season, playing at No 4 with the ever-present Webber at No 5. He lodged at the Bitterne home of Jim Angell, whom we've already encountered in two or three roles and who will inevitably feature again in the Eddie Bates story. This house was handier for reporting to Woolston police station, so Eddie left Mrs Penny's to move into the same digs as Harris. He became 'very, very close' to Harris, who became 'a very good friend of Tom Parker's'. Yet Harris's arrival at The Dell was not an occasion for universal celebration. It prompted the Board to worry about the expense that could be incurred if the Club were to 'avail itself' of opportunities to bring in 'more prominent players'.

A few such servicemen would be stationed nearby, but Bournemouth would grab some of them. Portsmouth would have a few sailors, but – most famously of all – Aldershot had the pick of the Army. The stories of star-studded Aldershot teams have been told too often – in Jack Rollin's *Soccer at War* and elsewhere – to need rehearsing here. Frank Swift in goal. Tommy Lawton getting goals galore. And the All-England half-back line of Britton-Cullis-Mercer.

Were Southampton jealous of Aldershot's good fortune? You bet they were. On 13 March 1940, the Shots achieved the double over the Saints with a 3-2 win at The Dell. Tommy Lawton missed a penalty when he blasted it straight at Eugene Henri (Hugh) Bernard. An amateur who had kept goal for the Saints a couple of times in 1936-37, Bernard would have a few war-time games but retire prematurely with a hand injury and then help with the juniors for many a season, part-time. There appears, from the *Echo* accounts, to be no justification for Rollin's suggestion that Lawton's penalty knocked Bernard 'into the back of the net' before the ball spiralled over the bar. That defeat completed the Saints' fixtures in the Football League South 'B', of which they finished bottom (although, to be fair, their well-served Hampshire neighbours fared little better). At the Board meeting the following week, Mr Wright offered to put his car and services at the disposal of Mr Parker should his fellow-directors wish him to go and get some of the 'prominent players' that abounded in the Aldershot area. Nothing seems to have come of this. Perhaps he couldn't get the petrol coupons.

There was an upside, though, to having fewer guests than most. Southampton could develop their young talent. Even as they lost 4-1 to Queen's Park Rangers to confirm their bottom position in the League South 'B', Charles Buchan, no less, was raving to his readers about the prospects of three of their 'immature youngsters'. There were several managers there to 'cast envious eyes' on 'Bates, a strong inside-forward who showed the makings of greatness', and who scored 'cleverly'. And Webber and Hassell both looked like 'future stars'. Tom Hassell, a 20 year-old local who had just signed pro, would have more than 100 war-time games for the Saints but never play League football for them – an indication, perhaps, of the Club's willingness to heed Buchan's message and keep faith with their youngsters.

That required patience, in the latter part of that first season, as the youthful side continued to struggle in the Football League South 'C'. This League amounted to another round of fixtures played almost end-on to the

What did you do in the War, Eddie?

'B' League – a compromise by the Football League Wartime Committee, involving a reshuffling to placate London clubs who had objected to being placed in the same league as South Coast riff-raff. As if to justify those complaints from the capital, the Saints even contrived to lose heavily in friendlies at Chelmsford and Guildford.

Two disappointing performers singled out in the manager's reports to the Board were Eddie Bates (so much for Charles Buchan's accolade) and Jack Bradley. The final day of this odd season, which came as late as the second Saturday in June, was a special day for these two inside-forwards. The evening game against Charlton at The Dell – in which the Saints were led by the Arsenal and England captain, Eddie Hapgood, in one of two war-time appearances for them – was to be Bradley's last game for them for a while. The waterfront was losing him to the RAF.

And, in the afternoon – before a 3-1 defeat in which he scored – inside-left Bradley had been best man at the wedding of his inside-right. Eddie Bates had married Miss Mary Smith.

Dressed for the Match

On 8 June 1940, Eddie Bates married Mary Smith at St. James's Church in Shirley. Then they went down Shirley Road, paused for a studio photo and proceeded to the game against Charlton at the Dell.

Chapter 4

Partners – Whist, a Wedding and a Wing

The groom's landlady and the bride's mother had been responsible for Eddie Bates and Mary Smith meeting at Hulse Road Labour Club in Shirley.

Situated just around the corner – or two, if you're counting – from The Dell, the club will be especially well-known, nowadays, to the many Saints' fans who drink there before the match. Mrs Penny and Mrs Smith were attracted there, though, as 'whist drive fiends'. The former would take her two young bachelor lodgers, Bates and Cutting, while the latter would partner her teenage daughter. Cissie Smith soon fell prey, however, to Eddie's eye for a free transfer: 'We sort of swapped partners', as her daughter puts it. And not only at the tables: 'I suppose he thought I was a good whist player, so he'd follow up the friendship'.

He followed up all the way to the altar of St. James's Church, Shirley on 8 June 1940. There was no photographer awaiting them as they emerged from the church. So they went down Shirley Road to pose for a studio photo', while their best man walked across to The Dell for the evening's game against Charlton. Their photo' taken, the newly-weds went to watch the match. 'On my wedding night!', the bride chortles. 'Going to watch the Saints – pretty novel!'

Their first home was literally a case of where Angells fear to tread. Jim Angell's sisters had been occupying a house in West Road, Woolston, opposite the offices of his building firm, but 'had gone off to Romsey', Mary recalls, 'to be safe'. So Jim offered the house to Ted and Mary. Their stay was short-lived. The Angell sisters appear to have shrewdly anticipated Germany's bombing tactics. In one of Southampton's early raids, on 24 August, a 250lb bomb landed in the garden of the home their brother was renting out to the Bateses. Mary remembers being in bed, 'having a bit of an argy-bargy' with Ted about how to react to the air-raid warning: 'should we go to the shelter or not? He refused to go and I got frightfully annoyed. I started off down the stairs and before you could say "knife", the bomb was down. Ted rolled off the bed and a piece of paving stone [from the roof] just missed his head. He was *extremely* fortunate'.

In a letter to Eric Webber, overseas, Tom Parker told him about the Bateses' bomb – and the practice match on the same day, of course. But, bombing or not, the Secretary-Manager seemed still to be thinking that the War would be short-lived and that 'the days gone by … will soon be here again, and I shall be grousing at you again'.

For Ted and Mary, the bomb meant a move – out to West Wellow on the road to Salisbury. Mary, who had been working as a secretary in the city centre, found a new job in the NAAFI accounts office at Petersfinger, near Salisbury. But not for long. Ted had become 'fed up with the War Reserve'. So he packed it in. On the principle that 'if you could play football, you could usually get a job somewhere', he went to work for Folland Aircraft at Hamble, along with 'a *lot* of footballers' who played for the works team under the management of 'football-mad' Tubby Wiseman. They included Bill Dodgin and Jack Scott from The Dell. At various stages, the three Saints would team up, there, with Chelsea's Dick Foss, Peter Buchanan and Harry Burgess; Charlton's Bert Tann; Barnsley's Mick Brennan; Carlisle's Harold Pond; Preston's George Summerbee; and several 'Pompey lads' – Jack Anderson, Cliff Parker, Bert Barlow, Jimmy Guthrie, Jim Allen, Bill Rochford and Bill Bushby.

You can see that, even by his conservative standards, Ted Bates is being cautious when he describes this as 'a fair side'. Bill Bushby more realistically remembers playing for 'a helluva team'. Buchanan had one cap for Scotland. Anderson, Barlow and Parker (2) had all scored when Portsmouth, captained by Guthrie, had won the Cup in 1939. Rochford had also played in that side. Allen, twice capped for England at centre-half in 1933, had been a losing finalist with Pompey in 1934, before joining Aston Villa. Bushby had arrived at Fratton Park in the 1939 close season as cover for Guthrie, the future Chairman of the Professional Footballers' Union who had been badly injured in a car accident, you may recall, and who would not play again until December 1939 – in Portsmouth's 4-1 defeat of the Saints at Fratton Park.

Tann and Pond would both turn out, during several war-time seasons, for the Saints, for whom Buchanan, Bushby and a few of the others would guest more occasionally. And Bushby and Rochford would both come to The Dell in the summer of 1946, the former to make a couple of appearances before moving on to Cowes, the latter to captain the side through those early post-war seasons. Foss would play mainly for Chelsea in subsequent war-time seasons – including Wembley finals in 1944 and 1945 – while continuing to rent a house with his wife in Netley, so handy for Follands. Ted and Mary became their sub-tenants and Mary took a job at Follands – as secretary to the Buyer. Ted cannot recall what his job involved. He seems to have been there less for his aero-engineering skills than for his football.

Partners – Whist, a Wedding and a Wing

He also represented Follands at cricket in the Parks League, though. If his cuttings are representative, this league was a lower-scoring affair than his summers in Thetford had been. There was, for instance, a game against NALGO when he top-scored with 31 not out in a total of 116 – sufficient to win, thanks to bowling that included Bert Tann's three for 12. An identical return for Bates the bowler helped to dismiss Vickers-Armstrong for 35 in another low-scoring game, while he and Jimmy Guthrie were joint top-scorers with 18 apiece when the high-riding Follands lost to Swallows.

In that 1940-41 season, Folland Aircraft FC played an unpredictable schedule of matches in the Hampshire War League and all manner of local cup competitions, plus friendlies against services teams. The League fixtures could not in fact be completed, with Follands stranded in second place to Portsmouth Reserves. But they did win both the Southampton and Hampshire Senior cups, plus the Russell Cotes and Silver Jubilee cups.

While expedient solutions may have been needed to the fixture chaos, certain standards had nevertheless to be maintained. For instance, players could still be sent off for 'misconduct' as Ted was reminded when Follands played away to RAF Gosport in January 1941. A 'Special Committee' of the Hants FA, before which he duly appeared, found that 'there was no case to answer' and exonerated him. The Secretary of the Hants FA wrote to reassure him that his 'football reputation is not in the least affected by the [referee's] report'. Amid all this, the untarnished Bates played only 11 times for the Saints that season and Dodgin did not play at all. With Bradley and Webber now in the Services, Tom Parker needed new blood – like Bill Ellerington and Don Roper.

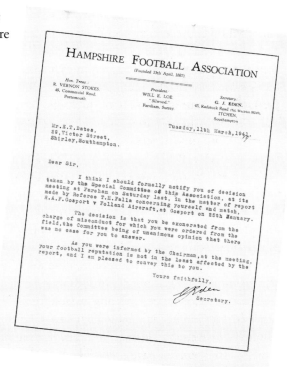

DELL DIAMOND

Ellerington had been born in Southampton in 1923. His father, a sometime Middlesbrough player, had turned out for the Saints during the First World War. By 1933, he was an out-of-work engineer in Southampton, 'jumping at' the chance of a job at Ford Paper Mills in Sunderland – there can't have been too many unemployed men pointing their bikes (and families) in *that* direction. His 10 year-old son found himself at Barnes Elementary School and making spectacular progress, football-wise. His first cap for England Schools came in 1937, in the same side as Jimmy Mullen, with whom he would win his two full England caps in 1949. In 1940, his family returned to Southampton. Tom Parker soon came 'knocking at the door' and took the young Ellerington, now nearing 17, to The Dell. He was already on Sunderland's books – he recalls standing reverentially aside in the corridor at Roker Park to let his idol, 'Mister Carter', walk by – so his 59 war-time games for the Saints were to be on guest terms.

Mr Parker faced no such restrictions in securing the services of another local 17 year-old. A prolific schoolboy goalscorer, Don Roper top-scored in his first season at The Dell and would head the Saints' war-time totals with 86 goals in his 166 games. He had been spotted by Toby Keleher, who had been managing the newly-formed 'B' team in its first, 1938-39, season. The young side had had a remarkable inaugural season, dropping only one point in its 26 League games and scoring 244 goals. Its ever-present captain and third-highest scorer (with but 41 goals that season) was Bill Stroud. A product of the Highbury Sports side that Keleher had been running, Stroud would play 175 war-time games for the Saints, converting from forward to wing-half along the way. Keleher's Highbury Sports also produced Alf Creecy, a full-back, who was a regular in Tom Parker's young side of 1940-41-42.

Only two players would turn out more often, during the war, than Roper and Stroud. Bates would make 181 appearances (for 66 goals) but full-back Albie Roles, another local in that pre-war 'B' team, would pip him with 188. Yet Roles's Football League career would amount to one game in 1948-49. One hesitates to talk of a career 'lost' to the War – some of their peers paid a much higher price – but you know what I mean. And so many of that generation would play plenty of war-time games and never make a post-war appearance that counted at all in the official records. Tom Hassell was mentioned, in this regard, in the previous chapter. Les Laney, likewise a local winger, was another. Having arrived from Cowes, pre-war, Laney spent the War as a plumber in the docks – with Mary Bates's father, Sam Smith, at Thorneycroft – and trained at The Dell two nights a week, all for 59 war-time games. That's eight more than Alf Creecy, whose Southampton career ended when his engineering skills merited a transfer, from a previously-exempt position with Thorneycroft, to the armed services overseas. When he returned home, he was not fit enough soon enough for the demands of the professional game.

'Other sides had top players' – but the Southampton side of 1940-41
was a bunch of youngsters led by guest John Harris.

The 15 characters who appear in the text are ❶ Charlie White, that season's 'keeper ❷ Harry Lanham, one of Jim Angell's temporary 'finds' for Norwich City (see Chapter 1); six of the youngsters introduced in this, or the previous, chapter ❸ Alf Creecy, ❹ Don Roper ❺ Bill Ellerington ❻ Bill Stroud ❼ Les Laney and ❽ Tom Hassell; the star guest ❾ John Harris; the managerial team of ❿ Toby Keleher, ⓫ Tom Parker and ⓬ Jim Angell (previously introduced as a Norwich scout and the Bateses' landlord); and three directors ⓭ G.W.A. Wright ⓮ J.R. Sarjantson and ⓯ A.E. Jukes.

Hassell made more appearances than anybody in 1940-41. And Laney managed to play a third of his war-time games that season – despite the arrival of a guest competitor for the outside-left spot. Bertie Mee, who had been on the books of Derby County and Mansfield Town, had joined up in July 1939 and had elected, on the outbreak of war, to go to the School of Massage, as it was then called, at Netley Hospital. This enabled him to work as a physiotherapist, to study for a civilian qualification in Physiotherapy and to run the football team. The hospital 'licked' the police – with all their ex-Saints – in that 1939-40 season and Mee suspects that this may have contributed to Tom Parker's acquiring his services on Southampton's left-wing for 1940-41.

DELL DIAMOND

It was not easy to combine this level of football with his work at the hospital, especially after The Dell was bombed in November 1940 and the Saints found themselves playing all their subsequent games away. This was a rather austere experience for the travelling Saints players:

> *We always used to put on board, at The Dell, these very big soup containers – to have a spot of soup and a roll on the way. That was our pre-match meal … I mean,* meals *didn't exist. We got sandwiches – or called in for fish and chips somewhere – on the way back from an afternoon game.*

And your travels could be even more harrowing if your final destination lay across the River Itchen from Southampton, which meant taking the Woolston Ferry over to the Supermarine Works at a time when 'Southampton was being pretty well hammered with bombing raids'. So, if you needed to cross there for Netley Hospital, you faced a long wait when you returned from an away game to find that the ferry was closed until the night's bombing stopped. Mee has a '*vivid* memory' of waiting at the crossing, on the Southampton side, 'crouching down – just looking at everything, the flames, bombs flying everywhere – and keeping our fingers crossed … I had to sit it out until four, five or six in the morning till the ferry started again, before I could get back to Netley'.

When this routine became 'far too much', he asked Tom Parker to count him out: he needed to concentrate on his war work and on qualifying as a physiotherapist, who would, of course, stay in the game – running the Treatment of Injuries course at Lilleshall for 20 years, towards the end of which he would become the Arsenal physio, before going on to be such a successful, double-winning, manager at Highbury. Bertie Mee played 16 times for the Saints in that 1940-41 season. One of his two goals came in a 6-4 defeat at Southend, a scoreline that encapsulates the Saints' dismal season of F53 A111.

Partners – Whist, a Wedding and a Wing

The bunch of youngsters, forever on the road, was held together by John Harris, who continued to play in nearly every game. His brother, Neil, an accountant, arrived and signed for Saints that season. He soon impressed the *Echo* with heading skills redolent of Dixie Dean, but would manage only six war-time appearances for them. The Harris brothers and Bertie Mee apart, there were few guests in that second season at war. Indeed, Southampton's dependence upon its own youngsters was favourably noted in the Brighton programme, when the Saints went there on 19 April 1941, to incur their third defeat at the Goldstone Ground in the space of six weeks. Applauding these resilient young travellers, the writer claimed to have assured Tom Parker repeatedly that, 'if he can only hang tight to this team he is going to save his directors a goodly sum'. Recalling how the manager tried to pass on such articles of faith to his young players, Les Laney rues some of the larrupings they had to endure: 'Other sides had *top* players'.

These were players to be held in some awe, of course, by the youngsters being thrown in at the deep end. Like Bill Ellerington coming into the first team, aged 17, and finding himself playing against Frank Swift and Tommy Lawton. He likes to relive a move in which both of these distinguished visitors featured during the game against Aldershot at The Dell on 5 October 1940:

> *Swiftie picked up the ball and threw it like a tennis ball – not over-arm – to roughly the half-way line, outside-right. This fellah went about ten, twelve yards and hit a long, diagonal through-ball. Lawton's off and catches this on the half-volley. And that ball – no exaggeration – hit our cross-bar and landed practically in the centre-circle. Charlie White [the 'keeper for most of that 1940-41 season] is still stood there and the bar was 'Throb! Throb!' God, didn't he hit it?*

He hit plenty *under* the bar, too – enough to bring him 337 war-time goals – and we shall have more stories of Lawton's visits to The Dell in an Aldershot shirt.

⁓

There would be no such visits in 1941-42. Aldershot and Portsmouth had gone off with the London clubs, leaving Southampton to play but four southern neighbours several times each. So they arranged six friendlies against the Army and a couple against the Navy to complete their fixtures. This meant swapping Tommy Lawton for his great hero, 'Dixie' Dean, whose goal-scoring record Tommy would have broken, he insists, had the War not interrupted the march of Everton's Championship side of 1939. Having gone across Salisbury Plain to play an Army XI at one of the camps

DELL DIAMOND

– Warminster way, it seems – in September 1941, Tom Parker's young lads were surprised to find themselves up against Dean. He scored twice in the Army's 5-2 win and left a lasting impression on Bill Ellerington: 'Big Dixie! I mean he's got thighs as big as my waist. And, yeah, he was playing against *us*. What you've got to put into perspective is that I'm a young lad of 18, who's been dreaming about Dixie Dean. And there he is! Marvellous!'

The odd season of 1941-42 began a fortnight later. The Dell was still not ready, so the Saints entertained Cardiff at the Pirelli-General Sports Ground in Eastleigh. The *Echo* enjoyed the novelty of the setting: 'Nearby the pitch … there were tennis courts – in use – and a pavilion comfortably nestling along near the sidelines – a most pleasant spot'.

The next month, they were back at The Dell. But not Ted Bates – except when Follands played a cup-tie there. He turned out entirely for Follands that season – with and against other Southampton players. There was the friendly for the 'Aid to Russia Fund' in February, against a Cunliffe-Owen side, captained by Arthur Holt and including a handful of on-loan police. And most of those ex-Saints police officers were out in force for the Hampshire Senior Cup Final at The Dell. No fewer than eight of the former Saints who had joined the Borough Police played for them in the side that beat Follands. The losers lined up with eight League players: Brennan (Barnsley); Townsend (local), Tann (Charlton); Dodgin (Saints), Allen (Villa), Bushby (Portsmouth); De Lisle (local), Bates (Saints), Ryans (local), Foss (Chelsea) and Anderson (Portsmouth).

Against the Law
The Follands team – with manager, Tubby Wiseman (seated left), and Mr Folland (standing right) – that lost to the Police, in the Hampshire Senior Cup Final of 1942.
Back row (left to right): Dodgin, Townsend, Brennan, Tann, Allen, Bushby.
Front row: De Lisle, Anderson, Ryans, Foss, Bates.

Partners – Whist, a Wedding and a Wing

This time, though, Follands won the League from Portsmouth Reserves. It was also a better season for the Saints. They started with their youngsters. Joining in the chorus of approval for young men taking a thrashing – this time by 6-1 at Dean Court to a Bournemouth side that had 10 guests – the *Echo* applauded this long-term strategy and likened it to the Club's youth-recruiting policy of the First World War. A few more guests arrived, though, including Walley Barnes, whose autobiography, *Captain of Wales,* recounts, in some detail, his interlude at The Dell. His recall has several glaring inaccuracies, but let's start by accepting his claim that Tom Parker had offered him and his brother John 'attractive terms' in 1938. But not attractive enough to stop the pair of them signing amateur forms for Portsmouth, instead. During the 1941-42 season, however, Barnes bumped into Mr Parker again. His regiment was at Blandford, where his Bombardier, Willie Watson – of subsequent fame as an England international, both at football and cricket – occasionally guested for Bournemouth. Watson took Barnes to watch Bournemouth entertain Southampton – something the Cherries did four times that season for a remarkable aggregate of 16-5 – and Mr Parker was so 'amiable' as to forgive his having preferred Portsmouth in 1938.

So it was that Barnes came to play a few games at inside-left for the Saints late in 1941-42. For his second game, away to Bristol City, he recalls being picked up at Salisbury in a Rolls Royce, which he shared with three other players. An improvement, then, on the transport arrangements experienced by Bertie Mee? Not necessarily. Taking the team across Salisbury Plain in three cars had proved problematic when Bristol City visited The Dell earlier that season. Only one car had arrived in time for the Christmas morning fixture. Fortunately, it included the kit. But only two players. So the visitors had to borrow nine men, including Les Laney and a few other Southampton players. Trainer Jimmy Gallagher – a war-time arrival not to be confused with the 1950s trainer of the same name – also obliged and scored for the visitors in their 5-2 defeat. The crowd was said to be 2,250, but three of them were called to the colours of Bristol City. Even by war-time standards, this degree of improvisation earned the game top billing in the chapter on 'Unusual Happenings' in Rollin's *Soccer at War*.

Posted, in the summer of 1942, to the Southern Command PT School at Winterbourne Dauntsey just north of Salisbury, Barnes was available to play 28 games for the Saints in the 1942-43 season, when Ted Bates returned to play a similar number of games at inside-right. Barnes does not have happy memories of the opening day. The Saints were back in the big-time – with Portsmouth, Aldershot and the London clubs – and Aldershot's 5-1 win at the Recreation Ground gave them an immediate taste of what they had been missing. For the return game, on 28 November, extensively reported in his autobiography, Barnes lined up with John Harris and five of the season's new guests. Bert Tann and Harold Pond were taking an occasional outing from Follands. George Tweedy, the Grimsby and England 'keeper, would have a few games for the Saints, all of them that season. Centre-forward Alf Whittingham, of Bradford City, would stay much longer – for 78 games in which he would score 84 goals. And the Manchester United left-winger, Charlie Mitten, would guest for a couple of seasons from his cosy quarters in the New Forest. Like Barnes, Mitten was a PT Instructor, in his case in the RAF. With his family quartered in a nearby bungalow, Charlie found life at RAF Beaulieu 'a piece of cake'. He had met Bill Stroud at a match somewhere and Bill had suggested he come to The Dell.

The full Saints line-up in that win over Aldershot was Tweedy; Tann, Roles; Pond, Harris, Stroud; Bevis, Bates, Whittingham, Barnes and Mitten. Aldershot had Tommy Lawton leading their attack, with Jimmy Hagan (of Sheffield United and, later, England) at inside-forward. Of Aldershot's famous All-England half-back line, only Cliff Britton was playing, while Frank Swift cried off late to be replaced in goal by Denis Herod of Stoke City. Barnes's match report – only slightly abridged and with clichés retained – reads as follows:

> From the whistle we peppered the visitors' goal. Billy Bevis, on leave from the Navy, soon found his land-legs and was unlucky not to score … with a low cross-shot, while Alf Whittingham, Ted Bates and myself also put in shots that would have defeated a goalkeeper in less brilliant form than was Denis Herod … It was Billy Stroud, advancing with the forwards, who gave us the lead after about twenty minutes' play …
>
> Aldershot piled on the pressure. Cliff Britton hit the post with a free-kick and Jimmy Hagan cast magic spells all over the field with his twinkling toes, but we counter-attacked and Mitten, Bates and Bevis … came close … Then, just before the interval, Tommy Lawton scored a fine equalizer. He took the ball in his stride, crashed through the defence and hammered the ball past Tweedy.
>
> Despite this set-back we were determined to keep a grip … and soon after the interval Eddie Bates gave us the lead, a lead that we maintained until the end.

You will have noticed that Bates was back in partnership, for this game, with Bevis, while Mitten was on the left-wing, where older fans will remember him – as in Manchester United's cup-winning side of 1948 and later at Fulham. Southampton played him on both wings that season. When Bates and he were paired on the left for the first home game, the *Echo* felt they 'would form an admirable wing if they could be kept together'. A few weeks later, 'Commentator' was confessing that he had 'not enjoyed a winger's play, in war-time football, more than … Mitten's' and urging that he be played on the left, where 'Bates is the man' to partner him. Mitten agrees on both counts: he was 'always a left-winger' and he liked playing with Bates, because 'Ted's a football player' who would give him 'the right pass at the right time and at the right strength'. Come February, 'Commentator' was revelling in his ideal Mitten-Bates 'co-ordination' – albeit on the right – when the pair provided 'one of the most entertaining features' of a 4-2 win over QPR. And three weeks later, when the Saints beat Palace 5-1, they were 'a right wing good to watch from the stand and a headache to the Palace defenders'.

After the Aldershot game, the Saints faced Arsenal, who would be the high-scoring winners of that season's League South, at The Dell. There is a touch of 'we wuz robbed' about Barnes's match report on Southampton's 3-1 defeat. Two of Arsenal's famous goal-scorers – Ted Drake and Alf Kirchen – were absent on RAF duty. This pair personifies the pillaging of young talent, from the likes of Southampton and Norwich, with which the Arsenal had consolidated their dominant position in the mid-thirties. We touched on Drake's beginnings in Chapter 1: joining the Saints as an 18 year-old from Winchester City in 1931, he had roared almost straight into the first team – a journey that Terry Paine would repeat in 1957. After 74 games and 48 goals, Drake became George Allison's first signing in 1934. Kirchen had had only 18 games for Norwich before Tom Parker sold him to the Arsenal in 1935.

Even without this duo – not to mention other stars required by the Army or RAF – Barnes considered the visiting team to be 'strongly representative', with a forward-line that included Cliff Bastin, Reg Lewis and Denis Compton, their three main scorers that season. For their part, Southampton fielded a one-off guest. Tom Finney. The 'Preston Plumber' would feature high in anybody's postwar 'Hall of Fame' – Preston-born Eddy Brown, who would leave his home-town club to be the Saints' centre-forward in 1950, ranks 'Sir Tom' (and he was calling him that long before the Queen caught on) as second only to Duncan Edwards.

"TURF" CIGARETTES

TOM FINNEY
PRESTON NORTH END & ENGLAND

50 FAMOUS FOOTBALLERS Nº 41

DELL DIAMOND

In 1942, though, Finney was, he insists, 'an unknown' who was thrilled to be facing the Arsenal in their pomp – a modest self-assessment for somebody who had played against them, 18 months earlier, in the war-time Cup Final. Yet he had certainly remained unknown to Southampton earlier that year while he was doing his tank training at Bovington, and was allowed to return north without a game. After a period at Catterick, and a few games for Newcastle, he was back in the Saints' catchment area at RAC Tidworth and expecting to head further south – they didn't order you to pack your tropical kit for December on Salisbury Plain. Even then, Finney suspects that Preston had to alert Southampton as to his availability. There was time, before he sailed from Southampton, for just the one game against the Arsenal: 'It was just a question of shaking hands and saying "Where are you stationed?" – and then it was "Goodbye" and I was off'. That fleeting acquaintance with his inside-forward was sufficient, though, for the *Echo* to feel that Tom Finney 'hit up a grand partnership with Eddie Bates'.

Two games later, the Saints had a new scoring partner for Whittingham. Jackie Stamps of Derby County. A knee injury had been keeping him out of football when Charlie Mitten recruited him on Waterloo Station. He duly scored in a 7-2 win at Reading, in which Whittingham got four. The Saints were now rampant, apart from a 2-0 home defeat by Portsmouth on Boxing Day. In the six games either side of that set-back, they scored 29 goals, culminating in an 11-0 home win over Luton. The players signed the ball, to be formally presented, at the next home game, to Whittingham, who had scored eight. We are left to wonder whose ration coupons, or whatever, paid for a new match ball.

The high-scoring guest from Bradford City got 15 of those 29 goals. Bates was keeping pace with Stamps and the Saints finished fifth in the League South, their best war-time placing which they would equal in 1945.

Their season was not over, though. It was the end of February. There was still a Cup competition to be played and a managerial upheaval to be endured.

Chapter 5

Parker Knell

The two South Cup games against Clapton Orient – the sides played three opponents home and away in qualifying leagues – were notable for quite different reasons.

The game at The Dell on 6 March provided another strange example – if hardly comparable with the Christmas chaos of the season before – of the *impromptu* loans that were necessary when players failed to arrive. Orient needed to borrow but two players, of whom Jack Scott was one. He made an immediate impact. Literally so – he collided with Bert Tann, who went off concussed. The visitors now had 11 men to the Saints' 10. True, Tann returned, but the oddity of rules that allowed on-the-spot loans but no substitutes will be apparent.

When Tann left the field, Barnes moved to right-back, where he 'enjoyed' himself. He'd played at full-back before and would play further South Cup games there (ignore his autobiographical claims to the contrary), on either flank. And he'd go on to do so, of course, for Arsenal and Wales.

He attributes his move to the Arsenal to boardroom interference before the return with Orient. With several players injured, Tom Parker was ready, Barnes alleges, to bring in reserves – until one of the directors 'ordered wholesale positional changes'. It was this incident, he claims, that 'caused Tom Parker to fall out with this official and leave the club at the end of the season'.

That seems to be a simplistic account both of cause and effect. It's not clear, for a start, what positional changes were at issue in a team that included newcomers Jones of Northampton in goal and Rudkin of Lincoln City at outside-left. By war-time standards, it was a remarkably orthodox line-up: Jones; Tann, Barnes; Pond, Harris, Stroud; Mitten, Bates, Tomlinson, Stamps and Rudkin. What's more, a split between Mr Parker and the Board appears to have been developing for some time. At the end of the previous season, perhaps having decided that his prediction of a short war was misguided, the Secretary-Manager had asked the Board 'to consider relieving him of all responsibilities for the duration of war'.

Nothing came of this, but Tom Parker was clearly intent, towards the end of that 1942-43 season, on obtaining both a better immediate deal and a longer-term guarantee. In a letter to Toby Keleher on 10 February, he confided that he had already had 'two offers to leave the town, one at once, with a war job found for me, and the salary that cannot be easily pushed aside'. He was still hopeful, though, of achieving his ambitions by remaining at The Dell: keen though he was 'to get to the top in football management', he remained 'very loth to leave the town, for I am convinced that given the right encouragement and support, I can realise my ambition right here in Southampton'.

Mr Parker appears to have raised these matters with the Board in broadly similar terms. He first asked 'where exactly he stood' on 6 March (the day of the home game with Orient). For, although 'he was not desirous of making a change', he had been 'invited', as the Minutes elegantly put it, 'to interview a gentleman re another appointment'. An exchange of letters during April failed to meet Mr Parker's concerns. Then, at a special meeting on 7 May, the Directors determined to pay him a lump-sum of £75 in respect of the season just ended and to raise his weekly pay to £5 in the season and £3 out of season.

Tom Parker replied that he had declined the interview elsewhere, since he wanted 'to play the game by Southampton'; suggested that his value to the club must be £500 a year; but offered a formula that would give him £460 – almost twice the Board's offer. When the Board refused to budge, the Secretary-Manager 'asked to be relieved forthwith of his duties ... for the duration of the War'. He agreed, though, to accept the £75 bonus on offer and to remain until the end of June, in order to prepare the accounts for that successful season of 1942-43.

On 1 June, he wrote to inform Toby Keleher that he had resigned 'for the duration of hostilities, you are not surprised at my action, and I think you would have been disappointed in me had I remained with the club after their recent decision for the future of the club'. It is not abundantly clear what this decision was – save that the Board had declined to discuss its expectations as to post-war football.

~

Whatever the explanation for his going, Mr Parker was not the only one on the way out. He summoned the players to his office, one by one, Barnes recalls, to tell them that, 'owing to a difference of opinion, he was ending his contract with Southampton'. It didn't stop there: Tom Parker offered, Barnes contends, to broker a move to 'another club' if any player preferred to leave The Dell.

Walley Barnes was *told*, he says, that he was going to the Arsenal – as a left-back. This arrangement was duly confirmed in writing by the two managers, but Barnes still needed Portsmouth to release him from his amateur registration. But where would his postwar future have been, we might ask, if Tom Parker had not conscripted him, seemingly out of pique, to the Arsenal? The irony is, of course, that Southampton would recruit their initial postwar left-back by going to Portsmouth, for Bill Rochford of their Cup-winning team.

Nor was Barnes the only player to be drafted by Parker to Highbury. Cyril Smith, another Toby Keleher discovery, had signed professional for the Saints, and had one game, at the end of the 1939-40 season. He played another nine in 1940-41 before his family was bombed out – whereupon 'we got our clothes over our arms, went up to the bus station and got on the bus and that's how we arrived in Salisbury'.

And that was the end of Cyril's Southampton career. Although only 22 miles from Southampton and despite overtures from Tom Parker and Toby Keleher, he found it 'very difficult' to get away from his work as an engineer: 'you weren't allowed to run around the country when you wanted to'. In that occupation, you went where the Ministry directed you. He played for various Home Guard sides – 'anything to keep fit' – until Mr Parker approached him, in the spring of 1944, with an offer of another kind: the kind that Walley Barnes had felt unable to refuse almost a year earlier.

Barnes had, as it happens, returned to The Dell, on 15 April 1944, to play in a friendly for the Saints against Portsmouth (and meet Tom Parker, perchance?). Despite having established himself as a full-back for the Arsenal, he guested at inside-left in a Saints line-up that included three future international right-backs. Alf Ramsey was back to play centre-half and Eddie Shimwell, who had made 15 guest appearances that season, was at No.2. Barnes scored twice in a 3-0 win. Three weeks later, Cyril Smith was playing for the Arsenal, after Tom Parker had approached him, out of the blue, to ask whether he would like a trial for Mr Allison. Coincidence? Or had Tom Parker and Walley Barnes met and conspired to this end?

Whatever the explanation, Barnes became Smith's minder when – with travelling restrictions by now considerably eased – he began to commute to London. Never more so than after his second game, away to Luton. When the Arsenal players returned to North London from Kenilworth Road, Barnes accompanied him to Waterloo. Cyril was surprised when he learned that his companion wasn't catching the train: Walley had ushered the rookie through the underground system 'purely from a friendship point of view'. A nice touch from the more successful of Tom Parker's two gifts to George Allison. Although Cyril Smith did not fulfil his mentor's ambitions for him – just half-a-dozen games for the Arsenal – it seems appropriate, in a study of longlasting loyalty, to pause for a tribute to this Parker protegé who had been bombed out, liked Ted Bates, during the 1940-41 season. In 1947, he settled down with newly-formed Salisbury, where he has served, in some capacity, nearly ever since – a marathon of loyalty in its own right.

DELL DIAMOND

Tom Parker, meanwhile, had gone out of the game. When he quit The Dell in June 1943, he was able to concentrate full-time on his job as a ship's surveyor in the docks. The Board met on 8 June to decide how to cope with 'the temporary retirement' of its Secretary-Manager: Mr Parker had been relieved, remember, only 'for the duration'. In order to 'avoid the temporary appointment of anyone outside the club', John Sarjantson came to the rescue. A Saints' director since 1914, the Chairman provided his colleagues with 'a happy solution', by resigning from the Board to become the Club's Secretary-Manager. Mr Jukes was elected Chairman in his stead.

Assured by Mr Parker, at its next meeting, that the books were in order, the Board asked him to account for a statement by John Harris that, 'now Mr Parker had left the club he would no longer be playing for us and that there were several [other] guest players who would similarly act'. But were they intending to move as a protest or because, as Walley Barnes implies, the manager had raised the possibility of their doing so – even if their passages might have been less *assisted* than his? Tom Parker assured the Board that he was not responsible for any exodus and 'repeated his declaration of loyalty to the Club'. That was not enough for the new Chairman who wanted to hear that assurance again – and again. Mr Parker gave it, in no fewer than five forms, minuted *verbatim*.

Meanwhile, Alderman Wright had met with some of the disgruntled guest players, including Harris, Mitten and Whittingham, who were proposing to defect to Stamford Bridge. The reasons for their disaffection, he reported, were less straightforward than previously rumoured. Chelsea were benefiting, according to his enquiries, from 'an undercurrent of feeling against [the Board] connected with the matter of a Christmas box and extra payments which it was hinted other clubs had been known to pay to cover broken time, etc'.

Charlie Mitten who defected,
with John Harris and Alf Whittingham, to Stamford Bridge

There had been more than a 'hint' of such extra payments a few months earlier: in the week that the cup-ties began, Mr Parker had reported to the Board that Bill Dodgin – the Southampton half-back who was guesting for Clapton Orient against the Saints in these ties – had claimed that Orient were intending to pay double for Cup matches. Harris had asked, as captain, that Southampton do likewise, but Mr Parker had instead reported Dodgin's statement to the Football League South. The Board approved.

Mitten insists that money was not the issue – 'it was just a bigger club, that was all' – but Harris and he were gone. Both would play for Chelsea – along with the Bateses' sub-lessor, Dick Foss – in the 1944 League South Cup Final at Wembley. Although he had half-a-dozen games for

The first of the League (South) Cup games of 1943, for which Clapton Orient were allegedly paying double – thereby provoking an exodus of Southampton guest stars to London.

Chelsea in that 1943-44 season, Alf Whittingham of RAF Christchurch in fact continued to guest mainly for nearby Southampton – for whom he would keep on scoring.

If that reprieve was something to be grateful for, the Saints had lost three quality players – Barnes, Harris and Mitten – to London clubs and were left with doubts in the boardroom about the extent to which the departing manager had contributed to that migration. The same Board meeting that received Mr Wright's report also learned of the two ex-players – Arthur Dominy and Arthur Holt – who would 'take charge' of the first team and of the Reserves, respectively, under the new Secretary-Manager. Holt, you may remember, was often keeping Ted Bates out of the first team in the last two seasons before the war and played regularly in the first war-time season. Dominy had scored 146 goals in a long career (369 games from 1913 to 1926) for the Saints, as they progressed from the Southern League to the Football League in 1920, with promotion to Division II in 1922. In his last eight seasons for the Saints, Tom Parker was a regular team-mate. Dominy played in that 1925 semi-final which was such a catastrophe for Parker.

DELL DIAMOND

The first Sarjantson-Dominy season – 1943-44 – was barely under way before the Board returned to Mr Wright's theme that there were soldiers to spare in Aldershot. This time their target was specific: Mr Sarjantson had been dispatched to Aldershot in the hope of securing the services of Stan Cullis as a replacement for the departed Harris. The Shots' manager, Billy McCracken, had told the Saints' envoy that the England centre-half was far too popular for such a move to be countenanced but he had undertaken to help find a replacement for Mitten. His recommendation, Bonass of QPR, duly arrived to play against Charlton on 18 September. He was immediately injured and soon gone. Wilf Grant of Manchester City would feature rather more, that season and the next, on that problem wing and would later sign for the Saints.

In fact, there was rather a lot of coming and going in 1943-44, with 53 players turning out in a side that conceded 105 goals in its 36 games. Their worst defeat – by 10-1 – came at Aldershot in November, when Tommy Lawton got six – although the *Echo* claimed that 'Aldershot's nine goals' margin exaggerated the difference between the two teams'. Nor were they scoring so freely. Even Whittingham, after his flirtation with Chelsea, was reduced to a single hat-trick. Roper, like Roles an ever-present, also got one.

Ted Bates missed only one game. Although he scored but eight goals, his right-wing partnership with Roper began to receive, that season, the sort of notices that he had enjoyed with Bevis before the War and with Mitten the previous season. Reporting on their opening day draw, 2-2 at home to Aldershot, the *Echo* predicted 'bright prospects' for this pairing. In the next home game – Bonass's unfortunate debut against Charlton – this right-wing duo 'made some of the best forward movements of the match'. Even in that 10-1 humiliation by Aldershot in November, Bates and Roper contrived to be 'a good right-wing' and the side's 'chief source of danger'. And so it continued, through to the Saints' dire performance, come February and March, in the League South Cup, when the right wing pair were 'the stars of Southampton's attack' in a 5-1 hammering at Upton Park.

The season's new arrivals included another young soldier who had signed amateur forms for Portsmouth in 1940. According to his autobiography, though, Fratton Park had never acknowledged the registration of a young centre-half in the name of Alfred Ernest Ramsey.

Joining up in June 1940, he eventually arrived at Barton Stacey in Hampshire as Sergeant Ramsey of the Duke of Cornwall Light Infantry and captain of the football team. He was at centre-half in the Army XI that came to The Dell for a pre-season match on 21 August 1943. Alf Freeman, who was later to join him in Saints' colours, was at inside-right in a battalion side that went down 10-3. Bates and Roper scored two each.

Parker Knell

In his first experience of professional opposition, the visiting No.5 was 'bewildered' by their 'speed of thought and movement'. Seven weeks later, though, Sgt Ramsey *(right)* was summoned to his CO's office to receive a request, from The Dell, to report to Southampton Central Station the next day. According to the *Echo,* he was due in town anyhow to captain the Army against the Reserves at The Dell. If we accept his account – notwithstanding that, like Barnes's, it contains obvious inaccuracies, in this case compounded by his biographer, Max Marquis, telling a different story with different errors – then Ramsey duly arrived at the station, collected his tuppence-ha'penny expenses from Mr Sarjantson and signed amateur forms for Southampton on the train, on which he sat next to Ted Bates.

A meeting, then, of two errand boys. Like Ted, Alf's first job had involved delivering groceries on his bike. And he, too, had played in the shop-boys' Thursday afternoon team – although Five Elms United doesn't have quite the ring of 'Thetford Thursday'. Their destination on 9 October 1943 was Kenilworth Road. A late goal from Don Roper gave the Saints a 3-2 win and spared the blushes of the debutant who had conceded the penalty from which Luton had come back to 2-2. In a more objective account of Alf Ramsey's arrival, the *Echo* reported that 'the defence as a whole functioned satisfactorily'.

His next game, three weeks later, was in a 7-0 defeat at Loftus Road. Wilf Heathcote, QPR's high-scoring centre-forward, gave him 'the run-around' and got four of Rangers' goals. After three more games for the Saints in 1943-44, a posting to County Durham took Ramsey out of contention. Returning south in 1944, he duly signed professional for Southampton. He reports, with an apparent sense of lasting *chagrin,* that he never received 'the usual £10 signing-on fee players are handed when they become professionals'. What Ramsey does not reveal is that players still serving in HM Forces were not entitled to such a fee – an explanation later given to him by the young woman who arrived at The Dell in August 1945 as Mr Sarjantson's assistant. Mary Bates.

Mr Sarjantson's appointment of an assistant had been almost 18 months on hold. The Secretary-Manager had sat next to Mary at Don Roper's wedding, in March 1944, and had asked whether she would like to work for him after the War. Come the armistice, though, Mary went to work for the Southampton Labour Party for the duration of the General Election campaign. The election won, the local Party – in which both of her parents were active – wanted her to become its permanent secretary. But soon after the return of a Labour Government in the election of July 1945, she moved to The Dell to take up Mr Sarjantson's offer.

Presentation Party

Ten of the side that beat Watford 3-1, with a Whittingham hat-trick on 4 March 1944, retired to the Polygon for tea with the Board and for a presentation to Don Roper and his fiancée, in celebration of their marriage the following Saturday.

The line-up had an unusually high number of guests, including three in uniform at the front.

Back row (left to right): Bert Head (cashier), Stroud, Bates, Whittingham, Tann, Dodgin, Mr Prince (director), Arthur Dominy (team manager), Mr Cosgrove (director).

Middle row: Mr Wright (director), Roper, Mr Sarjantson (secretary-manager), Mrs Roper (designate), Mr Jukes (chairman), Mr Hoskins (director).

Front row: Jimmy Gallagher (trainer), Drinkwater, Jones, Hamilton, Roles.

The season between job offer and job start had started with a bang – 18 goals scored in the first three games of 1944-45, with Whittingham and Roper getting six apiece. Bates, Roles and Stroud each played in all 36 games, which produced 205 League and Cup goals (F125 A80).

Bill Stroud attracted some unusual notices that season. On successive Saturdays at White Hart Lane – against Arsenal and Spurs – the *Echo* approvingly noted his long throw-ins. Stroud says that this feat involved a sleight-of-hand which he had been taught by John Arnold, the former Saints' winger and longstanding Hampshire opener who had the remarkable record of being capped once at each sport. Not to mince words, the perpetrator says they were 'foul throws'. Arnold had become the landlord of *The Criterion* in St Mary's, Southampton, and Stroud would go there to practise propelling the ball deceptively with one hand.

Meanwhile, the Bates-Roper wing was again flying. The London correspondent of the *Echo* felt that 'their skilful interchange of position had much to do with Southampton's decisive win', by 4-1 at Millwall on 9 September. The more he saw of this pair, 'the better they seem to play'. Their high-spot, though, came away to Arsenal on 30 December when they turned it on before an England selector. In a match report headed 'My Present To FA', Alex James – Ted Bates's schoolboy hero – commended Roper for the 'nonchalance' of a Matthews and recommended him to the England selectors as the successor to Matthews. True, the former Scottish international went on to praise the Saints' *team* – 'easily the best' he had seen all season – for their 4-2 win, but it was Roper's 'remarkable' display that made the headlines, with Bates's contribution to it being generously noted. As the *Echo* remarked, 'Bates, an untiring forager and a great shot, was never subdued, and Roper was even more outstanding'. Elsewhere, Bates was credited with 'a grand goal with a magnificent shot from the corner of the penalty area after a run from half-way – a feat in itself'. Other reports called it 'really brilliant' and predicted that much would be heard of 'this enterprising young wing partnership'. Their Arsenal triumph even made the news in Norwich, thanks to a City supporter who had witnessed it and who wrote to the local 'paper in praise of 'the best right wing [partnership] he had seen in South League matches [all] season' and of Bates, 'the Saints' star forward'.

So, while Roper was being tipped for England, Bates was getting good notices in his own right – as for a goal, away to Watford in the Cup, that the *Echo* thought 'a model of individualism', and, in the return game, for 'a gem of footwork'. Roper was 'out of touch' in that match, as he had been the previous week, when he was suffering from boils on his arm. That did not stop Bates having 'a grand game' as the Saints beat Luton 12-3. They rattled in 29 goals in their six cup-ties, including seven by Dick Dorsett, that season's star guest from Wolves. His 23 goals in 16 games included a hat-trick of penalties when Chelsea came to The Dell in the League. Whittingham was guesting for Chelsea, but he came back to hit eight Cup goals, including four of the 12 against Luton when Ramsey, who was standing in as an inside-left, also scored four.

Jack Bradley was captaining Luton that day but was back, scoring well for the Saints in the last four games of the War. The climax was a 5-3 win at Aldershot, a consequence, the *Echo's* Aldershot correspondent felt, of 'lively' forward play and of Frank Swift being out of 'international' sorts. Saints thereby completed a double over the Hampshire neighbours – Dorsett had got another hat-trick in the 7-2 win at The Dell – whose famous guests they had coveted.

DELL DIAMOND

The *Echo* heralded the win at Aldershot as 'a fitting end to a good season'. The season was not over, though, for Ted Bates who offered to play for Aldershot at Brighton, the following Saturday, and to take Bill Stroud with him. This entailed exchanges with the Aldershot manager that offer an insight into the ponderous communications with potential guest players when few of them were likely to have a 'phone. The Fosses had by now given up the Netley lease and returned to London, so that Ted and Mary had moved to Shirley, to live with her parents at 29 Victor Street. On the Tuesday, Mr McCracken accepted the first part of the Bates offer by letter to that address and undertook to let him 'know later about Stroud by wire'. Or Ted might prefer to ring him at the Recreation Ground, on Thursday evening, on Aldershot 11. The manager's telegram on Wednesday afternoon circumvented this: he confirmed that both players would be needed on the Saturday.

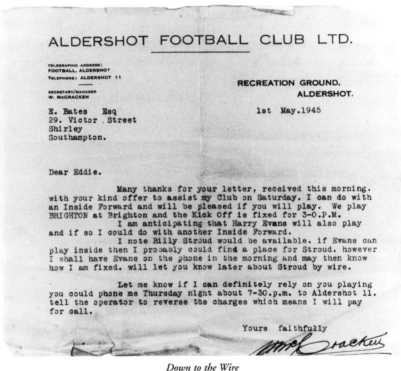

Down to the Wire

When the Aldershot manager wanted Bates and Stroud to guest for him, he was not sure whether Ted understood how to reverse the charges to Aldershot 11. So he wired the team news to him.

That game at Brighton was on 5 May 1945. Three days later came the armistice. Then, two months later, the election. And then it was August, with Mary joining Ted for a new phase at The Dell.

Chapter 6

Peaceful Interlude

It was to be a strange season. Guests would continue to be allowed. There would still be no Football League but the League South was expanded to 22 teams, extending to Wales and the Midlands. The FA Cup would resume, albeit with each round played over two legs.

So Portsmouth would at last have to defend the trophy they had 'held' since 1939 – a fact of which they reminded the Saints' directors when they went to Fratton Park for the third game of the season. The FA Cup was placed on the Boardroom table, sporting the holders' ribbons. Portsmouth won 3-2.

The first two games had been against Plymouth, a 5-5 draw at The Dell being followed by a 3-0 win for the Saints at a bomb-ravaged Home Park. With none of their stands having survived the blitz, Argyle brought in a double-decker bus as a directors' box. Alf Ramsey scored twice in each game – from his latest position of centre-forward. The inside-left experiment – which had seen him score four against Luton, remember – had been discontinued when, by his own admission, he had been 'a complete and utter failure' in the next game. Nor was this latest arrangement intended to last. As the *Echo* reflected, he did 'not pretend to be a centre-forward', despite his 'shooting power and forcefulness, which makes him a dangerous man near goal'. Relief for the reluctant No. 9 came in the form of a guest centre-forward – Brooks of Burnley – for the Portsmouth game. Although the guest never stayed, Ramsey had now reverted to centre-half. This meant the introduction, at centre-forward, of Bobby Veck. Having joined the Club as an 18 year-old amateur in 1938, Veck had spent the War on active service and was only now returning to play. He was essentially a left-winger, but this would not be the last time he was drafted to centre-forward.

Ramsey was soon back at centre-forward, and getting a hat-trick in a 6-2 win, when Jack Bradley failed to arrive for the game at Newport on 6 October. Bradley's travel arrangements were the problem. He liked to hitch-hike and try to claim his train fare from Mary Bates. Amid this chopping and changing upfront, The Bates-Roper wing remained constant and was receiving notices consistent with the close season expectations of Leslie Yates of *Sporting World*. In a special feature on the prospects for 'a popular southern club of great traditions', Yates was moved to 'single out Ted Bates for special praise':

DELL DIAMOND

Apart from a brief spell, Bates has held down the inside-right berth throughout the war and before finally dove-tailing with Don Roper struggled gamely to get the best out of a variety of wing partners.

A ninety-minute man, Bates combines thoughtful football with the ability to hit the ball where goalkeepers like it least, but his strongest suit is the through pass to his winger on the blind side of the back.

Ready for action: Ted Bates pictured at Stamford Bridge in September 1945, early in his busiest-ever season, in which he played 45 games for the first team.

While Bates was now considered a pre-war player 'of experience' – he was 27 – Yates gave 'pride of place' among the war-time arrivals to Don Roper, 'of whom much will be heard. An athlete from tip to toe'.

Roper was the only ever-present in 1945-46, with his right-wing partner missing but one game. Doug McGibbon was again available at centre-forward. He was still working as an aircraft fitter at RAF Shellingford in Oxfordshire, but would manage 33 games that season, commuting on his Rudge Whitworth motorcycle. After the Ramsey experiment, he was the next wearer of the No.9 shirt. Stroud and Evans missed few games at wing-half. Harry Evans had arrived in 1943. He would play in the four FA Cup legs of 1945-46 but manage only the one 'official' League game the following season. And, although Albie Roles continued to be the main full-back, Bill Ellerington was coming into contention. When Wolves came to The Dell on 20 October, he was at right-back, marking Jimmy Mullen, his pal from England Schoolboys days. A 4-2 defeat by Wolves was the start of a six-game run in which the Saints conceded 20 goals and took only one point.

The run ended when a new guest arrived to keep goal – at home to Birmingham City. Ian Black of Aberdeen had played in the Chelsea side, along with Foss and Harris, that had won the League South Cup in 1945. Reporting on the 1-1 draw with Birmingham, Thomas Moult – he of the famous poetic obituary of Herbert Chapman – described Black's performance as that of 'a young leopard'. But, then, it was a display that drove the man from the *Echo* to lyricism of his own. Not 'for a very long time' had he 'seen so many pile-driving, almost point-blank drives at goal saved so superbly ... Black did all his work with the calm assurance of a top-class player – sure in anticipation, agile, smooth'.

When he came over from Bordon to guest for the Saints, Ian would stay at the Bitterne home of Bill and Gladys Dodgin, a house that appears to have been something of a refuge, too, for the wives of guest players who were stationed nearby. Mrs Dodgin especially recalls Mrs Stamps stopping there when Jackie was guesting at The Dell in 1943-44, but generally reckoned to make her home available in this way: 'That's how everybody was during the War'. For the 21 year-old Black, this arrangement gave him 'a second mother and father'. 'Daddy Dodgin', as he was soon to become known, was now 36. On 11 November, the Board appointed him trainer-coach. It was to be on a weekly basis and he would continue to play for a while.

This first stay of Ian Black was short-lived. He could manage only five games before being posted to Malta. Fortunately, he would return to The Dell two years later. Eric Day was also under embarkation orders when, a week after Black, he made his 'debut' – although only the Cup games would count, this season, as official appearances – away to Birmingham. He had been pressed upon the Saints by Bill Luckett, his PTI in the RAF. Luckett had had 219 games for the Saints between 1928 and 1937 and would be returning to the training staff at The Dell. His discovery had taken up football in the RAF, only when a hand injury kept him from rugby, the sport he had played at Watford Grammar School. This late-developer made an instant impression upon the *Echo* reporter as 'the most promising left-winger seen in the Saints' side this season'. Having disappointed in his second game, he, too, was gone. But, like Black he would be back – only sooner and for a lot longer.

Meanwhile, the right-wing pair continued to attract attention. At White Hart Lane, the following Saturday, when Saints lost 4-3, the *Echo* thought that 'Bates was undoubtedly the best of the Saints' forwards' and acclaimed 'a typical Roper goal' from long range. George Allison was there, watching Roper for the Arsenal. The direct, goal-scoring approach of the Saints' right-winger made him an obvious replacement for Alf Kirchen, whom Mr Allison had snatched from Tom Parker in his Norwich days. But, according to Mr Sarjantson, who was interviewed at that game by Frank Butler, Roper was not for sale. Nor were Bates or Stroud, who were both interesting other clubs. As a measure of Southampton's financial buoyancy, the Saints' secretary-manager told Butler that the club was now only £15,000 in debt, compared with more than £40,000 in the early 1930s. Hereupon, he volunteered the arithmetic reported in Chapter 1: when George Allison had paid Southampton £6,000 for Ted Drake in 1934, only £250 remained after the most pressing bills had been settled. There was no question of a repeat, Mr Sarjantson insisted. The Board would not be 'tempted to starve the club of talent to pay off the debt. It will be cleared in about two years without selling'. So hands off, Arsenal!

DELL DIAMOND

And so to the final game of 1945, when 23,439 – the highest Dell gate since the outbreak of war – turned out for the visit of Chelsea.

The 'Bank of England' team had recently bought Tommy Lawton, who'd enjoyed all those guest goals for Aldershot against the Saints, to play between England inside forwards, Joe Payne – of 10 goals for Luton fame – and Len Goulden.

Lawton had gone into Christmas on a roll – 10 goals in six games – and Chelsea had won 8-0 at Millwall on Boxing Day. Yet it was the Saints' Doug McGibbon who was to capture the headlines, with six goals in their 7-0 win. This included the fastest goal yet scored from a kick-off, eclipsing the December 1938 record of 9.6 seconds by Villa's Bob Iverson against Charlton. That's according to the stopwatch of George Searle, the referee. Mr Searle, the manager of the Salisbury Swimming Baths, was proud of his watch, with which he also timed swimming and boxing events. When he showed this watch to McGibbon, as they returned to the centre-circle, it was stopped at 4.6 seconds from the kick-off for the second half (*not* the first half as Jack Rollin records in his *Soccer at War*).

But, then, the record books tend to focus on goals scored from the original kick-off. Rollin's various *Guinness* records suggest that, since 1958, three or four players have done that in six seconds. But *Ian St John's Book of Soccer Lists* includes three 'claims' for faster goals, including one at 3.5 seconds, since 1965. Whatever the merits of these competing claims, it appears that a goal in 4.6 seconds was some kind of record in 1945. It came from the four-touch move that Bates and Cutting had worked out in their bedroom before the War. You may remember (from Chapter 2) that, when it resulted in a goal against QPR Reserves in 1939, Cutting had got in ahead of McGibbon to score. This time, though, the centre-forward would start and finish the move, with Ted Bates still the second man and with Bill Stroud now the third. Doug McGibbon takes up the story:

> *We were winning 3-0 at half-time and it was our kick-off for the second half. I just tapped the ball to Ted Bates and Bill Stroud had to pinch a couple of yards without the referee looking ... Ted would kick straight across there on the diagonal. By this time, Bill had got to that point and, in the meantime, as soon as I'd touched the ball, I'd run as fast as I could down the centre – which was like a ploughed field. Bill received the ball and put it straight across on the other diagonal. I just trapped it with my left foot and hit it with my right foot, a daisy-cutter a foot inside the post.*
>
> *The Chelsea goalkeeper didn't know what day it was ... That was it. It was only because we pinched this little bit without the referee looking that it worked.*

This account concurs with that in the *Echo,* although, upon reflection, McGibbon felt that his 'daisy-cutter' was more of 'a mud-cutter, really'. And Stroud confirms that he 'infiltrated into their half … I was fortunate: the ref was facing the kick-off and had his back to me'. For good measure, several sixty-somethings – including Rob Holley and Norman Hull – have contributed their teenage terrace memories of the goal. Rob recalls the move 'exactly' as the scorer has described it as – 'ploughed field' or not – the play swept towards him at the Milton Road end. The *Echo* noted that the Saints had 'often employed this move' although McGibbon stresses that it could be used only 'once every match. Another occasion I hit the post. You couldn't do it more than once in every match; otherwise, the other team would cotton on, wouldn't they?'

Three-man move:
Stroud, the infiltrator (top),
Bates, the inventor
and McGibbon,
the record-breaker.

I guess they would – if you can imagine them with neither reconnaissance reports on upcoming opponents nor video replays of some new tactic. But, then, McGibbon had other ways of scoring that day. After all, he did get six. Bates added the other one.

6-goal McGibbon scores in $4\frac{3}{5}$ sec. —the fastest-ever

DOUGLAS McGIBBON, the Southampton centre, will remember the match with Chelsea—and not only because he scored six goals.

One of the six was scored 4 3-5 secs. after the start of the second half—more than halving the record held by Iverson, who, playing for Villa, scored 9 3-5 secs. after the kick-off in the match with Charlton on December 3, 1938.

McGibbon's time was stop-watched by the referee, Mr. G. V Searle, of Salisbury.

McGibbon is an aircraft worker at Swindon and the son of an old Southampton centre.

AND BUCHANAN

The victory was all the more remarkable because Saints' inside-left Bradley did not turn up and they borrowed Buchanan from Chelsea. Buchanan played a brilliant game, two of the three first-half goals coming from his openings. Lawton had little chance to get going against the quick tackling of the Southampton half-backs. Chelsea altogether had a bad day. Goulden missed a penalty kick and Williams, injured, spent half an hour of the second half in the dressing-room.

As we saw in the previous chapter, eight goals in a game got you the match ball, signed by your team-mates. Doug's six counted for nothing, though: the ball went, he assumes, to the winner of the *Penny On The Ball* competition. He recalls another, more informal, lottery, familiar to those of us who stood on the Dell terraces in those early post-war seasons. A group of fans would draw the names (usually by tearing up the programme) of the ten forwards (those were the days!) and pay up whenever one scored. '*Years* later', Doug met a man who'd drawn him – 'everybody wanted to draw Lawton, of course' – and who had 'cashed in' on his six goals.

DELL DIAMOND

That deferential aside to Lawton is typical of McGibbon's recall of what was such a great occasion for *him*. To beat the 'Bank of England' team was 'really something … They were, on paper, the best team in the country and we beat them seven-nothing'. He was in especial awe of Lawton's ability to 'put in whopping headers from the 18-yard line'. In that game, though, 'poor old Lawton' was 'bottled up' by Bill Dodgin. Norman Hull's 'strongest memory' is of Lawton inadvertently kicking Dodgin and then putting the ball into touch so that the Saints trainer could get on. A photographer then captured Lawton, supporting Dodgin to the touchline. The photo' also shows Lawton's two black-eyes: a souvenir from Boxing Day. When he climbed above the two-fisted punch of the Millwall 'keeper, Charlie Bumstead, to head one of Chelsea's eight goals, those two fists met him, one under each eye.

Lawton's only memory of a miserable afternoon at The Dell is of turning up with his two shiners courtesy of Bumstead. It was generally a bad day for the Chelsea forwards – Goulden even missed a penalty – although winger, Peter Buchanan, had a field-day. Rob Holley 'can see him now … rampaging down the wing and putting over cross after cross'. The centre-forward on the end of those crosses was not, however, Lawton. It was McGibbon. Jack Bradley, the Saints' inside-left and wayward hitch-hiker, had again failed to show, so Don Roper moved over from the right wing to take his place. And Chelsea loaned Southampton Buchanan, their Scottish international 12th man who had been with Bates and Dodgin at Follands, remember, when he had guested a few times for the Saints. In fact, the home side had had some difficulty in raising a team.

Armed Escort: Having kicked Bill Dodgin (stripes), Tommy Lawton (black eyes) helps him off the pitch, supported by trainer Gallagher and supervised by referee Searle.

With neither Ellerington nor Emanuel available, they had gone to the Isle of Wight for a guest full-back. A war-time cap for England, Huddersfield's Reg Mountford had been playing for Cowes. All in all, then, it was as well that McGibbon got to The Dell that afternoon – *just!*

As ever, he had to work on Saturday morning before riding his motorbike from RAF Shellingford to his in-laws at Bursledon, on Southampton's eastern outskirts, where his wife was awaiting the birth of their second child and where he could 'smarten up' and be driven, in his father-in-law's car, to The Dell. That had become his matchday routine. But it had been raining at Shellingford 'for a solid week' and he set off amid conflicting reports about the extent of flooding down through Newbury. All was going well until he rounded a bend and found himself in three feet of water: 'I rode straight into it and the motorbike stopped. I put my feet down and my foot slipped. I fell over and the motorbike fell over as well. I thought "Well, this is it. I'll never get there"'. Having picked up the bike and pushed it out of the water, his next thought was 'to find a telephone and tell them I won't be there'.

In desperation, though, he 'tickled the carburettor' and, much to his amazement, the bike started. But, by now, he was 'wet-through and getting absolutely frozen and had to keep stopping'. So, by the time he reached Bursledon, his father-in-law had left for The Dell:

I don't think I'd ever been so dejected in my life ... I hadn't had a drink or anything and my wife gave me a spoonful of rice pudding as I stood on the doorstep; and off I went. When I got around by the Polygon [400 yds from the ground], the roads were absolutely blocked with people, who couldn't get in ... I got off this motorbike and I was pushing it – and, of course, nobody could recognise me with all the blooming gear I had on – and I was begging them to let me through. Eventually, I got there, about 20 minutes before the kick-off.

I don't think I'd ever felt less like playing football in my life and I went on the field and scored six goals, including this world record – at the time – of four and three-fifths seconds.

Shortly after the Chelsea match, he was late again. This time he missed the game, but in such a way as to earn him an appearance, 38 years later, on *This is Your Life*. The occasion, at Loftus Road on Wednesday, 30 January 1946, was the second leg of the FA Cup, Fourth Round. Yes, *fourth* round. For only the second time since their semi-final appearance in 1927, the Saints had survived a third round tie – winning both legs against Newport County with a 6-4 aggregate. In the first leg at home, Ted had scored what would be his only FA Cup goal.

In the fourth round, QPR won the first leg 1-0 at The Dell. For the second leg, four days later, Doug McGibbon decided against riding his Rudge Whitworth to London. He'd let the train take the strain. On the morning of the game, though, he accepted a lift from his clerk of the works, who 'wanted to stop at every pub we passed' and hadn't 'the faintest idea' how to get to the ground. McGibbon arrived to find the team already on the pitch, with Roper again switching, this time to centre-forward. The *Echo* reported that it had been 'doubtful, in the morning, whether McGibbon could get leave, and also doubtful if he was fit to play'. So the versatile Roper was on stand-by to play at No.9. McGibbon dismisses that account: 'they just make these things up, don't they?' All that stopped him playing, he insists, was an unreliable driver. Planned or not, Roper's switch was lost upon the two BBC trialists in the commentary box. As one of them, Brian Johnston, has confessed in his memoirs,

> *I knew little about the teams but noticed a headline in the previous Sunday's paper describing a QPR match on the Saturday. Their centre-forward scored three goals and the headline read: '3-GOAL McGIBBON!' So ... [we gave] the QPR centre-forward ... the full treatment. 'There goes 3-goal McGibbon' ... [Then] we read in the evening papers that McGibbon had withdrawn unfit at the last moment and we had been describing his substitute! Neither of us ever became a soccer commentator.*

Whether or not that mistaken identity merited his banishment to cricket commentaries and cream cakes, Johnners might have been expected, when later explaining his error, not to compound it with ludicrous inaccuracies. Leave aside whose unfitness – McGibbon's or his driver's – caused his absence: Johnston could surely have ascertained that McGibbon was the *visitors'* regular No 9 and that nobody on either side had contrived to score three in the Saturday's 1-0 leg.

Yet, when Thames TV sprang McGibbon upon him for his 1984 *This is Your Life,* Johnners continued to proclaim Doug's *three-*goal fame. And the myth of QPR's three-goal McGibbon persists in Tim Heald's 1995 biography of Johnston. In fact, Doug McGibbon of Southampton never scored three that season. Several twos. And that six against Chelsea, to thrill the crowd that had flocked to see the great Tommy Lawton.

McGibbon's team-mates managed three without him that afternoon at Loftus Road, but QPR won 4-3 to go through 5-3 on aggregate. It was an unhappy afternoon for Len Stansbridge, the Saints' keeper, whom the *Echo* blamed for three of Rangers' goals, including a rare header from Alec Stock. With the half-back line also disappointing, the *Echo* wondered whether Ellerington, with his 'hall-mark of class', might be converted from full-back to centre-half. Trainer-coach Dodgin was, indeed, on his way out. His place at centre-half was filled, though, not by any relocation of Bill Ellerington but by the demobilization of Eric Webber, who would make the position his until February 1951.

～

In February 1946, after an 8-1 defeat at the Baseball Ground, Ted Bates, now almost 28, was belatedly called to the military service that Tom Parker had counselled against in 1939. The *Echo* gave him the headlines – 'Saints Losing Their Best Inside Forward to Forces' – which meant fewer column inches for an inquest on the Derby result. Stationed near Northampton, he was greeted in turn, by the local *Chronicle & Echo,* as 'an outstanding performer' for whom 'several clubs, including Chelsea and Brentford' had made 'substantial offers'. He would be guesting for the Cobblers on the morrow and whenever the Saints did not need him. In fact, he played only that once, and scored once, for Northampton and was able, as noted earlier, to complete 45 appearances for the Saints that season.

But the key events of February-March 1946 concerned the redistribution of some of the powers of Mr Sarjantson, the Secretary-Manager – mainly to a new Team Manager but also to his Assistant Secretary. The case for a post-war reduction of his burden had been considered by the Board a year earlier, when it was agreed that the dual role of Secretary-Manager was no longer sustainable. What was needed was a Business or General Manager, who would be the Company Secretary, and a Team Manager who

> *would be fully employed with the securing and maintaining of his team, their training and coaching and general welfare. He would ... have full control over all the players without any interference from either the Directors or the Business Manager.*

At that meeting of 20 March 1945, with the armistice seven weeks away, Mr Sarjantson had agreed to continue as Secretary-Manager 'for the coming season and for one post-war season if so desired'. In February 1946, however, Tom Parker declared himself 'willing and anxious to complete his [suspended] contract as Secretary-Manager'. The Board preferred to pay him for the unexpired period of his 1937 contract and he accepted. That left the directors free to appoint a Team Manager capable of fulfilling its 1945 blueprint. The hot tip in the nationals was that he would be a former

London club player. More specifically, the *Daily Mail* suggested, he would be 'a former famous London centre-forward'. Ted Drake, perhaps? The post did go to a former London player – Bill Dodgin, the ex-Charlton and Orient half-back who had come to The Dell in 1939. His promotion from trainer-coach was formalised at a momentous meeting of the Board, on 5 March 1946, that approved a considerable devolution of John Sarjantson's powers.

Daddy Dodgin
The March 1946 side, of which Bill Dodgin had just become Team Manager:
Back row (left to right): Dominy (outgoing Manager), Stroud, Ellerington, Warhurst, Jones (the sole guest) Roles, Mr Sarjanston, Smith, Gallagher (trainer), Wilkins.
Front row: Evans, Bates, McGibbon, Dodgin, Roper, Veck and Webber.

First, the directors clarified Mary Bates's position. She had come, seven months earlier, to a job that had no title. But, somewhere along the way, she had become known as the 'Assistant Secretary'. In fact, the *Echo* had used that label, the previous week, in a front-page piece on 'one of the very few women associated with a Football League club in an official capacity'. The Board now ratified her title and approved a salary of £4 a week. It then appointed Bill Dodgin to be Acting Team Manager at £9 a week, 'upon the same conditions as those applying to Mrs Bates'. If that order of priority causes you to smile, consider next how the Board went on to approve a common induction for the two positions, from the omnicompetent Mr Sarjantson, who 'undertook to do his best in training both Mrs Bates and Mr Dodgin for their respective posts and to help them in every way to make a success of their appointments'.

That was what it meant, then, to unravel the power that had been collapsed into the dual role of Secretary-Manager. But who could take seriously, anyhow, the idea of a woman as an Assistant Secretary at a Football Club? The *Echo* had done so. And so had the *Daily Mail,* in its February story predicting that a former London centre-forward would be the Saints' new manager. But then the story was picked up by the *Daily Mirror.* On the day after the ratification of her position, the 'Sports Mirror' stooped to triteness of a kind we have long since come to think of as sexist. Headed 'Mary puts a kettle on', the piece began by suggesting that, 'because she is tops at tea-making, Mary Bates landed a job no woman had ever had before: assistant secretary to posh, tradition-soaked Southampton Football Club'.

Sports Mirror

Mary puts a kettle on—

BECAUSE she is tops at tea-making, Mary Bates landed a job no woman had ever had before: assistant secretary to posh, tradition-soaked South-ampton Football Club.

Because she is also tops at office-running, Mary Bates is soon to have a bigger job: THE secretaryship.

What manner of woman is Managing Director J. Sar-jantson's right hand man ?

In the efficiently tidy, carefully-dusted office underneath the grandstand, we found her yester-day, settling the players' PAYE (" It's quite easy when you know how . . ."),

Brown-haired, brown-eyed, brown-costumed . . . twenty-fivish, five-foot threeish . . . expert at the soft answer that makes the wheels run smoothly. . . .

"How do I like the job ? Oh, fine, thanks. . . ."
"How did I get it ? Well, during the war I

To a football league club she's the manager's righthand man . . . the inside-left's wife.

This story had two further references to Mr Sarjantson's dependence upon the tea-making skills of his 'right hand man'. The *Mirror* did acknowledge that Mary was 'also tops at office-running', but this was defined as keeping a 'tidy, carefully-dusted office', doing the tax returns and being an 'expert at the soft answer that makes the wheels run smoothly'. No mention here of how she was having to learn the game's laws and regulations and take over many of such matters, from Mr Sarjantson, as the authorities prepared for the return of 'proper' football. Notwithstanding, the tea-maker would 'soon' succeed him as Secretary, the *Mirror* announced.

DELL DIAMOND

That prediction had already been made by the *Mail* and would be taken up by the *Weekly News,* which confidently proclaimed that the next season would see the appointment of 'the first woman secretary of a big time football club'.

If any of the directors had that in mind, it was not apparent at that ratification meeting of 5 March. Mr Sarjantson 'wanted the Board to appoint me as Secretary when the time came', Mary says, 'but the Board wouldn't consider that'. She also remembers his asking her whether it would 'upset' her or Ted if she 'finished up earning more, in the football world', than her husband. She said neither of them would mind. It would never happen.

But let's take stock. This transitional season may have been coming to a strange ending for the Bateses, with Ted away on military service and Mary's position attracting the press. The Club generally, though, had arrived at a new managerial structure and the season was ending with a bang, as each of the Cup finalists came, in April, to The Dell. Charlton were seen off 3-1 on Good Friday, eight days before the Final. Then, on their way home from Wembley, the cup-winners, Derby County, stopped off at The Dell to be beaten 4-2.

Derby paraded the Cup at half-time to provide a strangely symmetrical ending to war-time football at The Dell. The truncated season of 1939-40 had begun with Portsmouth coming there to show off the FA Cup (see the photo' in Chapter 3). Now, the trophy having been wrenched from Pompey at last, it was immediately on display at The Dell.

There would be more than the FA Cup to play for in 1946-47. League football would be back.

Chapter 7

Daddy Dodgin

There was no summer revolution for Bill Dodgin. His post-war reconstruction would have to be a more gradual exercise than the radical Mr Parker had attempted nine years earlier.

Two players remained from those Parker signings of 1937 – Ted Bates and Billy Bevis. Would they be re-united as a right-wing pair? Just one of many questions for the Team Manager as he surveyed his inheritance. With the benefit of hindsight, it is possible to identify five particular problems – concerning goalkeepers, scorers, the right-wing, full-backs and leadership – that he would need to sort out.

First, find a goalie. Sam Warhurst, who'd been in possession when war broke out, had hung up his cap to join the training staff. So it was a case of Pick Your P.O.W. Len Stansbridge had been at The Dell since 1936. He'd mainly been in German hands in Poland during the war – giving rise, in the sick humour of the dressing room, to the nickname of 'Stalag' – but had come home for a few games in 1945-46, including that cup-tie to be forgotten at Loftus Road. George Ephgrave had arrived for the last few games of that season, after four years as a prisoner in Odessa. The two of them would share the 'keeper's jersey for a season and a half – until Ian Black came to rejoin his 'second father'.

Next, who would score goals? Despite his commuting problems of the previous season – though soon after his flooded road to fame against Chelsea, he had swapped his motorbike for a car – the prolific McGibbon had finished the campaign with 29 goals in 33 games. It was hardly surprising, then, that he opened the 1946-47 season at No.9 – with a hat-trick. What is surprising – nobody seems able to explain it – is that, 12 games and nine goals later, he was gone. Could it be that George Lewis, a summer signing from Watford, was considered good and ready, even if he was almost 33 before he got his break? His hat-trick in a Third Round trouncing of Bury and 12 goals in 28 League games was a tolerable return, if hardly of McGibbon proportions. The main League scorer, though, was Jack Bradley, now clearly the *inside*-left, while the No.11 shirt went from wearer to wearer, as it would continue to do for many a season. Bobby Veck would begin and finish the season on that flank. But Eric Day, returning for a very long stint – of 11 seasons – would start it at No.11. And war-time guest Wilf Grant would return south in October from Manchester City to play mainly on the left – despite a preference for the right.

It wasn't as if the right-wing was settled territory, either. Billy Bevis, having survived no fewer than three torpedo attacks and a mine to boot, was back to compete with Don Roper. Bevis played only 14 times before he gave up the game. Roper had 40 games, that season, but few of them at No.7. Bates managed 22 games and most of these were at left-half.

His first game in that position was on 23 November, two days after Bill Dodgin had watched him play there for the British Army against an FA XI. The FA's centre-forward also noticed Ted: Nat Lofthouse remembers this as the only time he played against him. Perhaps when you've had to kick-off nine times – the Army won 8-3 – the opposition long remains etched on your memory.

Ted was mostly at No.6 when the Army played against the other services, the Belgian and French Armies and pretty well any other opponents they could cram in, it seems. The other wing-half was invariably Billy Wright. Gil Merrick was often in goal. George Lowrie and Trevor Ford were sharing the No.9 shirt.

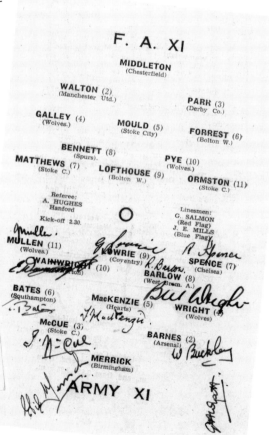

The spring of 1947 was an especially busy one for Pte E.T. Bates (who became Cpl E.T. Bates in mid-schedule). In March, he was in Paris (v. French Army) one week and at Goodison Park (v. RAF) the next. Then five games in a fortnight over Easter, at No.6 for the Saints – with new signing, Joe Mallett from QPR, at No.8. Then another flurry of Army fixtures, with only one more appearance for the Saints. With Mallett now at No.6 – for six seasons, that's all – Ted had his first game since November at No.8, when he scored in a 2-0 win at home to Fulham. He was again partnering Don Roper,

Enchanté: Billy Wright introduces Ted Bates to the French Army's representative in Paris.

but you can see why that pairing operated only six times that season and the Bevis-Bates wing only three.

Yet the right-wing of Bates and Roper had been acclaimed even by the Dublin press when the Saints travelled to play Bohemians in a pre-season fixture in August 1946. In a build-up to the game, Dubliners were introduced to this 'outstanding pair'. The report on the Saints' 4-1 win had an interesting variation on this theme. Although it had the customary assessment of how well Bates 'fed his partner', it especially praised 'the right-wing triangle of Stroud, Bates and Roper'. This concept of a 'triangle' down the wing is one I associate with the Saints' side of the mid-60s, when Wimshurst played behind Paine and O'Brien – a matter to which we can return in Chapter 17. In the reports of the 1930s and '40s, though, the 'wing' pair was generally all the rage.

If you've become a football fan in the last 30 years or so, then all these references to who formed a 'wing' with whom may seem odd. But you'll have noticed that the football reporters of that era repeatedly wrote about the efficacy of a pairing; that Ted Bates was judged for his ability to supply

DELL DIAMOND

Bevis, Mitten and Roper in turn; and that his game was deemed to have suffered from the lack of a stable relationship. The significance of a 'wing', consisting of an inside-forward who fed his outside-forward, is reinforced if you ask Eric Day about the relative merits of different Southampton full-backs playing on his flank. The question means little to him as a winger. The back's job was to get the ball to the inside-forward (perhaps via the wing-half) and *he* would supply Eric.

That is, of course, an over-simplification – and would especially be so once Eric had switched, the next season, to the right, with Ramsey at No.2 to advise him on 'the correct position' (his autobiography says) for receiving a direct pass from him. George Curtis suggests that it was more subtle than that: if Day dropped back towards Ramsey and tempted his marker to follow, this 'decoy' run would create a space into which Alf would play 'a flighted ball for Charlie Wayman to whip out and get it'. Whatever! – but it all revolved around Ramsey's wanting to change the way in which backs and wingers played. And not just at Southampton.

Readers of his autobiography will know that Ramsey had studied Sam Barkas's distribution when the Saints lost 1-0 to Manchester City on Easter Saturday 1947 and that he was soon giving advice to his outside-right at representative level – Stanley Matthews.

～

But we have jumped ahead to Ramsey the full-back (and the arrival of Charlie Wayman into the bargain). The season opened with Alf leading the Reserves' attack. He had been tried at full-back the previous season but his chance to make the No.2 shirt his for a couple of years came courtesy of the North East winds and of Bill Ellerington's disrespect for them.

Dressed for the occasion
The squad of 12, that had gone to Whitley Bay for the FA Cup Third Round tie at Newcastle, line up with their golf clubs and in their heavy jerseys. But note Ellerington's open neck. He caught pneumonia and Ramsey came in, at right-back, for the next 91 games.
Back row (left to right): Warhurst (trainer), Stroud, Freeman (12th man), Ellerington, Webber, Ephgrave, Rochford, Smith.
Front row: Bevis, Roper, Lewis, Bradley, Day.

That was in January 1947 when the squad encamped at Whitley Bay, prior to the Fourth Round cup-tie at Newcastle. When the players went golfing, they all wore the heavy polo-neck jerseys that the club supplied. All, that is, except Sam Warhurst and Bill Ellerington. The latter's room-mate, Bill Stroud, recalls how 'Big Ellie' woke up the next morning wringing wet. Pneumonia ruled him out. After half-a-dozen games in this position, Ramsey was playing right-back before the largest crowd – almost 56,000 – that he, and surely most of the Saints' side, had ever seen. Newcastle won 3-1. Centre-forward Charlie Wayman got all three. He, too, was getting used to a change of position, having until recently been an inside-forward. Tom Emanuel having returned to Wales after a few games in 1945-46 and Albie Roles having been called up, Bill Ellerington had begun the season in partnership with Bill Dodgin's major close season signing. Bill Rochford. The manager had played with 'Rockie' at Follands, of course, but Ellerington was not so familiar with the pedigree of Pompey's cup-winning left-back, when he was introduced to him in May 1946. Rochford had come to Bournemouth to partner him in an end-of-season friendly, prior to signing for the Saints during the close season. Ellerington recalls thinking that the 33 year-old full-back was 'getting on a bit' but he soon came to revere him. He still does and will tell you about his mentor for as long as you've got. Despite his concern about Rochford's lack of speed – 'I could run backwards round the track faster than he could run forwards' – Ellerington adduces three reasons for his new partner's ability to turn it on for his new club, even when he was opposing a fast winger.

First and foremost, he could 'read the game'. His younger admirer has 'never seen *anybody* – anybody *ever* – who could read a game like he could'. Ellerington, a 'very enthusiastic' learner, would watch his mentor and think how 'he made that look easy and he's only walking about'. Rochford certainly didn't expect to run too much and was philosophical when Ellerington expressed doubts about facing a nippy winger: 'Look, son, if all fast wingers had brains, we'd be out of business'. A second explanation, then, for Rochford's being in control. And, finally, it seems to be widely agreed that he was a *master* of the offside trap. Ellerington recalls his exhaustion after that introductory game alongside Rochford at Dean Court: 'I had never taken so many free-kicks in my life through offsides. This fellah played the offside-trap like no-one who's ever existed or ever will do'.

This all meant that this new signing from along the coast 'never got many chasings'. And, if he *was* struggling, he would rally his team-mates all the more. This did not endear him to left-wingers who had to drop back and help him. Bobby Veck is especially bitter. Eric Day, who started, as we have seen, on that flank, recalls Rochford's demands – 'his head was saving his legs. The more he could get someone to help him with the opposing right-winger, the easier his job was going to be' – but he is not resentful of them. To be fair, it wasn't only a question of 'helping him out'. As Augie Scott, a 1947 close season signing who would sometimes play at No.11, points out, Rochford liked to lay off short balls (the habit that Ramsey was trying to develop on the other flank), so the left-winger was 'no good' to him standing in the opponents' half: 'you've got to get back to get the ball'.

That said, Rochford's expectations of his outside-left do seem to have been a recurrent cause for complaint. Clements recalls how it was for Grant:

> In those days, all the wingers stayed upfield. They never came back. Bill Rochford used to shout to poor old Wilf to come back – to cut out that ball, so that he didn't have to do it. He couldn't get up there, could he? Wilf used to say 'How can I come back and cut it out when I've got to get up there?' Of course, then the ball would be put up to where he should have been and Wilf was never there, was he? And so he used to get the flak. Instead of just accepting it, he used to argue about it.

And so did Ernie Jones when he arrived in 1949. Although he'd been expected to score goals for Spurs, he was accustomed to 'going deep to *collect* a ball' – but 'not to chase another winger'. Rochford was by now 36, though, and Ernie was, at one level, willing 'to help him out'. While he accepted that, 'from the team's point of view it may have been a good thing', his dilemma was the same as Grant's: 'I couldn't be in two places at one time. In the event of me chasing back and the ball was cleared, I was on our own goal-line. So, consequently, as far as everybody else was concerned, Ernie Jones was out of position, see. I objected … I made it absolutely clear that I was a winger and not a third full-back'.

Jones was the last Southampton left-winger to have an extended run with Rochford at left-back. Like most of those who wore the No.11 shirt in this period, Ernie could play on the right. You will have noticed that Bill Dodgin had a tendency to buy wingers, often in a part-exchange deal, who would have preferred the right-wing but ended up on the left. Perhaps that is explanation enough of why he never found a settled No.11. During that 1946-47 season, he tried to buy a left-winger who had played with Rochford, and scored twice, in the 1939 Cup Final – Cliff Parker, who had also played (you may recall, from Chapter 4) with Rochford, Dodgin and the gang at Follands. He failed. Maybe Parker knew too much of Rochford's expectations – you surely have to wonder how much Bill Dodgin's failure to find a contented outside-left owed to the captain's cries for cover.

For Ellerington, though, Rochford's demands on others were symptomatic of his strength as a *leader:*

> *We can all be great skippers if we're having a blinder and everything is going well and the crowd is saying 'Good old Bill'. But to be a good skipper when your tongue's down here* (points to midriff) *and you're getting chased, up hill and down dale, and still keep us going, that's a good skipper … When he did [get a rare chasing], you always knew he was playing and he wouldn't let you stand around. He would always drive and drive and drive.*

The other feature of that leadership *on* the field was Rochford's capacity to change the game-plan. This was apparent even to the player least likely to be affected – Ian Black in goal:

> *He could alter things during a game if things weren't going too well, which was all important because it's not easy for a manager – sitting in the dug-out or up in the stand – to communicate with players on the field if he wants anything different. I'm not saying Bill Rochford did that all the time but he did that when he felt it necessary – with Bill Dodgin's cooperation. That was*

the great thing about them, the way they co-operated and the way they thought. I am not saying they thought everything in the same light but most things they did.

Eric Webber reflects similarly on the influence of Rochford, who 'knew the game inside-out, not only his own position' and on the way he helped Dodgin to move the team 'up a gear or two, from what was – if you like – a family-run operation in Division Two into something that could compete and, with a bit of luck, get into the higher grade and compete again'.

For the final third of the season, Rochford would have a lieutenant. Joe Mallett was briefly introduced earlier in the chapter. A former Charlton team-mate of Bill Dodgin's, he arrived, now 31, from QPR. As already mentioned, he started in his familiar position at inside-forward – where he had played in QPR's two-legged FA Cup defeat of Saints the previous season – and scored on his debut at Plymouth. In the system at Loftus Road, Joe hadn't played 'the normal inside-forward game. I played a bit deep … It was a role that Arsenal used to play with Alex James'.

Then, as I say, he went even deeper for the last two games of the season. Joe Mallett was on his way to becoming a fixture at left-half, where he would play over 200 games for the Saints, going beyond his 37th birthday. Alf Ramsey has described Rochford as 'one of the greatest tacticians' he 'ever met in football' and Mallett as 'one of the finest of all soccer brains'. To talk to others who learned from them at The Dell is to appreciate that these were not exaggerations. What he calls 'the Dodgin format' is most succinctly described by Ernie Jones: 'Bill Dodgin was in the office managing the team, Bill Rochford was on the field managing the team and his assistant was Joe Mallett. That was the Southampton administration, from the team point of view'.

Nobody will tell you different from that.

~

If there were five problems for the new manager to resolve, at least he had a fairly settled half-back line. Eric Webber was back to stay. George Smith and Bill Stroud started the season at wing-half. Smith had got into the first team a couple of months ahead of Webber, just before a war that he spent in the RAF. His subsequent appearances had been mainly in 1945-46. Stroud, on the other hand, had 175 war-time games: you may recall, from Chapter 4, that only Roles and Bates had more. His peace-time games for the Saints were to be limited, though. When Southampton returned to St James' Park, in February 1947, to avenge their Cup defeat with a 3-1 League win, he scored his favourite goal. But three more games would be his lot. In the close season, he would be gone – to Leyton Orient.

Daddy Dodgin

Just before the new season started, Don Roper, the leading war-time scorer – you may remember that, too, from Chapter 4 – would also be on his way to London. Taking over from George Allison, Tom Whittaker would succeed where his predecessor had failed. He would sign Roper. It was a long slog, though. As he explains in his *Arsenal Story*, the wooing of Roper, who was so 'necessary' to his plans, was not completed until 11 August, when Don signed for him 'over a cup of tea in a little café hard by the Arsenal Stadium. It had taken eleven trips to Southampton to persuade him to come, and finally Southampton's manager Billy Dodgin brought him up to town and departed with a £12,000 cheque'.

Not to mention Tom Rudkin and George Curtis, who formed part of the deal. One commentator, valuing these two at £3,000 and £9,000, respectively, concluded that Roper had moved, effectively, for £24,000 – compared with the record-breaking deals of £20,000 (Lawton) and then £20,050 (Shackleton). But, then, the valuation of Rudkin at £3,000 may have been over the top. Tom Whittaker neglected even to mention his inclusion in the package and the peace-time impact at The Dell of this war-time guest would be modest and short-lived. On the other hand, George Curtis – 'Twinkletoes' to admiring team-mates – came straight in at No.8. Mallett was no longer contesting that position, remember: he was installed at No.6. And Bates, who had played at No.8 so often, would soon settle in at No.10. But not for the first 11 games of that 1947-48 season, when Bradley was still in possession and scoring freely.

Then, suddenly, as with McGibbon the previous season, the leading scorer was sold. In this case, there was an explanation. Both Jack Bradley and Bill Dodgin will tell you that the player's behaviour – Bradley admits to being 'awkward' and to having had 'a few beers' on a close season trip to Germany – had upset the manager. And Southampton also received £8,000 from Bolton Wanderers, plus yet another winger who would play very few games for them. Why did everybody want to offload their surplus wingers to The Dell?

At least Billy Wrigglesworth provided some amusement. Indeed, he continues to do so. It's just about impossible to mention his name to a former team-mate, without provoking a chuckle and a reminder that Billy was wont to trap the ball with his backside. It spoils the novelty value a bit when Charlie Mitten claims that he liked to perform the same trick, but he does confess to learning it from Billy when they were at Old Trafford. Wrigglesworth would help Southampton into the Fifth Round of the Cup – even if it was Rudkin who would play in it – for the first time since 1927. Before that Cup run began, though, Mr Dodgin had two more big signings to complete.

DELL DIAMOND

On 25 October, his side lost 5-0 at Newcastle. Some of the Geordies in the team stayed up for the weekend, Augie Scott recalls. The manager hung about, too. His brother, Norman, had been at left-half for Newcastle that afternoon, but a family re-union was not at the top of Bill Dodgin's agenda. He had a train to meet. Newcastle Reserves were returning from their game at Hillsborough. The party included Charlie Wayman, out of favour at St James' Park. Turn to any history of Newcastle United and you're pretty well guaranteed to find an account of how Charlie had been dramatically omitted from the side that lost 4-1 to Charlton in the semi-final the previous season. So, eight months after his three Cup goals against the Saints, he was willing to sign for the man who was waiting for him at the Station Hotel. Bill Dodgin had ear-marked him, during the war, as the kind of goal-scorer a manager would want in his side. Or so he told John Graydon of Newcastle's *Evening Gazette:* as a Southampton player, he had been given 'the hardest time' he could remember when Wayman the sailor guested for Pompey in 1944-45.

Graydon was appalled that a fee of £10,000 – a record for Southampton – had brought to £750,000 the sum spent, over the past two seasons, on transfers. Urging that 'something … be done' about a market that had gone 'completely hay-wire', he suggested that £10,000 be the limit. Southampton were not complaining, though. They were soon getting a return on their £10,000. There was enough left of that 1947-48 season for Wayman to play 31 times in Cup and League, to score 19 goals and to establish himself as a massive favourite at The Dell.

The final block in this team-building phase was Ian Black. Demobbed from the Army and unwilling to stay at Aberdeen, the 'young leopard' was determined to rejoin 'Daddy Dodgin' whom he considered 'such a good manager'. He signed in December and played his first game at Leeds on 3 January. When the players returned to The Dell late that evening, there were 'huge queues', he recalls, of fans wanting tickets for the big Third Round tie the following Saturday – against Sunderland. Eric Webber starred in a game which the Saints won with a solitary goal from Eric Day. Next, another home tie, again First Division opposition. Blackburn were seen off 3-2 with two more for Day. He was scoring well from the wing – 13 goals that season – in true Roper fashion. When Third Division Swindon were reduced to 10 men after 10 minutes, Southampton cruised to a 3-0 win in the Fifth Round. Second Division rivals, Tottenham, were next up at The Dell.

The Saints were at White Hart Lane the previous Saturday for a 0-0 draw in the League. Snow that had fallen in the week was heaped around the pitch. Ian Black will 'never forget' how difficult it was to play, with 'a gale-force wind' blowing the heaped snow across the pitch: 'Ah! A tremendous game. In these days, they'd probably call it off'. The players again returned to see fans waiting in the snow for Cup tickets. One of them was Peter Ansty, who recalls going off to find coal for one of the braziers that burned around The Dell that night. Some of those who were turned away without tickets were sufficiently restless for the police to provide an escort for the two women who had been selling them – Mary Bates and her mother, who had initially joined her daughter's office to help in the unaccustomed task of selling Cup tickets.

Unsolicited mail: despite announcements that tickets for the Tottenham cup-tie would be allocated to personal applicants only, Mary Bates received 15,000 letters – and, subsequently, a police escort

For those Saints' fans who succeeded in being among the 28,425 at The Dell on the day, the game was an anti-climax – especially if you were of Mary Bates's generation. Mary had been but a tot when the Saints had last known Cup success in 1927 and she had cycled to The Dell with her father in the barren thirties, 'when they used to have hundreds of bicycles parked in the carpark'. So she was due a Cup run and was '*so* disappointed' when Les Bennett scored the only goal of the game that she cried – for 'the only time *ever* over a football match'. The Southampton players seem also to be haunted by that goal – or, rather, by the *manner* in which Bennett scored it. He used his *left* foot. This was 'the joke' in the visitors' dressing room after the match, as their outside-left, Ernie Jones, recalls: 'the players couldn't believe that he'd literally scored with his left foot'. It was no joke, though, for Eric Webber, who didn't think Bennett

'S' is for success: the emblem of the 1948 FA Cup run. The 'S' men, from the top, are Bill Dodgin, Rochford, Black, Ellerington, Ramsey, Smith, Webber, Mallett, Day, Curtis, Wayman, Bates, Wrigglesworth and Sam Warhurst. The background shot – as if you didn't know – is from the League South game against Aston Villa in March 1946

Straight Up! – Ted Bates demonstrates his vertical take-off in the cup-tie against Spurs. Ted Ditchburn appears to signal 'Six', while Bill Nicholson (centre) studies the man with whom he would fly regularly to Scotland 20 years later, haggling over a price for Martin Chivers (see chapter 22).

had 'ever scored a goal with his left foot in his life before', yet he'd managed to put the ball 'in the only place that Ian Black couldn't get it'. Joe Mallett agrees: 'He couldn't kick a ball with his left foot; and he scored with his left foot. I can see him hitting the ball with his left foot. I thought to myself "He's never scored a goal with his left foot, Les Bennett". It went right up in the corner'.

Whether or not Ian Black could and should have had that corner covered and whether Eric Webber was sucked too wide by Len Duquemin to create the gap for Bennett are matters for lasting debate, displaying shades of opinion. What rankles universally is that Bennett used his wrong foot to put the Saints out of the Cup.

The side, for that memorable Cup run, remained almost unchanged: Black; Ramsey, Rochford (but with Ellerington getting one game); Smith, Webber, Mallett; Day, Curtis, Wayman, Bates and ... er, um, er, Wrigglesworth, Rudkin or Grant (who took it in turns in this problematic position). If the League side was less settled – only Ramsey was ever-present that season – Bill Dodgin had assembled a group of players that was beginning to bond. He was helped, in this regard, by the Board's decision, just before the season began, that, *in order to give that little extra 'energy' to players, which, it was generally agreed throughout the sporting world, was lacking because of insufficient food of the right kind, … a daily luncheon be provided for them.*

Floor plan:
Bill Dodgin, watched by Sam Warhurst (left), demonstrates tactics on the innovatory pitch on the dressing room floor. Left to right: Wayman, Bates, Rochford, Day, Wilkins, Black, Ellerington, Webber, Grant, Mallett, Curtis.

These lunches became occasions for an extension of the tactical discussions that were taking place in a dressing room that now had a miniature pitch on the floor, where the game-plan could be demonstrated. This mini-pitch, which began to attract reporters and photographers, was, Joe Mallett believes, the first of its kind. He valued the way in which Bill Dodgin used this setting to let players have their say: 'It wasn't just the manager doing the talking: it was a consensus of opinion, very often, with players like Bill Rochford, myself, George Curtis – anybody who wanted to say something … And, because Bill Dodgin was in his early management career, he was willing to learn and listen to what the players had to say'. This debate continued, as I say, when the players foregathered for lunch. Ian Black enjoyed getting onto the same table as Rochford and Mallett, the leading tacticians. But did a 'keeper need, I wondered, to be part of their tactic talks? You bet he did: 'That was all part of the learning – because, after all, I was really the *boy* compared with them, experience-wise'.

George Curtis also courted Mallett's company, not so much at lunch but for a game of head-tennis in the carpark at The Dell. It was an activity that became such an addiction with Bill Dodgin's team that he could book them into Butlin's at Clacton-on-Sea as performers. The players and their families would get free keep in exchange for a demonstration of head-tennis each morning – 'not a bad racket' in Eric Webber's book. Many would say that head-tennis was never much more than that: a seaside cabaret act. But not so George Curtis, who remains extremely passionate about his games in the carpark. Having gone on to coach in many parts of the world, including a spell in charge of Norway's national team, George still insists that head-tennis is a neglected form of training: 'I say that there's no greater activity than getting your players to play head-tennis. That is admirable for developing techniques – the ball coming over quickly; even the volleyed ball comes over and dips'. Head-tennis remains, then, 'a *fantastic* activity' for George Curtis. 'People have said to me "No, George. That's old hat!" I say "No. That still pertains"'.

Joe Mallett was such an 'extremely good' performer that George would 'almost *plead*' to get a game in his 'group of many talents', in which Ted Bates and Charlie Wayman made up his favourite four. There was an extent, though, to which Ted was excluded from some of the gang's activities. As Mallett sympathetically explains, there was no way Ted could be 'popular' among his team-mates: 'Off the field, he was a little bit of a loner – not by choice. He was very unfortunate in the fact' that Mary was the Assistant Secretary:

> *Now Ted was in the terrible position – really, for him – that players used to think, because of this association, that he got in the team like that … He didn't, for me, but a lot of players used to think that and that altered his standing and his way of life, really, because we were a very friendly club … All the players used to go to lunch every day and I always thought Ted was uncomfortable, particularly when players used to have a go. It was jocular. But, on the other hand, … he was very unfortunate, Ted.*

'It was jocular', Joe assures us, *but* … This will not be our last encounter with that disturbing question about the nature of dressing room humour: how far are any of the barbs *meant?* But, then, that must be true of many a workplace, where the success of some colleagues over others will be explained away, surely, with all manner of specious reasons – just joking *or what?*

In this particular instance, the jobs of *two* people were up for questioning by badinage: was Ted Bates getting picked more often than he deserved, by virtue of his wife's closeness to the powers-that-be; and what on earth was a *woman* doing in that position, anyhow? In the most innocuous version of the first question, as Bobby Veck recalls, 'some of the boys were laughing: "Oh! She picks the team!"' OK, so players have to have *something* they can blame for the harsh reality that some get preference over others. If you're not going to go storming into the manager's office to *demand* a rational explanation – Tommy Mulgrew (1954-62) appears to have been the undisputed champion when it came to this approach – then inventing less rational ones, to be bandied around in the dressing room, becomes routine, it seems.

Some were less comfortable with that routine than others. Eric Day disliked some of the 'under-hand' joking about Ted. Not that Eric can recall any of the wife-in-power ribbing. He remembers Ted's being the butt of dressing room humour for quite another reason: he was the yokel in their midst, who'd worked in the fields and lunched, under the hedge, on cheese and pickles. Ernie Jones, who recalls examples of the ribbing Joe Mallett has described – 'Married into the Club. Mary will see you're all right' – says that Ted was 'thick-skinned' enough to let it ride with a 'yeah! yeah!' shrug. Ted, for his part, remembers none of this and wonders why footballers should need to engage in 'conjecture' about what went on in the separate 'world' of the Club's office. If we leave aside the mere question of memory – we don't have a lot of option, after all – I would suggest there are two good reasons why Ted could have been oblivious, at the time, to much of this mickey-taking. First, whether because his mind was focussed elsewhere or because it's not his kind of humour, banter tended to go straight over his head. George Kirby's analysis of how that helped Ted, as a manager, to survive a wickedly sarcastic dressing room is one we'll come to later (Chapter 18). Secondly, Ted was obliged, as Joe Mallett puts it, to be something of 'a loner' because his team-mates needed to sound off about Them Upstairs when he was not around.

Mary's first recorded presence at a Board meeting was in January 1947, when she deputised for Mr Sarjantson. And, from the start of the following season, she was there, in her own right, as 'Minutes Secretary'. As far as she is concerned, it was never a problem either that she would regularly hear complaints about players or that Ted had to function in a dressing room culture that included complaining about the Board: 'It didn't seem to present any problems at any time – none that I knew of, anyway. We didn't allow it to'. Both when he was a player and even when he became manager, Ted and she 'had a wonderful agreement', Mary says, whereby she '*never* discussed with Ted anything I didn't think was anything to do with his side of the Club. It could have caused conflict if I'd said "so-and-so said so-and-so about so-and-so, player-wise"'.

The 'so-and-so' being discussed in front of Mary could even be Ted, of course. On 4 September 1947, when Mr Cosgrove reported on the performance of the Reserves at Portsmouth, Mary was obliged to record that Bates and Ballard had been 'the weakest links in the side'. The manager wasn't buying that – Ted was back in the first team the next week for a run of 18 League games (worth 10 goals) and four cup-ties – but it does suggest that directors felt able to talk frankly in front of Mary. They trusted her, in other words, to organise her married life and professional responsibilities in the way she has recalled it 50 years on. But having the Board trust in her discretion is one thing. What a sceptical dressing room made of it all is another matter.

It might help you (as it did me) to get a better handle on all of this if you ponder a much more recent example of dressing room mistrust – as reported to Karren Brady, as Managing Director at Birmingham City, when she went public on her relationship with one of the players, Paul Peschisolido. The Manager, Barry Fry, complained that 'the players don't think they can talk around Pesch because he lives with Karren, it has created a bad atmosphere and we've got to sort it out'. Brady records, in her *Diary of the Season,* the solution on which Fry 'insisted': the player must go.

By that yardstick, Ted did well to survive any such concern – as Joe Mallett implicitly acknowledges. Yet not every player saw Mary as somebody Upstairs with the Board. To Eric Webber, she was 'a good servant' of the Club, who 'did everything', while Mr Sarjantson 'was really only a figure-head'. As he saw it, her principal role was external, relating to the public: 'she never had any direct dealings with the players at all – other than pay their wages, out through the window in a little brown pay packet, each Friday'. Even so, Ernie Jones felt that Ted had to 'live down' with some of the players the fact that he was married to the Assistant Secretary. Or, as Eric Day puts it, this 'didn't do Ted a helluva lot of good with a lot of the other players [who] didn't go much on the idea'. It never occurred to Eric, though, that you therefore needed to avoid talking in front of him:

> *I never thought that anything I said would go up to the Boardroom ... The only time you really spoke to Mary was when you went up there for your wages ... She knew what we were earning, but so did practically everybody in Southampton in that day and age ... I never thought that she went tittle-tattling. I would never think Ted would do that. I didn't know Mary very well, but it never dawned on me that she might ... If you're going to go through life thinking that everyone's like that, you're going to have a pretty worrying life, aren't you?*

Indeed you are, but even if people don't 'worry' about how to explain departures from the working norm – like a woman doing a man's job in a man's world – they may nevertheless feel the need, I have been suggesting, to deride. Mary Bates's arrival as Assistant Secretary was such a departure and stimulated, you may recall from the previous chapter, some silly journalism about her tea-making qualities. If such sexist nonsense would be unthinkable in the comparatively egalitarian 1990s, Karren Brady has had to put up with that other age-old explanation of how women get to the top: she must be 'bonking the boss'. They didn't talk like that in the 1940s, of course, although there were 'all sorts of rumours going around', as Ernie Jones recalls, 'about Mary being Sarjie's plaything. You know, that sort of thing … It was a lot of rubbish'. Which meant – I'm told by fans of sixty-something – that it was quite the teenage giggle of the day.

A Man's Game

Assistant Secretary Mary Bates lines up with the lads for the 1946-47 season,
flanked by her husband and Manager Dodgin.
Between Warhurst (left) and Cann, in their white coats, the players are
Back row (left to right): Ramsey, Freeman, Stroud, McGibbon, Wilkins, Bushby, Gregory
Middle row: Bates, Bradley, Ellerington, Stansbridge, Ephgrave, Webber, Lewis, Veck
Front row: Bevis, Rochford, Evans, Smith

As I say, Eric Day couldn't remember Mary's name featuring in dressing room banter; and if 'Sarjie was very fond of her', as he saw it, what did that matter? Not a lot among the players, it seems. If there was anything or anybody for them to be jealous of, then, as far as Bill Stroud was concerned, it was Ted: 'She was a very, very pretty young lady'. But, then, a woman who makes it in a man's world is more likely to be stereotyped, Brady 'sadly' concludes, by other women. So should I have interviewed a few players' wives? The Mary factor was not on my agenda but a couple of wives wondered whether I'd 'heard'. One of them recalled the 'tittle-tattle', when the wives got together, about the Secretary and his Assistant Secretary. All of this behind Mary's back, since 'she wasn't one of the girls – very friendly, mind, but always just that little aloof'. And necessarily so, says Mary.

DELL DIAMOND

Although Ted and she mixed with other players and their wives – 'they just treated me like another player's wife' – she felt obliged to remain apart from the wife-to-wife socializing. She was 'always very good friends' with Gladys Dodgin – shopping together when there was an away game in London and the like – but she generally *had* to keep her distance from the 'chit-chat and gossip' of the wives' circle. Which made it much easier, of course, for her to be the *object* of the gossip.

The other wife who raised the matter brought together the two stereotypes at issue: Mary shouldn't have allowed Mr Sarjantson, who had a way of flirting with the young wives and girlfriends at the Club's social functions, to do so with her. And if she was disinclined to stop him, then Ted jolly well should have. But, then, he was doing all right, even though some good players she could mention were spending too much time in the Reserves.

So, it may have been little more than a typical workplace joke – of a kind that has survived into the more egalitarian working environment of the 1990s – but we stand at that dicey junction where joking mingles with jealousy to nurture the feeling, in some quarters, that Ted benefited, as a player, from Mr Sarjantson's esteem, whether professional or aesthetic, for his wife. Mary says she never had to put up with any of this banter to her face: she was protected by being distanced from a circle in which it seems especially to have flourished. And if Ted has no recall, either, of any ribaldry to this effect, I have suggested that this could be similarly explained, at least in part, by the enforced exclusion to which Joe Mallett alludes.

The more nudges and winks I encountered and the more I tried to reconcile them, the less surprised I became. And Karren Brady's account of back-biting at St Andrew's in the 1990s helped me to put into perspective the Dell gossip of the 1940s. In an industry where opportunities come and go in all manner of ways that seem less than rational, conspiracy theories are likely to flourish, all dressed-up in the wicked humour of the dressing room to provide a rationale for the irrational.

If we want to be rational about it, then why, asks Mary, was Bill Dodgin always seeking to replace Ted? The most overt replacement was August (Augie) Scott, although his purchase, from Luton in the 1947 close season, could be explained by Ted's being still in the Army. Alf Freeman, who'd long since arrived with the Army (in Chapter 5), was still there but getting very few games. He'd get none at all in 1947-48: Bates got the nod for the Cup-ties, while Scott and he each played in about half the League games, sometimes in the same team. Alf is blunt about it: Bill Dodgin had favourites and Ted was one of them. Augie elaborates more gently on the obstacles in his way:

Let's be honest. Ted had been there for a long time, hadn't he? I think there was a little bit of favour there … He does have a little bit in his favour when he's been there since 1937 … When I came, Ted was in the Army. And when he came out of the Army, he was near enough straight in. He was good with his head, but he wasn't so great on the floor.

So is Scott saying he was better than Bates on the ground? 'I would have thought so – quicker!' Stan Clements agrees: Augie was a quick, 'neat little player' who combined well with Wayman, 'but the point is, he didn't have the height'. That is to say that, at 5ft 5ins, he lacked the heading ability that Bates supplied – even at 5ft 9ins – alongside 5ft 8ins Wayman.

So there you have it. Two players competing for a position to which they bring quite different plusses and minusses. As a team-mate sees it, it was question of who complemented better a star whose place was guaranteed. But the more recently signed player felt that the established player was inevitably the favourite son. 'Twas, surely, ever thus – unless, of course, the newcomer is competing with a local lad. In this scenario, Jack Gregory argues, then the home-grown player 'always gets shoved out a bit': he can be exploited because he is less likely to want a move. We'll encounter that complaint again, don't you worry, when Ted is managing. Meanwhile, what all of this says to me is that professional footballers can find quite enough reasons to explain who gets the nod over whom without needing to introduce a wife-in-the-boardroom dimension, with a nod and a wink about a hands-on patron thrown in.

~

As Bates and Scott played Box and Cox in 1947-48, there was one game in which Augie's inclusion embarrassed Eric Webber. It was the Saturday after the Sixth Round disappointment. On the Friday evening, Mrs Webber gave birth to a son. When the news reached Eric by telegram at the team's hotel on the Saturday morning, he boldly declared to his team-mates that he would name the boy after whichever of them scored first at Highfield Road that afternoon. He was obviously partial to having a son called 'Charles'. Wayman had been scoring most of the goals. 'Edric', as in Bates, was the in-form striker; but, as I say, Scott was in for him. You will by now have anticipated the punchline. August Scott scored his first goal for the Saints. Webber reneged.

In fact, that was the only goal of the game as the Saints bounced back from their Cup exit with a strong run that enabled them to finish third in Division II. The week after the Coventry game, they got some revenge for that 5-0 defeat that had preceded the signing of Wayman when they beat Newcastle 4-2 at The Dell. It was a special triumph for Webber and

DELL DIAMOND

Wayman. Eric was doing well, for the second Saturday running, against George Lowrie, Ted's Army team-mate, who'd moved expensively from Coventry to Newcastle during the week. And Charlie was scoring twice against the club that had rejected him.

It was FA Cup semi-final day and a convoluted chain of thoughts went through Eric Day's mind: if the Saints had beaten Spurs in the Sixth Round and had then played, in the semi that day, the way they were playing against Newcastle, then they would have been on their way to Wembley. But, come Cup Final day, the Saints would be winning their fourth game in a row, the penultimate game in a stirring run, after that Bennett left-footer, of 13 matches of which they lost only two. The second of those defeats was the home game against Plymouth on 10 April, when Len Stansbridge momentarily reappeared. Ian Black was otherwise engaged at Hampden Park, winning his first and only Scottish cap in a 2-0 defeat by England. Despite this surge, the Saints were out of contention for promotion when their season finished with a goalless draw at Filbert Street.

They would sail for Brazil the next morning.

Chapter 8

An Awful Lot of Lessons in Brazil

The idea had been to tour the USA. Councillor Rex Stranger, a former Mayor of Southampton and a director of Southampton FC, had returned from America in 1947 with a plan for 'the advancement of soccer in the United States'.

Make no mistake about it – it was to be a missionary expedition. The tourists would not only fulfil eight fixtures but would kindly allow the natives to join in their training sessions. And any profits would be left in the USA so that Americans could buy new grounds or bring their old ones up to standard 'by erecting covered stands'. When the Board's plans to educate North Americans fell through early in 1948, Mr Stranger came up with an alternative in South America. They would go to Brazil as guests of Botafogo FC.

Brazil should have been a 'natural' destination for Southampton FC. The reason has been documented in several places by Dave Juson – most notably, for his fellow-Saints' fans, in *The Saints Magazine*. That reason is named Charles Miller. Having attended Banister Court School – little more than a Bill Stroud throw from The Dell – and had a few games for the Saints in 1892-93-94, the 19 year-old Miller returned to his native Brazil, in 1894, with a football under each arm. It was fitting, then, that the man who had brought the game from Southampton to Brazil, and to São Paulo in particular, should kick-off when the touring side arrived in his home town from Rio. Yet Miller, by now 73, had not been a variable in the planning of Cllr Stranger's alternative tour. The imperative came from the relationship, so strong during the war, between the City Council and the Brazilian Consulate in Southampton.

In his new book on Miller's legacy, Aidan Hamilton reveals that the Brazilians had long since been led to believe, by the British Embassy in Rio, that they would get the Arsenal. The team they'd all wanted to play against during the war were romping to the First Division Championship of 1948. Brazil would have to wait for them, though, until 1949. Meanwhile, his hosts asked Mr Stranger whether the Southampton party might include a couple of international guest stars. His fellow-directors instructed Rex

DELL DIAMOND

Stranger to reject this suggestion and to point out that 'we have several players in our own team of International standard'.

At the same Board meeting of 11 March – only seven weeks before they were to leave – travel arrangements had still not been finalised. But the directors accepted that 'several members of the team were against air travel', so the party would hope to go by sea. With the last game at Leicester having been brought forward to Wednesday 28 April, they would be able to sail the following morning for Rio. Passengers normally came aboard the *Andes* the evening before she sailed. But not so the Saints party. They arrived in the morning, from their overnight hotel, and proceeded to hold up the boat's departure, while they were sent off in style. The Mayor led a round of farewell speeches in the ship's lounge, the team lined the rails for photos and the *Echo's* shipping reporter took a roll call of the numerous civic and consular dignitaries who were there to see them off. And plenty of 'dockies' wanted to join in the farewells, according to lounge steward, Ted Meech. The docks were 'crammed full' of them – 'up the masts, up everywhere, to cheer them on'. And Alf Ramsey, having stepped aboard for the photos, was also waving them off. He would be flying out to join the party once he had completed the FA's tour of Italy and Switzerland that was to see him capped for England 'B' in Bellinzona.

All Aboard the Andes
Preparing to disembark – once Ramsey and the Mayor have stepped ashore –for Rio.
Back row (left to right): Smith, Black, Rochford, Horsfall, Curtis, Bill Dodgin, Grant, Ramsey,
Commodore H.F. Way, Clements, Ellerington, Mallett, Webber, Day.
On the steps (ascending from left to right): Wayman, Bates, Ballard,
Scott (behind the Mayor, Cllr Frank Dibben), Sam Warhurst (seated) and Wilkins.

An Awful Lot of Lessons in Brazil

Bill Dodgin and trainer Sam Warhurst sailed with a squad of 16 and a travelling referee. George Reader – a one-time Saints player (three games in 1920-21) – had become a schoolteacher in Southampton and a football referee of some repute, with several international matches, including Great Britain v. Rest of Europe in 1947, to his credit. Cllr Stranger had suggested to the Brazilians that the 51 year-old Reader join the party 'to confer with the referees in Brazil'. But as Rex Stranger would report home – in the first of a series of letters to George White, the *Echo* Sports Editor – their hosts took such a shine to Mr Reader that he was immediately invited to referee all seven matches. He agreed to do so.

George Reader would also be sending dispatches to the *Echo*. His series of match reports has been drawn upon by Aidan Hamilton in *An Entirely Different Game* – a title borrowed from Ted Ballard's verdict on the tour – and I do not propose to rehearse, here, those match-by-match details. A word, though, about the squad. Ian Black was the only 'keeper, though trainer Warhurst was, of course, on hand. Pending Ramsey's arrival, Ellerington could partner Rochford. There was no place for Jack Gregory, who'd had a feel, in 1946-47, of the first-team football he was to experience 68 times for the Saints. Ted Ballard, whose seven games to date had all been at left-half, could double as a full-back, the position he would fill in his remaining 40 games for the Club. He had come from Leyton Orient, as part of the Stroud deal, in 1947 – for once, Bill Dodgin had not got a redundant winger in exchange.

The regular half-back line of Smith-Webber-Mallett was reinforced by three young reserves. George Horsfall will be better known to Saints' fans for his 30-odd years on the coaching staff from 1955. But he'd come to The Dell as a sailor in 1943 and turned out for the Reserves. His two first-team games, to which he would never add, had been at the end of the 1946-47 season. Len Wilkins had played, as a teenager during the War, for the same Cunliffe Owen's side as Arthur Holt, who had brought him to The Dell. He had three games in 1945-46 – he remembers a debut at centre-half against Swansea's free-scoring Trevor Ford (41 in 41 that season) in the Saints' 5-2 win at The Dell – but would not make his 'official' debut until later in 1948.

Centre-half Stan Clements was, by comparison, a veteran of 15 games. He had arrived from Gosport Borough, via war-time appearances for Portsmouth, to be Eric Webber's understudy. And so he would remain. In fact, he would outlast Eric, staying on until 1955, but for only 120 appearances. Today, he would be a regular substitute. In his day, he watched numerous games from the bench – forming lots of opinions of use to our discussion, like those on Rochford and Grant in the previous chapter.

DELL DIAMOND

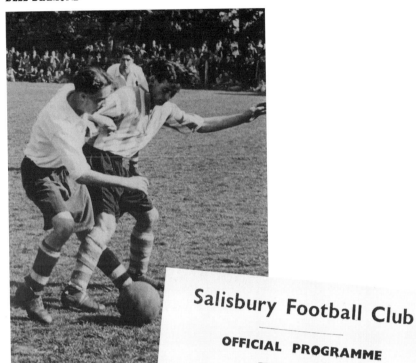

Missing men: Bobby Veck and Jack Gregory might have expected to be in the party for Brazil. But, on 8 May 1948, while the chosen 16 lived it up on the *Andes* (as dressed for First Class accommodation, opposite), they played for the Reserves at Victoria Park, Salisbury, where the crowd spilled down to the touchline to watch them compete for the St Dunstan's Cup.

The photo above shows Veck (right) being tackled by Cyril Smith, the Salisbury stalwart who had been bombed out of the Southampton team in 1940-41.

Salisbury Football Club

OFFICIAL PROGRAMME

Price 2d.

SATURDAY, MAY 8th, 1948. ST. DUNSTAN'S FOOTBALL CUP.

SALISBURY
White Shirts, Black Shorts.

1
FOUNTAIN

2
DUNCAN

4   3
ABBOTT   5   SCULLARD
            WILLIAMS

7   8   6
ROGERS   SMITH   COLMER
                  9
                FISHER   10   11
                          PARKER   CHILD

Referee :
Mr. AMOR,
Larkhill

VECK   *Linesmen :*
11   Mr. L. PINNER
      BEATTIE   Mr. T. DOWTY
      10   LEWIS
MIGNOT   9   FREEMAN   RUDKIN
6   WITT   8   7
      ROLES   5   SALWAY
        3   4
              GREGORY
              2
        STANSBRIDGE
              1

Red and White Stripes
SOUTHAMPTON

SALISBURY FOOTBALL CLUB, SEASON 1947—48.

	P	W	L	D	Goals F	A
Western League	34	29	4	1	145	33
F.A. Cup	4	2	1	1	6	3
F.A. Amateur Cup	5	3	1	1	19	6
Wilts Cup	2	1	1	0	7	8
Friendlies	1	0	0	1	1	1
TOTAL	46	35	7	4	178	51

'We lived like fighting cocks', said Bill Ellerington (right) of the way the crew ('75 per cent were Southampton – football *daft*') indulged them. Eric Webber (left), Bill Dodgin and Joe Mallett are also being served.

DELL DIAMOND

There were only six forwards on board: Day, Curtis, Wayman, Bates, Scott and Grant. Bobby Veck had hoped to go as well. He had signed as an amateur, a year before war broke out, and had made his debut as far back as 1946 in that flurry of Cup activity. But he had damaged his cartilage at the turn of the year. Although the Board had been assured, in February, of his recovery, Veck feels that this injury stopped him being a seventh forward in Brazil.

If that is so, then the measure of his misfortune can be gauged from events of 8 May 1948. While he turned out for the Reserves in the annual St Dunstan's Cup match at Salisbury, the 16 tourists were relaxing 10 days out at sea. It wasn't all relaxation, of course. They were up early to train – 'religiously', Bill Ellerington insists. Ted Meech vouches for their early start – 'those that weren't sick', that is – the first morning out, as they entered the Bay of Biscay. The casualties notably included Len Wilkins, who spent the first six days in his bunk – so sea-sick, he recalls, that his team-mates came in to drape a Union Jack over his head, in solemn preparation for his burial at sea. The survivors of the Atlantic waves made such a commotion, that first morning, as they made their way up from their First Class quarters on the Lower Deck – 'it was a terrible noise', Ted Meech recollects, 'running up the stairs, bouncing their balls' – that other passengers complained. So these enthusiastic athletes had to find a less obtrusive route to their training area up near the funnel. They also opted out of the First Class dining room. Ted Meech could see why:

> They're only ordinary fellows, these footballers. The upper society – some very wealthy people, big meat barons, used to travel in those ships – had dinner at eight. [The players] wanted to eat at five o'clock. They were hungry. They were young lads that were kicking a ball about. They didn't want to wait. On top of that, people in the First Class all dressed up [in more formal attire than the] blazers and club-tie – Dodgin was very demanding of that … They felt a little bit out of place – a big mob of them coming into the dining room. I think a lot of these upper crust people looked down on them a bit, because they weren't exactly quiet when they moved about.

They did, however, endear themselves to those passengers whom they entertained – as we know from Mr Stranger's letters to the *Echo* – with 'exhibitions' of George Curtis's favourite form of training: head-tennis.

This exercise may not have been enough, however, as the team headed (in both senses) across the Atlantic, to work off the effects of over-eating. Bill Ellerington blames the dietary leap from 'strict rationing' at home to the plentiful spread at sea. To put things in perspective, you need to countenance a nation where bread was still rationed and where the weekly food allowances for the average man were 13oz of meat, 1½oz of cheese, 6oz of butter and margarine, 1oz of cooking fat, 8oz of sugar, two pints of milk and one egg. The players were coming from that regime to the *Andes,* where '75 per cent of the crew were Southampton – football *daft.* And they say, "if there's anything on the menu, just tell us; you'll get it". We lived like fighting cocks'. Ted Meech blames this over-indulgence on Charlie Biddlescombe, the Chief Butcher – 'a very powerful man on the ship' – and Alf Carter, the Chief Pantryman. Mr Biddlescombe was 'a fanatic Saints supporter. He gave his orders: "*Anything* they want to eat! Let me know if it's for the Saints". He gave them all the best food'. And Mr Carter, who determined what was served, 'doubled up on everything' for these famished footballers.

'There's no greater activity' – said George Curtis ❶ who gets a chance to play head-tennis, on deck, with two of his 'group of many talents', Ted Bates ❹ and Joe Mallett ❷

Not that they were *that* under-fed. Ration books or not, Eric Webber points out that footballers were already feeding 'reasonably well': your 'average man in industry' didn't have lunch on match days at the Royal Hotel. Not to mention the weekday lunches that the Club had recently introduced, you may recall from the previous chapter, to give them extra energy. And yet, even by those standards, Eric still thought the journey out was 'a holiday in itself' as the waiters invited them to 'go through the card: they've only got seven courses on the card, that's all!' Even without their fans force-feeding them, Eric Day feels that the shift from rationing to 'food you never saw on the mainland' was not what these athletes needed – especially with such 'slight facilities' on board for training. So they 'weren't *pushed*' and, consequently, 'when we got there, we weren't fit'.

DELL DIAMOND

And then more high-living awaited them. There was no food rationing in Brazil: 'Steaks?', asks Ellerington, 'you just name it and we had it'. Their lavish hosts 'couldn't do enough' for them. 'Nothing', Ian Black felt, 'was too much trouble'.

Sugar Loaf tourists
Sightseeing at Pão de Açucar in Rio
Back row (left to right): Clements, Wilkins, Ballard, Smith, Curtis, Horsfall, Ramsey, host.
Front row: Host, Warhurst, Dodgin, Stranger and Bates.

An Awful Lot of Lessons in Brazil

All of which meant that the players could be cacooned in luxury, amid poverty. Notwithstanding the deprivations of his early teens, Ted Bates had never previously 'come in contact', his sister Alice feels, 'with real poverty … I think that really did shake him up at the time. It was something he talked about – the contrast between people'. But Botafogo FC could shield their guests at Rio's Luxor Hotel, from the grandeur of which they could watch the 15-a-side games on the Copacabana Beach. The hotel where the England party was to stay, two years later, for the World Cup, it struck Billy Wright, the England captain, as 'a splendid, modern building, with the cool waves of the Atlantic almost coasting into the reception hall' and with bedrooms that were 'out of this world'. If the Luxor was grand enough to faze the England captain, by then a comparatively seasoned international traveller, what hope was there for Mr Stranger's innocents abroad?

Even so, Bill Ellerington *lost* weight – three quarters of a stone. Quite simply, they'd not come prepared for the heat of late autumn in Rio: when you went to bed, 'you'd feel the sweat running down your face. We used to get up at six in the morning and start training. Then, at nine, we couldn't do anything else if we wanted to'. Ian Black explains what it was like to *play* – even in goal – in such 'oppressive heat', after only a few days' acclimatisation and without the benefit of oxygen that their hosts generally expected, it seems, to take at half-time:

The first game we played was about 95 degrees … I can vouch – you may think this is exaggerating, but it isn't – at half-time, George Smith had to have oxygen, because he was so exhausted. And I took my jersey off and I wrang it out … Not a thick jersey. It was one of their jerseys – a thin, cotton-type of jersey. And I'm in goal – not running about!

The oxygen was available to the visitors in their dressing room, although Ted Ballard and Joe Mallett 'didn't know what it was' until Botafogo demonstrated its use in training. Not that his introduction to oxygen was a huge help to the exhausted George Smith: he was so disoriented that he lined up in the wrong half after the interval and was replaced by Ted Bates. So? What did any of this matter? Overfed. Undertrained. Overheated. Under-acclimatized. So what? These were British footballers coming to teach these Brazilians a thing or two. It was as if nobody had thought to rewrite, for South America, the missionary plan that Mr Stranger had drawn up for North America. Brazil? 'None of us knew anything about football in Brazil', Joe Mallett admits. It was 'a mystery tour', Bill Ellerington confesses. 'We hadn't a clue what to expect'. Ignorance fostered complacency. They arrived confident, according to Eric Day, of showing their hosts 'how to play football'. And they were re-inforced in their self-esteem and self-deception by the way their hosts and the local media fêted them.

Welcome to Rio
The 'festival atmosphere' that greeted the Southampton party.

As they disembarked in Rio on 10 May, they received an 'extremely cordial reception'. Streamers enveloped them as they lined up in pairs to be kissed by 'two gracious senoritas' of British extraction. Or so said the evening paper, *Diário da Noite*, under its banner headline, 'Festival Atmosphere on the Arrival of the *Andes*'. The visitors were said to be strong, happy and healthy, even though they were sweating profusely in the early morning sun and notwithstanding the age of their captain: the reporter was somehow persuaded that a 34 year-old Briton was the equivalent of a 23 year-old Brazilian.

Their self-confidence was re-inforced when they had their first practice session under what Mr Stranger described as 'special night-light equipment', but what Ted Bates, in a postcard to Mary, was already calling 'floodlights'. Rex Stranger assured the *Echo* that the team was 'on top form' and playing as they had, in March, against Newcastle – that semi-final day performance that you may recall Eric Day drooling over. Of course, they'd needed to borrow six players from Botafogo to make up the numbers. Mr Stranger thought them 'very fast' and 'clever', though 'too greedy in the box'. Nothing to fear here then. This 'false sense of security' continued, Bill Ellerington reckons, when the tourists went, the next evening, to watch a

An Awful Lot of Lessons in Brazil

Rio league game. They may have marvelled at the skills of the kids on the beach, but Ted Bates wrote home to Mary that the professionals were 'very individual players' who did 'not seem to have a lot of method'. What Bill Ellerington and the rest of them were soon to appreciate was that the skills of those they were watching 'more or less cancelled each other out. We thought "Ooh, isn't bad, this; yeah, we'll do all right here"'. Ted Ballard dismissed the spectacle as 'a load of rubbish' and thought 'we'll paralyse them'.

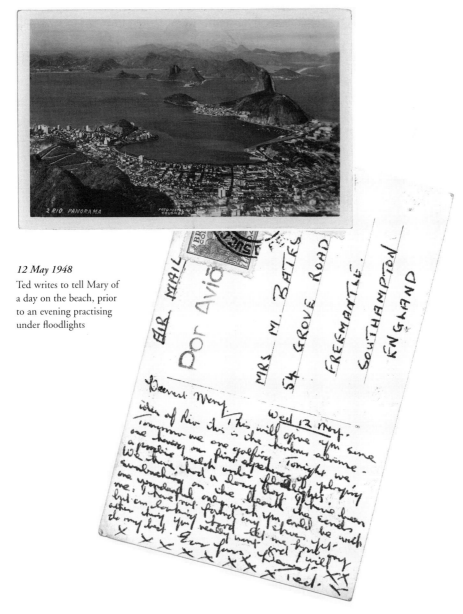

12 May 1948
Ted writes to tell Mary of a day on the beach, prior to an evening practising under floodlights

DELL DIAMOND

The first game, against Fluminense in Rio, gave them cause to re-assess the quality of Brazilian football. Paralysis was on the other foot. 'They walked all over us', Day confesses. 'The way they played football was out of this world'. Joe Mallett soon realised the difference between watching two Brazilian teams and playing against one of them: 'We didn't appreciate their skills. They had speed and skills. When you see them playing each other, it's a different game because they're playing the same game' as each other. But it was such 'a different style, a different system' from what he and his team-mates had ever played. Moreover, those skills were not confined, Ian Black stresses, to 'a *few* players'; it ran through 'whole teams'. Ted Ballard very much appreciated his introduction to what we would now call 'total football':

> They were all footballers in the team – eleven footballers which British football never used to be then. You played to the position you were in. We had full-backs who were good kickers of a ball but couldn't beat a man to save their life. And that was playing for England, as well ... It was an entirely different game. They paralysed us.

Fluminense won 4-0. 'And if it hadn't been for Bill Rochford', Ellerington reckons that 'it could have been 10. He kept playing them off-side ... The skill was phenomenal – Even the goalkeepers could do it on their shoulders'. Do what on their shoulders, exactly? Eric Webber explains:

> I watched this big fellah training. He's kicking the ball up against the wall. He's taking it back on his knee. He's lifting it off his knee on to his shoulder. He's putting it off his shoulder on to his head, then on to his foot, foot to the wall, back ... And I said – pidgin English, you know – 'Inside-forward?' 'Reserve team goalkeeper' (laughter) Reserve team goalkeeper! ... We had outfield players that couldn't have done it – never mind goalkeepers! I thought 'Christ, what's his inside-forward like?'

The answer, according to Bill Ellerington, is that they were all 'light years ahead of us'. Thanks to Rochford and Mallett, Bill felt he 'was beginning to know a bit about football', but this was something else: 'I can't remember anybody beating one of our defenders with the ball. When they attack you – and, my God, they attack straight at you – they always had a couple of supporting players. If we broke it up, by the time we got it through [to our forwards], there's about seven of theirs saying "Here we are. Have a go at us, now"'.

And this skill and technique was backed up by off-field preparation and resources, with training that Ted Ballard found 'very hard – very tough; very deep'. In fact, 'they were right up-to-date with everything they did. First aid. Oxygen … That's how far Brazil was in front of the world'.

All in all, then, the intended pupils were able to teach their visitors 'a tremendous lesson', Bill Ellerington reckons. Some aspects of that lesson would be of longer-term value – like how to play under floodlights and in 'carpet-slipper football boots', which Eric Day found 'very comfortable to play in: you got the feel of the ball much better'. But these lightweight boots went with the lighter balls their hosts were using. It 'would have been very hard work', Eric muses, to wear these carpet slippers with the heavy leather balls still in use in England.

Getting into gear: Ian Black, flanked by Ellerington (left) and Rochford, demonstrates the Brazilian jersey and knee pads he had acquired – but with no sign of adapting to their hosts' footwear.

TEMPORADA INTERNACIONAL DE FOOT-BALL DO

SOUTHAMPTON F.C.

19 46

PROGRAMA OFICIAL

BOTAFOGO F. R.

DELL DIAMOND

In the short term, though, there were games to be won. Losing the first four was not a promising start. Rochford's offside tactics continued to keep the defeats to respectable proportions. As the *Gazeta Esportiva* reflected on the third game, against São Paulo, here was 'a tactical resource used with perfection and art'. But not enough perfection to prevent a 4-2 defeat. Much of the problem was upfront. 'Up the middle to Charlie' may have been a popular chant, and a regular goalscoring ploy, at The Dell, but Wayman was bemused by his first acquaintance with a *libero*: 'I was running here, I was running there, wondering why the ball wasn't coming to me'. His puzzlement was shared by a key supplier. Mallett could not understand, initially, what was happening: 'I used to play a lot of balls into Charlie Wayman's feet and he was very clever: he could turn his marker. When he turned his marker in England, next was the goalkeeper, almost – he's through. When he did that in Brazil, he was running onto what we call a *libero*'.

As a corollary, of course, the full-backs were free to overlap in a way the visitors had never seen: 'they used to cut through like wingers'. Adjustments were needed – and quickly. 'That's what the game is all about', Ellerington reflects. 'If you keep doing the same stupid thing, you ask for what you get'. But with games coming up every four or five days, Black was pessimistic about what changes could be achieved 'overnight'. Moreover, it needed more than a change of approach. It needed a change of attitude. Mallett was concerned lest a squad that had travelled out 'with the wrong attitude – we thought we'd gone there on a trip' – might find it difficult to achieve this change.

Fortunately, they found some kind of solution, he explains, in diagonal balls, played in behind the advanced full-backs, especially from left to right, taking advantage of Eric Day's speed. This meant that Wayman, who was used to getting balls played up to his feet, had to rely more on meeting Day's crosses, but the Saints were rewarded, in their fifth and sixth games, for their adjustments. They had still not learned to cope with the overlapping full-backs – Mallett says they 'never really did. They used to break that quickly' – but these two games brought the two wins of the tour: 2-1 against Corinthians in São Paulo (the game for which Alf Ramsey joined them and missed a penalty); and, back in Rio, 3-1 against Flamengo (when Rochford was rested and Ramsey captained the Saints for the first time). Ted Bates wrote home to Mary that he had supplied the passes for the two goals against Corinthians and he felt that the whole side had 'played really well'. And George Reader reported to the *Echo* that Ramsey had 'played a magnificent game' against Flamengo , co-starring with two-goal Wayman. The players were so pleased with their improvement, says Ellerington, that 'you'd have thought we'd won the Cup'.

An Awful Lot of Lessons in Brazil

The penultimate game, against the South American club champions, Vasco da Gama, was 'one of the best matches' Ramsey had ever played in. Saints lost 2-1. Not a bad scoreline when you consider Aidan Hamilton's calculation that the home team fielded seven players who would make the Brazilian World Cup squad in 1950, including six who would play in the final against Uruguay – refereed, of course, by George Reader, an undoubted success of this tour. As the British Ambassador, Sir Nevile Butler, put it, Mr Reader had 'had all the bouquets that is good for one man to receive'.

The tour ended with a 1-1 draw in Juiz de Fóra, against a State side, Minas Gerais. So, after four defeats in the first four games, they'd won two and drawn one of the next four. Some credit for learning fast, then? Ramsey felt that Southampton had made a 'good impression' by their continued efforts to 'play real football', but the Brazilians had massively re-inforced his view that 'a defender's job was also to make goals in addition to stopping them'. This would equip him, he boasted, for 'singular success' with Spurs and England.

But what would it all do, in the coming season, for a Southampton side intent on finishing higher than third?

In the middle for Charlie
Charles Miller deposes Charlie Wayman (second left), in São Paulo, in order to demonstrate a Brazilian kick-off. Ted Bates (left), George Reader and George Curtis study what Miller learned in Southampton and honed in Brazil.

Taking the Shirt Off Their Backs
Even Len Wilkins (sea-sick for half the journey) was fit to jog in Rio, wearing a Botafogo shirt (left) and
supported by Ted Bates and George Horsfall

Chapter 9

After the ex-Mayor's Show

There were those, according to Alf Ramsey, who had predicted that the Saints players would be 'stale' after such a long summer tour.

Instead, they continued to play the 'brilliant football' they had latterly achieved in Brazil. They were soon atop the Second Division, with performances that were being hailed as of 'First Division class'.

Ted Bates was not an initial part of this renewed quest to play at the level his father had fleetingly achieved, more than 40 years earlier, with Bolton. He missed the first seven games, including the visit to Cardiff on 28 August. A pity, that! It could have been a poignant return to the city in which he had watched his father play cricket for his adopted county. Glamorgan had just won the Championship for the first time in their history. And, in John Arlott's BBC interview with two of the victors four days earlier, tributes had been paid to a handful of stalwarts, including W.E. Bates, who had laid the foundations.

Ted himself had now forgone his last chance to become a professional cricketer. Hampshire had wanted him to come for a trial in 1947, but Army commitments meant that he 'couldn't fit it in'. And the tour to Brazil had ruled out any thought of trying again in 1948.

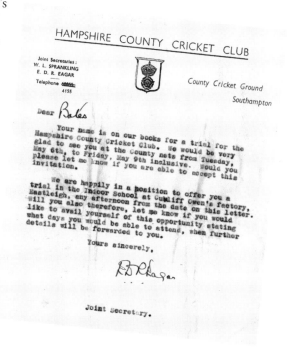

A letter from Desmond Eagar invites Ted Bates to Hampshire's May 1947 trials

DELL DIAMOND

So now the all-round sportsman who might have been a professional cricketer, had his father been around to take an interest in him, would have to settle for football alone. And, to signal his future in the game, he had completed, in July, the course leading to his FA coaching certificate – as duly acknowledged in a letter from Stanley Rous, informing him that he had 'obtained a high standard'.

This was not 'a standard letter', Sir Walter Winterbottom stresses. 'Oh no! We used to add that last paragraph to let them know it was a high standard'.

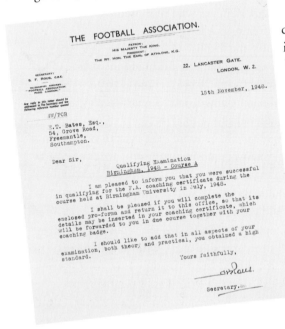

As Director of the FA's coaching schemes immediately after the War, Winterbottom was impressed by the ability of uneducated men, like Ted, to 'talk and coach. Their ability to lead – to lead men – was quite astonishing. They had no teacher-training, but a lot of them had gained a lot through the PTI system'. Lots of footballers had been PT Instructors throughout the War, of course, many of them playing for Aldershot in those regular thrashings of Southampton's war-time youngsters that we

Qualified Success: Ted Bates achieved a 'high standard' for Walter Winterbottom (see his 'WW' reference) as signified, here, by Stanley Rous.

relived in Chapter 4. We're talking especially of Joe Mercer, whose early involvement in the FA's courses was crucial, Sir Walter contends, in 'converting so many managers to the idea of coaching'. If an England international could join him – initially at Carnegie College in Leeds or at Birmingham University and ultimately at Lilleshall – then there was a hope of challenging 'the deep-seated feeling that either you had it or you didn't have it'. A Johnny-come-lately like Ted, who'd not joined the Army until there was only the Cold War to be fought, had some catching up to do. Being a PTI was a vital first step: 'I thought to myself, "If you can do this in the Army, you should be able to coach". I knew football from back-to-front, really. What I learnt in the Army was how to express myself'.

After the ex-Mayor's Show

That ability to stand in front of people and demonstrate should not be taken for granted. By way of example, Sir Walter cites Ted's hero, Alex James: 'a talkative chap, but get him in front and try to organise anything and he couldn't do it. And, as for demonstrating and talking at the same time, and then getting other people to do it – that sort of thing – those skills were without him'.

Model behaviour: Joe Mercer (right), the crucial role model in the development of the FA's coaching scheme, fields a medicine ball at Carnegie. Ted Bates (third left) seems happy to hide his ball.

It was George Curtis, when he arrived at The Dell, who 'really got me going on coaching', Ted acknowledges. Their styles were very different. George was 'hail-fellow-well-met and lots of jokes', Sir Walter recalls, whereas Ted 'would be down-to-earth and get on with the job. An industrious fellow. He was easy to get on with. He'd get people to do things for him by goodwill more than anything else'.

Ted's contribution to one of the most sensational seasons in the Club's history was only temporarily on hold. Once he returned to the side in mid-September, then he settled in, mainly at No.10, for the season. Most of his games the previous season had been at inside-left – with four different wing-partners, but Wrigglesworth more often than not. Now it was Grant's turn. This was a pairing Ted liked – even if Wilf, like other Dodgin left-wingers, preferred to play on the right (especially if being on the left meant tracking back to help Rochford to the extent noted in Chapter 7).

As the Saints came from 2-0 down to beat Coventry 5-2 at The Dell on 9 October, Bates and Grant got three of the goals and an accolade for 'the best display on the left-wing given by the home side this season, and this pair may solve the club's forward problem'. Forward problem? What forward problem? The only problem was the recurring one of finding a settled No.11.

Charlie Wayman was certainly buzzing at No.9. In the next home game, he scored his 100th League goal, one of his five in a 6-0 trouncing of Leicester City. He 'couldn't believe' how he was beating the visiting centre-half 'on the run all the time', fed principally by Eric Day. As one report put it, 'Day never seemed to be where the City defenders thought he would be'. Forward problem? What forward problem?

Apart from a 2-2 draw with Bradford on 18 September – the first goals they had conceded at The Dell – the side just kept on winning at home.

DELL DIAMOND

When that dropped home point was followed by successive away defeats at Hillsborough and Oakwell, however, the manager expressed his alarm to the Board. He assured the directors that 'he had been extremely busy trying to secure new players [and] frankly criticised the half-hearted attitude of certain players'. Yet he 'felt sure that this was only a passing phase': the side that had lost 3-0 at Barnsley had been 'considered by the Barnsley people to be the best side to visit them so far this season'. The Board thereupon gave the manager a remarkable vote of confidence:

> *It was generally agreed that Mr Dodgin was facing up to difficulty with courage and sound judgment and he was assured that the Board was firmly behind him in his efforts and that he was free to proceed with any negotiations with confidence that he would have their utmost support.*

Bill Dodgin would acquire a couple of forwards – inside-left Roland Wheatley from Forest in December and Billy Heaton, yet another left-winger, from Leeds come February. At the same Board meeting to which he reported signing Heaton for £6,000, the manager mentioned his enquiries after two Newcastle forwards: Stobbart, who had replaced Wayman for that 1947 semi-final, would cost £15,000; and Milburn, who had generally taken over from Charlie, was not for sale. As Wayman was not for sale either, Ted Bates would presumably have been the man displaced. But look at the price! Stobbart was nothing special: he would very soon head south for a lesser life in Luton and London – another 200-odd games with a scoring rate of 31 per cent. Yet his asking price would not be equalled, let alone surpassed, by Southampton until they bought Tony Knapp in 1961. If, after Chapter 7, you're still wondering how Ted Bates kept his place, consider the cost of finding a half-decent replacement.

Meanwhile, the only immediate change, after Bill Dodgin's alarmist report in October, was the introduction, at right-half, of Len Wilkins for George Smith. That would be the end of Smith and the first of 274 games, over the next 10 seasons, for Wilkins. But, then, there was a hardly a crisis to be halted. It would be 22 January before the Saints dropped their second home point and 9 April before they lost at The Dell.

When they had gone 10 home games undefeated on 4 December, the *Echo* applauded the 'solo effort' by Ted Bates that won the game against Chesterfield. That was the fifth consecutive home game in which he had scored. At the halfway point in that run, when the Saints beat Spurs 3-1, Stanley Russell told his readers that 'it would be a pity' if either side were to miss promotion: such was the 'high-class football, high-speed thinking and sheer hard graft we have come to expect from these clashes'.

After the ex-Mayor's Show

Eric Webber, compensating for any suggestion of an error in that cup-tie the previous season, 'obliterated Duquemin', while the 'hero', upfront, was Ted Bates, who made two goals before obliging with one of his habitual headers.

It's probably fair to say that we don't expect our 5'9" forwards to score most of their goals with their head. But Ted Bates would disabuse us – with his near post headers, especially flicks from corners. He was 'dynamite' in those situations, as far as Bill Ellerington is concerned. And he needed to be 'a very brave player', as Joe Mallett explains:

He used to score goals and we used to sometimes question how he got them. He'd go in where I wouldn't go in – where other people wouldn't go in. He'd put his head in. He'd slide in. He got a lot of goals from around the six-yard box because he was very brave. He had good anticipation when the ball was coming in. He was a good character. He was a 100 per cent player ... Ted was a limited player, but he got the best out of himself with determination and bravery and he was dedicated to the game ... If you take away his smelling – the way he smelled out the goals, around the box – he didn't have a lot. But the fact that he would always nip in where angels fear to tread – with his head or with his feet – and get goals in the box was a big thing for us.

Ted's willingness to 'be the first to go in where it might hurt' was valued by team-mates like Eric Webber. For 'courage and fortitude on the field, there weren't any better', in Eric's estimation, than Ted: 'He would shirk nothing'. And, like others who played behind Ted, Eric appreciated that 'he was one of those you could always find in space'. Bill Stroud agrees. He was 'brilliant' for a left-half, looking for a forward in space: 'Ted Bates always found the space and made it easy for you to find him'. So, there was more to Ted's game, it seems, than looking after his winger.

In today's terms, of course, a Ted Bates would be assessed less on how he linked up with the player outside him than for how he worked with the principal striker. His dependable supply of 'good support for Charlie' was appreciated by Joe Mallett: 'Two different players – Charlie got his goals by trickery, skill, a few headers, whereas Ted got them the other way: he'd go in where Charlie wouldn't go. And that was a good combination'. Ian Black seconds that:

Ted was not – what shall we say? – a classy player but he worked. Ted would run about all day, which was a terrific combination with Charlie – because Ted was a forager. He was up-and-down, up-and-down, all over the place. A successful team needs somebody like that to do a lot of the running about, a lot of the donkey work, for want of a better expression ... Ted didn't get all the credit he deserved for the amount of work he used to put in. Because, you see, the other inside forward, George Curtis, was not a runner and a chaser. George was a ball-player. He liked the ball at his feet and then he could use it. But Ted was the one who did all the running and chasing about.

Reading match reports of this side's elegance and class, one can appreciate how much it needed a runner and chaser. One position where style was guaranteed was right-back – whether the man in possession was Ramsey or Ellerington. The football writers of this period liked to ponder 'Matthews or Finney?' for England. But you can while away an hour or two on 'Ellerington or Ramsey?' for Southampton if you're talking to their team-mates about the make-up of Bill Dodgin's team.

As a full-back, Albie Roles was impressed with the way in which Ramsey, who'd been so 'full of hustle and running around at centre-forward', converted to right-back: 'He adapted so quickly to it – and so good. He [now] showed signs of being a tip-top footballer'. Even so, Roles preferred Ellerington: 'He tackled harder. He was more direct, more decisive, with his tackling. And he could hit a ball right up along the ground. He didn't have to lob it. He could hit one right up to his winger, if necessary, or right across the field. Alf Ramsey may have been a better positional player, but Bill was a good footballer'.

George Curtis, who'd played for Essex Schoolboys with Ramsey, was an admirer of that positional sense with which Alf compensated for his lack of speed: 'His reading of the play [meant] he could almost walk to the next situation. He'd seen it happening miles before anybody else'. Ellerington thought his rival was limited 'with the ball behind him, but a good player with the ball in front of him. Anything played inside or over the top, he struggled. He was a bit thick in the thigh and couldn't turn quick'. The 'push-and-run' system he would soon join at White Hart Lane would be 'right up his alley: I mean, the furthest he ever had to kick the ball, practically, was from here to the other side of the road – 12 yards'. Bill is 'not knocking' Alf – he had to be 'good' to play so long for England – but most of their team-mates came down in favour of Ellerington.

If you want a meticulous argument on their respective merits, then try sitting Ted Ballard alongside Joe Mallett. On balance, it didn't make 'any difference at all', to Joe, which of them was at right-back:

Bill Ellerington had things that Alf Ramsey didn't have and vice versa. Bill used to clear his lines whereas Alf used to try and play the ball out of danger – which sometimes wasn't the right thing to do. Bill's all-round defensive game was better than Alf's. Alf Ramsey was always beaten by speed and players that took the ball up to him – tricky players; quick players. But he was a brilliant user of the ball. That was how he got his name, on his usage of the ball: good passing, very good passing; but sometimes he used to take chances with short ones, in the danger area around the goal.

Ted Ballard disagrees: 'Alf was a much better all-round player. Bill was a great kicker – one of the best kickers of the ball I've ever seen. Alf played football; he'd play a ball towards midfield and he was accurate with it, whereas Bill cleared his lines'. So Ted would 'sooner have Ramsey' in his side: 'a technical player. I don't think Bill was a technical player (Joe concurs). Great kicker. A great tackler'. In practice games, Ballard expected Bill to stop him, but he 'could beat Alf sometimes, because I was faster than Alf. But, taken all round, Alf was a great player'.

~

They were an analytical bunch, that Dodgin Class of 48-49. Analysis, analysis. Bill Dodgin had to *decide*. Ellerington could cover for Rochford and even revert to his original right-half spot for a couple of games in 1947-48, but Ramsey remained in possession of the No.2 shirt he had inherited in January 1947. What's more, he wore it for the Football League in September 1948 and, on 2 December, he won his first England cap in that position against Switzerland at Highbury.

Yet his Southampton career was about to hit the buffers. His last full game for the Club would be the 2-1 defeat at Hillsborough, on 8 January, in the FA Cup Third Round. The Saints were due at Loftus Road the following Saturday, but QPR's Cup replay took precedence. With Sheffield Wednesday's opponents also involved in a replay, Bill Dodgin asked Wednesday to bring forward their February League fixture at The Dell. They declined. Plymouth were also without opponents, but the Saints had already completed the double over them. So the two sides agreed to play a friendly at Home Park. Ramsey damaged his left knee and never played for Southampton again.

Since he came in for that cup-tie at Newcastle, Ramsey had had a run of 91 games. And yet Joe Mallett argues that it wasn't the injury at Plymouth that cost him his place so much as a disagreement about tactics, at Hillsborough, the week before. With the forwards disappointing – 'Bates, alone, was nearer to his form than any of his line', the *Echo* said – the visitors' defence struggled. Cue Rochford's offside trap, then. Mallett blames

105

DELL DIAMOND

Ramsey for spoiling the plan. It might help if you imagine Joe, dressed in football shorts – he was in his 80th year when he performed this for me – dancing nimbly around his living room demonstrating the positions involved. And you have to accept his principle that, if a full-back is going to play opponents offside, it has to be the *covering* full-back, on the opposite side of the field to the ball. But Alf had 'got into the habit', Joe regrets, 'of putting his hands up: "Offside!"', even when the play was on *his* flank:

> Now you can't do that because you don't know what's happening over here [inside you and] behind you. This is the reason that Alf Ramsey was transferred to Tottenham Hotspur. Sheffield Wednesday had an outside-left who was a quick, small player. Alf went up: 'Offside!' They broke away. They scored. And at half-time, in the dressing room, there was a row – between him and Bill Rochford [who] said 'You've got to keep playing the man. You've got to run. Even if you think he's offside, you've still got to go with him'. Referees are only human ... So you've got to go with your man. So that was the reason that Alf Ramsey took umbrage and left the Club.

The *Echo* reporter tells it a bit differently. Ramsey generally played Dennis Woodhead 'splendidly', but had 'slipped' when tackling him in the move that led to Wednesday's 'brilliant' opening goal. The winning goal, in the second half, came down the other flank, in a move that left Rochford 'completely baffled', according to another report, while Bill Dodgin told the *Echo* that he thought the scorer was offside.

Still smiling
Photographed at The Hawthorns in November 1948, this was the eleven that David Bull would see, in his first exposure to the Saints, a month later.
Back row (left to right): Ellerington, Wilkins, Ramsey, Dodgin, Black, Rochford, Mallett, Warhurst.
Front row: Day, Curtis, Wayman, Bates, Grant, Webber.

Yet Joe Mallett has repeated his concern, to Ramsey's latest biographer, about Alf's tendency to 'take liberties' with Rochford's expert offside tactics and has described his 'lasting impressions' of how that cost them the game at Hillsborough. Moreover, that inopportune shout for 'offside!' and the reprimand from Rochford left quite an impression on the young right-half who'd had but a dozen games in front of Ramsey.

Len Wilkins – who, the *Echo* says, was dummied by Woodhead after Ramsey's 'slip' – talks of that cup-tie against Sheffield Wednesday as Alf Ramsey's 'Humpty Dumpty' match: this was the moment of his great fall, from which the Southampton management and Board would never re-assemble the pieces. It's an interesting twist to the received wisdom about the significance of the injury at Plymouth. Whatever the contribution, at Hillsborough, of Ramsey to the first goal or Rochford to the second, the same reporter who thought the latter was 'baffled' felt that *both* full-backs were 'brilliant' on the day.

Make of those different accounts what you will. Out of favour with his captain or not, Ramsey's injury meant that it was Ellerington's turn, anyhow. Bill was in for the rest of the season, even stepping in as the penalty-taker, as the Saints appeared to be racing away with the Second Division championship. With ten games to go, they won 3-1 at Leicester. Wayman scored twice to bring his League tally to 31, breaking the club record, and was invited to stand by for the FA's summer tour. In the ten games starting on 27 December – a 2-1 win over Nottingham Forest at The Dell and the first game I ever saw – he scored in every game bar one. The Saints were unbeaten in those ten fixtures and would bring the run to 12 games, with only two points dropped, at White Hart Lane on 2 April.

Preparations were being made to celebrate promotion, if not the Championship itself. On 30 March, the Board considered a letter from a Mr Patience (not an especially apt name in the circumstances) suggesting that, should promotion be secure by the time of the last home game (v. West Bromwich on 23 April), a special souvenir programme be issued. The Board empowered the Secretary to act accordingly.

Other clubs had been acclaiming the runaway leaders in their programmes – Reserves programmes even. As early as 19 February, when the Reserves played at Highbury in the Football Combination Cup, the Arsenal programme offered 'their seniors sincere congratulations on a splendid record which now sees them heading the Second Division table. May they gain their goal!' By 28 March, when the Reserves were at Upton Park in the same competition, the West Ham programme envisaged that this goal would be attained, so that the Hammers, then lying seventh in the Second Division, would not be meeting the Saints the following season.

DELL DIAMOND

At the end of that week, the rampant first team came to north London, supported by at least 10,000 fans, the *Echo* estimated, in a White Hart Lane crowd of 69,265. Some gate for a Second Division game – especially when you consider that another 10,000 were said to have been locked out and that the First Division leaders, Portsmouth, had but 35,000 at Fratton Park, that afternoon, to see them beat Liverpool. Fourth-placed Tottenham were entertaining a Southampton side that was six points clear of the field, with eight games to go, prompting the Spurs programme to join its neighbours in predicting the Saints' promotion: 'only a series of unlikely disasters' could now deny them. The first 'disaster' occurred that afternoon.

For, although a Wayman goal – which brought him to 32 in 35 games – gave Saints both points, increasing their lead to eight points with seven games to go, that would be Charlie's last goal of the season. Early in the second half, he pulled up lame. He went off but returned to hobble on the left-wing and to watch Bates,

King's Lynn, and Clacton Town.

THE SOUTHAMPTON TUSSLE

The League side are at home this afternoon to Southampton. We congratulate them that a series of brilliant performances in the League have taken them into what appears to be an unassailable position. They are No. 1 in the table with 49 points from 34 games, and Fulham, their nearest rivals, have six points less. West Bromwich Albion are third with one point fewer, and the Spurs are next with a gap of eight points between them and Southampton. The outlook for our visitors is of roseate hue. They have not yet had First Division football at The Dell, but only a series of unlikely disasters will deprive them of it in 1949-50. Southampton have our best wishes for their success, and may we still hope that a fortuitous run of events will enable us to be runners-up to them? Well, while congratulating the Hampshire club on its outlook we admit to a tinge of envy on their prospects as compared with our own. The Spurs have slipped. We all regret it. Southampton kept pegging away, and they are to-day where they are on merit. They carry with them for the rest of the season our hearty good wishes. What a triumph for Hants if two of its leading clubs carry off the two plums of the Football League.

VARIA

One of the greatest surprises in F.A. Cup history was the

ROOM FOR 60,000 UNDER COVER		
Football League—Division II. April 2nd, 1949 Kick-off 3.15		
TOTTENHAM HOTSPUR O		
White Shirts, Blue Knickers		
RIGHT WING	GOAL	LEFT WING
	DITCHBURN	
	1	
	BACKS	
TICKRIDGE		LUDFORD
2		3
	HALF-BACKS	
NICHOLSON	CLARKE	BURGESS (Capt.)
4	5	6
	FORWARDS	
COX	BAILY	DUQUEMIN	BENNETT	JONES
7	8	9	10	11
Referee: Mr. P. C. ANNETTE (Hants.)		
Linesmen: Mr. L. S. Brunsdon, Berks. (Blue and White Flag)		
Mr. L. G. Aylott, Surrey (Red and White Flag)		
11	10	9	4	7
HEATON	BATES	WAYMAN	CURTIS	DAY
		FORWARDS		
6		5	4	
MALLETT		WEBBER	WILKINS	
		HALF-BACKS		
3			2	
ROCHFORD (Capt.)			ELLERINGTON	
		BACKS		
		BLACK		
LEFT WING		GOAL		RIGHT WING
	SOUTHAMPTON		
	Red and White Striped Shirts, Blue Knickers		
ANY ALTERATION WILL BE NOTED ON THE BOARD		

Premature congratulation
The Tottenham programme on 2 April 1949
failed to allow for 'unlikely disasters'.

who had moved to centre-forward, hit both posts after beating Ditchburn to a back pass. Then, with little more than 10 minutes to go, Wayman scored what the *Echo* hailed as a 'story-book' goal. 'How I got there', says Charlie on the video of the Saints' history, 'I don't know'. Likewise, it will 'always remain a mystery', to the *Echo* reporter, that a player who had been hobbling on the touchline was suddenly in the goalmouth to receive the ball and score. How the ball reached him is clear, though: 'by a combination of skill, strength and sheer pluck', Bates ran through, 'battling against odds and close tackles by two opponents, [and] forced the ball across to Wayman'.

Two years later, in the *Daily Mirror* series, 'My Greatest Goal', Wayman nominated this one. His recall in 1995 was remarkably faithful to that of 1951: 'I don't know how I got to that ball ... I hit it and it came back off the goalkeeper and I hit it with my other foot – the one that worked ... Then they carried me off'. That is to say, in the epic prose of James Connolly, that 'his colleagues ecstatically carried their injured hero back to the centre line and handed him over carefully and tenderly to manager Bill Dodgin on the touchline'. Not that there was anything tender or caring about obliging Charlie to join those 'ecstatic' team-mates for an evening at the Palladium: 'talk about in pain!' Mary Bates had booked the tickets and the show must go on.

The football show, alas, must go on without Wayman. He would play in only two of the remaining games, in which the Saints would score only two goals, get only four points and finish third. Few of the players involved would demur from Ian Black's assessment of those four April weeks being 'probably the biggest disappointment in all our careers ... It was just incredible the way that, in the last few games of that season, everything just went wrong'. So what did go wrong, Ian?

> *We just don't know ... We played Grimsby twice, Bury, West Brom, West Ham. And in all these games, we had the best of the play but we just couldn't score goals ... And in all these games, I would say, without fear of contradiction, that we had the majority of the play. Of course, it was a tremendous blow Charlie being injured ... Even so, we had the chances, but they just would not go in.*

Now we've all heard such excuses for losing the odd game. But how does a side that has played 35 games with a record of W22 D7 L6 then have a run of W1 D2 L4? It's a question the fans – well, the sixty-somethings – are still asking. And answering with a passion. Having to cope without Wayman may be mentioned. That the club 'didn't want to go up' most certainly will be.

Alternatively, we can listen to the players. For them, missing Wayman was a prime factor – although it didn't help that they wuz robbed by more than one dodgy offside flag. And, of course, *they* desperately wanted to go up.

DIVISION II

	P.	W.	L.	D.	F.	A.	P.
Southampton	35	22	6	7	67	30	51
Fulham	34	18	9	7	61	33	43
West Bromwich A.	33	18	8	7	53	35	43
Tottenham	35	14	8	13	55	34	41
Cardiff	34	15	9	10	50	41	40
West Ham	34	15	11	8	47	45	38
Chesterfield	35	12	10	13	45	42	37
Sheffield Wed.	34	14	12	8	56	49	36
Luton	34	12	11	11	44	46	35
Leeds	35	11	13	11	53	56	33
Bury	33	14	14	5	52	61	33
Queen's Park R.	35	12	15	8	36	53	32
Coventry	35	13	16	5	50	54	32
Plymouth	34	11	14	9	39	48	31
Bradford	34	11	14	9	55	60	31
Grimsby	34	11	14	9	60	64	31
Barnsley	34	9	13	12	49	52	30
Brentford	33	10	13	10	34	39	30
Blackburn	35	11	17	7	46	56	29
Leicester	31	8	11	12	50	59	27
Lincoln City	36	7	18	20	49	80	25
Nottingham Forest	35	9	20	6	35	48	24

Only seven games to go
and certs for the Championship
– barring 'unlikely disasters'.

DELL DIAMOND

As the teamsheets for that run of seven games show, Bill Dodgin had no obvious cover for Wayman. On the afternoon of the Spurs match, Bobby Veck, whom we have hitherto encountered as a left-winger, finished the Reserves' game at centre-forward, with both of the goals in a 2-0 win over Palace Reserves – led, ironically, by Southampton reject, Alf Freeman. Two days later, Veck was leading the first team attack for the first time, in a 2-0 defeat at Bradford. He lasted two games. Bates and Wayman shared the remaining five.

But was Charlie fit for the two games he played in? Bill Dodgin insists that he was, but nobody else – least of all Wayman himself – seems to think so. The more interesting question is: where was the reserve centre-forward? Len Wilkins suggests that he was playing full-back in the Reserves. Had not Alf Ramsey scored a few goals as a No.9?

If that was one neglected alternative, we can say, with the benefit of hindsight, that there were two replacement centre-forwards, playing on the wing for the first team or the Reserves. But it would be four seasons before Eric Day would convert to a sensational goal-scoring No.9, while Wilf Grant would have to move to Cardiff City, the next season, for his ability in that capacity to be realised.

In 1948-49, though, Wayman was the goal-getter, with Bates the only other player in double figures.

So were the team too dependent upon Wayman and unequipped to replace him in the event of injury? Bill Dodgin admits that he had no cover for Charlie. But, then, how could he? – 'Charlie was half the team'. It was he who had made Southampton 'the best team in the League'. Ellerington takes a similar line: 'It isn't a matter of being too dependent. You play a certain way, don't you? If you get the same – more or less – people together, you keep playing that way because you're getting success all the time'. Ian Black elaborates:

> It would be very, very hard to get somebody near his class and ability to score goals. And, even if you had, you wouldn't be able to keep him in the Reserves. That's something that a lot of people don't understand. They say 'Well, Charlie was injured. There should have been somebody to take his place'. But who are you going to get to play in the Reserves to be good enough to take Charlie's place when he's injured? We'd some very good reserves – there were a lot of good reserves who came in and did their stuff – but, you see, not somebody in Charlie's class to score goals.
>
> It's an entirely different aspect somebody coming into the middle of the field or a defender, to play his particular game, than to get somebody to come in at centre-forward and to do what Charlie was doing.

And, so, wuz they robbed? When they went to Park Avenue, two days after the Spurs game, Bradford had gone 10 games without a win – compared with the Saints' 22 points out of the last 24. What an anti-climax! Having beaten high-riding Spurs before a crowd of 69,265, their 2-0 defeat by Bradford was watched by 9,293. From their highest gate of the season to the lowest. Rochford and Curtis were also missing. Albie Roles and Roland Wheatley each came in for his only game of the season. The captain had 'a slightly pulled muscle', the *Echo* said, but Curtis was 'resting'. George 'certainly wasn't injured'. It was, he says, an act of 'foolhardiness', on the manager's part: 'when you're having such a good season, it's a question of persevering with those 11 that have got you so far'.

'There was no better forward than Bates', the *Echo* reported, as the re-shuffled line had two 'good goals' – in Eric Day's estimation – disallowed for offside. 'It was just one of those days', 'Observer' concluded in his Portsmouth *Football Mail* column, when 'fickle Miss Luck had a lover's tiff with her favourites'.

He was wrong. Miss Luck had left them in the lurch and there were more days like this to come. Starting with the Saints' first home defeat of the season by West Ham. Bates was down with flu'. He remembers Bill Dodgin coming to see him: 'I was weak. I could hardly stand up. He talked me into playing'. But not for the West Ham game. Southampton were without the pair who had scored 43 of their 67 League goals to date. Four minutes after West Ham had scored, Bill Ellerington had a chance to equalize from a penalty. He 'blasted' his spot-kick and it 'sticks in the craw', to this day, that 'the 'keeper took off and he tipped it round the post, a brilliant save'.

So Bill would be relieved of this duty were his side to win a penalty at Blundells Park on Good Friday. They did – in the last minute, with the score 0-0. Rochford had lined up Heaton for the job. But he twisted a back muscle during the game and Ellerington was re-instated. As the 'keeper went the wrong way, Bill stubbed his studs into the ground so badly that the ball 'trundled' (as the *Echo* put it) into the goal and the scorer of the game's only goal collapsed in pain.

Miss Luck's reappearance was but fleeting. The Saints took only one further point from the holiday games. The defeat at Bury is blamed upon a substitute linesman who had emerged from the crowd after a volley from Joe Mallett had laid out the referee. Ted Bates, the stand-in No.9, 'scored' what appeared to 'Observer', in the *Football Mail,* to be a 'perfect goal'. 'We all trot back to the centre-circle', Bill Ellerington recalls, only to see that the volunteer linesman has 'got his flag up. The referee goes across and gives them a free-kick'. To add insult to injury, Bury came straight down the field to score the only goal of the game.

A £20,000 effort

Eric Day (left) wheels away after heading his lucky equalizer against West Bromwich Albion.
George Curtis's *We're going up* signal proved premature. The goal did not, after all, achieve promotion,
valued at £20,000, but West Brom went up.

If Ellerington is to be believed, the reporter who says that Grimsby 'had to defend for three parts of the game' on Easter Monday is under-estimating. According to Bill, the Saints had 'ninety-nine, point nine, nine recurring' of the game. Well, that's when the ball was in play: the visitors 'were kicking it over the East Stand, over the West Stand, up in the air, anywhere you like, and they hung on'. Nil-nil.

When West Bromwich came to The Dell five days later, for a four-pointer, there was, of course, no souvenir programme for Mr Patience. But there was a record-breaking Dell attendance of 30,586 to watch the 1-1 draw. Having 'murdered' their visitors, the Saints were 'lucky', Ellerington reckons, 'to get a point in the end'. Eric Day agrees that his headed equalizer three minutes from time was indeed lucky.

At Chesterfield, Day was a surprise spectator. As the team prepared to leave their hotel for the ground, he learned he wasn't playing. Augie Scott took his place, only to be put 'out of the game', he recalls, when Norman Kirkman (who would join the Saints a year later) drove the ball into his stomach. So Day watched Wayman have 'a good goal' disallowed. Bad luck or not, though, the dropped winger felt that 'the team was a shambles' that afternoon: they 'never performed. That's all there was to it'. There was, of course, a lot more to it. The manager's reshuffling of his attack was 'a fatal mistake' according to reporter Harold Swan. Bill Dodgin today accepts that judgment – 'football is a game of mistakes'.

Regardless of the fact that Eric Day 'hadn't been having a particularly good time' in the run-in, Eric Webber thought it a mistake, 'psychologically', to leave him out. But, then, he reflected, the whole side played so badly that, 'if you'd been watching as a neutral, uninformed observer, you would have wondered which side was which, which was the one that had something to be aiming the highest for'.

⁓

So what had happened to motivation and morale? Joe Mallett suggests that complacency had crept in and Ian Black agrees that he's 'right in a way':

They may have thought it was cut and dried, being so far ahead, which is easily done in any sport – when you're so far ahead and you think 'Oh Well! It's all over now'. And then it becomes a mind factor, doesn't it? It's not what you can do on the field, then; it's the way your mind reacts.

From there, it's only a short step to suggest that some players were not trying. And, before you know where you are, you can be uttering that great line of Southampton FC folklore: there were those who didn't want to go up. Mr Jukes, the Chairman, told reporter Bernard McElwaine – in early March when their lead was five points – that the club had received 'letters hinting that we were not trying to go up to the First Division'. Having 'snorted angrily' at this suggestion, the Chairman advised McElwaine that Bill Dodgin had a wastepaper basket big enough for such 'ridiculous letters'. Indeed, the Board would be discussing, the next day, how to increase the ground capacity. The season's lowest home gate had been just short of 21,000 on New Year's Day and a postwar record, of 29,445, had been set when Sheffield Wednesday came to The Dell in February (to be broken, of course, by the visit of West Bromwich in April). So the Club would be looking to accommodate more than 30,000, Mr Jukes said, in 'the bright days ahead'.

And not necessarily by expanding The Dell. The Board had tabled a statement, at its meeting of 7 December 1948, of approval 'in principle' for 'a new ground for the Southampton Football Club on the reclaimed ground near the Central Station'. The directors stressed that the scheme 'would incorporate running and cycle tracks of International Standard and a dirt track', all of which would justify 'stands capable of housing 60/70,000 spectators'. None of which suggests a Club lacking First Division ambition.

The difference in rewards between the top two divisions may have been less stark in 1949 than with today's TV-financed Premiership, but journalist Maurice Smith valued it at '£20,000 maybe. Perhaps even more', when he calculated that Eric Day's point-saving header against West Brom might take

Saints up, after all. Yet there was a hint, in the way I first heard this piece of Dell folklore, of divided goals: the players had responded to their manager's enjoinders to 'run your blood to water for Daddy Dodgin' and had deservedly become favourites for promotion; it was the directors who didn't want to go up. It must have been four or five seasons later, when I was 13 or 14, that I heard the story from the pensioner whose *Football Echo* I used to deliver on a Saturday evening. In his version, if memory serves, a fan had wished Bill Rochford good luck before the Chesterfield game and hoped the Saints would win. The captain had, of course, replied that they daren't. I couldn't put that story to Rochford, alas, but was able to repeat this heretical suggestion to several of his team-mates.

Eric Webber dismissed it as 'a load of hooey' and Bill Ellerington as 'ridiculous' – I had to be joking. 'The players themselves [had] everything to gain', Webber reasons. 'And there's no way that any director, or the manager, is going to come down to the dressing room and say "Look, I'm sorry, lads. This club can't afford to go up" … So, no! As far as this club is concerned, there's no way they'd have deliberately avoided the chance of going into Division One'.

It's not entirely true, of course, that the players had 'everything' to gain. As George Curtis points out, you could be better-off, in the days of the maximum wage, picking up bonuses for winning games in Division II than you would be losing week after week in Division I. That said, most professionals would surely 'want to go in where the best players play'. George had already been there, of course. Eric Day was among those who wanted to get there and 'can't believe what the public said – that the players didn't want to go up … Maybe somebody in the Club didn't but the players did. So far as I was concerned, it was the ultimate to get promotion to the First Division'.

For whatever reason – from losing Wayman to lousy linesmen – they were denied promotion. Fulham came through to finish first on 57 points, with West Brom second on 56. Southampton, on 55, were third. There was, moreover, a sting in the tail. It concerned two international right-backs and a manager.

~

It was Bill Ellerington's turn to round off the season with representative honours. First, he played for a strong Football League side that beat the League of Ireland 5-0 in Dublin. We have lasting proof that Rochford really did call Ellerington 'Son' – in the form of the 'Best of Luck, Son' telegram that he sent to Dalymount Park. Then, as for Ramsey in 1948, there was a European tour – the one for which Wayman had been on stand-by before his injury – this time involving full internationals. Ellerington would win two

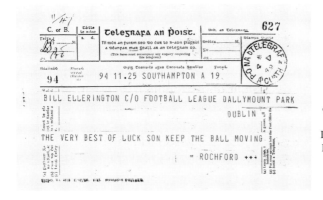

The Very Best of Luck, Son!
Proof that Bill Rochford really did call his full-back partner 'son' – on the occasion of Bill Ellerington's first game for the Football League, a 5-0 win against the League of Ireland in Dublin.

caps, in Norway and France, each time lining up with Jimmy Mullen from his England Schoolboy days. Portsmouth's Jimmy Dickinson made his debut, too, in Norway, and kept his place, like Ellerington, in Paris. Reporting on the latter game, Charles Buchan's *News Chronicle Football Annual* declared the two newcomers to be 'outstanding successes'. But, whereas Dickinson would win 48 caps for England, these were to be Ellerington's only two.

He would give way to Bert Mozley – until, of course, Alf Ramsey settled in for a four-year stint as England's right-back. It is remarkable that Ramsey should have played for the Football League in September of that 1948-49 season and for England in December, while Ellerington waited patiently in the Reserves – standing by to assume not only his Southampton shirt but, as it turned out, his international one.

As Bill Dodgin told reporters, Ellerington 'never moaned once all the time he was in the Reserves'. Alf Ramsey was less content to wait. While he insists that he 'did not object to playing for the second team', he claims that the manager was insensitive, a month after his injury at Plymouth, to tell him that he would find his place 'very hard to regain'. This slight to his feelings became an 'obsession' with Ramsey, who asked for a transfer. All of which called for a special meeting of the Directors on 8 March. The Chairman had already met with Ramsey and tried to dissuade him, but Mr Jukes had found the player 'adamant in his desire to be transferred to some other Club, his stated reason being that he felt he was lowering his chances of becoming an International player, by being played in the Reserve Side and he thought his opportunity of returning to the First Team was remote'. Whereupon, the whole Board interviewed Ramsey and pleaded that 'it would be far more to his advantage and future reputation if he remained with the Club and went up with them, as we all hoped would be the case, into the First Division'. Ramsey would not relent and told the Board 'he was willing to go anywhere'.

DELL DIAMOND

On the Saturday before the transfer deadline, Alex James interviewed Bill Dodgin. He was told to expect the unhappy Ramsey to leave. Sheffield Wednesday were interested but Alf wasn't. Spurs came in and he was. It was too late, though, to beat the deadline so Ramsey played out the season in the Reserves, climaxing in the Combination Cup Final. Bournemouth beat Saints at Fratton Park 5-3 after extra time and the *Echo* applauded a performance by Ramsey that 'could not have [been] better had he been wearing an England shirt'. On 16 May, Ramsey met the Spurs management to revive the deal. In the week that saw Bill Ellerington make his England debut in Oslo, Alf Ramsey moved to Spurs with Ernie Jones, the Welsh international winger, and £6,000 coming to The Dell.

Yet another left-winger arriving as a makeweight in an exchange deal, then? Not really. Jones, who'd played in that cup-tie at The Dell the previous season, had been in Bill Dodgin's sights for some time. When Wilf Grant was out for seven games in September, the manager tried six players at No.11 and enquired after Jones. Ernie recalls Bill Rochford meeting him in London and asking how he'd feel about a move to Southampton.

When the exchange was eventually effected, Bill Dodgin was not around. He had returned to Brazil – this time as a guest of the Arsenal. So it's easy to see why Bill Ellerington talks of a 'deal done between the Board and Spurs', while the manager was away, as a sufficient explanation for Bill Dodgin's resigning, after his return from Brazil, to become manager of Fulham. This assessment of cause and effect is not borne out, however, by the facts.

We have just seen that the decision to sell Ramsey had effectively been taken well before the end of the season. What's more, the Board kept the manager informed. Gladys Dodgin recalls being at the hotel reception in Rio, 'waiting for our rooms', when her husband was handed a telegram from the directors, indicating Spurs' final offer. He told John Thompson of the *Daily Mirror*, who was following Arsenal's tour, that he had cabled back three words: 'GO AHEAD – DODGIN'.

He was reluctant to do so, as Ramsey was one of those players – like Rochford and Wayman – who could 'think for others', whereas Ellerington 'left it to other people: he couldn't help the others, like Rochford and Ramsey. Neither of them could run, but they couldn't half think'. What's more, as a general rule, 'you don't let your good players go. If it's flash-in-the-pan players, you sell when they're flashing. But these two players were so consistent. You want to keep them'.

Ellerington feels that there was room at The Dell for both him and Ramsey: each had shown himself capable of playing at left-back, where Rochford, by now 36, 'wasn't going to last much longer'. That, Bill claims, 'was the idea'.

So, if both the Board and the manager consented to Ramsey's going, what provoked Bill Dodgin to leave? Ian Black takes a circumspect view:

It's hard to say really, because a lot of talk must have gone on behind closed doors that the players didn't know anything about. I think, really, that probably the most important factor is that, in the light of all that Bill had done for the club – and he'd done a tremendous amount for Southampton in the short time he'd been manager – that they didn't give him, and they weren't prepared to give him, as much support as he deserved in the way he wanted to run things.

There was, indeed, a lot going on 'behind closed doors'. When Bill Dodgin returned from Brazil, he sorted out a number of matters with the directors at their meeting of 6 July. The issues dividing them might be 'considered frivolous by some', Mr Stranger observed, but the manager was taking them 'very seriously'. One matter that was resolved was the status of the two 'trainers' – Sam Warhurst, who'd been travelling with the first team and Sid Cann who'd been minding the Reserves. Cann, who'd won a losers' FA Cup medal with Manchester City in 1933, had later played at Charlton with Bill Dodgin, who had brought him to The Dell, as a qualified physiotherapist, in 1946.

In clarifying their respective roles, the Board determined that Warhurst would be 'designated Trainer and Coach and be … in entire charge of the Dressing Rooms and players under this heading', while Cann was to be 'designated as Physiotherapist to the Club and be in charge of all players for all medical purposes and be responsible for the conduct of the treatment rooms'.

All job descriptions would be up for grabs, however, as a consequence of a bombshell from Mr Dodgin, nine days later, when he asked the Chairman to release him from his Agreement with the Club. This came as a 'complete surprise' to Mr Penn Barrow, who had succeeded to the Chairmanship when Mr Jukes died on the Monday after that watershed game at White Hart Lane. The Board (now joined by Mr Jukes's son, Reg) proceeded to offer Bill Dodgin increases both in salary and control. Mr Sarjantson even volunteered to give up being 'Secretary and General Manager' and become 'Secretary', so that Mr Dodgin could be designated 'Manager' instead of 'Team Manager'. Bill Dodgin proved as obdurate, however, as Alf Ramsey and his Agreement was cancelled as from 3 August 1949.

He had turned down an offer from Fulham a year earlier. Frank Osborne, a former Saints and Fulham forward who had played for England, had – as Fulham's *Complete Record* puts it – 'stepped down', after 13 years on

the Board, to become manager. Now, having taken Fulham to the Second
Division Championship for which the Saints had been odds-on favourites,
he was stepping upstairs to be General Manager. If Bill Dodgin wanted
more freedom to manage, this doesn't seem like the most obvious set-up.
He says he welcomed the opportunity to work for a 'boss' who had 'played
the game', but – as Charlie Mitten tells it, the Fulham players felt that he
was Osborne's 'stooge'.

According to Gladys Dodgin, though, there was another, less
conspiratorial reason for her husband's move: she wanted to get back to
London. Whatever the reasons, it sticks in Eric Day's craw that Bill Dodgin
should have joined the very team that had pipped Saints for promotion:
'I was disgusted. I was shocked … I couldn't believe it. They preach, preach,
preach and then they turn their backs'. At least Day wasn't losing a father
figure – or even a manager he rated highly:

> He'd talk. He was not even a good tactical man, I wouldn't say. But, then, in
> those days there weren't all that many people talking about the finer points of
> the game. We were living in a bit of a dead period, if you like. We were only
> too glad to be playing after the war was over and everyone was enjoying
> themselves.

For somebody who played in a side full of tacticians and coaches-to-be, it is
not surprising to hear Eric Day claim that he 'played football by instinct –
nothing else': after all, he'd taken up the game, remember, only in the RAF.
Uncoached and fancy-free, he nevertheless valued shrewd management: 'If
we'd had a manager like Arthur Rowe, we would have had promotion. Not
the slightest doubt about that'. But Arthur Rowe was about to take over at
White Hart Lane: having signed Alf Ramsey, acting manager Jimmy
Anderson would hand him over to the incoming Rowe that same month.

So whom would Southampton appoint to succeed Bill Dodgin? His
would be a hard act to follow. For even if Eric Day did not lament his
going, so many of his team-mates had been willing to 'run their blood to
water for Daddy Dodgin'.

Chapter 10

No Cann Do?

'Have a little chat together', the Chairman pleaded, 'on matters concerning the Club'.

Mr Penn Barrow and his Board needed to fill very quickly the gap left by Bill Dodgin's resignation. Mr Sarjantson and he soon met with trainers Cann and Warhurst and captain Rochford. Warhurst was made 'temporary Team Manager', pending an appointment, although Cann would 'be in temporary charge of the Dressing Room' – the territory that had been designated as Warhurst's domain only four weeks earlier. Mr Penn Barrow invited any of them to apply for the vacancy but suggested they talk it over between them – the delicately-worded minute (above) presumably meant that he'd like them to agree which one should apply.

Each man made a pledge of allegiance in the cause of morale. There was, said Cann, 'a feeling of tension and gloom hanging over everyone' and the 'old team spirit' would need to be rebuilt. Committing himself to 'do all he could' to that end, Rochford said it would be 'useless to say that the players were not under a cloud as a result of Mr Dodgin's departure'. For Ian Black, it was more than a case of his losing a 'second father': the team was 'shattered … I think the general feeling within the club – from the players' point of view – was that it was a tremendous blow, after what he'd done'.

Having played with Dodgin, Bill Ellerington had subsequently enjoyed him as a manager: 'He had a way with *people*. You couldn't help but like him. I liked him tremendously – always a laugh and a joke and always a nice smile and a homely face'. George Curtis had similarly appreciated having a manager who 'was full of fun and light-hearted'. He'd been 'really popular' with the lads, Charlie Wayman suggests, because he was himself 'one of the lads'. But he would be missed, Black reckoned, for more than his sense of fun. There was 'his knowledge of the game, his terrific enthusiasm':

> *He could instil that enthusiasm into the team, which is all-important. There are quite a lot of managers, who are good enough managers in a sense, but they can't transfer that enthusiasm to the players. And that's a very, very important aspect in any manager. His whole attitude and approach were first class in the sense that he was such – what shall I say? – a friendly character generally: you know, he never got really upset and started throwing his weight about … Bill had lots of plusses in his make-up.*

DELL DIAMOND

Given their hurry to restore morale – the new season would kick-off on 20 August – the directors did not advertise the vacancy. And when they met, six days later, they decided to make a temporary appointment, for one season only, from among the three internal candidates: Cann, Rochford and Warhurst had all accepted the Chairman's invitation to apply. There were those, like Ian Black, who had not given much thought to who might succeed. But Bill Ellerington claims that, despite the allocation of temporary positions the week before, 'everybody would have bet £100 it was going to be Bill Rochford':

> When it was announced in the boardroom, the Chairman got up and he said 'You'll be pleased to know who the new manager is … ' – and we all thought 'Yeah, we know who he is, Bill Rochford' – and he said, 'You'll be pleased to know, it's Sid Cann'. I've never had a more embarrassed 30 seconds in my life. Because Sid was stood there with the Chairman and everybody was looking at the floor and up at the ceiling and scuffing their feet and everything.

Warhurst would be designated Head Trainer and Rochford would become Player-Coach. Announcing this distribution of responsibilities to the *Echo*, the Chairman said that an internal appointment was 'the best way to keep continuity of ideas and the right spirit'.

~

The Board's solution was a way of promoting all three candidates, but Stan Clements contends that the directors should have got rid of Warhurst. A nice enough chap, but he 'wasn't a technician'. With him out of the way, Sid Cann could have commanded the background. If that sounds back-handed, it *is*, nonetheless, a compliment.

As Clements sees it, Cann had every qualification imaginable for such a position. He was an FA coach *and* a physiotherapist. He'd brought in heat lamps and so many other innovations, and all to a Second Division team. He was involved in so many ways – all of them 'more background than foreground'.

If Ellerington is especially partisan about it, nobody seems to think that Cann should have been offered the foreground. Not even Eric Day, who had not 'rated' Bill Dodgin. Without wanting to be 'unkind', Eric did not think Sid Cann had 'a lot to offer'. Ellerington is quick to insist that he had been 'outstanding' as a manager of the Reserves, but the qualities needed in that job would not necessarily, and did not, transfer to the first team. Bringing the 'kids' on was one thing; hacking it with 'seasoned pros' was another. And his introverted style disappointed Dodgin's disciples. There was, for Ian Black, 'such a *vast* difference between the two people':

No Cann Do?

Sid Cann was – what shall I say? – a very withdrawn person; kept everything very close to his chest. There wasn't the same discussion, atmosphere and spirit – nothing like there was when Bill Dodgin was there … Sid had qualifications as a coach, an FA Coach, but that's not the be-all and end-all. There's a lot more to being a manager of a club than being an FA Coach … He couldn't communicate with people, really, and I think the whole atmosphere and outlook of the team and the Club – not just the first team – deteriorated.

George Curtis takes a similar position. He was a passionate disciple of Walter Winterbottom. His visits to Lilleshall, to which he would accompany Sid Cann, were touched upon in the previous chapter. Yet he admired the wisdom of Rochford and Mallett and was 'saddened' that they never joined Winterbottom's crusade: 'it was a vital loss to many, many players that their type would not go to Lilleshall and spread the football gospel'. But never mind coaching certificates: if you were 'looking for a manager, the most *complete* bloke', in Curtis's estimation, 'would be Joe Mallett'. And, of the candidates available, he would have preferred Bill Rochford. He would have been *'ideal'*. He could 'push out information' from his 'vast experience' and 'had character: once he'd said anything, that was it'. Cann had the 'knowledge of the game' and was 'quite an intelligent thinker'. What let him down was his communication. He was 'not a smiler' like Dodgin.

So would Rochford have been, as Ellerington believed, the answer? Ted Bates is doubtful. Although 'surprised that Rochford didn't go further than he did' as a coach and although he had expected him to succeed Dodgin, he feels Bill was 'perhaps a bit short in management qualities' and not 'built to stand the pressure of football people'. Clements takes a similar line – 'it didn't necessarily follow' that this very popular captain had the 'something extra' that he'd have needed to become a good manager. But, then, as Stan points out, it wasn't just a case of replacing a manager but of replacing a style of management, a style that depended upon the captain and his

Good Luck, Boss!
Charlie Wayman (right) hands a black cat – for luck? – to new manager, Sid Cann, watched (left to right) by Day, Webber, Ellerington, Edwards and Jones.

lieutenant – the three-fold 'administration' that Ernie Jones described in Chapter 7. For Clements, this triumvirate had operated with Bill Dodgin as 'the talker, but the thinkers within his team, for running [things on the field], were Joe Mallett and Bill Rochford – which basically was OK, because it was a strong force'.

If Dodgin had depended upon Rochford, there seems to be no dispute that the captain had in turn depended upon Mallett. Despite his acclaimed ability to change things on the pitch, Rochford lacked 'the educational background', Clements feels, to articulate his thoughts off the field. That's where Mallett – who 'was educated, both on and off the pitch, and could talk football' – came in. 'If you could put Joe Mallett and Bill Rochford together in managing, and if they could have worked together as a manager', then that, Stan Clements concludes, 'would have been fine'.

But this was not a solution in the minds of a Board hurrying to replace one manager with another before the season started. And if their choice of manager had no support among the players, then the shortcomings of Rochford seem to have been almost as apparent – even to his disciples. Although dubious about Bill's capacity for management, Eric Day considers that 'defensively, he would have held the team together'. But, then, Eric had found Bill Dodgin unduly 'defensive-minded'. Ian Black feels Rochford 'would have been a much better bet' than Cann but suspects, rather like Day, that the Board perhaps thought him 'a bit too forthright in his outlook but at least he was straight and honest and you knew what he meant and what he was trying to get home'.

Rochford was certainly forthright enough when the Board offered him the position of player-coach. He demanded and received an assurance that he would 'undertake and supervise the coaching of all the players – First team, Second team and even the Nursery side'. He had told the Board 'frankly' (so say the Minutes) of

> a difference of opinion in the Dressing Room regarding the coaching ... All players should be coached and trained on a common plan so that ... a reserve team player [could] come into the First Team Side with the same ideas as to the plan of First Team play generally. Instead of this, through a lack of co-ordination, he came into action with a different outlook and a different style of play, and even an experienced player would be under a disadvantage if this plan of action was continued.

That looks like a scarcely-veiled swipe by Rochford at the way Sid Cann had been coaching the Reserves. As Clements saw it, it was the style of football that Cann had played at Charlton under Jimmy Seed and Jimmy

Trotter. It had served Charlton well – 'they were a *solid* side' – but Clements echoes Rochford's complaint that it was not preparing players for the quite different style of the first team.

So how could the directors give Rochford the authority to get rid of this approach? It hardly needs the benefit of hindsight to declare this a suspect assurance. If the Board were to abide by it, then Bill Rochford had established a powerful new position.

~

Moreover, Rochford was still at left-back when the Saints started the 1949-50 season the following week. He had a new outside-left to work for him. Ernie Jones had arrived, remember, to wear the 'graveyard' shirt. And, while Nos 1 to 9 just about picked themselves, Jack Edwards had come from Forest, before Bill Dodgin departed, to open the season at No.10. A less than obvious replacement for Ted Bates, who was yet to start a post-war season, Edwards was a ball-playing inside-forward in the Curtis mould.

After the side had taken only one point from four games, though, Ted came in to score the only goal against Preston at The Dell and otherwise add, the *Echo* felt, 'a lot of punch to the attack'. Curtis moved, 'with distinct success', to right-half, where he would remain for most of the season. Wilkins, in turn, went to right-back.

How odd that the position so recently contested by two England right-backs should now be taken by an inexperienced player converted from wing-half. But with Ramsey gone and the position his, Ellerington was injured for much of the season. He would partner Rochford at full-back less often than Wilkins would partner Ballard – also converted, after sitting out the whole of the 1948-49 season, from wing-half.

Yet it was Webber and Bates whom Sid Cann most wished to replace. As he told the Board after six weeks in office, he needed to spend and especially on those two positions. When Mr Sarjantson said that no more than £10,000 could be available for transfers, the manager pointed out that he had nobody to offer in part-exchange. The likes of Wayman, Ellerington and Curtis 'would be asked for and naturally no such request could be entertained'. Curtis would be the season's only ever-present in a most unsettled side – while Webber, despite Cann's misgivings, was well into a run of 134 consecutive League games and would miss only the FA Cup Third Round replay with Northampton at The Dell.

He had finished the 1-1 draw at Northampton, limping on the left-wing, a position vacated by Ernie Jones, hospitalised in a brutal encounter. Clements, waiting patiently for an opening through Webber's long stint, came in for the return at The Dell and stills rues the slip that gave McCulloch, the visiting centre-forward, a run on goal. And yet, although the

DELL DIAMOND

Saints may have missed 'the stopper qualities of Webber', the *Echo* asked what other defensive deficiencies might be blamed for Northampton's coming back from 2-1 down to win 3-2, when each of their wing-halves scored from a corner.

'Commentator' further reflected that 'it was unfortunate that so many experienced first-team players were out of this game'. A diplomatic comment on the casualty list from the County Ground, but also a reference, of course, to the loss of both full-backs. Rochford would, in fact, play his last match for Southampton the following Saturday, completing 134 games for a club he had joined at the age of 33. As Ellerington says, Ramsey wouldn't have had long to wait. Bill would be back – until April 1956, in fact – but, for the moment they were without all three of their star full-backs of 1946-49, not to mention the winger they had traded for one of them.

Ernie Jones's injury created an opening initially for Tom Lowder – although Edwards would play more than half the following season at No.11. It had been bad enough for inside-left Bates to have a succession of outside-rights playing reluctantly on the left, but he found it more difficult to have Edwards out there. Yet Jack would be neither the first inside-man (think back to Augie Scott) nor the last (in his first 15 months as a manager, Ted Bates would, ironically, do it to Johnny Walker) who would be required to wear the dreaded No.11 shirt. Lowder, by contrast, would play all but one of his 39 games – in fits and starts over four seasons – as an outside-left. He came from Boston United in October 1949, as a job-lot with wing-half Bryn Elliott.

Sid Cann was rebuilding, then. But could he rebuild the 'old team spirit' – the task he had identified in his mission statement to the Chairman? As far as Ellerington was concerned, things had 'started to go down when Bill Dodgin left. It's as simple as that. If Bill hadn't have gone, I still think we would have won something'. Likewise Ian Black: 'There wasn't the same spirit in the team … I'm not saying everybody was going about with long faces, making a big fuss of things, but you could sense that there was a different atmosphere within the club' – so much so that he thinks it 'remarkable that we did so well'.

Doing 'so well' meant missing promotion by an even narrower margin – 0.063 of a goal – than in 1949. Despite the low morale and a manager that few, if any, of the team respected, the side ended the season with a flourish that was the opposite of 1949. A visit to White Hart Lane was again the watershed. This time they lost 4-0 – before an even bigger crowd of 70,302 – to the team that was running away with the Division II Championship. There were 12 games to go and, no matter that Wayman would miss four of them, the Saints would lose only once. Charlie was in for consecutive games against their two rivals from Sheffield, crucially scoring each time in a 1-0 win.

So it was that this once demoralised team went into the last game, at home to West Ham, knowing that a win by a three-goal margin should enable them to pip both Sheffield teams for promotion. Two Southampton players claim that a deputation from the visitors offered not to try too hard if the home team would hand over their win bonuses. Really? Not a story that is readily corroborated, almost half-a-century on, although both men – including the one to whom the approach was allegedly made – name the same source of the offer. If they have correctly recalled its terms, there seems no reason to doubt their insistence that these were roundly rejected: West Ham promptly took a 2-0 lead. Although the Saints came back to win 3-2 – with Rochford out of the side, Ernie Jones felt free to go forward and score a couple – the two points were not enough to take them up.

They finished on 52 points, along with Sheffield Wednesday and Sheffield United. Sid Cann's re-shaped side, with its makeshift full-backs, had conceded the same number of goals as Wednesday. Its problem lay in having scored three fewer. Wayman had played his part with 24 goals in 36 games and Bates, with 16 in 33, achieved his best-ever strike-rate. But Wednesday's superior goal average – by just 0.063 of a goal, as I say – took them up with Spurs.

Sheffield United would have to wait another three years and Southampton a little longer.

～

Not a bad season, though, for a team still licking its 1949 wounds and lamenting a lost manager.

If that's how it felt to devotees of Daddy Dodgin, how did the team spirit seem to Sid Cann's new boys? We can get an idea from three men who arrived at different stages of his two-year stint and a fourth who was coming through from the ranks. Bryn Elliott's signing from Boston in October 1949 has already been logged above. Frank Dudley arrived from Leeds in February 1951. Don Featherstone came as the physiotherapist in August 1951 after a spell with Hounslow Town in the Athenian League. And, the following month, Peter Sillett made his first team debut. The son of Charlie Sillett – who was at right-back when Ted Bates made his debut in Chapter 2 – Peter had signed as a 15 year-old amateur during Dodgin's last season and as a pro at the end of Cann's first.

Arriving at intervals, the newcomers formed the same impression: they were entering a 'divided camp'. They were fairly consistent, moreover, about two of the reasons they adduced for that divide.

DELL DIAMOND

The first, hardly surprising, was that the division of labour among the three candidates had not been accepted by the losers and/or their supporters. As Elliott saw it, 'whoever got the job, there was going to be back-stabbing from the other people'. So Dodgin's disciples were still siding with Rochford. Mallett and Ellerington, especially. And perhaps Black, although Ian is adamant that, whoever had become manager and even if Saints had been promoted, he would still have wanted to follow his mentor – as he did at the end of that season – to Fulham. By the time Don Featherstone arrived, Rochford had gone, but the 'back-biting' continued: 'Sid Cann didn't get on with the others and they didn't get on with him. Nobody had any respect for anybody'. Warhurst remained a problem, he felt, for Cann. 'A very, very strong character', who 'had no time at all for team-talks on tactics or anything like that', the head trainer regularly undermined the team manager. Featherstone had never worked at a league club before so tended to judge the atmosphere at The Dell against his experience in the Army – some of the machinations reminded him of the Sergeants' Mess – and his job with Hounslow: 'There was far more discipline at Hounslow Town than there was at Southampton'.

Cann seemed to the new physio to be largely out of control of 'a very funny set-up'. As Elliott saw it, 'he was probably too nice a bloke for the job' and 'didn't have a lot of chance' of succeeding. Similarly for Frank Dudley: he found Cann to be 'a very affable sort of chap' who did not know 'how to handle strong-minded people'. Joe Mallett had by then become a 'very strong-minded' successor to the Rochford mantle.

After playing that last game in January 1950, Rochford agreed to 'have a go' at a new set of duties. These included watching young players. He was soon reporting negatively on Ron Reynolds, Aldershot's 22 year-old goalkeeper, who was so keen to come to The Dell that he wrote, during the close season, and asked them to have him. His plea went unanswered, so he went to Spurs instead. Southampton would be chasing him, of course, 10 years later.

Nor did the Club sign a promising teenager whom Rochford brought to The Dell from his native North East. The lad seems to have been widely admired, during his trial period, by Rochford's team-mates – not least by Joe Mallett, who remembers him arriving 'with his little case' and coming back for a meal with him and his wife, Bertha (who chips in her own fond memories of the evening). But, to general dismay, Sid Cann let him go. Ted Bates 'couldn't believe it: we couldn't understand why Sid didn't sign him. We thought he seemed promising enough. For some reason he didn't fancy him'. This would have added, Ted feels, to Rochford's problems with Cann: 'There was no way that he was on the same lines as Sid'. Indeed! It seems that this impressive youngster was a victim of The Dell's divide. We know, from the trialist's autobiography, that Rochford was 'upset at the way Southampton had treated me'. So Bill Dodgin was alerted and he duly took the young Geordie to Fulham. *Bobby Robson!*

Peter Sillett, just two weeks older than Robson, remained oblivious to any such 'split', so long as his acquaintance with the first team dressing room was confined to boot-cleaning duties. At the end of the 1950-51 season, though, he began to travel as reserve, when he roomed with his idol, Bill Ellerington, and Ted Bates took him 'under his wing'. When Ted told his young charge that the team was 'a little bit split', Peter wondered why Ted should enquire whether he was 'a meat or a fish man'. So Ted translated: was he a Catholic; or was he one of the 'hooligans'? If the notion that religion was a feature of the divide was a joking matter for Ted Bates, Don Featherstone treated it in a similar vein: 'There were "The Pope's Boys" and the other lads' and the former would soon be joined by the Irish invasion of Kiernan and Traynor. Bryn Elliott seems to have taken it more seriously and to have alerted Frank Dudley to it. As Bryn saw it, Rochford, Black, Ellerington and Mallett were Catholic buddies who 'stuck together when Dodgin left'.

Three pigeons
When Frank Dudley arrived, this gave the forward line three fast runners. Dudley says they could surge forward together and cites this goal against Swansea, in November 1951, as an example.
Brown (on the line) has cut the ball back for Dudley (right) to score, while Day is also up with the play.

DELL DIAMOND

Ellerington roundly dismisses any such explanation of the 'inner circle' from which Dudley felt excluded. Having previously found the side to be 'a jolly good set of fellahs', Frank wondered what was going on. Whatever the explanation, there seems to be no disputing that Rochford had handed over power to Joe Mallett, with Ellerington as his lieutenant. Featherstone liked the two of them – 'they were a very sharp pair, [but] not unpleasantly so'. They were 'the Godfathers [who], in a way, ran things'. Dudley, too, is a Mallett fan: 'a wonderful player, who knew his football' and who became 'a first class coach'. You will detect an echo, here, of Curtis's comments earlier in the chapter: Joe Mallett was an outstanding thinker and communicator, but he didn't fancy joining Sid Cann – along with Bates and Curtis, and very soon Dudley himself, on their expeditions to Lilleshall.

For his part, Ted just 'couldn't stop' coaching. He so enjoyed travelling across Hampshire, over to Isle of Wight, 'all over the place', passing on what he'd learned on those trips to Lilleshall. And he found a niche at the University of Southampton, coaching the 1st XI. The 1949-50 side was captained by Steve White, who'd played with Alf Creecy and Bill Stroud for Toby Keleher's Highbury Sports before the War. Ted took it seriously, going to watch the Wednesday afternoon games, Steve remembers, 'to see how we were doing and whether we were listening to him. He was a great enthusiast – absolutely brimming with enthusiasm. That brushed off on the team'.

Lilleshall together: A 1951 gathering at Lilleshall includes a strong Southampton contingent of ❶ Dudley, ❷ Easson, ❸ Bates, ❹ Curtis and ❺ Cann. The other numbered participants are ❻ Ron Reynolds, whose transfer to Southampton in 1960 (see Chapter 15) would owe much to his Lilleshall meetings with Ted Bates; ❼ Walter Winterbottom; and ❽ Alan Brown, who would become the coaching mentor, in later years, of several Southampton managers/coaches.

No Cann Do?

'U' Certificate: Ted Bates lines up, as coach with the Southampton XI of 1949-50, captained by Steve White, a member of Toby Keleher's Highbury Sports side to whom you were introduced in Chapter 4

Here, though, we have Dudley's third 'divide' – Frank feels that the coaching coterie were resented by some of their unqualified colleagues, not least because the men with badges could spend their afternoons coaching in schools, thereby supplementing their limited wages as players. For Henry Horton, Frank is missing the point. Henry's concern was not the money they earned but the energy they expended. In the course of praising the attributes of Curtis and Dudley, he slips in a gentle rider: 'They went out coaching, quite a few afternoons a week, and I don't think this exactly improved their performance on the field. I think there were times when, with a bit more energy left, they'd have been playing to their full potential. They enjoyed it and got paid for it. I think it cost them a little bit of form'. Like Dudley, though, Curtis felt that their earnings were the 'basis' of their team-mates' objections – even if '"resentment" may be too strong a description'.

However you label it, this phenomenon was not peculiar to Southampton. As Walter Winterbottom recognised, these afternoon pickings could be 'quite an additional factor to their salary'. But here was a club where the top *brains* – first Rochford and now Mallett – seemed to epitomise the 'natural' School of Coaches: teaching schoolkids is all very well; now show us what you can do on the pitch on a Saturday afternoon. Sir Walter found that kind of attitude widespread among managers of that era – that 'deep-seated feeling' that, if players 'were natural footballers, they were *born* with the ability and you couldn't do anything to change that'. And much more to that effect, as noted in the previous chapter. It was but a short step from there to the belief that only lesser players would go off and get certified to teach schoolboys. That's why the decision of Joe Mercer to join Winterbottom's crusade made such an 'extraordinary' contribution to that cause; but it is not difficult to appreciate why Frank Dudley may have felt that the 'naturals' at The Dell might tend to deride the Lilleshall lads.

Despite these schisms, though, Dudley found The Dell 'a great place to be'. If he was in awe of Mallett and his 'inner circle', this owed much to a concern that he was 'perhaps not quite up to the standard' that Joe demanded of his wider circle. He was rudely introduced to those demands, he says, during the manager's *post mortem* on a friendly at Bournemouth, Dudley's fourth game, on FA Cup Sixth Round day. In his second game on the day of the previous round, in a Dell friendly with Middlesbrough – the team he had helped to remove from the Cup before he left Leeds for Southampton – Frank had scored once. Then, on his third appearance, he had scored twice in a 3-2 home defeat by Raich Carter's Hull City, made possible by the efforts of Southampton Fire Brigade to clear most of the water and by Carter's skill in 'hopping about in the dry spots', as Frank Dudley puts it. But then Frank found himself waiting with the visitors, after the game, for the London train: 'Raich Carter came over to me and paid me the biggest compliment I'd ever wish … He said "Well played, son!" That's all he said'. That's all – but it *was* Raich Carter.

So Dudley had every reason, it would seem, to be pleased as he completed a 1-2-3 goal sequence with a first half hat-trick at Dean Court. But when Bournemouth came back with two second-half goals – one of them by our old friend and record-holder, Doug McGibbon – Frank was 'dumbfounded' to be blamed, in Monday's inquest, by Joe Mallett. Like a succession of outside-lefts who had tracked back too seldom for Rochford, Dudley had failed, as a goalscoring inside-left, by leaving his left-half exposed. Frank would not be the last inside-forward to be criticised by his defenders for letting his marker come through unchased: 'That's right', George O'Brien is said famously to have retorted, 'but where was he when I scored those two goals?'

~

That discussion of the 'divided camp', at which Dudley would arrive during the 1950-51 season, has taken us ahead of ourselves. We had left Sid Cann's slightly re-shuffled, and sometimes demoralised, side just missing promotion – again.

In the 1950 close season, Rochford gave up his alternative assignment to join his old Follands team-mate, Jimmy Allen, who had just taken Colchester United into the Football League. His effective replacement was Jimmy Easson, a former Scottish international forward, coming – as Rochford had four years previously – from Portsmouth. 'A fabulous guy', says Brian Clifton, who describes the main lesson he learned from this 'very clever man'. As an inside-forward, you should 'drive the winger up the line and wait for the ball to come back from the dead-ball line'. The key word here was 'wait': Jimmy 'used to say "Wait! Wait just outside the box and then come in. You've got time to come in"'. As a young player joining the Club towards the end of Easson's brief stay, Clifton might have been expected to pick up, and treasure, a tip or two. What is odd is that Ted

Bates, who was 32 when this 'tremendous football person' arrived, found that it wasn't too late for him to learn the same lesson:

I always remember one thing that he taught me as an inside-forward. He said 'Make sure, when you're close to your attacking goal-line, that you hold your ground'. One of the big problems in football, as he says, is that, when wingers get away, forward players run so that they get level with them. So they shut out their space and opportunity to get in it. 'Holding your ground' means getting behind the person with the ball so you've got some space to receive it. Jim was always on to me that, the nearer somebody came to the by-line, the more you came out. You open the angles so he could get the ball back to you. It's a simple thing ... I was getting on then and nobody had pushed that into me before – which is amazing, isn't it?

It is rather. As I say, Ted was 32. And he'd had his coaching certificate for two years now. Perhaps the Old Dog had acquired too many of his old tricks from defenders – Parker, Dodgin, Rochford, Winterbottom and latterly Cann.

Sid Cann had completed a more satisfactory probationary year than must have seemed possible and was confirmed as Secretary-Manager. The Board had the prudence, after its experience with Tom Parker, to insert a 'War Clause' into his contract, 'covering the Club against liability for salary should there be any suspension of League Football on account of War, Strikes, etc'.

Unfortunately, there was no clause to prevent a double evacuation – of Ian Black to Fulham and Charlie Wayman to Preston. As I intimated earlier, Black was determined to follow Dodgin, even though it meant leaving a club that he 'valued so highly'. And he still *does:* 'It was the best club that I've been at – *streets* ahead of Fulham'. An exchange of internationals brought Northern Ireland's Hugh Kelly from Craven Cottage to The Dell.

Two different explanations have been offered for Wayman's departure: the manager's anxiety about his fitness; and the player's anxiety about his wife. Ernie Jones feels that Wayman was dispatched from The Dell, as he himself was later, because Sid Cann had misdiagnosed him as 'a crock' whom the Club should 'unload' as soon as it could. True, Wayman's knee had troubled him during the close season tour of Denmark and he had had a cartilage operation in June. The story of his departure is more usually explained, though, by his having broken one of football's most fundamental rules: if you marry a home-loving lass, don't move from her home-town team. His wife had been reluctant to leave Newcastle and was unhappy in

Southampton – not least, Charlie admits, with the hours he kept and the company he kept them with. By all accounts, Mrs Wayman tended to express her displeasure in a manner that broke another rule: if you live in a club flat, then remonstrate quietly or the neighbours will hear.

Charlie's neighbour was in the dressing room. If none of his team-mates wanted him next-door, they all wanted him as a player. And so, most vehemently, did the fans – to the extent, Charlie recalls, that they sent a representative up to Preston on an eleventh hour mission to beg him to stay. If returning north was his solution to his domestic problems, then Preston is still a long way from Tyneside. But Newcastle was not among the four interested clubs reported to the Board on 25 August, with the season already two games old and with Ted Bates deputising at centre-forward.

Fulham – Bill Dodgin fancied having him again – Burnley and Bradford were no competition for Preston North End. An exchange was eventually completed in time for Eddy Brown to make his debut in a 2-0 home win against Leeds on 9 September. Maurice Smith admired 'his neat footwork, his perfect positioning and readiness to chase every ball', a combination that gave John Charles 'an uncomfortable afternoon'. The great Leeds centre-half is philosophical about having experienced such discomfort, both in general – 'I would do, aye. I always did do against these small fellows' – and in particular: Eddy Brown was 'quick', he recalls. Qualified compliments – and with the benefit of hindsight. But Maurice Smith's instant reaction was to assure his readers that 'Southampton won't miss Charlie Wayman at all'.

That's not quite how it turned out, of course. Tom Finney makes no bones about it: Preston 'had a fantastic bargain … Charlie was a really superb centre-forward'. What's more, Eddy agrees with that evaluation. You get the feeling that he'd concur with anything his great hero says about football; but, even so, there is something disarming about the way Brown talks of his own 'lots of lack of ability'. You may remember that self-effacing one-liner as being from the video of the Saints' history. If you haven't seen it, then picture Eddy standing with Charlie Wayman, pointing down admiringly and telling his predecessor that he 'could shell peas with that left foot'. He's still at it today, reminiscing about 'a wonderful player' for whom Southampton got, in return, 'a right-footed runner, still learning, not ready yet and foreign to their way of caressing, holding and spraying the ball around'.

Joe Mallett, who had liked to caress the ball forward for Wayman to hold and to spray, found Eddy a 'very limited' replacement: 'He had speed; he was strong; other than that, he had very little'. While Wayman was a 'skilful, *technical* player and a joy to play with', Brown 'couldn't pass'. Similarly, Ted Bates found Eddy 'an entirely different type of player to Charlie: an upfront-chase-it type of player. He wasn't as neat and tidy as what we'd been used to … It changed our style around'. Ted's complaint here, though, went beyond his new attacking partner. The team had gone 'from playing *football* to playing it long. We had a different type of centre-forward with Eddy Brown, who chased everything. The whole system changed. It was very difficult … For me, it wasn't so enjoyable. I mean, always as an inside-forward, I'd been getting the ball'. A fetch-and-spread-it inside-forward could be by-passed as the team played it longer and 'looser'.

Even so, Joe Mallett, who wasn't given, we have seen, to tolerating inferiority, was 'good' to him, Eddy recalls. His main admirer in the dressing room, though, appears to have been Ernie Jones. He felt Eddy 'played for the team'. And what he lacked as a ball-player, 'he made up for with his speed' – speed that gave the team three 'runners' in the shape of Day, Brown and Jones. Ernie's enthusiasm for that formation is somewhat academic, though: the three men played together only twice. The forward line in which the flying No.9 was soon playing had a different balance: Day, Curtis, Brown, Bates and Edwards.

Eddy Brown lumps his footballers into three categories – runners, ball-players and kickers – and this line had for him the ideal balance of the three. He and Day were the runners. Eric says it made no difference to him to have a runner down the middle. But, then, he was never impressed by systems: football was for playing, not for theorising. Curtis and Edwards were the ball-players. Especially George: 'he was the controller – he orchestrated the runners'. That left Bates as the 'kicker' – albeit metaphorically in so far as Eddy especially admired him for his heading: 'He didn't have to have a *running* jump. He jumped like Zebedee. Straight up!' And if 'Ted did not have all the ability in the world, his plusses outweighed his minusses'. Those plusses included his temperament: 'Never moaned, Ted … *Always* positive. He was a nice man and football is *not* a nice game'.

Maybe not, but unlike Elliott and Dudley, Brown 'didn't notice any discontent' or divides in the Southampton dressing room. And, as somebody who had been preparing for the priesthood, he thinks it 'strange' that anybody should have seriously thought religion to be at all a factor there.

⁓

Eddy Brown's model forward-line was going well throughout November and up to Christmas, in a run that included only one defeat – at Preston, of all places, by the odd goal in five. Eddy scored from a lob after an exchange with Ted Bates, but Charlie Wayman had already taken the honours with two early goals. A 4-0 defeat at Brentford on Boxing Day was, however, the start of a dismal run, lasting until St Patrick's Day. The 5-1 win, at home to Grimsby, that broke this sequence did not stop the Board from holding a special meeting, the following week, 'to discuss the decline in form of the team'. This resulted in a committee of three directors being appointed to conduct an enquiry, in which players and staff would be interviewed.

The only win during a League spell of four draws and five defeats had been in the FA Cup Third Round, when 'four beautiful goals' by Southampton beat 'three scrambling affairs' by Tommy Lawton's Notts County at Meadow Lane. A triumph for 'the tricky ball-play and immaculate passes of the Southampton forwards', John Camkin concluded, with the two runners each scoring from '40-yard lone dashes down the middle'.

Eddy Brown's balanced line was disturbed in February, though, by the arrival of Frank Dudley from Leeds. Sid Cann had been looking for 'an inside-forward of the thrustful type' and was surprised when Major Buckley agreed to sell him Dudley, who had gone into Christmas as Leeds United's leading scorer. But Frank had then lost his touch, so much so that he couldn't even score against Ted Bates. When the Saints lost 5-3 at Elland Road on 13 January, Hugh Kelly was concussed and left the field for 15 minutes. Ted took over and is ashamed at the way he conceded a goal: 'I'd always rattled on about being beaten at the near post – how *disgraceful* it was for goalkeepers. I hadn't been there 10 minutes before I was picking one out at the near post. I tell you something: when you get between the goalposts, you learn a lot more than when you're looking into them – particularly when there's about 40,000 [officially 29,253] round the ground'.

Dodgy 'Keeper!
Ted Bates's 15 minutes, deputising for the injured Hugh Kelly at Elland Road. Eric Webber looks on anxiously. Frank Dudley (left) had been Leeds United's leading scorer. But, after failing to score against Deputy Bates, he was transferred to Southampton.

Dudley, as I say, did not get on the scoresheet that afternoon – or ever again for Leeds. Two more games and he was a Southampton player. So keen was Sid Cann to sign him that he and Chairman Penn Barrow completed the formalities on the train south and made the headlines in doing so. Dudley was accommodated at No.10, either by omitting Bates or by Curtis dropping back, as for much of the previous season, to No.4. Either way, it meant you now had the three runners that Jones had fancied, but with only one of them wide. Brown agrees that this 'does seem over-balanced'. Naturally, Eric Day never noticed. Frank Dudley admits that 'there were times when maybe we got in each other's way'. But, then, it can be a waste, he counters, if nobody can keep up with the man who's raced ahead with the ball.

Rail-roaded Signing: Journalists considered it newsworthy that Southampton should sign Frank Dudley (seen here boarding at Leeds) on the train south.

Whether or not it worked to have three forwards who could 'catch pigeons', the idea of racing them against each other appealed to promoter Charlie Knott, to the extent that he promoted a 100 yards race at The Stadium. Unfortunately, Brown had to cry off. As Dudley remembers it, Day, who was so fast over 10 yards, went off well. But Frank, who reckoned to pick up at 50 yards, won easily enough. It was never resolved whether he was faster over 100 yards than Eddy Brown. Southampton was also a congenial setting for Dudley the fast bowler. Several of the footballers he had joined fancied themselves as cricketers. Ted Bates may have given up his county cricket aspirations, but there was still some cricket to be played for fun – notably in that July/August period when training had begun, but the football had yet to kick-off.

Meanwhile, back at The Dell, Eddy Brown had been doing better than his declaration of limitations would suggest. As the Saints recovered a little from their barren spell, Eddy was finding the net regularly. On 31 March, he again had the satisfaction of scoring against Preston – twice this time to Wayman's once – in a 3-3 draw at The Dell. According to Percy Holmes, he 'gave a brilliant display of pluck and perseverance, and outshone Charlie Wayman'. The draw ended a North End run of 14 wins on the trot but Tom Finney remembers that this 'real cracker of a game' was sufficient to clinch promotion and justify a celebration dinner on the train home.

Preston duly went up as Champions. Charlie Wayman was in the First Division. But Eddy Brown had hardly let the side down, with 20 goals in

36 games – not so far short of Wayman's 24 in 36 the season before. What's more the goals were better shared across the forward line this time. Eddy's fellow-runners weighed in with 20 between them – an aggregate of 40 goals in 88 games for the flying trio. And Bates, the heading 'kicker', added a creditable 10 in 29. So the side scored more goals (66) than in 1950, but dropped to the bottom half of the table, thanks to a porous defence (73 conceded). Mallett had been ever-present but Webber had completed his unbroken run and gone to be Torquay's player-manager. And the Club fielded no fewer than five left-backs and four goalkeepers.

The left-backs included Norman Kirkman – a member, you may recall, of the Chesterfield side in that fateful game at the end of 1948-49. Having spent the following season with Leicester City, he started the 1950-51 season as Southampton's left-back. He was injured in the second game and out until the FA Cup game at Meadow Lane. There were two young debutants among the 'keepers. England Youth international Eddie Thomas would play only eight times for the Saints before he dropped out of League football, whereas John Christie would span the 1950s with over 200 appearances. After the stability provided by Ian Black – in his stay of 104 games, he had missed only five – Hugh Kelly's in-and-out season was especially disappointing. It ended, literally, with a bang.

With three games left, the Saints were away to Leicester. After their 3-1 defeat, they stayed up there to play a friendly against Boston United – part of the deal that had brought Elliott and Lowder to The Dell. Following a Sunday evening out, Kelly brought Ken Chisholm, the former Leicester forward, to the team's hotel, along with a couple of females. Nothing naughty. Just socializing downstairs among the tea and sandwiches with the other players. But beyond the team's bed-time. It fell to Jimmy Easson to part Kelly from his guests. 'He must have done it five times', according to travelling reserve, Peter Sillett (although the official count, in the Board Minutes, made it only three). Either way, Kelly was not budging and eventually Easson threw a punch that left the goalkeeper with a 'purler' of a black eye. The Board's response was unequivocal. Kelly was immediately placed on the transfer list and would never play for the first team again.

So the Club was looking for a new goalkeeper. And it would soon be looking for a new manager, with left-back Kirkman playing a novel role in the Board's manoeuvres. With Mr Penn Barrow resigning in May, this double search would be conducted with Mr Sarjantson in the Chair.

Chapter 11

Exchange and Part

The search for a goalkeeper proved easier than the search for a manager.

Yet, with 11 games gone, the side had fielded three 'keepers. Len Stansbridge (aged 32) and Eddie Thomas (only 18) had each played his last three games for the Club. John Christie had had a run of five games, conceding 14 goals, and relief came in the form of Fred Kiernan. Signed from Shamrock Rovers, Kiernan would become a Republic of Ireland international and share the Southampton goalkeeper's jersey with Christie for five seasons. For the rest of that 1951-52 season, the position was his.

As in 1950-51, the side would concede 73 goals, 26 of then coming in an eight-game spell starting at the end of October. The final game of that run – which included an 8-2 drubbing at Bury – was the 3-0 defeat at Everton on 15 December. At its meeting the next week, the Board 'resolved that Mr Cann be released from his duties as Secretary forthwith'. And the 'Manager' part of his title went, a week later, 'by mutual consent'. The Club would start the New Year without a manager. Meanwhile, a sub-committee (calling itself the 'Management Committee') of three directors would meet weekly with the coaching threesome: Warhurst and Easson were still there and would be joined, 'for the purpose of reporting on Players and Teams', by Bill Luckett. The former Southampton player – introduced in Chapter 6 as the PTI who discovered Eric Day – had returned to junior team duties at The Dell and was now the Reserves' trainer. Their minuted 'purpose' was a euphemism for picking the team and reporting back to the Board.

In one of its initial attempts at team selection, the Management Committee confessed to 'a divergence of opinion regarding the centre-forward position'. Wally Judd, who'd made his debut the previous season, had been in for Eddy Brown since the defeat at Everton. Discovered at Nomansland and signed in 1949, Judd had scored four times in six games. But the Board decided, at its meeting of 24 January, to put the No.9 shirt to the vote, for Saturday's game at Cardiff. Brown got it by three votes to two, with the Chairman abstaining. The Saints lost 1-0 at Ninian Park. Judd returned for the rest of the season and Brown never played for the Club again.

There is no mention, in the Board's record of selection by Committee, of any player involvement. In the *Complete Record* of Chalk and Holley, three players – Mallett, Clements and Horton – are said to have been included in the process. Yet there is considerable vagueness, even among this threesome, as to how this player representation worked. What is clear is that this trio spent much of that 1951-52 season swapping the No.5 and No.6 shirts between them. Captain Joe Mallett was mostly in his regular left-half spot, but Stan Clements had failed, with the departure of Webber, to make the No.5 shirt his own. Henry Horton had played for Blackburn Rovers when they were the Fourth Round victims in the Saints' Cup run of 1948. A versatile player, he wore all three half-back shirts during that 1951-52 season and had two games at No.10. Horton will be remembered as the last of that breed, of which the Saints had known so many, who played both football and cricket professionally. But, although he had played for Worcester's 2nd XI, Henry did not come south to play for Hampshire. For the moment, he would have to settle for the annual round of July/August friendlies.

Selection by committee ended in March when the Club came up with a novel way of finding a manager. It involved trading a player. The Board's target was George Roughton, who had been managing Exeter City since 1945. Their exchange package was Norman Kirkman. Given the feudal nature of players' contracts in the 1950s, 'package' is perhaps the word. Winifred Kirkman remembers how she discovered that Norman was to leave The Dell to become Exeter's player-manager, with George Roughton heading east.

She was walking down Shirley High Street, when she saw a newspaper placard, informing her that her husband was leaving Southampton. When Norman got home, he denied all knowledge of any move, but then the rat catcher came to the door – not as part of the deal, you understand, but to attend to their rodent invasion: 'He said "I believe you're moving, Mr Kirkman" … I thought "This is not very good. The rat-catcher knows more than us"'. But the rat catcher was soon followed by the manager catchers – two cars arrived at the Kirkmans' door, bearing the Southampton and Exeter negotiators. Not that a player had a lot of room for negotiation if he was moving as a player-manager: 'You couldn't stand and argue about it. You'd no job'.

George Roughton had been a better-than-average full-back in the 1930s, initially with Huddersfield and then with Manchester United. He just missed selection for the Huddersfield side that lost to Tom Parker's Arsenal in the 1930 Cup Final but toured Canada that summer with an FA XI. Football League honours followed. In 1945, he moved to Exeter City as player-manager, but soon gave up playing to manage a Third Division (South) side that was consistently in mid-table throughout his tenure. With Exeter always out of the FA Cup by the Fourth Round, George Roughton had done nothing to make obvious his attraction to Southampton.

Exchange and Part

And he seems to have done nothing very much, in his three-and-a-half years at The Dell, to convince anybody that he had what was needed. As Eric Day succinctly puts it, 'I don't think he made any impression on any player. He certainly didn't on me'. A lovely man, yes. Everybody says so. 'A nicer man', says Mary Bates, 'you wouldn't wish to meet'. But a manager? No. 'He was a nice enough man', Ted agrees, 'but if you're too nice to footballers, they'll tread all over you'. Consequently, Roughton 'wasn't ever really comfortable with himself', Ted feels, 'management-wise. He didn't get at the game enough'. He was 'out of his depth', Bryn Elliott and Stan Clements argue, when 'the Club was looking', as Clements saw it, 'for leadership'.

Let's look at George Roughton's balance sheet, though. He was soon taking his new charges down to Division Three, but he also took them beyond the FA Cup Fourth Round; he let Ted Bates run the Reserves, starting that season, in such a way that he could succeed to the Manager's job; and he brought trainer Jimmy Gallagher to The Dell.

The Cup run of 1952-53 may have ended in the Fifth Round, but it is such a part of the Club's folklore that you can easily forget that Southampton were relegated that season for the first time in their history.

Ted Bates had hung up his boots in time to miss the excitement of the Cup and so was well out of it by the time relegation followed. Having for once started the season, Ted had played 15 times up to and including the 2-1 defeat by West Ham at The Dell on 20 December. He had scored three times, his final goal coming in a 5-1 home win against Hull City on 29 November. In one of those strange twists that football trivia are made of, three of the other four scorers that day – Frank Dudley was the odd one out – were scoring their first goal for the Club. For Bob McGarrity, it was his debut goal and his only goal for the Saints. The inside-forward from Morton would have but five games. Bryn Elliott would top 250 games but score only one more goal. And Peter Sillett's penalty was the first of his four goals in his second and last season at The Dell.

DELL DIAMOND

Ted didn't do a lot in his last game against West Ham and the *Echo* concluded that 'more staying power' was needed at inside-forward. But he did end his career with an 'assist', setting John Hoskins off on the run from which he scored the Saints' only goal. It was Hoskins's third game after signing from Winchester City. Ted had played his entire inside-forward career at Southampton, looking for a stable partnership, mostly on the left. It is ironic, then, that the goal-scoring Hoskins would become the most settled outside-left the Club had had since Ted's arrival at The Dell.

By finishing when he did, Ted missed the two Christmas exchanges with Fulham. John Christie – in for a 20-game spell – recalls how Bill Dodgin was boasting that Fulham would take four seasonal points from his old team, struggling near the foot of the table. They should have started with two points at Craven Cottage on Boxing Day but Christie saved a late penalty from Charlie Mitten to secure a 1-1 draw. Even in those days, a goalkeeper might be expected to practise what John calls 'the psychology of penalty-taking' or what fair-minded observers would describe more simply as 'gamesmanship'. But when Christie wandered out for a chat with Mitten, Charlie apparently told him 'get back on that line and pick this out the back'. Unflinching, John told him 'Charlie, you could never beat me to save your life'. A bold claim to a man whose biographer describes him as a 'spot-kick king *extraordinaire*'. All the reports say that Mitten put this one straight at Christie. Unabashed, John takes full credit for the save: 'If you get your hands up to one of Charlie's, you're doing well. He couldn't half hit them'.

In fact, the memory of Mitten failing with a penalty is the lasting memory of that match for an 18 year-old playing the first of his 594 League games for Fulham. So many of the Saints' side will tell you that they remember this as Johnny Haynes's debut and some will insist that they'd initially thought the slip of a lad warming up was the mascot. Exaggeration, maybe – although I am able to vouch for the fact that he looked young enough and small enough for the job. The next day, when Fulham came to The Dell, I had to be persuaded by Bedford Jezzard, their centre-forward, to hand my autograph book to the nipper standing alongside him as they waited for the train back to London.

Not that Haynes played at The Dell: 'it was pretty muddy', he recalls, so he was left out. So, too, was Bobby Robson, who was having a good season for Fulham, as a goal-scoring No.8 and fully vindicating the judgment (from the previous chapter) of Bill Rochford and his bewildered team-mates. It meant a return for The Dell, though, for Ian Black and Charlie Mitten. Perhaps it was Charlie's war-time knowledge of the ground that helped him to evade the mud, to say nothing of Bill Ellerington. Bill would certainly prefer to say nothing of the opening skirmishes in which Mitten flourished while he floundered and Fulham took a 2-0 lead. But then a shift of covering tactics – Bill would not be sucked in so far as the team's system usually demanded – put a stop to Mitten's free runs. Yet Peter Sillett and Henry Horton both insist that the main breach was not at right-back, anyhow, but at left-half. The attack-minded Alex Simpson was not containing Stevens and was leaving a gap, what's more, for the visiting right-half, Jimmy Hill, to come through as well. Simpson had recently arrived from Notts County, in an exchange deal involving Jack Edwards. 'He was a good player, Alex, but on this particular occasion', Horton recalls, 'he wasn't in touch with the man or the game'.

What did it matter, though, that the Saints eventually conceded three goals that afternoon, if they scored five – including a hat-trick by Frank Dudley – past Ian Black? Henry Horton can picture Dudley outstripping Jim Taylor, Fulham's England international centre-half: 'It was just like a horse coming up the home straight and leaving the field, because every pace that they took, Frank was drawing away'. This 5-3 win was one of three eight-goal encounters that season – the other two being against Sheffield United. Having lost 5-3 at Bramall Lane in November, the Saints drew 4-4 at The Dell in late March to end a dismal run of defeats. These two results say something about that 1952-53 season in Division II: Sheffield United won the Championship despite conceding 55 goals; and Southampton went down despite scoring 68 – four more than when they'd narrowly missed promotion three season earlier.

Nine of their 68 goals came in the last two matches, but the four points were not enough to save them. Eric Day went to No.9 for both of these two games. Starting there with a hat-trick, he had found a new position that he would enjoy: 'You're in the game! If you score goals, you enjoy the game, don't you? You're in the game in the middle more. In those days, the winger went up and down the wing, waiting for passes, virtually'. Put like that, it sounds like a goal-scoring machine had been idling on the wing. An exaggeration, obviously – although it does rekindle the question raised in Chapter 9: might Day have been tried there at the end of the 1948-49 season, as Bill Dodgin desperately passed Wayman's vacant shirt around the dressing room?

Eric Day was the fourth centre-forward to be used by George Roughton in the last seven games. Frank Dudley's appendix was to blame. When he was rushed into hospital with appendicitis before the match at Barnsley on 4 April, it was the latest set-back for an injury-prone side. Parker and Simpson had each broken a leg, Horton his jaw and Purves an arm. Joe Mallett was twelfth man for the game at Oakwell. Putting on the No.9

shirt, he treated the 'crowd' of 6,466 (Barnsley were so bad that they finished 15 points adrift of their relegation companions) to a sneak preview of the deep-lying centre-forward formation that the Hungarians would bring to Wembley later in the year. 'My idea was to draw the centre-half out of his central position', Joe explains, 'and make space for other players to infiltrate into scoring positions'. He 'enjoyed the game', with his team-mates playing the ball into his feet according to an improvised game-plan, but George Roughton was not, it seems, impressed. The country would have to wait for the spectacle of Nandor Hidegkuti, while the Southampton manager gave Jack McDonald, Peter Sillett and Eric Day two games each as his centre-forward.

A goal-scoring left-winger, McDonald had played in the Fulham side that pipped the Saints for promotion in 1949. Displaced by Charlie Mitten, he had joined the Saints in time to start the 1952-53 season at outside-left.

Along the Line
When Ted and Mary lived, from 1948, in the club flat at 64 Archers Road, the Hampshire FA was downstairs, with the club laundry outback.

Jack McDonald (left) attracted photographers in search of odd poses. Bryn Elliott and Ted Bates joined in this one. Kath Dawkins (right), who ran the laundry, would later care for Mr Sarjanston (see Chapter 14) at his home.

His main function at The Dell seems to have been one of humouring photographers by appearing in unlikely settings with Ted Bates. His two games at centre-forward would be his last for the Saints. Sadly, the same goes for Peter Sillett.

After two seasons switching between the two full-back positions, as his father Charlie had done for much of the 1930s, Peter emulated his dad's alternative trick of donning the No.9 shirt. He scored at The Dell in a 1-1 draw with Birmingham City, but then faced a back-from-Bogotá Neil Franklin in a four-pointer at Boothferry Park. He barely touched the ball, he says, as the Saints went down 1-0. Then there was Day.

Before it ended prematurely in a Doncaster hospital, Frank Dudley had had an in-and-out season. He top-scored with 14 goals in only 23 League games, but it's the goals he missed when Blackpool came to The Dell for an FA Cup Fifth Round replay in February that they talk about to this day. John Christie, a first-half spectator at the other end, can still see George Farm, Blackpool's Scottish international goalkeeper, standing on his line, as Frank 'absolutely blasted it past him' – and back off the woodwork.

To accompany the story, John rotates his his head from side to side – like a tennis spectator – to imitate Farm watching the ball flash repeatedly across his goalmouth. But only once – a first-half goal by Johnny Walker – into his net. There were so many missed chances, with Dudley the chief culprit, that the Saints 'should have been at least four or five up at half-time, without question', Christie contends.

It is an assessment shared by his opponents. Stanley Matthews comes up with the same numbers and blames Dudley's prodigality, in particular, for the Saints' leading only 1-0 at the interval. Matthews even had the indelicacy to mention this verdict to Dudley himself when they met again some 40 years later. This is *not* a game that players on either side have forgotten. Johnny Walker says that Harry Johnston, his manager at Reading (where Johnny went from The Dell in 1957), was always going on about how many the Saints should have had by half-time. Johnston captained Blackpool in that famous Cup run of 1953 that he has charted in his *Rocky Road to Wembley.* If 'it takes luck as well as skill' to reach the end of that road, then Blackpool's round of luck came at The Dell: 'Southampton could have been three or four up at half-time', Johnston admitted. 'It seemed a question of: how many would Southampton get?'

There are competing autobiographical accounts – Johnston's and *The Stanley Matthews Story* – of how Blackpool plotted to turn it around in the second half. If the captain and his outside-right claim differing degrees of credit for who suggested what to whom, the home players are agreed on two things.

First, Matthews had been played out of it in the first half, just as he had been at Bloomfield Road. Dudley can picture the maestro standing on the halfway line at The Dell – 'all by himself: a disconsolate figure. I thought to myself, "This isn't right. The greatest of all English players hasn't had a kick of the ball yet"'.

The stifling of Matthews – for the first match-and-a-half of this tie – has been variously attributed to the attentions of John Hoskins and Peter Sillett. Hoskins had his winger's job to do – laying on Walker's goal was part of it – but Christie points to his tackling back and adduces photographic evidence (see overleaf) of just how deep the young outside-left was prepared to come.

There is newsreel evidence, too, from the first game. Watch Hoskins, on the video of the Saints' history, dashing out to balk Matthews, down towards the corner flag. Walker and Christie agree that Hoskins was 'brilliant' at doing what he had to do. It may not have involved a lot of tackling – 'John couldn't have tackled a jelly baby', Sillett reckons – but it seems to be agreed that there was what the *Echo* called 'an anti-Matthews plan'; that it required Hoskins to interfere with the 'supply' and generally 'make it difficult' for Matthews; and that the novice accomplished his mission.

These Eight Can Stop Matthews:
George Roughton sets out his plans for stopping Blackpool's main man, even though Matthews's marker, Peter Sillett, was in the RAF and unable to join in any planning.
Those who attended were Christie (standing) and (left to right) Walker, Day and Hoskins.

Plan in Action:
Goalkeeper Christie looks on approvingly as Hoskins (supine) comes all the way back to the six-yard box, this time to tackle Mudie.

Yet Sillett still gets oodles of credit, from his team-mates, for marking Matthews out of the first 135 minutes of the tie. The performance of the young full-back, over the two games, is the more remarkable in that he was in the RAF, not keeping 'terribly fit' and finding it difficult to get away to play, let alone train with, his team-mates. There was certainly nothing rehearsed, then, about his late free-kick at Blackpool, from which Henry Horton headed the equalizer. As Henry explains, 'time was running out and I thought "Well, I'll go up for this one"'. If his memory serves, it was Bryn Elliott who encouraged him and volunteered to stand by his man. So forward Henry went, timing his amble to perfection: 'I went round the back and came in on the blind side. I couldn't believe that, when I came into the penalty area, this ball was coming floating down. I met it, of course, with a header and it went in the far corner of the net. They were stunned. I was stunned – even more!' Eat your heart out, all you dead-ball strategists. Perhaps a 1-1 draw did not reflect the home side's possession, yet Bill Ellerington insists that it was 'a good draw with full honours'.

Matthews's 20 year-old conqueror was doubtful, though, for the replay: would the RAF release him from a prior engagement? The Dell replay clashed with the RAF's Inter-Command Cup Final. With only seven first-team games behind him, 19 year-old Tommy Traynor – imported from Dundalk the previous summer – was on standby and nervously doubting his ability to emulate Sillett. Jackie Mudie, due to play against Peter in the RAF match, soon secured leave to play for Blackpool. But Sillett – and Traynor – were kept waiting. Eventually Tommy obtained his reprieve and Stanley Matthews would have to wait a while to torment him.

The Saints had, as I say, a 1-0 interval lead at The Dell. Peter Sillett was pleased to have 'kept Stanley fairly quiet'. So quiet that Matthews wandered abroad in the second half. It's generally agreed that he went over to Blackpool's left flank. Most reports say that he popped up at deep-lying inside-left, collecting the ball from George Farm or from left-half Hugh Kelly and setting off from there, Henry Horton recalls, with the ball 'glued to his foot'. So who should have picked him up? Eric Day – mirroring the Hoskins role – maybe? Or Bryn Elliott, if Matthews was, indeed, at inside-left? Everybody has his theory, it seems, although Alex Simpson – the Saints' fifth captain of the season – felt you had to follow instructions. Gone were the days when Rochford would have re-organised his troops: they were waiting for a word from the bench.

Whatever happened, witnesses for the Southampton defence deny that Matthews took his 'bodyguard' with him in the way he describes in his 1960 autobiography. The problem was that *nobody* went with him. Sillett and Ellerington could each play on either side, so they discussed swapping. But they felt they should wait for the word. The word never came. Even Eric Day – not given, as we have seen, to subordinating impulse to strategies – feels that the manager should have made some tactical adjustment to combat a genius at large. Adjustment came there none.

Blackpool scored twice – helped as much, it must be said, by a Horton howler as by Matthews magic. The Saints' saviour at Bloomfield Road toe-ended a Perry shot out of Christie's path and into his own net: 'John had it covered perfectly. It was a nothing shot and I heard him shout. But I thought I could reach it without any trouble … I took it right out of his grasp. I don't know why the devil I stuck my foot out. Unnecessary!'

But necessary, of course, for the creation of one of the great romances of the FA Cup – the 'Matthews Final' of 1953. Yet some of the vanquished blame, more than Henry's toe-end, the manager's lack of a strategic response. And *everybody* blames Frank Dudley. One way or another, Blackpool survived, in their captain's estimation, the trickiest of their obstacles along the 'Rocky Road' to Wembley.

DELL DIAMOND

It was 'one of the most disappointing results' in Dudley's career. Without seeking to dodge his share of the blame, he raises nevertheless the possibility of another contributory factor. His story begins at a cinema in Blackpool on the Friday evening before the first game. As they waited for the supporting feature, the Saints' players spotted the Sheffield Wednesday side sitting behind them. Having themselves gone out of the Cup at Bloomfield Road in the Third Round, Wednesday had come over for a First Division game at Deepdale. Bill Ellerington was waving to Jackie Sewell, a team-mate on the FA Tour of Canada in 1950. But, as the Saints turned to greet the team that had won their Division the previous season with 100 goals, the big attraction was Derek Dooley, the centre-forward who had scored 46 of them in only 30 appearances. And he was now topping the charts in the First Division. Dudley, and Christie likewise, can picture leaving that cinema seeing Dooley going down the steps in front of them.

Older followers of the game will recall that Dooley's career ended at Preston the next day, when he broke a leg in a collision with the home 'keeper, George Thompson (whose father had kept goal for the Saints in the late 1920s). The Southampton players learned of this injury from a porter, as they changed trains at Preston that Saturday evening. On the morning of the replay, Dooley's leg made the headlines: it had been amputated after gangrene had set in and his condition remained critical. Mr Howarth, the Football League Secretary, described this as 'a cloud over the whole of football'. That cloud lengthened over the Saints' dressing room, Dudley recalls, when word reached it before the kick-off that Dooley had died: it felt as though 'we had lost a personal friend – because he'd been with us, in the pictures the previous Friday night, as large as life'.

The story was corrected after the game. Dooley had come through and was soon issuing, from his hospital bed, that famous statement that he'd do 'anything [to] stay in the game. I don't care if they stick me in the ground and use me as a corner flag'. But his cinema-going 'friends' from The Dell had played one of the most talked-about games in Southampton's FA Cup history, thinking he was dead. Even though they'd 'all played really well', Frank Dudley wonders about the possible impact of Dooley's reported death 'lingering in our minds … We all felt dejected and I think that might have had some effect on us – on our concentration. I don't know'.

And we shall never know. Nor will we know what effect the result had on their League performance in the 13 games that remained. John Christie is convinced that defeat, in 'a game that we should have never ever, ever lost, cost the Club their Second Division status – because everyone was so deflated'. That explanation doesn't totally hold up. If there was an effect, it was on home performances – just two wins in seven games at The Dell. But they would win half of their remaining away games, starting on the Saturday at Luton. The team was unchanged from the cup-tie and Ted Bates travelled with them.

Coach in charge
The team beaten by Blackpool went to Luton for their next game, with Ted Bates the new coach.
Back row (left to right) Elliott, Horton, Ellerington, Christie, Sillett, Simpson.
Front row Day, Purves, Dudley, Walker, Hoskins.

Ted now had a coaching agreement that he shared with Jimmy Easson. He had joined the coaching staff in October, shortly before he finished playing. Having appeared in nine of the eleven games up to the end of September – the kind of start he had achieved only once before – he had been displaced by Johnny Walker, a record signing (at £12,000) from Wolves. With two other inside-forwards having arrived in 1951 – Tommy Bogan, from Aberdeen, and Charlie Purves from Charlton Athletic – Ted appeared not to be needed as a player. The *Echo* announced on 13 October that he would henceforth play only in an 'emergency'. When Roy Williams joined the Saints in November, there should have been no more games for Ted. He would have a flurry of six more appearances, though, before Williams took over from him in December. Ted could now concentrate on coaching.

He hadn't planned it this way. All he knew was that he wanted to be a manager and that he wanted to manage in England. That's why he had turned down, in November, an offer to coach for the Bermuda FA: 'That was an interesting proposition and a great opportunity, but it was the isolation from English football that worried me'. There were other offers: 'Walter Winterbottom wanted me to go more in with the FA. Again, it would have taken me away from professional football'. Or he could have gone to Switzerland. The FA was 'always being asked for people from England to go coaching'. George Curtis would be one of the people who responded to that call. But, while he championed the cause of head-tennis around the world, Ted stayed at The Dell. His joint coaching assignment with Easson would be short-lived. In May 1953, he would take charge of the Reserves. More of that in the next chapter.

Meanwhile, George Roughton was bringing Exeter's trainer to The Dell. When the Roughton-Kirkman exchange took place, Jimmy Gallagher stayed behind. In the 1953 close season, though, Warhurst retired and Gallagher was re-united with Roughton. It was to prove an inspired appointment, not least in that he would be such a chalk-and-cheese complement to Ted Bates once Ted became manager. Stories about ex-Sgt Major Gallagher abound, so let's get some of the more hackneyed ones out of the way right now.

You have to envisage a man who believed utterly in the efficacy of kaolin poultices. You have to picture him, boiling up his kaolin in his cluttered treatment room. Cluttered, you ask, how come? Had Sergeant-Major Gallagher not been in charge of the stores? So they say, but here was a less-than-orderly storemaster who, Terry Paine insists, had lost a tank but had a wheelbarrow to spare. And he couldn't even guarantee to heat the kaolin to the right temperature: 'Don't worry, son', he would say, 'I'm great at burns'.

And so on. He didn't know a great deal about football, by all accounts. And 'he didn't know a lot about physio either', in Paine's estimation, 'or the treatment of injuries'. If that seems to be the general view, then there is, equally, universal support for his attributes: 'Jim was a character', Terry assures us. 'A great guy'. Ted Bates takes a similar line. When he later became manager, it didn't matter too much to him, either, that his trainer 'didn't have too much knowledge of football'. Ted could handle the football side of things, confident that he could rely on Jimmy Gallagher to be 'great at getting the players together'. That's very much how Bobby McLaughlin, who would arrive in 1953-54, remembers it, too: 'Jimmy Gallagher was one helluva trainer – an absolutely brilliant, physical trainer, he was. Ted was the brains. Ted was the clever man as far as football was concerned – the quiet man that got you to do things on the field'.

All of which explains why Terry Paine feels they 'got a lot of good years with Jim'. A lot of years with Bates and Gallagher in tandem, taking the side from the Third Division to the First.

It makes quite a story. But first Ted had to serve an apprenticeship with the Reserves.

Chapter 12

Something in Reserve

Southampton had had a long run in the Second Division.

They had been there for 31 years, longer than any other team in it. Quite an achievement for the Southern League side that had been in at the formation of the Football League's Third Division in 1920 and had needed only two seasons to be promoted to the Second. It would take a little longer this time.

They would be there for seven seasons – five in Division Three (South), followed, after a re-organisation of the League, by two in an unregionalised Division Three. Their first two seasons down can reasonably be characterized as a first team disappointing under George Roughton while Ted Bates won his spurs with the Reserves. Ted had been officially appointed, on 27 May 1953, to the position of '2nd Team Trainer and Coach', at £12 a week in season and £10 in the summer.

Life in the Third Division would begin without Peter Sillett. After those two games at centre-forward, he would revert to full-back. But not for Southampton. Mr Sarjantson had told him, in the absence of George Roughton on holiday, that half-a-dozen managers were lined up to meet him, some at the Polygon Hotel, others at the Royal. He had 'never thought of moving on', he says. 'I just wanted to play for Southampton. My mind was just boggled. I loved the New Forest'. The only manager who impressed him was Sheffield Wednesday's Eric Taylor. But then Ted Drake arrived on the scene. He knew all about Southampton selling a young discovery when they were hard-up: you may remember, from Chapter 1, how it had happened to him in 1934. Now here he was at the end of his first season of managing Chelsea. He wasn't on the official shortlist of interviewers, as Sillett recalls, and wasn't going to talk to the son of a former team-mate in a hotel. So, arriving at The Dell, he exploited Peter's habit of bringing in new-laid eggs for Jimmy Easson: 'Pete, take me to see Mum. I've got to have some eggs like Jimmy's got here'.

Mrs Sillett was willing to let Ted Drake have some fresh eggs *and* her son. She'd even throw his younger brother in too: John was a 16 year-old amateur at The Dell. It remained, of course, for Mr Sarjantson to sanction the bargain. Little old Southampton had lost another goodun to London.

McDonald, the photogenic success and playing disappointment, also moved on and Dudley soon followed – to Cardiff in exchange for another

wing-half of Elliottesque proportions: Bobby McLaughlin. That left Eric
Day to settled in at No.9 for the best part of three seasons. He started well
– with 25 goals in 42 games at centre-forward – in that first season down.
The other goals came mainly from the wings, from two local lads. John
Hoskins had made an impressive start, as we saw in the previous chapter, in
an ailing side. John Flood had come in for the last two games, as Eric Day
switched to the centre.

Fred Kiernan had finished that relegation season as the favoured 'keeper
and had played the first two games of 1953-54. But then, after a 4-3 defeat
at Selhurst Park in the second game, John Christie was in for the rest of the
season. It included a disappointing Cup exit. The relegated Saints were
playing in the First Round of the Cup for the first time since 1925. And
that's as far as they got, losing 3-1 in a replay with Bournemouth at Dean
Court on 25 November 1953.

To add insult to ignominy, the replay meant forgoing the trip that the
Club had arranged to Wembley – you may have recognised the date as the
occasion of England's 6-3 defeat by Hungary. Just because they were in the
Third Division, though, it didn't mean they couldn't discuss the lessons to
be learned from England's first home defeat by a side from beyond the
British Isles. Might there be something to be gained, for instance, by
copying their diet? The Hungarians favoured pre-match steaks, as John
Christie recalls, so Fred Kiernan was glad it was they who had ended
England's home glory and not the Chinese.

The next season, the goalkeeping fortunes were reversed. On the opening
day, Christie conceded four goals at home to Brentford and gave way to
Kiernan for most of that 1954-55 campaign. Yet the Saints had won that
first game 6-4.

Tommy Mulgrew, newly arrived from Newcastle along with Welsh
international winger Billy Foulkes, had needed only 15 seconds to register
the first of his 90 goals for the Club. By half-time, the home side had six,
including a hat-trick by Johnny Walker, who would have his best season at
The Dell, missing only three games and scoring 16 League and Cup goals.
Brentford – just relegated from Division II and captained for the day by
Frank Dudley who had spent but three months at Cardiff – retaliated with
three second-half goals. Christie seemingly took the blame. Pat Parker, back
from the second broken leg that had kept him out of the relegation battle of
1952-53, had taken over from Stan Clements who had enjoyed his fullest
season (38 League and Cup games) in the first season down. But Pat gave
way to the versatile Wilkins who re-adopted the No.5 shirt that he had
worn for a while in 1951-52.

Something in Reserve

Frank Exchange

Returning to The Dell, Frank Dudley (left) clearly takes the captaincy of Brentford seriously,
but Len Wilkins can't help laughing at the referee's *coiffure*.

The faithful Clements was back in the Reserves for good, having had a
reasonable first-team outing after under-studying Eric Webber's remarkable
ever-present run that had lasted more than three years. In that 1954-55
season, the Reserves won the Football Combination Cup and Ted Bates
took much of the credit for his management of the side. The secret, as John
Christie remembers it, was that Ted 'got all the players behind him':

> *He got everybody involved in various moves, set-pieces, certain things to do
> and he became very successful at it … The launching pad, so to speak, would
> be the set things that we did. If I collected the ball on the left, the right-winger
> would be back to change the play: I immediately knew he'd be back and, as
> soon as I turned, he'd be there; I could throw it out … He was always trying
> to introduce something – even if it was simple – if it was successful.*

And, as Pat Parker recalls, he was a good motivator: 'Ted made you want to
win games'. That can't be easy in the mix that makes up a reserve side –
even more so when only a non-playing 'twelfth man' travelled with the first
team. What is a Reserve team? – long-term understudies like Stan Clements
wondering where the next first team game is coming from; youngsters being
given an opportunity to develop; the odd first-teamer recuperating from
injury; and, just to make it really difficult, players who feel that they've been
unjustly omitted from the first team. How do you get a team out of that
lot? 'It's not always easy to get the best out of them', Ted says with under-
statement: 'To get teamwork from them is something you have to work very
hard at'.

DELL DIAMOND

Hard work was never going to be a problem and Ted somehow managed to instill a winning habit – starting in practice matches against the first team: 'Ted would say "Get out there and have a go"', Bryn Elliott recalls. 'We used to beat them every time we played them'. Ted agrees with that account: 'I used to take pride in getting them to play. Even in practice matches, I wanted to beat the first team if I could … I wanted to win things'. Bill Ellerington finds that a difficult concept: 'You see, to me, a Reserve team is not there to win things. Don't get me wrong. Everyone wants to win – I'm a rotten loser; even when I used to play tiddlywinks with the kids, I wanted to win – but to me a Reserve team is there not to win but to bring the youngsters on'.

But *win* Ted's Reserve team did. The win they all talk about was against Norwich City in the 1954-55 Combination Cup Final, with ten men after Doug Millward was stretchered off in the second minute. Pat Parker remembers going to watch the FA Cup Final at the end of that season and meeting some of the Norwich side they'd beaten 3-1: 'They said "You must've been on a big bonus the way you played". They couldn't believe that we only had 10 men and we beat them quite easily. Everybody ran themselves into the ground that night – tremendous! Honestly'.

'Well done, Ted!'
The crucial victory, in Ted Bates's apprenticeship with the Reserves, was their 3-1 Cup win over Norwich.
Standing (left to right) – Ted Bates, Gregory, Christie, Williams, Elliott, McGowan, Parker, Flood, Oakley.
Kneeling – Millward, Gaynor, Digby.

Something in Reserve

The Southampton directors were also impressed – to judge from the way they came into the dressing room after that game: 'Well done, Ted!' 'Well done, Ted!' is how Elliott remembers it. So was that giving credit where credit was due? The *Echo* seemed to think so: 'A special word of praise … is undoubtedly due to Assistant Trainer, Ted Bates, whose enthusiasm has done so much to inspire members of the team'. Bryn Elliott agrees: 'There must have been a helluva team spirit for 10 men to beat 11 for 85 minutes. It's got to have something to do with the chap who was in charge … That was probably the match that made the Directors realise that Ted was the chappie for the job'.

But not yet a while. George Roughton was re-engaged, on 30 June, for another year. Then, on 18 August, Ted's good friend, Joe Mercer, was appointed to his first managerial position at Sheffield United, two days before the 1955-56 season kicked off. It didn't take him long to decide that he needed an Assistant. Ted Bates was an obvious choice. He had worked with Mercer often at Lilleshall and 'had got to know him outside of football' – not least when Mary and he had met Joe and his wife, Nora, on holiday in Sardinia. By Monday 22 August, Ted was at Bramall Lane to watch a goalless draw with Charlton – he remembers being introduced to Jimmy Hagan and the team before the game – and to discuss Joe's offer. It wasn't what he was looking for:

> *I came away, thought about it seriously and I thought "I've got my own mind on football and I don't want to change it really". I thought if I went with Joe, as his assistant, I'd have to fall in with him on some things which perhaps I didn't agree with. That's how I felt talking to him, sometimes, about the game.*

Alec Stock appreciates those sentiments: 'Ted's not an assistant, is he? He wants to make his own decisions, doesn't he? You don't want someone else having to ask his opinion, because you finish up with sweet bugger all'. Joe Mercer would go on, of course, to establish one of the most successful Manager-Assistant relationships of all – at Maine Road with Malcolm Allison. A brilliant fusion of contrasting personalities. Perhaps Ted and Joe were too similar to have forged a successful partnership. More than once, I've heard them likened spontaneously to each other. Denis Howell volunteered, for instance, that Joe Mercer had had 'a lot of admiration for Ted Bates'. They were two of a kind: 'whole-hearted football men, with high principles about the game and their conduct'. And Mike Summerbee, a Mercer protegé whose father had played with Ted during the War (as you will know if you were paying very careful attention in Chapter 4), needs no bidding to compare these two 'fatherly' managers: 'all the players were their children'.

DELL DIAMOND

Neither Ted nor Joe had had a lot of opportunities, by 1955, to develop a paternal style – or any other kind of managerial style, for that matter. But Ted knew enough about the style he wanted for himself to turn down Mercer and bide his time at The Dell. He hadn't long to wait for the top job there. After a home win, on the opening day, against Swindon Town, the Saints took only one point from the next four games. The Board thereupon held a special meeting at the Bassett home of Reg Jukes on Wednesday 7 September, where it

was unanimously resolved that Mr Roughton be asked to tender his resignation forthwith and that E.T. Bates be appointed as Team Manager at a salary of £1000 per annum plus first team bonus from tomorrow September 8th.

When the Board re-convened at The Dell the next morning, Mr Roughton obligingly 'tendered his resignation and was handed a cheque' – for the remaining 10 months of his contract. The Directors weren't hanging about: 'E.T. Bates was then called in and was formally appointed Team Manager as from today'.

MINUTES OF SPECIAL MEETING OF THE BOARD HELD AT
"OAK LYNNE", BASSETT CRESCENT WEST, SOUTHAMPTON,
ON WEDNESDAY, SEPTEMBER 7TH, 1955, AT 4.30 P.M.

Present: Messrs. J.R. Sarjantson, C.J. Cosgrove, E.C. Chaplin,
             R.W. Jukes, G.E.H. Prince, G. Reader and
             W.E. Toomer.

The nature of the business of this Special Meeting had previously been conveyed to the three Directors who were unable to be present, Lt. Col. Meyrick having been written to on 6.9.55.

It was unanimously resolved that Mr. Roughton be asked to tender his resignation forthwith and that E.T. Bates be appointed as Team Manager at a salary of £1000 per annum plus first team bonus from tomorrow, September 8th.

Messrs. Corbett and Stranger were advised by telephone of the above decision.

This ended the business of the Meeting.

15-9-1955-

The minutes further record that the players, trainer Gallagher and the *Echo* 'were then notified'. What that record doesn't show is that the players were about to leave for Newport where they had a match that Thursday evening. Ted travelled with them as their new manager – starting out, as he had as a player almost 18 years before, in South Wales. Bill Ellerington was taken by surprise: 'I was amazed when he took over, I'll be quite honest with you'. Ted's success with the Reserves cut no ice with Bill. Remember that he'd seen Sid Cann promoted to first team manager on the back of such an achievement.

~

Ellerington was Ted's longest-standing team-mate in the side that lost 1-0 at Newport that night. But two others – Eric Day and Len Wilkins – went back a long way with their new manager. The full side at Somerton Park was Christie; Ellerington, Gunter; McLaughlin, Wilkins, Elliott; Flood, Mulgrew, Day, Walker and Page.

Christie was taking over from Kiernan, as ever, after a bad start. Gunter was in for the fourth of seven games scattered across his only season in the first team. Page was playing his third and last game as a left-winger. He had come to The Dell as a youth from Mytchett, where his manager was an old friend of Jimmy Easson. He had made his debut at No.11, partnering Ted Bates in the away 'leg' of those two goal feasts with Sheffield United in 1952-53. After Christmas, he would become Ted Bates's centre-half, a position he would contest for the next three seasons with Pat Parker. And when Pat got the nod at No.5, John would be competing with Len Wilkins for the No.2 shirt.

Bill Ellerington would grace that shirt only six times under his old mate. Towards the end of that season, he would re-appear for one last game at left-back. He had 'a shocker' against Leyton Orient: 'A little fellah called White gave me the chase of my life'. Rochford's advice on surviving fast wingers had expired. Only in respect of first team duties, though. Duly appointed player-coach, Bill would play on with the 'A'-team. If you had any doubt that Bill still considered himself a player, you had only to look at the team photo' at the start of the season. Right through to 1958-59, you'll find Bill pictured, in the *Complete Record* line-ups, not in his coach's tracksuit but stripped to play.

The other significant change of personnel was at No.8, where Ted brought in Derek Reeves as a goalscoring partner (19 goals in 35 games) to Eric Day (29 in 48). George Roughton had blooded Reeves at the end of the previous season, during which he had signed him from Bournemouth Gasworks. Towards the end of the 1955-56 season, Ted separated this duo, switching Day back to the right-wing and handing the No.9 shirt to Reeves.

But finding the best scoring combination was not the new manager's main concern. The side that he had taken over with an aggregate of F8 A14 had ended the season on F91 A81. That's why they finished only 14th, while the three sides that scored more than they – in fact, they all topped 100 – were the first three in the Division. Top of them all was Leyton Orient, who did the double over Southampton. Continuing in the Roughton tradition, Christie took the blame for the 4-0 defeat at Brisbane Road in November. He thinks he was 'possibly to blame for a couple' of Orient's goals – and so do the match reports – including one when he was too slow to close down his opponent in what we would now call a one-on-one situation: 'Ted wasn't happy about it'.

If finding a regular 'keeper was a problem Ted would not solve until Eric Martin saw off Campbell Forsyth in 1969, he had more than that to think about as he left the Brisbane Road pitch with the Orient manager, Alec Stock. The two men went back a long way. Stock had been at inside-right for QPR Reserves that day in 1939 when Ted's kick-off ploy first brought a goal: indeed, it would have been his job to cut out the diagonal ball from Ted to his left-half. And Alec's goal – when that 'nice fellah', Len Stansbridge, let his header 'go through his hands' – had helped to knock the Saints out of the Cup in 1946, in the game of the phantom McGibbon at Loftus Road.

Only a year older than Ted, Alec Stock had stolen a managerial march on him – and their generation generally – by becoming player-manager of Yeovil Town at the age of 29 in 1946. After their legendary Cup run in 1949, Stock had moved on to Orient. So he was already a manager of some experience, when Ted Bates asked him 'how do you do it?' Stock's answer was pragmatic: 'Ted, we're bloody good at the back: we can keep 'em out. Up front, we can knock 'em in. Across the centre-circle, we are bloody terrible'. In other words, Stock explains, 'I tried to tell him that we were not totally endowed with good footballers'.

A comprehensive prescription for Ted to follow. And, as he got down to it, that autumn, Mary was taking sick leave, with TB, to enter a sanatorium for six months, while her remarkable mentor, John Sarjantson, was retiring from the Board that he had joined in 1914 and handing over the Club Chairmanship to Mr Cosgrove.

In a farewell speech, recorded by the *Echo*, Mr Sarjantson noted that he had 'seen eight managers come and go' in his 40-odd years. Saints' fans who have suffered the turmoil of the 1990s, will smile at such stability. Who would have predicted, against that history recorded by Mr Sarjantson, that the newly-appointed young manager was settling in for 18 seasons? In a demob-happy reference to this appointment, he claimed that Ted Bates already had the team 'playing better and more attractive football', after eight weeks, 'than for seasons past'.

Ted's top priority was a new centre-forward. Derek Reeves would revert to inside-right and Eric Day would not see out the season at No.9 – a position in which he had achieved a remarkable record of 85 goals in 131 games: a strike-rate of 65 per cent. At the end of the season, as he approached 35, Eric wanted to prepare for his future. So he asked whether he might work in a garage – 'train as normal, full-time, but go and do the paperwork for this firm in the afternoons'. Eric was 'shattered' by the way in which Mr Cosgrove rejected the idea: 'It shook me and I don't think I got over it for three or four years'. And he was 'annoyed' at Ted's failure to come and talk about it.

The outcome was unsatisfactory on all counts. The career of a player who had mocked his late start by completing 422 games for the Club (with 156 goals), petered out with only 13 games, all in his old No.7 spot, during that 1956-57 season. The Board fretted about his contract, at meeting after meeting for six months, and at least three directors became involved in discussions with different brewers to find him an off-licence instead. It seems that this was seen as a form of earning that a footballer could combine with a full-time contract, whereas Eric's garage job smacked of the part-time. But, as negotiations over an off-licence stuttered along, Ted was asked to negotiate a part-time deal with his old team-mate.

That was the last thing he wanted. In George Roughton's final season, the directors had resolved to make half of the squad part-time. This was the ultimate step in a series of economies. The finances were so bad by March 1955 that the Club's bank manager had attended a special meeting of the Board, to be informed of the possible 'serious consequences' of selling off the silver – in the form of 'at least one of our leading players' – as the 'only means of carrying on to the end of the present season'. Other cuts were found. Don Featherstone, the physiotherapist, was given two months' notice. Then, at its meeting of 28 April, the Board asked the manager whether 'he could carry on with one trainer only', the following season. He said not. So Ted Bates still had a job, along with Jimmy Gallagher. But the Vice-Chairman told the Board that the two trainers had 'each offered to accept a reduction of 10s.0d. per week in their wages'. That would not be enough to satisfy the bank manager, though. It was at this meeting that the Board produced an unorthodox 'Retain-and-Transfer List', with 11 of the 23 retained players asterisked to indicate that they were 'to be invited to accept part-time terms'.

It had not come to that and Ted says he told the Board – not a condition it wanted to record, it seems – that he was not interested in managing a Club with half of its players on part-time contracts. Even when it came to having a 35 year-old play his last season as something less than a full-timer, Ted objected on principle – and on the record.

All in all, then, it was a sad end to Eric's career. He scored only three goals in a season when the team's tally was generally down. Reeves, mainly at No.8, top-scored with 19, one more than the new centre-forward, Jimmy Shields. Backed by a loan from the Supporters Club, Ted had taken Mary to Whitley Bay for a holiday, where he 'dumped' her at the hotel, she reveals, and set off to sign a Sunderland reserve. Shields had arrived at Roker Park from Crusaders two seasons before, but had never made the first team.

There was room at The Dell, though, for 'a real hard, grafting, run-around, enthusiastic, typical, tearaway centre-forward', as Johnny Walker describes him without drawing breath. Jimmy went straight into Ted's attack, with Reeves alongside him, and scored on his debut against Bournemouth at The Dell. He kept scoring – 11 goals in the first 12 games – and, by November, he was a Northern Irish international. Just the one game. Scotland. Hampden Park. George Young. Walker and some of the other Scots at The Dell enjoyed teasing him about the prospect of facing Young. So how was it on the day? 'Oh! I had three kicks. Two on the knee and one on the shin'. Or 'something like that', we're reliably informed.

Jimmy Shields took the ribbing in his stride – Irish caps? 'You can buy 'em in Woolworths, Jim' – and carried on scoring. Not quite at the rate he'd started at, but well enough to finish with 18 goals in 35 League games (with Reeves getting 19 in 41). Nobody else was getting very many – as I say, Day had dropped down to three – and the side finished with but 76 goals. Only one team in the top eight scored fewer than that and Alf Ramsey's Ipswich won the Division with 101 goals. And yet the Saints finished fourth – by virtue of conceding only 52, the best defensive record in the Division. Having a settled defence had reaped dividends, it seems. Christie in goal, Wilkins and Traynor at full-back and McLaughlin at right-half each played in 39 or more of the 46 League games. And Pat Parker, after all that bad luck with broken legs, was ever-present – four cup-ties made it a round 50 for him – and he played for the Third Division South against the Third North.

In the New Year, though, there were comings and goings upfront. Don Roper, Ted's right-wing partner from those days (back in Chapter 5) when they talked of a 'wing' pairing, returned from Arsenal, in January, to play mainly at No.8. And then, in March and May, two new wingers made their debuts. Competing for the places of the two locals, Flood and Hoskins, were two more local youths.

Their arrival, at the end of an historic season for the Youth team, is a chapter in itself.

Chapter 13

Ted's Teenies

Ted Bates had two strokes of luck in establishing a youth policy. They were called Ernie Jones and Charles Henwood.

Ernie returned to the area in 1956. He had left The Dell in 1951, unhappy about Sid Cann's attitude to his injuries, and, after a spell with Bristol City, had been managing Rhyl. But, still fancying a game at 36, he had come down to play for Poole Town. It was all the rage. Managed by Stan Rickaby, the former England full-back, the Southern League club had attracted Wilf Mannion a year earlier. Ernie Jones stayed just long enough to score 'the second best individual goal' of his life and decided he wanted something else.

He went to see Ted. They talked about Ernie's talents, which included engineering – while managing Rhyl, he had helped design and erect the floodlights. This gave Ted an idea. Charles Henwood, who owned the local engineering works, CPC, had expressed an interest in being involved in the Club – not as a shareholder or director, but simply by putting up the money to run a nursery team in the Hampshire League. This arrangement had been agreed, in broad terms, in February 1956. Now Ernie Jones could be an opportune link. Suppose he were to go and work for Mr Henwood not only as an engineer but also as CPC's football coach? Henwood would have a cracking team of lads sporting his firm's name. Some of them would play also for Ted's Youth team, wearing the 'CPC' badge on their Saints shirts – sponsors had not been heard of – and they, too, would be coached by Jones, whom Ted wouldn't have to pay. Director John Barber could supply a training ground at Rownhams.

All in all, quite a deal – even by the cheapskate standards of ingenuity for which Ted would become renowned. And an utterly remarkable deal when you consider that it produced the first side ever to beat Busby's Babes in the FA Youth Cup.

From the start of that competition in 1953, Manchester United had not lost any of the 42 legs they had played in. In their 43rd and 44th legs – the semi-final of 1956-57 – they met Ernie Jones's tyros, who had stormed through the previous rounds. When they beat Spurs 6-0 in the quarter-finals, their manager – Ernie's old team-mate, Bill Nicholson – told the *Echo* that Spurs 'did not mind being beaten because the Saints lads played so brilliantly' and he commended to others the CPC 'example'. The first leg of the semi-final attracted a crowd of 19,320 to The Dell. In the first minute, Terry Simpson missed a penalty which he has never been allowed to forget – 'a bloke at work keeps reminding me' – and United assumed control to win 5-2. Yet there was sufficient interest left in the tie for 16,876 to turn up at Old Trafford for the second leg. They came to salute the all-conquering Babes. But the young Saints won 3-2. Wes Maughan made the headlines with his two goals, although goalkeeper, Tony Godfrey, was everybody's Man of the Match.

Ted's Teenies – aka Jones's Juniors?
Whatever you want to call them, they burst the bubble of Busby's Babes.
Wearing their CPC-sponsored shirts, the 1957 FA Youth Cup team lines up, with Ted Bates (left)
and Ernie Jones (right), for their Fourth Round Replay against Bristol Rovers:
Standing (left to right) – Walker, Scurr, Harley, Flood, Holmes, Stickler.
Seated – Paine, Simpson, Maughan, Vine, Sydenham.

They had lost 7-5, but they had burst the bubble. It was time for words of wisdom from Matt Busby. He went into the away dressing room, the *Echo* proudly recorded, to praise Jones's lads for 'a great performance' – so perhaps Peter Vine is being a bit ungracious to recall that the United manager, who had been reeling in schoolboy stars from across the British Isles, was unable to comprehend how his compendium of talent had been beaten by 'a bunch of yokels'. Compared with Busby's Five Nations catchment area, this was certainly 'a local team. The only foreigner', Ernie Jones observes, 'was Wesley Maughan, from the Isle of Wight'.

For his part, Ted Bates welcomed the opportunity, after 18 months of management in the Third Division, to converse with the manager of that great pre-Munich side that was about to win the Championship for the second successive season:

He was somebody that everybody respected in the game. I talked to him about the game, about every aspect of it, to try and listen and learn from him. He made a classic remark to me, which always stood me in good stead. We were talking about Boards. He said 'With Directors, Ted, let them have their say – and do as you want'. That was very useful. You see, in Board meetings, if you're not careful, you can start shouting your mouth off to people you could only upset. It's far better if you let them talk, listen, rather than aggravate them all.

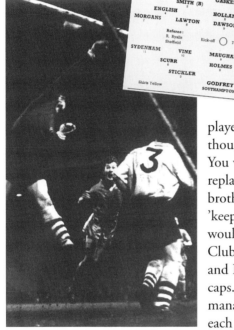

As Terry Paine will constantly remind you – he's at it again in the foreword – this side contained an unusual number of players who made it as professionals, though not all of them with the Saints. You will spot Tony Godfrey. He'd replaced the injured Brian Flood, brother of John and then the reserve 'keeper in the England Youth team, and would go on to play 149 times for the Club. John Sydenham, Colin Holmes and Peter Vine all won England Youth caps. Yet Holmes and Vine would manage only one first team appearance each – two fewer than Scurr.

Good Godfrey!
The Man of the Match tips one over in the Youth team's historic 3-2 win at Old Trafford.

⁓

It has been Colin Holmes's misfortune to become known as the player who was Terry Paine's team-mate in the British Rail works team at Eastleigh and who signed professional for Ted Bates with Terry – but who then played just 803 games fewer than his mate for Southampton. Terry insists that Ted had locked him and Colin in his office. They could leave once they'd signed professional. Both aged 17, they had been playing for the Youth team, during 1956-57, as amateurs, while serving their railway apprenticeships. Ted had not moved to clinch their professional signatures, they had been to Highbury for trials and were expected back. Terry later learned that the somebody in Arsenal's office had neglected to send the right forms at the right time.

DELL DIAMOND

Had Paine joined Arsenal, a few ex-Saints would have been in a position to contemplate the local lad who'd got away. Bill Ellerington had first met Terry some time before. His father-in-law ran the Highcliffe Corinthians team for which Terry played – that is until two other former Saints came to sign him for Winchester City. Their manager, Harry Osman, had been the other inside-forward the day Ted made his debut for Southampton (see the line-up in Chapter 2). Usually an outside-left, he held goalscoring records for a winger that would be shattered by the teenager his assistant, Bruce Howard, wanted him to watch. Howard occupies an odd place in the Saints' history. He played just twice during the War, but one of those games was the strange 5-2 win on Christmas Day 1941 – described in Chapter 4 – when Bristol City turned up nine short. Bruce scored four of Southampton's goals.

Harry Osman has generally had most of the credit for 'finding' Paine, playing him as a 15 year-old in Winchester City's Hampshire League side and recommending him to his former team-mate at The Dell. But it seems to have been a work-mate, Johnny Walls, who advised Ted Bates that he'd better hurry to beat the Arsenal to Paine's signature.

It was a lot simpler with the other winger. John Sydenham just cycled up to The Dell one day, put his name to a form, collected £10 and 'raced home to tell all my friends'. His first team baptism was the final game of 1956-57 – a 3-0 win over Newport at The Dell. He was still only 17. Terry Paine had also been 17 when he made his debut, seven weeks earlier, in a 3-3 draw at home to Brentford. It was all happening for Paine. On 6 March, he and Sydenham were in the forward line that ran riot against Spurs in that Youth Cup quarter-final. Three days later, he was playing his first game at outside-left for the Reserves, laying one on for Terry Simpson, his right-wing partner in the Youth team. Johnny Walker, partnering him on the Reserves' left-wing, scored twice in their 4-0 win over Bristol Rovers and told Ted Bates 'what a wonderful player this lad's going to be'.

The next Saturday, Walker and Wonderlad were paired on the left again – but for the first team at home to Brentford, managed by Bill Dodgin (who had left Fulham for Griffin Park in 1953). The *Echo* liked the way Paine made 'holes in the experienced Brentford defence [and] put over a good many fine centres'. And his tendency to 'cut in

One Down – 803 to go
Debutant Terry Paine 'cuts in from the wing'

from the wing when occasion arose' suggested 'a scoring winger' in the making. We did not have to wait long for Terry to realise that hope. A week later, on his 18th birthday at Aldershot, he cut in – just like the man said – and scored the first of his 185 goals for the Saints. 'Observer' thought it 'one of the best individual efforts that a Saints' player has produced this season' and considered it 'fairly certain that a good deal more will be heard of Paine'. As on the previous Saturday, the opposition was being managed by a war-time team-mate of Ted's. Harry Evans – whom Ted would have to keep away from Terry in later years.

My own recall is of going home to Camberley and telling my father that I'd seen a newcomer who would surely play for England. Rash talk, I grant you, for a 17 year-old judging an 18 year-old, but I'd never seen

anything like this before. I was able to see my new hero again, two days later, at Reading. 'Observer' enjoyed another 'excellent performance' by Paine, who scored one, laid one on for Roper and had a shot parried for Walker to score in a 4-2 win. Was there no stopping him? Not according to the man from the *Mail* – 'you can throw me in the Southampton docks if Terry Paine doesn't become a household name before he's much older'.

And yet, as Ted Bates advised this reporter, Paine was out of position on the left-wing: he was 'a much better outside-right'. The switch came on the last game of the season. Sydenham came in at outside-left and Paine moved to the wing that he would colonise. John Sydenham's 397 games for the Club may look insignificant alongside Terry Paine's 804, but it still adds up to a lot of games in which Southampton fielded a pair of home-produced wingers – 1175 of them for Ted.

Many a fan will have forgotten, though, the other three forwards from that Youth side – Simpson, Maughan and Vine – but, coming back to Terry Paine's point, it is surely amazing that this entire forward line made it, at least once, into the first team.

DELL DIAMOND

Terry Simpson would manage only 25 games before joining Jimmy Hagan first at Peterborough and then at West Bromwich – which meant he was playing in the First Division some time before Paine and Sydenham. Wes Maughan would gain attention for his goalscoring feats for the Reserves but get only seven run-outs with the first team. But, then, that was six more than Peter Vine. If you blinked, you will have missed his one game at Bury in March 1959. Yet all the other players in that forward line are agreed, along with the managerial staff involved with that team – Jones, Ellerington and Bates – on one incontrovertible truth: the greatest talent in that side was Peter Vine.

So what went wrong? Peter doesn't know: 'There's no answer, really. I probably had the wrong attitude. I don't know. I probably didn't try as hard as the other lads … I *wanted* to make it. I'd always wanted to be a footballer'. Ted Bates was frustrated by the waste: 'Terrific ability, but he just wouldn't work at it. That's what used to annoy me – to get somebody special like him and he didn't work at it. And if you don't work at the game, you won't get far in it, will you?' Indeed, but how far do you go, as a manager, before you give up? 'We hung on and hung on', Bill Ellerington recalls, lest Vine be released only to succeed elsewhere. Bill needn't have worried: Peter was eventually transferred to Crystal Palace, where he enjoyed Arthur Rowe's coaching methods but never made the first team. 'Talk about throwing a life away!', says a rueful Ellerington. 'Two great feet. In fact, I thought he was as good, or better, passer of the ball than any of the pros'.

Terry Simpson goes even further than that. He can think of only two footballers he's seen kick a ball as well as, or better than, Peter Vine. Bill Ellerington himself is one: 'The finest. No effort. Beautiful – like a golf swing'. Bobby Charlton is the other. Indeed, for all-round skill, Simpson puts Vine on a par with Charlton. 'Anybody I speak to', Simpson says, 'he's Number One'. And that, as I say, is what they all wanted me to tell you.

Yet Peter Vine suggests that there were other young talents – like youth international, John Bailey – greater than his. Without blaming the training methods at Southampton for his own truncated career – after all, he never made the first team at Selhurst Park, either – he wonders how much Bailey's failure to make even one appearance for the Saints could be attributed to methods that were 'wrong' in that 'everybody did the same programme. Everybody ran round the track. Everybody lifted weights'. That was fine for those who 'need that type of training, but other kids need to play with a football'. And Bailey was, for Vine, 'a classic example' of a player who had had his 'magic' trained out of him and was 'frightened to do anything'. Shades of Tom Parker flattening a young Ted Bates for holding on to the ball (way back when in Chapter 1). But, by Terry Paine's count, a remarkable number of his promising contemporaries survived the training regime and made it as professionals – even if the one they most admired wasn't one of them.

It wasn't apparent, either, which first team places were especially threatened by those kids of '57. Paine may have found an instant backer in Walker, but it wasn't universally obvious in the dressing room that Johnny Flood, still only 24, should make way for him. Even if he had caused a stir at the end of that 1956-57 season, and had shown that he could play on either wing, it didn't follow that Paine would get 44 games the next season, with Flood making just two more appearances before he left for Bournemouth. Remember that this was the Third Division, so there was less need for the manager to cosset him in the way that an 18 year-old might be nursed (unless he's called Michael Owen) into the Premiership today. Sydenham had to be more patient, playing only 28 games, over the next two seasons, while he waited for Hoskins to bequeath the No.11 shirt.

If Paine's rapid elevation caused any resentment in the camp, it was softened, as ever, by those two mainstays of dressing room humour: sex and cynicism. Ted Bates must be receiving unmentionable favours from Terry's mum. Thick-skinned as ever – refer back to Chapter 7, if you need to – Ted backed his judgment. And who can argue with what he produced from one of the less recognised players in his Youth team line-up? Less recognised, that is, by the England Youth selectors, who were partial, as we have seen, to Ernie Jones's lads. Terry had been capped for England Boys' Clubs, but he never won a Youth cap. When England – managed by Ted's old team-mate, George Curtis – entertained Ireland in a youth international in May 1957, two months after Terry had burst into the Third Division, Mike Connolly of Doncaster Rovers was partnering Jimmy Greaves and would continue to do so. By the way, the right-back that day was Joe Kirkup, a West Ham youngster whom Ted Bates would chase for several seasons until he got him.

But, then, Southampton's success at Youth level should be judged not by the failure of Terry Paine to win recognition but by all the others who did. Sadly, Ernie Jones failed also to get the recognition that he felt he deserved. Mr Henwood was 'heartily congratulated' by the Board for the achievements of 1956-57, but there was no such mention of Ernie. The Directors did agree, though, to the manager's suggestion that he be paid £2 a week come the 1957-58 season. Towards the end of that season, they were concerned that Jones seemed 'to be trying to establish a full-time job in connection with our various junior sides'. All he wanted, Ernie insists, was to be designated Youth Team Coach – part-time with 'some sort of remuneration'. There was no such job on offer, but Jones the engineer was to be employed four days a week on ground improvements at Rownhams. In July 1958, the entire arrangement was terminated.

Jones's Juniors were history.

Wingers
Ted Bates with John Sydenham (left) and Terry Paine, the two young wingers who would play for him some 1,175 times, between them.

Chapter 14

Dealing with Charlie

The lessons of 1956-57 – you can finish as high as fourth if you concede the fewest goals in the Division – were not entirely heeded.

In 1957-58, Ted Bates's swashbuckling team scored 112 goals but dropped two places. They had let in 72. That aggregate was good enough, though, to give them 10 points more than Northampton in 13th place. In other words, they easily made the 'cut'. This was the final season of the Third Division (South) which Southampton had won in its first season (1921-22). By finishing in the top 12, they had survived its death and would be in the new, de-regionalised Division III in 1958-59.

It was all happening for the Bates family in 1958. In February, Mary left The Dell after 12½ years' service, as their first child was due. Josephine was born in May. And, after 10 years at the club flat in 64 Archers Road – you may remember the photo', in Chapter 11, of Ted in the back garden with the laundry – they were on the move to Chilworth, to live in the house that Mary had just inherited from Mr Sarjantson.

After 'Sarjie' was widowed in 1948, Mary became involved in setting up various caring arrangements for him. Kath Dawkins, from the Club's laundry (who's in that photo' with Ted), moved into an annexe at Chilworth. When she died, Ted's mother, Eva, took over for a while. You may recall, from Chapter 1, that Eva had been a nursing auxiliary and that she had been so reluctant to travel with her itinerant husband. But here she was, in her old age, visiting her three children, spread across the country.

Meanwhile, Ted and Mary had become regular Sunday afternoon visitors to the childless widower – latterly accompanied by their friends, the Worlocks. A professional pianist, Monty Worlock had long followed the Saints away when his engagements coincided with theirs. He had befriended Ted, who was his best man when he married Peggy, who would become a member of the expanding staff in Mary's office at The Dell.

When Mr Sarjantson died in 1958, the estate that he left to Mary included not only his house but his shares in Southampton FC. When Mary asked that these shares be transferred to Ted, the Board didn't know what to do. Could a manager hold shares in the Club? After consulting the FA and the Football League, the Board approved the transfer.

So the footballer who had benefited as a player – so the jealous tongues said – from his wife's link to Mr Sarjantson now had his shares in the Club and was living in style in his house. What would the rumour-mongers make of this? For some, it may have fuelled the old tittle-tattle about the Secretary-Manager's attachment to his attractive female assistant. You could join the Club in the 1970s, I'm told, and find that tales of that relationship still had some mileage.

They seem to have been superseded, though, by a new angle: Mary was Sarjie's daughter! And it's the way they tell them: it's all trotted out in such a matter-of-fact way. Perhaps it's not that surprising if inheritance of an estate suggests a blood-tie of some kind, but it's odd how these family trees take root. Ask Lawrie McMenemy and Lew Chatterley. They're not related in any way, but how many times have you heard them described as brothers-in-law?

Why can't people just accept that some of us get to like a few of our workmates more than most of the others? Here was an old widower who'd enjoyed the company of two younger colleagues from The Dell and, who continued to be visited by them in his retirement. If he wanted to remember them in his Will, what business is that of anyone?

OK, some will say, why have I made it my business to mention any of this? Quite simply, because it's part of the Ted Bates story. You could fill a book with tributes to this lovely man, who's achieved so much, but the complete story of the man and his achievements requires some acknowledgment of the jealousy that accompanied certain aspects and phases of his success.

Wishing Saints Well!
Ted and Mary, regular Sunday afternoon visitors to Mr Sarjantson at Chilworth, at his wishing well.

~

That 1957-58 season was one of promising bursts, interspersed with lapses. There were four spells, including the opening week, when the side won three or four games on the trot. And there were three seven-something wins at The Dell. The local derbies with Bournemouth produced 14 goals, the Saints winning 7-0 at home (having hitch-hiked ineptly, from Camberley, I missed all the goals) and losing 5-2 at Dean Court.

Dealing with Charlie

Most of the goals came from the twin strike-force of Derek Reeves and Don Roper. Don's 18 goals from 40 League and Cup games was impressive. Derek's 35 from 44 was something else. Jimmy Shields missed the whole season. He was playing for the Reserves in September when he put the ball past the Luton Town goalkeeper with his right foot and had his left leg broken by the 'keeper's challenge. Wingers Hoskins (who restricted Sydenham to 11 games) and Paine weighed in with 31 goals between them.

The second best scoring ratio that season – of seven goals in 12 games – belonged to a debutant who never got a clear run in the Saints' attack, even though he maintained a strike-rate of at least 50 per cent in the Third Division, whenever he was trusted with a forward's shirt. Brian Clifton.

Because Brian made his debut six months after Terry Paine, he is sometimes thought of as being in that same crop of Youth team talent. In fact, he had arrived from Whitchurch in 1953 when almost 19, had done his National Service and had been waiting around in the Reserves before Ted Bates gave him his break against Brighton in September 1957. He responded with two goals in a 5-0 win, followed by another two in the next home game – the 7-0 romp against Bournemouth. But the success of the Reeves-Roper combo restricted this powerful header of a ball – the Oz cartoon suggests a similarity of style to Ted Bates, himself – to only a dozen games.

In 1958-59, he maintained a 50 per cent strike rate when used as a forward, but finished at right-half, a position that Ken Birch had been contesting with Terry Simpson. Birch had arrived from Everton – effectively displacing Bryn Elliott after 251 games, over eight seasons – in time to play in the last 10 games of 1957-58, a strong surge that included seven wins. Put like that, it sounds like a significant signing. Indeed, Ted Bates had been so keen to sign Birch before the 1958 transfer deadline that he obtained the Board's authority, at a special meeting, to trade one of his outside-lefts for him. Everton settled for cash, but they could have had Sydenham for £30,000 plus Birch or Hoskins for £15,000 and Birch.

He wasn't worth it. Ted had bought a right-half who was not suited to his outside-right. 'He just couldn't keep the ball on the ground', Terry Paine explains. 'My neck! I had neck-ache. Every time he kicked it, you had to look up for it. He used to *launch* it'. Ted soon realised his mistake. By

169

November, Paine had Terry Simpson, his inside-forward from that Youth team of 1956-57, behind him at right-half. But then – and this still rankles with Simpson – Ted brought in Birch (and Christie for Godfrey, likewise) for the visit of Blackpool in the Third Round of the Cup: 'He went for experience. That's what he told me. That put me off Ted to a certain extent, but no malice … A big game – everybody wants to play against Matthews and I sat in the Stand'. Just as Tommy Traynor had done in 1953 – although you may recall, from Chapter 11, that he was none too keen 'to play against Matthews'. This time, though, there was no escape for Tommy.

A new anti-Matthews plan?
In training for the 1959 cup-tie against Blackpool, the squad appears to be rehearsing a new strategy to stop Matthews.
Left to right Birch, Christie, Hoskins, Godfrey, Traynor, Mulgrew, Paine (taking the ball), Reeves, Livesey, Hillier, Sydenham and Davies (feeding the other ball).

Traynor was much admired by his team-mates and his manager. Yet they all get a lasting laugh out of his problems with Matthews. He'd had a couple of practice runs in 1956 in floodlit friendlies at The Dell – just two of those games against All-Star XIs in various guises that the Over-50s will recall from the days when floodlights were the new toy to be celebrated and Southampton, inspired by their Brazilian experience, were among the pioneers. But now it was the real thing and there was no Hoskins to tackle back.

Dealing with Charlie

So might John Sydenham have done so? Ask a daft question and you get a smart answer: 'If they'd expected me to mark Stanley Matthews, then it would have been a pretty sad day, I think, for the Club'. Especially since Sydenham was, that day, too small for his boots. Literally. It was icy. So, while Matthews may have 'had all the right gear on', Southampton's resources, as John recalls, ran to a cupboard full of rubber boots. One or two sizes fit all. Grab what you could and hard luck if you took a size '5'. As in 1953, Blackpool won 2-1.

Notwithstanding the goal-scoring feats of 1957-58, Ted Bates had introduced a new centre-forward early in that 1958-59 season. Reeves, who had started in possession – scoring four in a 6-1 win, on the opening day at Mansfield – was injured in the next game. Enter Charlie Livesey. Charlie would get 28 League and Cup games, in that one season of his, in which he would score 15 goals. Not a bad strike-rate for a player who was not the most dedicated of professionals. Tony Godfrey, who was in digs with him at Morris Road, near the Polygon, was bemused by Livesey's priorities: 'He'd be out to three o'clock in the morning before a game – no thought about going to bed or anything like that – but he could score goals and he had lots of ability'.

Cue for another of those could-he-have-done-more-if-he'd-worked-at-it analyses? No. With all due respect to Livesey, an assessment of his one season in the Saints' first team is of less significance than the story of how Ted Bates sold him to the very club whose Chief Scout had brought him to The Dell – a crucial episode in any evaluation of how Ted succeeded in building a side fit to return to the Second Division.

The key figure, in this regard, is not Charlie Livesey, so much as Jimmy Thompson, who fetched him from east London. A former Chelsea forward with a fair strike-rate of his own, Thompson had become Chelsea's renowned finder of young talent, which he took to Stamford Bridge to be developed by Ted Bates's old Follands team-mate and Netley landlord, Dick Foss – by now Chelsea's youth team coach under Ted Drake. If you want to know more about Jimmy Thompson, the larger-than-life wheeler-dealer, if you want a feel of the 'melodrama' and 'cloak-and-dagger' shenanigans (as Terry Venables puts it) with which he found so many young players for Chelsea, then just read an early chapter in one of the biographies of Venables or of another famous find: Jimmy Greaves.

So what was Chelsea's famous scout doing bringing Livesey to Southampton? A favour to Mr Blagrave is the simple answer. Herbert Blagrave was the Saints' President and, in Ted Bates's book, 'a very, very good Saints' man'. A horse-racing man – he had stables at Beckhampton –

he used Jimmy Thompson to place his bets. When Chelsea turned down Charlie, the young forward who had hoped to play for West Ham signed amateur for Wolves but didn't take to commuting to Molineux. Then a skirmish with the law left him ready to leave London: Thompson even went to court to vouch for him and to assure the judge that he'd found him a good home at The Dell: 'I'm taking him to Southampton to play football, Your Honour'.

A great line – uttered not only by Livesey, but by John Corbett, a director at that time and the President when he repeated the story for me. A member of Mr Blagrave's racing fraternity, Mr Corbett says that the directors were happy to provide Livesey with the good home that Jimmy Thompson had promised the court. The Board was less worried by Livesey's record, he reckons, than Thompson's: 'they were a bit frightened of Jimmy'. Orthodoxy was not his strong suit.

That is to say that he operated by a set of rules that was not to be found at Lancaster Gate. Reflecting on 'the very thin line' that Thompson trod, Ted struggles for the right word to describe his wiles. The word 'spiv' is uttered but retracted:

> What a character he was! ... To call him a 'spiv' is not right really. He was just a very wise football man – on youngsters. That was his job ... He was a real one-off person. He'd have the readies in his back pocket ... He always had a pocketful of fivers. He'd give [parents] a few quid. Say he wanted to sign your son on. He'd come and knock at the door, have a chat with you and, before he left, he'd give you a few quid and he'd be signed on for Chelsea or whoever.
>
> I wouldn't say what he did was within the rules, but that was the way he worked.

Even if he always had a wad of 'fivers' in his pocket, Charlie Livesey recalls that Jimmy Thompson sometimes paid parents in kind – with a fridge, say. The outcome of his favour to Mr Blagrave – 'on the side', as Mary Bates saucily puts it – was that Ted Bates had a dashing young alternative to the high-scoring Reeves.

Livesey's first game was at home to Swindon. One commentator who 'didn't enjoy it much' was Mick Channon. But, then, he was only nine at the time and didn't see very much – until he was hoisted on to his father's shoulders when the Saints had a penalty. His view – or memory – needed to be better. It was not Birch, as Mick records in *Home and Away*, who took the penalty and scored. It was John Page who took it and missed. Roper scored in a 1-1 draw.

Dealing with Charlie

Nobody scored at all in the next three games and Livesey was due, he says, for the chop. He responded with four goals in a 6-1 win over Hull, followed by two in the next game – a 5-0 win against Halifax – to present Ted Bates with the kind of problem that managers love, we are told, to have: two goalscorers competing to be the centre-forward. Unless, of course, one of them could be moved to inside-forward. Ted resorted to this solution 16 times that season and it was invariably Reeves who surrendered the No.9 shirt he had worn so prolifically the season before. Each player maintained a strike-rate of over 50 per cent, but they never once scored in the same game.

The directors knew that Reeves was unhappy with the arrangement, but they valued Livesey so highly that they agreed to Ted Bates's suggestion, in March, to pay him at the top rate, along with Paine. Come June, though, Ted and the Board were opting for a different solution. Not unanimously – Mr Stranger felt so strongly that he resigned on the matter and went public on his reasons: you didn't sell your young assets. But Jimmy Thompson was now wanting to get Livesey to Stamford Bridge. He knew that Ted Drake 'was absolutely dying', as Ted Bates recalls, to sign the young striker Chelsea had previously let slip. Ted was ready to deal and knew whom he wanted from Chelsea.

Such was the talent in Ted Drake's reserve side that Ted had Bill Ellerington watch them, from time to time, on spec'. Bill had taken a fancy to a 22 year-old wing-half who had managed but half-a-dozen games for Chelsea that season. He recommended him to Ted: 'Strong, keen and workmanlike. Very destructive'. Cliff Huxford. 'Destructive'? Well, let's just say that 'Chopper' Harris, then an apprentice at Chelsea, puts himself below Huxford in his list of 'iron men'. More to the point, Ted endorsed Bill's assessment. He accepted Huxford and £12,000 for Livesey.

This was, in Terry Paine's view, 'one of the shrewdest signings that Ted ever made'. Terry liked Charlie Livesey. Fascinated by such 'a wide boy – a different kind of person to any I'd ever met' – he'd taken him home to tea in Winchester. He liked playing with him, too, but 'never thought that he quite finished off: I didn't think he was quite as good a finisher as he looked, put it that way'. Tommy Mulgrew preferred playing with Reeves. He found it 'far easier', because 'Charlie was a bit of an individual – he wandered'. But Huxford was a player Paine 'rated – for his heart. He wanted to win. The drive he had! You knew he'd be there fighting for you, thick-and-thin'. A good swap, then, in Terry's estimation. And £12,000 in spare change.

Ted knew how to spend the money. Ellerington had set his sights on George O'Brien before he had moved from Dunfermline to Leeds. George Rowells, one of his army contacts, had told Bill where he could watch the young soldier. Bill went to see and liked what he saw – even in the warm-up: 'You could see when he's kicking-in, there was something about him. Believe it or not, you can generally tell – how they kick in and bring it down'. But the price was not right for George Roughton, who was happy for Ellerington to tip the wink to Eddie Lever at Portsmouth. The Pompey manager did not share Bill's enthusiasm and it was left to Ellerington's great hero, Raich Carter, as manager of Leeds, to bring O'Brien south in 1957. Neither he nor his short-lived successor, Bill Lambton, gave George an extended run – just 44 games over two and a bit seasons, in which he scored but six goals. Ellerington took another look. 'I said to Ted "I still fancy him. Maybe I'm prejudiced but I still fancy him"'.

Bill Ellerington can apologise for this particular prejudice as much as he likes. Saints' fans will be eternally grateful that he had seen something in George that was lost on the management at Fratton Park and Elland Road. We must also be grateful, though, that Ron Hewitt wouldn't come from Cardiff. Ted rated the Welsh international inside-right, whose five caps included three games in the 1958 World Cup Finals. So much so that, when Mr Barber put him on the spot at the Board's meeting of 25 June, Ted said he'd prefer Hewitt to O'Brien. Within a few weeks, Hewitt had signed for Wrexham and O'Brien for Southampton. Instead of a 31 year-old international, Ted had obtained a 23 year-old who had simply not done it in the First Division for Leeds.

What we are talking of here, of course, is the ability to envisage how a player who is performing or not for one team will deliver for you. George O'Brien may have been a disappointment at Leeds – six goals in 44 games, indeed – but Bill Ellerington contrasts him with Johnny Walker. As we saw in Chapter 11, George Roughton signed him from Wolves for £12,000 – not only a Club record but more than Dunfermline had been asking for O'Brien a year or so later and twice what Ted Bates eventually paid for George seven seasons later. Walker had scored 21 goals in 37 games for Wolves, but Ellerington is not impressed: the service Johnny received at Molineux, even in the Reserves, was so good that 'he only had to stand in the six-yard box and keep putting them in' – whereas, at The Dell, 'he had to work and couldn't do it'.

Walker fans may find that a harsh verdict. If his Southampton strike-rate of 52 in 186 games falls below his Molineux level, I, for one, am not surprised. I remember 'Windmill Walker', arms rotating as he ran towards goal (as opposed to the *after*-scoring style that Mick Channon would later patent). My image is of a popular forager who could not be expected to be a six-yard box man as well. But Johnny wasn't a Bates or Ellerington kind of player. George O'Brien *was*. Bill's humbly-confessed prejudice had been justified and his patience rewarded. He had got his man and Ted Bates still had change from the Livesey money. Enough to buy Dick Conner, a wing-half from Grimsby, whom he'd been tracking for some time. Despite some concern, on the Board, that the Club already had 10 half-backs and that Page was not 'commanding' enough at centre-half, the manager was left free to sign two wing-halves – Huxford to destroy; Conner to construct. Ted had tried in vain to trade first Traynor (whose 'dressing room attitude' was causing problems) and then Hoskins for Conner. But the Livesey bargain meant that he could pay cash.

All in all, some deal! Even Ted thought it 'amazing'. As a piece of three-for-the-price-of-one manoeuvring, it would surely take some beating. And, if Bill Ellerington played no small part in the research, he admires the way Ted did the sums: 'He was very canny, Ted was, at deals. Weren't many beat Ted on deals, I'll tell you'.

Can't say fairer than that, Bill. After all, these three new signings would miss only six games between them (out of 52) as the Saints roared to the Championship and won a famous cup-tie at Maine Road.

Chapter 15

We are the Champions

Don Roper was on his way to Weymouth. To create space in the dressing room for his new signings, Ted let 14 players go in the summer of 1959. But the departure of his old partner on the right-wing is the one they all talk about to this day.

The talking point is not that he dropped out of the League – so too did Birch, McLaughlin and Parker in that summer clear-out – but that he didn't remain at The Dell in a coaching capacity. Whether or not 'it was common knowledge', as John Christie puts it, 'that he would have a job at The Dell at the end of his career', it's certainly common currency that, when Roper returned from Highbury in 1957, he was led by Ted to expect a position at the Club. Don didn't want to talk about it, or anything else for that matter, when I invited him to do so, but his reluctance to turn up to re-unions is generally attributed to his refusal to forgive Ted for reneging.

Ted is not exactly comfortable about this matter himself. As he sees it, Roper was 'getting on' – he was 34 – when he persuaded him to return: 'Perhaps in my mind then might have been the thought that he would have had a job eventually with us. I don't know, but I knew I needed his ability'. Isn't that evading the question of giving him an undertaking? 'Well, I didn't think I did. I'm pretty sure I wouldn't make a promise to any player about anything like that … I'm not sure whether I promised him a job or not. I wouldn't have thought I would have done'. Nothing very much there, then, to dispel the general belief that Ted must have said something to Don that has led him to nurse such a lasting grudge.

Christie thinks that it all 'turned sour' when Don helped out in October 1957, by filling in at right-back against Swindon. Don 'got a chasing' so Barry Hillier came in for one of his nine appearances at full-back. As Clifton and Reeves were enjoying a spell together upfront, there was no room for him there. In a word, he was dropped. And that, Christie reckons, was what the players believed to have been 'the beginning of the end'. Ted's recall is that Don and he fell out over wages. Ted had 'had to give him top money to get him to come back to Southampton'. But, when he failed, come the renewal of Roper's contract, to keep paying him in the manner to which he had become accustomed, Don was not pleased: 'I sort of lost him, really, a little bit then. He probably got a little bit suspicious of me, but we did have a difference of opinion which affected him'.

Whatever you make of all that, you have to be disappointed, surely, at this break-down of a relationship between two men who had been persistently discussed, by reporters in the mid-1940s, as a partnership – a 'wing'. You may recall, from Chapter 7, that there had been talk of a 'triangle', where this wing-pair was supported by Stroud. On the occasion of Ted's 75th, Bill went to plead with Don to restore their triangle – to let bygones be bygones. No joy. Don was so admired by Ted, as 'a terrific, two-footed, strong player' with whom he 'used to get on well' when they played together. It would not be surprising if Ted thought, in 1957, that his former wing-mate was another football brain he could use, long-term, at The Dell.

Terry Paine, playing outside him, valued Roper as 'an elder statesman', to whom he'd take his problems. And, more significantly perhaps, defenders like Davies and Godfrey remain grateful for the help he gave them. Ron Davies had arrived from Cardiff City towards the end of the 1957-58 season to end Len Wilkins's long stay at his home-town club. Like Godfrey, he testifies to the wealth of ideas that Roper had to offer in team-talks. As a young newcomer, he sensed 'that little bit of animosity' between Don and Ted in team-meetings that could become 'heated'. Godfrey likewise remembers how Roper 'used to argue and used to be annoyed with Ted Bates. So, whether Ted bought him and then thought "Oh! He's a bit of a threat" – he wants his job or whatever – I don't know'. If Don 'never appeared' to Godfrey to be thinking that way, 'he never seemed very happy'.

And he still isn't. A sad end to that war-time 'wing'.

～

The summer evacuation made way for more than just the three-for-the-price-of-Livesey. Ted also brought in Bernard Harrison from Crystal Palace and Pat Kennedy from Blackburn Rovers. It was a move of convenience for Harrison, a Hampshire cricketer, to be a reserve to Terry Paine. He would get three games in that 1959-60 season. That was one more than Kennedy managed. Having started the season at left-back, he lost his place to Traynor, who'd sorted out his 'attitude' problem well enough to manage 43 League games that season and a further 200-odd in all. In fact, no fewer than nine players appeared in at least 43 of the 46 League games and four of these – Davies, Huxford, Paine and Reeves – were ever-present. The only unsettled positions were in goal and at No.10.

The Championship-winning line-up was, then, Godfrey, Charles or Reynolds; Davies, Traynor; Conner, Page, Huxford; Paine, O'Brien, Reeves, Mulgrew (or Brown or Clifton) and Sydenham.

Ted made Huxford his captain before the season began. The Board's Management Committee wasn't too sure about this move. Col. Meyrick hoped that Terry Paine could be encouraged to give the newcomer the backing he needed and Ted was persuaded to make the appointment provisional. It was the first of many edgy interventions that season by the Board or its Management Committee. There may have been a remarkably settled side on the field but the directors seemed determined to fuss and fidget.

Tony Godfrey started the season as the No.1 goalkeeper. John Christie had moved on to Walsall, after 209 appearances for the Saints. He wouldn't miss out on a medal, though. Walsall would be promoted in successive seasons, so that by 1961-62, John would be playing against the Saints in Division II. Godfrey's career would see-saw during that time, precipitated by an injury at Halifax in September 1959. In just 11 games, he had conceded 25 goals. But who's counting? – the 3-1 setback at The Shay was only the second defeat for a side that had scored 34 times in winning six and drawing three. And they had just won four in a row, with Reeves scoring 10 in an aggregate of 18-9.

Before that goal-rush, Reeves was being criticised by the Chairman for missing so many goals that the side should have been top of the League, not ninth, after six games. Ted Bates thereupon gave the Chairman a lecture – a rare treat, indeed, for readers of the Board's minutes: 'Reeves had a part to play in the team and if they were to get promotion', the manager explained, 'he was one of the key members. The Board should remember that with a dry lively ball, the forwards will miss more goals than they will score.' He dutifully undertook, though, to 'bear the Board's observations in mind'. The Board was so concerned, the following week, that the manager was 'instructed to institute a search for another good full-back'. And a Reeves hat-trick had just lifted the team to eighth! The centre-forward was, as I say, on a roll and, even after the set-back at Halifax, they were still sixth.

After that game at the Shay, the side was staying up for a Monday night game at Shrewsbury. Ted needed a replacement for the injured Godfrey. Bob Charles travelled up to join the party. The 17 year-old son of a 'keeper who had played with Ted at Follands, Bob was in the Southampton Schools side that shared the England Schools Trophy in 1957, when Godfrey was keeping goal for that almost-as-successful Youth team. Charles not only followed Godfrey into that Youth side, but added England Youth caps, rooming with Nobby Stiles, to the Schoolboy honours he had already won.

After a 1-1 draw at Shrewsbury, the Board had a major inquest. The side was only one point better-off, and had a worse goal average, than at the same stage the previous season. This was 'not a promotion side'. A 'full discussion' was needed, the Chairman said. A full-back remained a priority, but the main topic of concern was a lack of co-ordination between Page, at centre-half, and his goalkeeper. The manager spelled out his dilemma:

getting 'a more experienced goalkeeper ... might help the centre-half' but then his 'two young 'keepers ... would not gain experience'. It was accepted that Charles needed a few games to settle in and he was not blamed for the two defeats that followed. It was Mulgrew's turn to be fall-guy and the Management Committee 'instructed the Team Manager to search for a good inside-forward'. Two weeks later, following a five-point burst that had taken the side to sixth, an inside-left remained the priority – along with a centre-half. In fact, it was revealed that 'some negotiations had already taken place [for] the services of a certain centre-half'. It became apparent that these negotiations involved an unnamed scout (now let me guess) who was expecting an 'under-the-counter payment' for him and the player. The Committee resolved not to countenance the deal unless it 'could be legally effected'.

There endeth the crisis of confidence. A 5-1 home win against Coventry, two days later, took the side to third. They were very soon second and the only way was up. From 20 February, they would be stuck at the top. In a 25-game run, in the League and Cup starting on 10 October, they lost only three times (including an anti-climactic Cup exit). Then, as the Ides of March and the transfer deadline threatened, Charles took the blame for successive defeats by 5-1 at Newport and 4-1 at Coventry.

So Ted turned, for his third 'keeper of the season, to the experience he had rejected in his October address to the directors. His choice was a player whom the Club had rejected in 1950: Ted could have been a team-mate of Ron Reynolds (as you'll know if you were concentrating really hard in Chapter 10) if Ron's begging letter had been better received. Reynolds had gone instead to White Hart Lane, starting as an understudy to Ted Ditchburn but graduating to 86 games in the First Division. Ron reckons that he must have been one of Ted's simplest-ever signings, as he hurried from training with Spurs in the morning to become a Saints' player by tea-time: 'I couldn't *wait*'. There was a double incentive. He doesn't subscribe to the widespread acclaim for Billy Nicholson, who had taken over as the Spurs' manager the previous season, whereas he had enjoyed the company of Ted Bates, as a fellow-coach at Lilleshall.

That was sufficient to overcome any apprehensions about the nightmare floodlights at The Dell. Ron had played under them in an historic Football Combination match on 1 October 1951, when Saints Reserves lost 1-0 to Spurs Reserves in the country's first-ever competitive match under lights. He had kept a clean sheet more by luck than judgment. The ball kept hitting him: 'You just couldn't see the damn thing!' The Dell lights were too low and 'absolutely hopeless for goalkeepers'. Tony Godfrey agrees. He 'used to dread playing under them'. To compound the problem for Reynolds, though, an eye injury, while he was with Spurs, meant that he now had to wear contact lenses. If Terry Paine is exaggerating when he likens them to ashtrays, you can imagine the mirth they caused in the dressing room.

But, joking apart, there seems to be considerable agreement that his services were seriously needed for the run-in. Bob's good friend, John Page, feels that the young goalkeeper was starting to get 'a bit dithery'. Another 'shrewd buy' in Terry Paine's estimation, 'for what it was meant to do – to try and cement promotion'. And they 'wouldn't have got promotion', O'Brien feels sure, 'if we hadn't got Ron': young Charles just didn't have the 'timing'. Reynolds played out the last 11 games of the

		Home			Goals			Away			Goals		
	P.	W.	D.	L.	F.	A.		W.	D.	L.	F.	A.	Pts.
Southampton	46	19	3	1	68	30	...	7	6	10	38	45	61
Norwich City	46	16	4	3	53	24	...	8	7	8	29	30	59
Shrewsbury Town	46	12	7	4	58	34	...	6	9	8	39	41	52
Grimsby Town	46	12	7	4	48	27	...	6	9	8	39	43	52
Coventry City	46	14	6	3	44	22	...	7	4	12	34	41	52
Brentford	46	13	6	4	46	24	...	8	3	12	32	37	51
Bury	46	13	4	6	36	23	...	8	5	10	28	28	51
Queen's Park Rangers	46	14	7	2	45	16	...	4	6	13	28	38	49
Colchester United	46	15	6	2	51	22	...	3	5	15	32	52	47
Bournemouth and BA	46	12	8	3	47	27	...	5	5	13	29	45	47
Reading	46	13	7	3	49	34	...	5	7	11	35	43	46
Southend United	46	15	3	5	49	28	...	4	5	14	27	46	46
Newport County	46	15	2	6	59	36	...	5	4	14	21	43	46
Port Vale	46	16	4	3	51	19	...	3	4	16	29	60	46
Halifax Town	46	13	3	7	42	27	...	5	7	11	28	45	46
Swindon Town	46	12	6	5	39	30	...	7	2	14	30	48	46
Barnsley	46	13	6	4	45	25	...	2	8	13	20	41	44
Chesterfield	46	13	3	7	41	31	...	5	4	14	30	53	43
Bradford City	46	10	7	6	39	28	...	5	5	13	27	46	42
Tranmere Rovers	46	11	8	4	50	29	...	3	5	15	22	46	41
York City	46	11	5	7	38	26	...	2	7	14	19	47	38
Mansfield Town	46	11	4	8	55	48	...	4	2	17	26	64	36
Wrexham	46	12	4	6	39	30	...	2	3	18	29	71	36
Accrington Stanley	46	4	5	14	31	53	...	7	0	16	26	70	27

THIRD DIVISION

season. It was a low-scoring run-in – W5 D3 L3 F18 A12. If that aggregate does not appear to be championship-winning stuff, then just reflect that this was a side that scored 106 and let in 75.

It had lost 11 games – 10 of them away from home. Their away record of W7 D6 L10 F38 A45 is hardly Championship stuff. It needed a home record of W19 D3 L1 F68 A30 to do the trick. And overall, it needed, as I say, 106 goals to offset the remarkable deficit of 75.

～

George O'Brien blames the high number of goals conceded on two kinds of shortcoming at the back. The purchase of Reynolds solved one of them. But, more fundamentally for George, Ted Bates couldn't buy defenders who could *defend*. The exception, in George's book, was Ron Davies. A 'very under-rated player' in Tony Godfrey's estimation, Ron played in every League and Cup game of 1959-60, mostly alongside the more attack-minded Traynor. Cliff Huxford contrasts the 'very steady, week-in, week-out' performances by Davies – 'he very rarely had a poor game' – with the 'more erratic, more swashbuckling, more adventurous' Traynor. For Cliff, this kind of 'contrast' ran through Ted Bates's new-look side: it was all part of the 'blend'.

A similar balance at wing-half – with Conner, the play-maker on the right and Huxford, the no-prisoners defender on the left. 'What a contrast in styles!', Terry Paine observes. 'But that was Ted again: he had all that planned'. Such a 'plan' for Nos 4 and 6 would be routine enough with today's formations, but it made quite a change from all those seasons with the rather similar Elliott and McLaughlin at wing-half. We still talked of a 'half-back line', though. And a solid line it was, with John Page – who was 'under-rated', in Huxford's opinion – at the centre of a threesome that between them missed only two of the 52 League and Cup games. Paine and O'Brien both valued Conner for his ability to deliver a good pass early. Terry thought him a role model for younger players – 'the way he passed it'.

Upfront, Reeves was ever-present and sensational. Mocking the Board's anxiety at his wayward finishing that brought him only four goals in the first six games, he finished with 39 League goals and another five in the Cup. Brian Clifton was so thrilled for him – in an uncomprehending kind of way: 'Derek was a real gentleman – *why* he was playing football, I don't know. The nicest guy you'd ever wished to meet – and you'd wish your son to be like'. So he named his first son, born in 1959, after him.

O'Brien was scoring well, too. He missed five games but still weighed in with 23, plus four in the Cup. Paine says his ability to find O'Brien was instant. George arrived, with the other new boys, to practise at Rownhams and they hit it off straightaway:

I get the ball. I give it to George. He gives it back to me. I give it to George. He gives it back to me. It was like that! Telepathy. It just worked. And, inside the box, he was some player! (whistles) *Could he finish!*

If you're as big an O'Brien fan as I am, you'll be as pleased as I was to learn how highly his team-mates rated him. Huxford and Paine are especially valuable witnesses, as each was in a position to compare George with one of the great goalscorers of their generation. 'I don't think I ever saw a player – even Jimmy Greaves – who was sharper in the six-yard box than George', says Huxford, who'd played a bit with the young Greaves at Chelsea. Paine likewise thought O'Brien 'very much on a par' with Greaves – 'at club level: George never played at international level and you never know if they're going to make that step up. But George was that kind of finisher. Jimmy did all of his work in the box. George did it all in the box. A lethal finisher, George!'

The question of whether George O'Brien should have played for Scotland is one to which we shall return in the next chapter. Among the reasons advanced for his not winning a cap, there's the state of his knees – so bad that he was expected to train very little. George Kirby felt this affected his turning circle: 'When George used to turn, it was like a big liner. He couldn't turn – he had to go all the way round. Otherwise, his knee would have gone'. But nobody expected him to run about a lot – just so long as he kept getting on the end of Terry Paine's crosses.

DELL DIAMOND

The Paine phenomenon is worth a chapter in itself (see Chapter 18), although it will inevitably involve contrasts with Sydenham. Yes, another 'contrast', as Cliff Huxford is keen to point out. Ted Bates's own contrast between the two is crisp: 'John gave us width and pace – a great left foot. Terry had great skill, a wonderful chipper and crosser of a ball – everything you could wish for in a player'. He volunteers the thought, though, that he may have given Sydenham less credit than he deserved: 'I used to accept his pace, his left-sidedness and use him in the team. But, when I look back and think, he was a good *team*-player, as well'.

Paine played every game in that 1959-60 season and Sydenham missed just the one. The No.10 spot was, as I say, the only problem here. Again, despite the Board's instructions to replace him, Mulgrew was there until February, when Clifton came in for three games. True to form, Brian obliged with four goals. Mulgrew was back, though, for those heavy defeats at Newport and Cardiff that cost Charles his place.

But hereupon, Ted Bates belatedly heeded the Board's order to buy an inside-forward. Gordon Brown arrived from Derby to make his debut, along with Reynolds, at home to Tranmere. Brown scored the Saints' goal in a 1-1 draw. And he scored again, the following Saturday, in a 1-0 win at Loftus Road. That was pretty well it as far as Gordon Brown's Southampton career is concerned. Five games (plus three the next season) and just those two goals. But vital goals, as you can see.

Clifton wasn't finished, though. He was back for four more games at No.10 and scored in every one of them.

The second of those came in the 3-1 win at Dean Court. Page got the other two – both penalties: 'I always used to put them to the right-hand side of the goalkeeper. I'd never had two in the same match, so I thought I'd stick it in the other side'. Fairly cool for a centre-half whose self-assurance had suffered, they said, from playing with young 'keepers. Yet this was, for me, Clifton's Match.

Perhaps that's because I missed the previous one, the 1-0 home win against Reading on Easter Monday. A crowd of 25,042, the Saints' biggest of the season, home or away – just try imagining that today – saw Brian win the game, and clinch promotion, with what was obviously quite a header. Everybody says so. The photo (opposite) shows so. And even the impossibly modest Clifton knows so:

I can always remember it going in. I couldn't believe it. It seemed to go right through Jonesie [Reading's 'keeper]. It went so quick ... I remember everybody going up [in the air] – the crowd. It's amazing. That one moment! ... Afterwards, George O'Brien said 'You lucky so-and-so. You know that goal's going to be remembered forever'. It's true! If I speak to anybody from down there [in Southampton], they'll always remember that goal, because it put us into the Second Division.

So why complain? Quite simply, because Brian feels that nothing should be allowed to detract from the fact that Derek Reeves scored 39 goals: how unfair that he should be remembered for one! All right, but let's just put it on the record that Clifton finished the season with at least one goal in each of the matches he had played at inside-left. Having made one goalless appearance, early on at wing-half, his final tally was eight goals in as many games. Really, he deserved a medal. And what's more, he got one. When the Championship trophy was presented, he was sitting in the Stand and Mulgrew was at No.10 (for a post-season charity match against Norwich City, the runners-up). The 11 medals went to the 11 most regular players, including Charles and Mulgrew. The *Echo* speculated on whether the Club might successfully apply for additional medals for Godfrey and Reynolds. Each had played in 11 of the 46 games, fractionally missing the customary qualification mark of 25 per cent. It hadn't occurred to 'Observer', it seems, that Clifton might get the medal that some of us (you'll have gathered I'm quite a fan) thought he'd earned.

'That goal's going to be remembered forever'
Clifton (stripes, right) lands after heading the crucial goal that won the game against Reading.

Champions!
The side that won the Third Division in 1960.
Standing (left to right) – Conner, Davies, Page, Reynolds, Huxford, O'Brien, Traynor.
Kneeling – Mulgrew, Paine, Reeves, Sydenham.

The solidity of that Championship side meant that there were few opportunities for any more of the talented 1957 Youth side to get in alongside Paine and Sydenham. David Scurr had one of his three first-team games at left-back, while Colin Holmes made his only first-team appearance a few games later. Wes Maughan managed three games, including the Cup defeat at Vicarage Road, when George O'Brien was suspended. George had had a problem with Ollie Burton, when Newport came to The Dell on Boxing Day: 'I was lying on the ground and he came up and kicked me. So I just got up and hit him. What can you do?' Ted's ploys to delay O'Brien's suspension backfired, so that – at a time when players were suspended for so many weeks rather than matches – George missed two League games and a Fourth Round Cup replay at Watford. That meant three games for Wes Maughan – sadly, his longest run, despite his promise in the Reserves – and it meant George sitting out a most anti-climactic Cup exit.

It followed a remarkable Third Round game when Third Division Saints visited First Division Manchester City. Bob Charles arrived at Maine Road in awe of opponents who included the great Bert Trautmann. It promised to be different from Division Three: 'A massive place! I said to Pagie, "I hope they don't get a cricket score here". Inside 20 minutes, Bob was 'picking the ball out' and thinking 'Bloody hell! 'Ere we go!' But then 'Reevesie got one'. And another. Half-time: 2-1. With less than 25 minutes to go, O'Brien added a third. Not yet time for Charles to relax, though:

> *Three-one. And when it got to 4-1 [Reeves's hat-trick after 67 minutes], I thought 'We can win this!' That's how nervous I was ... I've looked up at the clock and she's twenty past four. I thought 'Bloody hell! Another 20 minutes yet'. Then [Reeves's fourth with four minutes to go] – it's 5-1. And, at twenty five to five, I thought 'They're done now. They're finished, this side'. After the whistle, Bert Trautmann came up to me and he said 'Well done! What a load of rubbish I had in front of me!' And he had thrown three in – three of them were his fault.*

Trautmann's biographer implicitly exonerates him from blame for Southampton's 'avalanche of goals', but his display was 'one of the big disappointments' for John Page. Like Bob Charles, he'd expected the opposition to perform. That doesn't mean he wasn't impressed with his forwards' contribution to City's defeat: 'Sydenham and Paine ran riot. Terry absolutely skinned his left-back'. Paine agrees that he was able to turn Cliff Sear, later a Welsh international, 'inside-out: it was one of those days when things went for you'. They went so well that 'the score could have been 8-1', according to the *Echo*, 'so completely were [the Saints] the masters'. O'Brien reckons 'it could have been 9-1. It could have been anything. We ran all over them'. However many the Saints could have had, everybody seems to concur with the verdict of 'Nomad', in the *Echo*, that the home side was 'humbled, humiliated, outplayed and reduced to a shambles'.

While 'Nomad' paid tribute to 'a team win' and was reluctant to single out Derek Reeves (as did Oz) for his 'four fine goals', he felt he had a 'duty' to 'hand a large bouquet to Terry Paine ... I am positive he has never played better than on Saturday'. Terry is conscious that he 'left an impression there: they camped on my doorstep all that summer – illegally. Phoning! Jimmy Meadows [a City coach] came down and said "No, no, I'm just passing through on holiday". They were chatting me up'.

But Terry Paine wasn't going anywhere – except the Second Division.

On our Way to Watford
A celebration of the 5-1 FA Cup win at Maine Road that set up the anti-climactic exit at Watford.
Standing (left to right) – Charles, Conner, Jimmy Gallagher, Traynor, Page, Huxford, Davies, Paine.
Crouching – Ted Bates, Reeves, Mulgrew, O'Brien, Sydenham.

Chapter 16

Liverwho?

Back in the Division where he had played all his first-team football, Ted Bates was content to let his promoted lads have their heads. The side that had finished the promotion season was unchanged for a 1-0 defeat at Rotherham.

Ted's only new signing was a shrewd one. He needed cover for John Sydenham when his National Service became due. He encouraged his men to enlist in the RAMC, as he reckoned that a posting to Crookham would invariably allow for Saturdays off. That would work up to a point for Sydenham. But then he was posted abroad. John talks of fellow-pros who lost their places, during National Service, to the replacements their managers had brought in. So Harry Penk, who'd had three good seasons with Plymouth Argyle after failing to make it at Fratton Park, was a dream substitute for John Sydenham and Ted Bates: he was very keen to move back to the area to be near his wife's parents; he was more than good enough to fit in; and yet he was unlikely to pose a serious threat to a discharged Sydenham.

Harry's self-assessment – that he could never be 'a spectator's kind of player' in the Sydenham mode, but that he 'was doing a "player's player" kind of thing' for Ted – is borne out by appreciative team-mates, notably Terry Paine, who was 'smashing' to him: 'It used to give you all the confidence that somebody like that wanted you in the side'. The move also gave Ted Bates a chance to experiment with a winger who tackled back more than Paine or Sydenham. I mean *legitimately:* Terry was gaining a reputation for pursuing his full-back and clipping his heels and Harry 'couldn't believe that a player of his standing got away with murder like that'.

Part of Harry Penk's assignment at The Dell was 'to chase down fast opponents and put them under pressure'. In the best tradition of Southampton left-wingers, Harry boasted 'two good feet' and fancied his chances as an outside-right. But there were two good reasons why he would never wear the Saints' No.7 shirt. One was called David Chadwick, a patient standby for that position. The other was Paine's malingering. In a desperate bid to avoid National Service, he pretended to be hard of hearing. Harry Penk had escaped a call-up with a genuine case of a perforated eardrum. But Terry was trying it on. The amount of wax removed from his ears impressed his examiners, who were duly convinced, by his feigned inability to hear their test sounds, that he was in no fit state to wear a uniform. That was good news for Saints' fans who were happy to see him wearing the No.7 shirt with such regularity but bad news for Chadwick who would have liked a turn.

David had made his debut for the Reserves the previous season, when still only 16 (the youngest ever until Mick Channon). Having signed professional early in the 1960-61 season, he would get only 26 first team games in a stay of six seasons, often when Paine moved inside. For Terry Paine would seldom miss a game. Never mind the vengeful queue of left-backs out to flatten him: he would prove as nifty at dodging them as he had the military medics.

~

The Second Division seemed to suit Paine and O'Brien as a goalscoring pair. Both were ever-present until the last game and they scored 40 goals between them. Until they dried up in late March, hardly a game went by without at least one of them making his mark. And Paine amply outscored Reeves, who was not the force that he had been in Division Three. As Derek 'struggled' at this level, O'Brien explains, he himself 'could always find space'.

After the opening reverse at Millmoor, the team hit a winning groove with a 5-1 romp against Portsmouth sandwiched by a double over Liverpool. Pompey were in decline and had come close to swapping divisions with the Saints when they narrowly escaped relegation the previous season. Their reprieve was shortlived. They would go down in 1960-61.

But then there was Liverpool. Bill Shankly had arrived at Anfield the previous season: remarkably, Bert Shelley, who had left The Dell in 1936 – and Chapter 1 – was still there. Shankly was not pleased with Liverpool's first half performance at The Dell. Jimmy Melia, then at Liverpool, remembers that the visitors scored first and 'we were so full of ourselves'. But they were 3-1 down by half-time and Tommy Leishman, who'd scored their goal, made the mistake of being first into the dressing room: 'Bill Shankly was so mad with us. He tore into Tommy and gave him such a hard time, Tommy couldn't believe it'. Leishman wasn't to know that losing to Southampton was not something Shankly was going to take lightly – *ever!*

To rub it in, the Saints not only won the return game at Anfield a week later but went back in the League Cup in November to make it three in a season. As if being beaten again by this lot was too much for Bill Shankly to bear, Liverpool withdrew from the League Cup for the next several seasons. It would be 1967-68 before they entered this competition again.

Terry Paine was revelling in it, though. His two goals at Anfield meant that he had scored in every round to date. He turned supplier in the next round, on 5 December, when Derek Reeves went crazy in pantomime conditions. Having managed only four League goals at that stage of the season, he ran up five against Leeds in what 'Observer' described, in the *Echo*, as 'one of the most fantastic matches in the history of football'.

The bare facts of the game are these. After 10 minutes, the lights go out. A delay of 28 minutes before play resumes. Reeves heads the first of his five. Reynolds dives at McCole's feet, the lights go again as he does so and the Saints' keeper is stretchered off in darkness. At 8.54 pm, the game resumes with only 21 minutes' play completed. With only ten men and Huxford in goal, the Saints go 4-0 up, as Reeves completes a hat-trick before half-time and adds a fourth soon after the 9.25 pm resumption. Leeds rally to 4-4, but Reeves clinches it just before the final whistle at 10 past 10.

It was Huxford's first-ever game in goal. As he explained to the *Echo*, Ted Bates wanted to keep 'the regular deputy goalkeeper' in his attack. That deputy was Terry Paine, who would get his turn in goal at Fratton Park on New Year's Eve – this guy Reynolds was an injury collector. Meanwhile,

Cliff Hanger
Never having played in goal before, Huxford dons the jersey against Leeds United, hoping that nobody will be able to see him anyhow

Terry was impressing 'Observer' with 'another of his outstanding games' and 'an important share' in each of Reeves's five goals. That's five against Jack Charlton. One other Revie man in the making was playing that night. Billy Bremner was wearing the No.8 shirt that Revie himself had worn in the previous rounds of this new competition, of which the Saints were now in the quarter-final.

Their opponents at The Dell were the League Champions, Burnley. They lost 4-2. Tommy Traynor had a torrid time against John Connelly: 'By God, could he motor, that lad! He'd put a ball over my head and he was gone'. And Ray Pointer gave John Page 'a bit of a chasing – the best centre-forward I ever played against'. By this time, the Saints had already gone out of the FA Cup, after strenuous efforts to get a waterlogged Dell playable for their Fourth Round tie against Leyton Orient. They lost 1-0. As Terry Paine puts it, 'pump all the water off, talk the referee into playing and we get beat 1-0'. Another example, for him, of 'the shame of Cup football' – the sheer anti-climax after you have won the previous round 7-1. Especially if your humiliated opponents are on their way to winning your Division.

That 1961 Championship for Ipswich depended, in Ron Reynolds's opinion, 'purely on their method that Alf Ramsey introduced – a totally new form of attack', in which Ray Crawford, the No.9, would drop back to 'lure defences away'. Perhaps not totally new – Don Revie had, of course, worn Manchester City's No.9 shirt in this way, after the fashion of Hungary's Hidegkuti – but novel enough to take unwary opponents by surprise. In the Ramsey version, Crawford was a goalscorer in his own right, but when he and left-winger Leadbetter fell back, they would create room for Ted Phillips to come from a deep inside-left position to score – five years ahead of Martin Peters's time. In his recent biography of Alf Ramsey, Dave Bowler has been helped by Joe Mallett to explain the Leadbetter role by recalling Ramsey's Dell days. You may recall, from Chapter 9, that Ramsey had problems when wingers took a run at him. The Mallett theory on Leadbetter, as expounded by Bowler, is that the deeper a winger went the more he could puzzle a full-back: should the back cross the half-way line; or should he stand his ground and let his opponent work up a speed? For Ted Bates, though, the question was how to stop Crawford and Phillips coming through. In that Championship season, they scored 70 of Ipswich's 100 goals.

The Saints had incurred three of those goals in a draw at Portman Road, so Ron Reynolds and his team-mates were aware of how this 'simple method of attack could tear defences to pieces'. And so was Ted Bates. Which is why he deliberated aloud, with Reynolds and some fellow-defenders, when Ipswich were due at The Dell for the FA Cup Third Round: Ted 'was willing to listen', Ron remembers. 'He invited experienced players to discuss with him certain tactics'. On this occasion, Ted's tactical idea was to switch his wing halves so that Huxford could block Phillips. But Ron and the others thought that the attack-minded Conner might be demotivated by the implication that he couldn't change his game for the occasion and suggested that he be given the opportunity to do so. He was. He did. It worked. 'Phillips never had a look in'. Right-back Ron Davies found 'there was nobody out there to mark' and revelled in the freedom: 'I was in *their* box'.

Easy! The visitors even needed an opponent to score for them. A John Page own-goal was their only reply after the Saints had led 6-0 at half-time. Ted Bates told the *Echo* that the first-half display was 'even better' than the previous season's performance at Maine Road, while 'Observer' thought it 'the best' he had 'ever seen from a Southampton side'. While rejoicing in an all-round team performance, the man from the *Echo* praised 'a forward line that on its first-half form must be as good as any in the country'. And George O'Brien 'stood out as a schemer as well as a snapper-up of chances'. He scored three. It all proved to him that Southampton were a better side than Ipswich. Reflecting on the Saints' record of two League draws and a 7-1 Cup romp against Ramsey's champions, George blames Ted for his failure to outdo his old team-mate in the managerial stakes:

They got promoted and they went on and won the First Division [the next season]. Alf Ramsey got the England manager's job and then went and won the World Cup. Ted Bates could have done that – couldn't he? ... That could have been Ted, if he'd had promotion [in 1961], if he had made the signings he had to make when we went into the Second Division – which was a centre-half; Ted couldn't buy out-and-out defenders – make the managerial decisions that mattered, like Ramsey did ... It's all hypothetical, I know, but we were a class above Ipswich ... If Ted had done what he should have, if we'd have done even of bit of what Ipswich had done, that would have helped a lot of people, wouldn't it? Me, in particular, I suppose: if we'd have been in the First Division, you're really in the public eye [for international selection]. I think we were a better side than Ipswich. I'm sure Ipswich thought that as well. And Ramsey went on to get the England job. So we used to say Ted would have got that job.

So, if he had been smarter, and swifter, at buying defenders, Ted Bates would have been England manager and George O'Brien would have played for Scotland. Make of the first deduction what you will, but more than one of George's admiring team-mates question his conclusion that Ted cost him international recognition. Sydenham puts it all down to George's ongoing problems with his knees – which meant, as we saw in the previous chapter, that he seldom trained during the week. If it hadn't been for that, John is 'sure he would have played for Scotland'. So George should not blame Ted: 'Ted did quite a bit', John feels, for George's career, by patiently nursing him along with his 'terrible knee problems'. Indeed, George Kirby reckons that the way in which Ted 'put up with' O'Brien's knees 'shows how good a manager he was. He's sacrificing one aspect for another and that has to reflect in the team'.

DELL DIAMOND

Whatever else he had heard O'Brien moan about, Paine had not heard his beef about Scottish caps – although he does feel George has a legitimate grievance in respect of inadequate recognition by the Club: 'He was such a good player. And Ted knew he was a good player. But, somewhere along the way, it was never portrayed in that way to George … I always felt he didn't get enough credit for what we were doing at the time'. Terry agrees that perhaps Ted wasn't at his best when buying defenders, but is loth to criticise: 'It's easy to say those things and, as players, we would say them: "Why doesn't he buy him and why doesn't he buy him?" But, at the end of the day, how much are they going to cost you? Can the Club afford it?'

Ron Davies comes to the same conclusion – even though he starts from the O'Brien position. Of course, Southampton were better than Ipswich – 'you've got to be a bit better than someone to beat them 7-1' – and 'that's the time', Ron agrees, that Ted should have bought. But with what? Ted did 'OK with the money he had. Let's face it: he took us up on a shoestring'.

That said, O'Brien's concern about the defence is vindicated when you consider the line-up that would at last take Southampton into the First Division five seasons later. It showed more changes at the back than at the front from the side that had come out of Division Three and had finished eighth – 15 points behind Ipswich – in their first season in Division Two. You don't win promotion with a scoring record of 84-81.

～

You'll do a bit better with 77-62, but that scoreline was good enough only for sixth place in 1961-62. Shankly's Liverpool won the Championship, clinching it, at Anfield, with their first win over Ted Bates's Southampton, who clapped them off the pitch. Ted had strengthened his defence, when Tony Knapp arrived from Leicester City only hours before the season kicked off. The manager's hand had been forced a little by Page slipping a disc in pre-season training, but John's replacement promised to be a class act. The 24 year-old Knapp had toured with the full England squad, but had lost his place at Filbert Street after injury. That had attracted the attention of Bill Shankly, who was looking to shore up the defence that had conceded three defeats to Southampton. Knapp came close to signing for Liverpool but was a victim of some double-dealing, as Shankly's biographer effectively confirms. All the time that Knapp was negotiating with Liverpool, their manager was nursing a hope of prising Ron Yeats from Dundee United. When Shankly got his man, Ted moved in.

We're Better than Ipswich
Ted Bates (left) warms up, for another tussle with Ipswich.
Left to right – Page, Brown, Reynolds, Mulgrew, Davies, Huxford, Traynor.

Knapp needed neither an England tour nor a domestic queue for his signature to convince him that he was a good player. As Terry Paine puts it, here was 'a boy who believed in his own ability. Oh yeah! He thought he was the best'. Paine 'didn't think he was the best, if we're talking about' the need to buy better defenders. 'We thought he was well below what we needed'.

Tony would sometimes be 'punished' for that excess of self-belief, Huxford suggests, when he tried 'to take people on in the wrong areas'. He was not, alas, as good as he thought he was: Cliff had known where he was with John Page's simple style of 'stop it, get it and hit it long'. It seems that Knapp had an unsettling effect on the defence generally. Ted had the two full-backs into his office, Davies recollects, to discuss how they might cover him better. So how come Ted could spend a record fee on this near-international and then expect his backs 'to cover for him'? 'He's supposed to be better than us' Davies recalls Traynor protesting. Eventually, though, Ron feels that Tony came through that 'vulnerable' spell. He did what he'd been bought to do. A modicum of praise, then, for the record signing. Tony Knapp did have his fans – none moreso than Brian Clifton. Tony was 'so quick and he attacked the ball brilliantly', as Brian saw it. 'That's all he knew to do, was go for it'.

He didn't, by all accounts, know how to pass back to his 'keeper, though. If John Page's confidence was affected, we're told, by inexperienced 'keepers, it seems to be agreed that Tony Knapp took full revenge on behalf of centre-halves. Which is why Tony Godfrey is unsympathetic to George

DELL DIAMOND

O'Brien's grievance about Scottish caps: 'We could all say things like that, couldn't we? I could have said that, if it hadn't been for Tony Knapp and his back-passes, I could have been in the Under-23 side'. There was a time when Godfrey was being tipped for such honours and there was a long time, it seems, during which his team-mates despaired not only of Knapp's inability to pass back but of Godfrey's taking the blame. Ron Davies is most supportive of Godfrey in this regard. How could Ted blame his 'keeper for Knapp's recurrent inaccuracy? And how did he think it could be remedied by holding a special practice session for the centre-half and 'keeper: 'How can you have *practice* for back-passing?'

Terry Paine roars with laughter as he relives the spectacle of that session. It was no laughing matter for Godfrey, though. He was dropped early in Knapp's second season after a 3-2 defeat at Luton:

> *I think there were about four really bad back-passes. I think they scored from two of them. They used to complain about him, the other players. Nobody was really sure of him that much. Although he had a lot of ability, he wasn't the steadiest of players. He didn't really give goalkeepers confidence, I don't think … It's amazing the amount of games he played, because he was always very jittery. He would do the unexpected.*

According to the *Echo,* Luton did indeed take advantage of two wayward back-passes. The first was from Knapp, but the second was from Paine. There are no indications that Terry was called in for passing-back practice after that. His team-mates will tell you that he found an alternative solution: he never again dropped deep enough to attempt a pass-back. Ted's solution was to drop Godfrey. A player who'd come through the ranks at The Dell was dropped when a record signing screwed up. And another signing, Ron Reynolds, took over for what was to be an exciting season. 'I'm not bitter about *anything*', Tony insists, but he does feel that he was a victim of discrimination against the home-grown:

> *Ted Bates was always buying goalkeepers, but he was a bit that way that somebody he bought he seemed to favour a little bit – that was my opinion – against players like myself and Brian Clifton: players who he brought on and gave a chance to in the first place. But, then, he seemed sometimes to want [home-produced] players to fall back on.*

That complaint of discrimination against your own lads is not, of course, peculiar to Ted Bates's management: you may remember Jack Gregory making that point, in Chapter 7, about the way he was treated in the early seasons after the War. It doesn't hold up, of course, when you consider locals who got in early – like Paine and, later, Chivers – and stayed in. It wouldn't stop at Godfrey, though. Bob McCarthy and Micky Judd – who were even more 'local' than Godfrey and who would each make his debut five seasons later – both feel that Ted exploited this factor. 'Local boy. That was my problem', says Judd. 'If they'd paid money for me, then I would have had more games ... People like David Thompson [purchased from Wolves and of whom more later] – he was always going to get a game, more than me, because I hadn't cost anything'. The native player can be taken for granted, McCarthy reasons, because 'it's your home town and it's your team and I think you're a bit reluctant to move'. Which made the likes of him ideal for Ted to rely upon as quiescent 'reserve cover'.

While Godfrey cites Clifton as another victim of this tendency, Brian has a different explanation for his repeated exclusion from the chosen ones. If Ted was discriminating against him, perhaps it was because he was 'a steady-going lad' who didn't answer back: 'I wasn't brought up like that. I was brought up to conform. I've heard some funny stories about people chasing Ted round the table – the Mulgrews!' He wonders whether 'Ted might have been under pressure from [such] players. I don't know. But I suspect not: he was pretty fair'.

Notwithstanding his upbringing in this regard, Clifton does admit to another, more cathartic, form of protest. Having held his tongue when he was dropped, he thought he'd get his own back when he faced Ted on the training pitch:

> *I always remember Ted getting the ball and I thought 'I'm going to go straight through you'. I had the perfect chance. And I hit him, ball, the lot! He went up and came down in a crumpled mass. I stood over him, sort of clenched up: 'Go on. Say something!' He's getting to his feet, still cringing from the tackle, and he went 'Great tackle, son!' I was just deflated. I was expecting a great rollicking and he came out with that. I thought that was wonderful. I think he was a wonderful guy.*

Tony Godfrey owns up to a more Mulgrewesque manner: 'I think, sometimes with Ted Bates, if he had a bit of a problem who to put in and if he thought somebody was not going to shout and keep quiet, he would drop the quietest one and play the other one. I always used to go in and complain, thinking that I've got more chance of him giving me a chance'.

~

If the locals have a case, then Tony Knapp had it going for him: a record signing, who was soon made captain. He would start with 103 consecutive games, in Cup and League, and would miss only 21 games over the next six seasons. His team-mates may have felt that Ted was unduly patient with him and that this demanded unfair adjustments by some of them, but they'd said much the same, you may recall, about Terry Paine's introduction to the team.

The manager had bought himself a competitor for Paine. Ted now had two demanding young stars, competing to be both the top earner and the butt of dressing room cynicism. The joke that Terry Paine went into the manager's office to pick the team was already well-established. Harry Penk expected Paine to give him advance notice of his selection – 'he'd know before anybody else' – and doesn't 'think people bothered too much' about Terry 'nipping in' to see Ted.

That does seem to have been the general view. It wouldn't bother you, of course, if you thought Terry had no real influence: 'Ted might have gone along with Terry', Brian Clifton feels, 'and said "Yes. Yes. Yes", but I would have thought he had his own mind'. It was a problem, though, if you were supposed to be captaining the side. Cliff Huxford had found it so intolerable that he had resigned the captaincy:

> *The captain was the go-between between the players and the manager. Instead of me going in [to see Ted], he was going in. So there was no point in being captain. Terry had more or less taken over. In the end, I packed it in, because I felt my authority was being undermined by Terry going to the manager.*

But if Paine was forever in with the manager, then Knapp won a different kind of renown – for hovering *outside* the manager's office, intent on checking whether anybody was getting a better deal than he was. So the word in the dressing room became: knock the door before you leave Ted's office; give the eavesdropping Knapp time to make himself scarce.

The whole issue of players competing for the best deal would become an increasing headache for a manager with a reputation for paying everybody as little as he could get away with. Before the 1961-62 season started, though, Ted faced wage demands of a more collective variety. The maximum wage had been lifted during the previous season to end the industrial action led by the players' formidable Chairman, Jimmy Hill, and Tommy Trinder had kept his well-publicised promise to pay Johnny Haynes £100 a week. Nobody was going to get anything like that out of Ted Bates and his Board, but the players believed that Terry Paine had been offered 'a helluva lot more' than the rest of them. Ron Reynolds recalls it as the only time he ever 'had words' with Ted: 'I told him he was being very very unfair. He didn't deserve the support of the lads'.

Liverwho?

The matter was settled shortly before the season kicked off. As they stepped out to play Plymouth at The Dell, Ron Reynolds suggested to Cliff Huxford that this 'could be a great season for us'. Not for Reynolds, it wasn't. His season lasted less than half a match and Godfrey was in for the remaining 41 games. Ron landed awkwardly coming for a Plymouth cross just before half-time. This time, Paine and Huxford both went in goal. One at a time, of course.

It was a patchy season. The patches included two winning streaks of four League games each. The first, in September, was immediately followed by a League Cup defeat in a replay at Fourth Division Rochdale – a humiliation that would be tempered come April when Rochdale appeared in the Final. That said, this early exit from a competition that the Saints had so enjoyed in its inaugural year was a blot on an undefeated run of eight League games. This run climaxed in a 6-1 home win against Brighton – an unhappy return to The Dell for George Curtis, Ted's old coaching buddy. George would have many a coaching job, at home and abroad, but he struggled in what was to be his only attempt at managing in the Football League.

The second winning spell came at New Year, wrapped around an instant exit from the FA Cup. After that run, there were just four home wins, high-scoring ones in which the Saints averaged over four goals a game. In other words, the home side was functioning below par when they put only four past a 16 year-old Welsh debutant on St Patrick's Day. Gary Sprake, an apprentice and fourth-choice goalkeeper at Elland Road, was flown down on the morning of the game. Some accounts say he was sick on this, his maiden, flight. Most accounts agree that he did well to keep the score down to four. Southampton beat Leeds 4-1.

If their overall performance was patchy, there was one consistent feature: the three half-backs played in every game. Huxford kept his place at No.6 alongside Knapp, but Conner had gone to Tranmere. So Brian Clifton came in for 37 games at No.4, before finishing with five games at inside-forward – in which, needless to say, he scored four goals. Justice at last for this elegant, under-rated, undemanding player? Not really. He would play but four more games, in the Saints' dreadful start to 1962-63, before moving to Grimsby Town and finding his best position, he reckons, at centre-back: 'I should have stayed and played centre-half. When I played centre-half at Grimsby, it was wonderful. I played better – almost sweeping – at centre-half than I'd ever played in my life'.

So who could have made way for him at The Dell – Knapp or Huxford? An unassuming man, just brimming with compliments to his team-mates, Brian nevertheless feels he could have pushed out 'anybody' to play centre-back, even his good 'mate', Cliff. Given his admiration, noted earlier, for the way 'Knappie went for everything', Brian thinks that he would have complemented him 'perfectly': he could have 'just dropped off and picked everything up and looked good (laughs at himself). I had the distribution at that time: I could just play the ball out where I wanted. It's always very impressive, that – where you can just sweep up, step in'.

But Ted Bates was not about to try Clifton in that role. And Brian's place at right-half was about to become Ken Wimshurst's, as the Saints went on the FA Cup trail again.

Chapter 17

Cup Runners

Ken Wimshurst succeeded where Bobby Robson had failed. A Geordie find of Bill Rochford's, Ken was nevertheless acceptable at The Dell.

But not immediately. A Newcastle reject, he played a few times for Gateshead in their last two seasons – 1958-59-60 – in the Football League. Rochford, who had not lasted long at Colchester, was their trainer. As Gateshead kicked off the 1960-61 season in the Northern Counties League, he was telling *The People* that Wimshurst was ready to step back into the League. Rochford's old protegé, Bill Ellerington, went to watch his latest protegé. He reported back that he had had 'quite a useful game; nothing outstanding', though.

Ted Bates bided his time. Wimshurst moved onto Wolves, but was soon on Salisbury Plain, doing his National Service and playing for the RAF Netheravon Police School. He later learned that Ted Bates had watched him there: 'can you imagine the manager of Southampton watching a game on Salisbury Plain?'

Well, yes I can, actually. If you talk to those who worked with him, and more especially to Mary, you will be left in little doubt of Ted's appetite for the game at any level. And you will be reminded over and over again of the two other things that a Bates-like manager needs: trusted contacts who supply you with recommendations; and a capacity for *storing* all that information.

That's what it had taken, Ken reckons, for Ted to pursue Rochford's recommendation onto Salisbury Plain. Patience and perseverance. And a car that would withstand his driving.

Wimshurst was more than pleased with the outcome. Never having made the first team or signed pro at either St James' Park or Molineux, he felt as though he 'had won the Pools' when Southampton gave him a professional contract in July 1961:

Straight out of the Forces, after working in a factory for five years, I was playing football every day and getting paid for it … And not only that, I thought I was living in Majorca, living in Southampton as against South Shields. It was wonderful – walking round town in a polo shirt [with no need of] a jumper under your arm in case you walked into the shade in the north-east and got cold.

DELL DIAMOND

Wimshurst digresses to contrast his good fortune with the expectations of the 'kids' he has seen in the 1990s, in the Saints' School of Excellence at Bath: while they 'seem to *work* to be a professional footballer', his generation 'just played football and it was a *fluke* that somebody spotted you and you were *asked* to go and be a professional footballer'. In the 1960s, those who did the 'work' were, of course, the managers like Ted Bates, building networks of old team-mates scouting for them here and there, in the hope that their 'system' might cut down the 'flukes'.

The 1961-62 season had been Wimshurst's turn to bide his time. He hadn't had to wait long for his debut. After a hat-trick for the Reserves at Bournemouth – taken 'with the ease of a master', according to the *Echo* – he was in the first team, at inside-left, for a couple of games. He returned for the last five games at right-half, but lost that place, at the start of 1962-63, to Ian White. Ted Bates had gone back to Leicester City, this time for a 26 year-old Glaswegian who had started out with Celtic. Mulgrew had been let go after 325 games, 100 goals and a disagreement with Ted, who had 'lied' to him, he says, about who was being paid what.

～

So Ted now had three very different midfielders. Despite a good season, the elegant, goalscoring Clifton would be on his way, leaving Wimshurst, a ballplayer in the Conner mode, to dispute the No.4 shirt with White.

If Clifton wishes he could have become a sweeper at The Dell, he has no complaint about surrendering the right-half berth to such 'a great player' as Ken Wimshurst: 'Lovely on the ball. He knocked it about brilliantly'. Yet Brian feels Ken was 'perhaps a long time before his time. I think he'd be brilliant in this football today: he always reminded me of a foreign player'. Similar in style to Conner, Wimshurst had 'a bit more vision', Huxford feels. 'He could hit a longer ball. He used to change the play'. It was watching Wimshurst playing behind Paine and O'Brien that introduced me to the beauty of football played down the flank in a 'triangle', so I was interested to hear Huxford use this word to describe the magic this threesome worked down the right. If O'Brien had liked playing with Conner, he enjoyed Wimshurst, for the same reason, almost as much:

He had a good idea of the game and he gave me the ball in my *time … I don't want them to give me the ball when it suits them; I want them to give me the ball when I want it – not when they're getting rid of it. If I get the ball as soon as I can, then I can do something with it. That's what I needed and that's what Ken would do. He'd just give it to you. Dick was actually better than Ken to play with, because Dick would give it to you straightaway … That's what I liked – to get space and get the ball in my time.*

For those of us who can remember O'Brien performing in the six-yard box, getting onto the end of yet another cross from Terry Paine, it is revealing to listen to his job description for the perfect right-half feeding him further back. The problem – and Ian White surely represented the first of Ted's recurrent attempts to wrestle with it – was that a No.4 in the Wimshurst/Conner mode left the team vulnerable on the right side if O'Brien and Paine were to be indulged.

Given that George reckoned to leave the opponents' penalty area at nothing more than a stroll and Terry Paine's only purpose in chasing back was to clip heels, could Ted afford to have anything other than a grafter at right-half? Even Ian White appreciated the 'balance' – that word again – of having Wimshurst's creative 'talent' on the right: 'it really needed somebody free' on that side to balance the defensive Huxford on the other. But Ted had bought White to be a 'marker', who 'used to be taken to away games to do marking jobs'.

That kind of job was less needed at home, of course, and Ian can 'remember Batesie saying "What I'd really like to do is to play you away and to play Ken at home"'. Even today, when 14-men squads make it easier to Box and Cox, we still see managers opting for a settled side over horses for courses. Ted Bates did bring Ian White 'in and out' but not on a home-and-away basis. He just kept re-considering – not least, it seems, because Wimshurst, of his own admission, responded to the challenge of being dropped – which of these two different players to include. The following season, he'd often play them both – White would wear No.10. But it came down to this: White's inclusion meant that one of the play-makers, at No.4 or No.10, would have to make way for him.

By O'Brien's reckoning, Ted made this problem worse by replacing such an able defender as Davies at right-back with such an attacking full-back as Stuart Williams. Ron 'could mark people out of the game, but he couldn't clear his lines as well as most full-backs'. Stuart 'couldn't defend', though. 'He was good on the ball coming forward. He was brilliant. He couldn't defend, though … We needed a left-back as well. Tommy [Traynor] was alert on the ball, but we needed *defenders*'.

The 32 year-old Williams, with a load of Welsh caps and an 'excellent' reference from Pelé to his name (you can look it up in *My Life and The Beautiful Game*) was not, however, Ted's first choice. He had been hoping to sign a 29 year-old England international, whose own claims to fame included the suppression of Stanley Matthews in Chapter 11.

Peter Sillett was out of favour at Chelsea. Ted Drake had made way for Tommy Docherty and Sillett was hoping to return to The Dell. Much as he had enjoyed playing for Drake, he had never liked London. But he admits to inserting an unacceptable term into his discussions with Ted. He wanted 'a few bob under the counter' but the Board would not play.

When Ted made his alternative move for the West Bromwich full-back, Williams decided to study form: he read the match report on the Saints' visit to Stoke. With Matthews recently returned home from Blackpool, Stoke City would win the Championship. A tough assignment, then, for a side with a record of P7 W1 D1 L5, with only six goals scored. They lost 3-1 – David Chadwick scored his only ever goal for the Club – but Stuart didn't let that worry him: 'I looked at the team that played at Stoke and, when I saw the names there, I thought "Well, there's no way they should be down there, with those good players in the side"'. That was on the Saturday. He signed in time for Wednesday's game with Chelsea at The Dell.

~

Another tough one: Chelsea, who would be promoted as runners-up to Stoke, had beaten the Saints 2-0 at Stamford Bridge the previous week. A strapping 17 year-old local lad was playing his second game at centre-forward that night. Martin Chivers had moved very quickly into the first team – especially when you think how slow Ted had been to snap him up. So slow that Portsmouth had pursued him after watching him score loads of goals for Taunton's School. The Saints' networking was 'very loose in those days', Martin feels. 'I could have gone anywhere'. He didn't fancy going to Fratton Park, though, and answered an advert' in the *Echo* for trialists at The Dell. He was soon playing for CPC as a 16 year-old. He was 17 when Ted went, one Thursday evening by appointment, to talk to Mr and Mrs Chivers and their son. Martin signed professional, received his signing-on fee and was told he was in the team for Saturday's game at home to Charlton.

It 'takes a bit of doing', Ken Wimshurst feels, to sign a young player on Thursday and play him on the Saturday; and he admires the 'bravery from the manager' that this required. There was a limit, though, to such bravery: Martin Chivers was not yet ready to take over from the fading Reeves and Ted was in the market for a replacement. Another 17 year-old remembers his sneak preview of who the new centre-forward might be. Denis Hollywood was lodging with the Huxfords at the time and the next-door club house was vacant. So when a car drew up with potential tenants, a peep round the curtain was in order. Their new neighbour was to be George Kirby.

Not having quite made it with Everton in the First Division or Sheffield Wednesday in the Second, George had had a couple of good seasons for Plymouth Argyle. So the Southampton players had a fair idea what they were getting. In fact, some of them went to watch him playing for Plymouth at Fratton Park on the Wednesday evening between the defeats at Chelsea and Stoke. Ian White remembers Kirby savaging both Pompey full-backs in the first few minutes. Brian Clifton, who 'always rated George', nicely captures the team's ambiguity towards their new team-mate: 'We always liked playing against him when he was at Plymouth … A good lad. Tremendous! He was so aggressive. He was a real nasty piece of work. You'd always rather have him on your side than play against him'.

That's precisely what Stuart Williams thought as he watched his new team-mate 'put himself about' in the opening exchanges with Chelsea at The Dell. Coming from First Division West Bromwich, Stuart had never seen Kirby play before. Nor had the Chelsea centre-half, John Mortimore, whose side had just been relegated. Mortimore bumped into the Southampton players at Waterloo – as he often did on his way home to Farnham – on that Saturday evening after the game at Stoke. Knapp and he compared notes on the worst centre-forwards in the Division of which Tony had had a season's experience. Knapp warned him that Kirby was 'the worst bugger'. Mortimore soon had a chance to judge for himself. Four days later, he was marking Kirby at The Dell. George wasn't going to get involved, though, with Mortimore or with his centre-back partner, Frank Upton, a hard man who was on 'Chopper' Harris's list of two players – Huxford was the other, remember – who led the way as 'iron men'.

DELL DIAMOND

Confirming his fancy for full-backs that his new team-mates had noticed at Fratton Park, George chased across, straight from the kick-off, and took out left-back McCreadie. He also 'had a go at Peter Bonetti', Mortimore recalls, but his trademark was 'going in late, disturbing defenders, more than anything'. That's just how Ron Reynolds remembers it. The tackle on McCreadie was so late that it would have earned a red card today – 'no doubt about it' – and, once bitten early on, Bonetti was having to keep 'one eye' on Kirby as the crosses came in: 'nearly both eyes at times'. The Chelsea 'keeper could not prevent Kirby scoring on his debut.

The other Southampton goal was a first for Ian White, who had been wondering, after the side's woeful start, 'What have I let myself in for, here?' Ironically, he'd been expecting to join Chelsea, whose manager Tommy Docherty had attended the same Glasgow school as he, but the deal had fallen through. Cliff Huxford's recollection of Docherty, that evening, is of him walking along the track from the dugout, 'muttering' about Kirby and the referee's failure to sort him out. We shall return to that theme, come quarter-final time.

Meanwhile, Ted's team-building continued. With Chadwick at No.7, Paine had been playing at No.10. He would later fill this shirt more often as he lost a yard or two and wingers went out of fashion. But, for the moment, Ted wanted an inside-left, who could both score goals from Terry's crosses, when the two Georges were marked, *and* put passes into John Sydenham's stride.

David Burnside was capable of doing both those things, but wanted to carry on doing them at West Bromwich: just because he had been left out for a couple of games and had words with his manager, Archie Macaulay, he saw 'no reason to drop out' of the First Division. Three Second Division clubs expressed an interest. Burnside fancied the other two – Grimsby and Luton – even less than he did Southampton. He decided, though, that a day-trip to The Dell could do no harm. He told his wife he'd be home by eight 'at the very latest'. But he was retained by Ted Bates in more senses than one:

He talked to me about all the things that I thought were good in football – about skilful players expressing themselves, being allowed to do that. He talked about me – and he knew about me and all the parts about me, which I didn't realise anybody knew. He talked to me, as an individual, and convinced me that this was the place for me to stay ... He said things like 'You are a creative player and you want to score and create things for others. That's what I want. That's what I need. And that's what we'll allow you to do. We'll overlook some of the deficiencies in your game to strengthen your strengths'.

Although still only 22, Burnside had had five seasons at West Brom and had played for England Under 23's – against Turkey at The Dell, the previous season. But he was not accustomed to this kind of talk: 'No-one had ever ever talked to me like that before. Everyone, in the past, had said "Well, yes, you're quite good at doing a few things", but they always said "You can't do this; you've got to improve on that"'. Now, in contrast with 'all those negative vibes', here was Ted saying 'I'll allow you to do the things you're good at. We'll improve on the things you're good at and don't let's worry too much about what you can't do'. All of which 'convinced' Burnside that he 'could go and play at Southampton and do well … It was down to Ted Bates that I got transferred to Southampton. Him only – and nothing else!'

Burnside wasn't home by eight. And when he rang his wife, at 10, it was to tell her he'd signed for Southampton. He made his debut at Elland Road the following Saturday. As the team walked to the cinema on the Friday evening, the three new signings were at the rear with the manager. Ted felt the need to lecture them, Stuart Williams recalls, on doing their press-ups the right way. And, being the kind of coach who believes in demonstrating as he talks, Ted dropped into position on the pavement. Too embarrassed to watch, Williams and his bewildered new team-mates walked on, leaving Ted to attract alternative admirers.

Now, it has to be said that there is more than one version – that is to say location – of that story. Ted has publicly demonstrated the art of press-ups in so many towns, on so many pavements. Brian Clifton insists categorically that it happened in Southport, at the end of the previous season, before the game at Preston. And Terry Paine is just as adamant that it happened in Manchester's Piccadilly. Perhaps there have been fewer sightings of Bates press-ups than of UFOs, but I am inclined to treat them with a similar degree of salt. Or, if that's not fair, let's accept that it did happen in Leeds and Southport and Manchester and maybe all points north, even if the story has become embellished, randomly located and another piece of Bates apocrypha.

What *did* happen in Leeds was a creditable 1-1 draw against the side that was shaping up, under Revie, to win the Championship the following season. In the previous chapter, we met Charlton and Bremner by intermittent floodlight and Sprake on an emergency flight. They had now been joined by Reaney and Hunter, while Peter Lorimer was making his debut that afternoon. Ted Bates's own team-building was finished for that season. The side that played at Leeds that late September afternoon would stay together for as many as 20 more League games and all seven of the Saints' FA Cup matches. Yes, seven Cup games, going all the way to the Club's first semi-final since 1927.

This is not to suggest that the three signings were the sole cause of the resurrection. George Kirby, coming into a side that 'played more football than any team I'd ever played for before – they were a *passing* team, Southampton', had been bought, he feels, as a 'catalyst'. This was a recurrent feature, he reckons, of his roving mission through the Football League. He would repeatedly join a side whose manager 'needed somebody to liven up his team and give them a bit of *clout*'.

Whichever of the three newcomers especially helped to stimulate their struggling team-mates, it seems to be agreed that some of those already in residence responded by raising their game. This would be especially true of Wimshurst, who would be discussed, come the Spring, as an England prospect. As the newcomers settled in, Ken replaced Ian White and 'turned on some magical football', Stuart Williams remembers: it was a spell in which 'he was international class, really'. Or, as John Arlott put it, in a contemporary issue of *Hampshire: the County Magazine*, 'Ken Wimshurst suddenly began to play in the manner of the great ball-masters at right-half, bringing the ball confidently forward, working impossibly close and linking with Burnside to give the other forwards a subtle and constant service'.

Giant Killers
The side that played, unchanged, for seven Cup games (including three against Nottingham Forest) and won the *Giant Killers of the Year* trophy
Back row (left to right): Williams, Traynor, Wimshurst, Reynolds, Knapp, Huxford
Front row: Paine, O'Brien, Kirby, Burnside, Sydenham

The transformed XI that played together so often that season was Reynolds; Williams, Traynor; Wimshurst, Knapp, Huxford; Paine, O'Brien, Kirby, Burnside and Sydenham. Six survivors from the side that had clinched promotion three seasons earlier. And five newcomers slotting in in such a way as to keep that word 'balance' alive. Ted had found 'a *balance* there, in that team', which was, Wimshurst feels, 'as good as you'd get':

He never said a lot, but I think Ted knew what he needed in a team ... I think Ted was the master of really getting the best out of the individual players [for the team]. He had, in that team, a bit of everything. He had strong people. He had footballers. He had quick people. He had people with a lot of knowledge of the game – who had football brains. Tommy Traynor. Tom wasn't the ideal athlete, but a super football brain and a super left foot.

But what of George O'Brien's misgivings about attacking full-backs? 'Which way do you want it?', asks Ken. 'What Tommy gave you one way you'd maybe lose in another. So what do you want to do: do you want to cut the "Goals Against" down and forgo getting goals at the other end?' What's more, while he agrees with George's assessment of Ron Davies as a defender, Ken found Stuart Williams 'perfect' to play with:

I think footballers have got to have footballers to play with – who understand football. Stuart wasn't the greatest defender. That wasn't his strength. But when he got the ball, you could play with him, because he wanted to get it and pass it to me and get it again. Then he'd give it to Terry – he could link up with other people ... As long as the ball came over to that right side – Stuart, me, Terry, George – we'd create something. If you've got a non-footballer in that little area, it breaks down.

So there you have Ken Wimshurst's answer to George O'Brien. His notion of 'balance' involves 10 men with a mix of skills, but they must *all* have football brains. They had to wait to test this balance in the FA Cup. Thanks to the big freeze-up that put football on hold in January 1963, this side did not begin its famous Cup run until 13 February. The frozen standstill seems to have helped that run in two ways.

First, there were the ten-a-side games on the carpark in the afternoons – after the morning work-outs in the gym. 'We went out on that carpark, cleared all the snow and ice off and had a match', Wimshurst recollects. 'I wonder whether players would do that now. I think it created a bit of team-spirit and I'm sure that was reflected in the results we got when we started again'. Secondly, with suspensions still imposed for weeks rather than matches, the side-lined Kirby didn't miss a thing, as he sat out the freeze and nine postponements of the Saints' Third Round tie at The Dell. And Oz

'And if you really think Mr Bates needs you more than I do you needn't come back'

thought it worth a cartoon when the Club called for volunteers to clear the snow from the pitch – the players having reached their pick-and-shovel limits, it would seem, with the carpark. Yet Kirby believes that the pitch could have been playable during his suspension if Ted hadn't had it watered to ensure an ice-bound inspection. Hard to credit, but Paine wouldn't have put it past him. Anyhow, even when the game with York City was played, the surface was frosty enough, Wimshurst recalls, for him to slip as he scored one of the goals in a 5-0 win.

A 3-1 home win against Watford followed – revenge for the same round in 1960. Then the Saints had to wait a while for their Fifth Round opponents, from the still-frozen north, to catch up. First Division Sheffield United had yet to play their Third Round tie. Having beaten Bolton on 6 March, they won at Port Vale a week later. So when they came to The Dell on 16 March, O'Brien felt sorry for them as they 'dragged themselves on to the field'. His team-mates and he were happy enough, though, with the 1-0 win that took them to the City Ground for a Sixth Round tie against more First Division opposition. Ken Wimshurst remembers the game for the '*perfect* ball' with which George Kirby put Terry Paine through to lob Peter Grummitt, the Forest keeper, for the Saints to snatch a 1-1 draw: 'I'd have been proud of that pass: it was a helluva pass'. Grummitt was impressed, in turn, by Terry's impudent skill – 'in those days, you didn't get many people doing the lob' – but it was not an especially memorable game in *itself.*

Its significance lies in setting up two of the classic FA Cup-ties in the Club's history. The first of these two games – the Sixth Round replay with Forest on 3 April 1963 – was watched by a crowd of 29,479. I wasn't there – I was working and living in Exeter at the time – but it seems to have been my lot in life to hear about the game from nearly everybody who *was* there, including a 14 year-old called Michael Channon, an 11 year-old Paul Bennett and an 8 year-old Nicholas Holmes (who would all take part in Southampton's next great Cup run, 13 years later). The lucky young things! It was one of those games that evokes poetic accounts – notably and outstandingly by John Arlott – and invites hyperbole, as I found when it was relived for me by the entire Southampton team (with corroborative evidence from the visiting 'keeper, Peter Grummitt, and referee Denis Howell).

Forest went 3-0 up shortly after half-time, even though they had 'never', in George O'Brien's estimation, 'been in the game'. The home side 'just kept going forward and going forward' to no avail, with Forest 'packing their defence so tightly there seemed barely room', as John Arlott put it, 'for a ferret to have wriggled through it'. But, then, with half an hour to go, it all changed. Arlott has recorded how. First,

Paine ran in on a long free kick by Traynor and flick-headed it past Grummitt. The whole ground flared up – but, offside (There are people in Southampton who still believe that Paine's inward run was from an onside position, but that he moved too fast for the linesman's judgment). That decision would have knocked the spirit out of most teams, and out of most crowds, too. Yet, instead of the silence of disappointment, that single incident seemed to convince the spectators that Southampton could win. The roar mounted, took on a strange ... quality of exultation. Here were a Second Division team, three goals down to a well-ordered side from the First Division, with a bare half-hour left for play, yet there was an illogical but half-convincing air of triumph about the losing side.

Wimshurst now was moving with suave confidence, finding O'Brien and Paine, switching on the right; from time to time Sydenham went galloping down the left; Kirby was needling away in the middle. Now it was 16 minutes to go; Forest still led 3-0, when Kirby went up to a cross and headed a goal. Now belief was absolute. As Southampton rose, Forest fell back, rattled by the incessant stream of crosses as Paine, again and again, twisted clear and inwards on the right to search out the hungry heads of his inside-forwards, sweeping in against a defence that was losing its earlier discipline. Another cross and Kirby was in, butting his head into the ruck, and young Grummitt, only half an eye on the ball, pushed it into his own goal.

Only time was now the enemy. The packed crowd inside the closed gates and the less comfortable watchers, perched precariously in the trees across Archers Road, were merged in a complete unity and in a mass voice that lifted the team to an equal belief. Only one minute was left when Burnside, in a cold split second, measured his right foot shot and hit it low and accurately wide of Grummitt's right hand into his goal.

Jimmy Gallagher, the Southampton trainer suddenly popped out of his dug-out, ran on to the pitch and kicked a ball sky high: the impossible had been done. Pressmen tore up the copy they had half finished and began to write fresh stories.

DELL DIAMOND

They had little to write about the anti-climactic half-hour of extra time. What everybody remembers is that comeback from 0-3 to 3-3. Today, of course, a penalty shoot-out would have followed. But they did things so much better in 1963. The parties would re-assemble in neutral territory. It would appear that the uplifted Saints' fans re-assembled in greater numbers than the deflated Forest fans. John Arlott records an estimate of 25,000 supporters setting out for White Hart Lane, some of whom arrived in time to become part of a crowd of 42,256. As Ken Wimshurst puts it, 'Southampton *closed down*' that Monday afternoon. My father has recalled for me often the 'bumper-to-bumper' cavalcade of cars and coaches that Arlott describes. A bricklayer, he witnessed it from a roof on the A30 in Blackwater, slowly making its pre-M3 way, throughout that afternoon, to Tottenham: 'it didn't seem to stop'.

Forest were without Jeff Whitefoot, their injured right-half who was being tipped, like his Southampton counterpart, for England honours. The Saints were unchanged and so, it seems, were their tactics. 'We didn't change from the first game to the second game to the next game', Ken Wimshurst explains. 'We played exactly the same, because that was the only way the team that Ted had accumulated understood how to play. He just let people go on and play'.

Their opponents, though, used a formation which George O'Brien perceived as being designed to combat the threat from the Saints' right-wing pair: 'they played with a man *withdrawn*. They didnae play with an inside-left: they played with two left-halves. They played with a normal left-half and somebody behind him'. Describing this strategy for his *Daily Telegraph* readers, Donald Saunders perceived a different purpose: it was a 'precaution against undue aggression' by Kirby. What O'Brien and Saunders agree is that this created a hole for Wimshurst to play in and that he revelled in the freedom. For Saunders, 'the great difference between the teams was Wimshurst', while the *Echo* Sports Editor thought it 'one of the best wing-half displays' he had 'ever seen in a Saints' side'. Wimshurst scored the second goal and put Burnside in with 'a splendid through pass' for the third of Southampton's five without reply. Nobody would demur, it seems, from the verdict of the displaced Ian White that Wimshurst was 'majestic that night' and just 'strolled through it'. As Ken left the ground, he saw Ron

Reynolds talking to Danny Blanchflower in the carpark: 'I went over and I remember Danny Blanchflower saying "It's a good job they didn't come here and *attack* you or it might have been 10"'.

And then the team coach was following the cavalcade of cars back to Southampton. Cliff Huxford, who'd taken a knock on the leg, was resting it by standing in the stairwell at the front of the coach: 'I could see, for miles in front of us, the tail-lights of cars, in streams going back to Southampton. It was brilliant. We had a *fantastic* following that night'.

For the fourth time in four seasons, then, Ted Bates's cavalier side had won a cup-tie by scoring at least five. Yet if they still talk about that game at White Hart Lane, it seems for many to be overshadowed by the drama of the comeback that brought about that second replay. If the latter was Ken Wimshurst's game, the recovery at The Dell will be forever associated with what John Arlott politely described as 'Kirby needling away'. Wimshurst is more graphic: 'George absolutely *terrorised* the Forest back four. Paine was hitting corners in and George was steaming in – you know, anything goes – and they were all looking for him'. But that especially applies, it seems, to the Forest goalkeeper. Paine expresses the general view that Kirby 'frightened the life out of Peter Grummitt that night'.

It was a reprise, as Reynolds saw it, of what George had done, on his Saints' debut, to Bonetti. It was typical of how 'George could come in like a ton of bricks. If he made up his mind to go in, irrespective of whether the ball had gone three or four seconds earlier, he still went in'. In Ron's book, this was 'not good football, it's not nice football, but it certainly can disturb the opposition'. He 'felt sorry' for Grummitt that night. So did Huxford, in so far as he considered 'keepers generally to be under-protected in those days: as he chillingly puts it, they were 'decent targets'.

Each of the combatants is coolly philosophical about it. 'Any striker who attacks the ball is always going to have trouble', Kirby reasons, 'with the goalkeeper – if you attack the ball and the 'keeper is attacking the ball. I'm not making any excuses or trying to be fly'. And nor is Grummitt making any excuses about being on the receiving end of Kirby's aggression:

We used to know that, if we were going up for the ball, we were going to get hit. But it was always fair and square; and we used to enjoy it. It was part and parcel of the game. Nowadays, there isn't anything like that. If you touch the 'keeper, it's a foul.

But, 'part and parcel' or not, did Kirby rough him up? 'Oh, yes! He did. I got hit a few times by him – but I expect it … As far as I can see, it wasn't that dirty. It doesn't worry me. It didn't worry me at the time'.

It worried Andy Beattie, his manager, though. So much so that –
according to Denis Howell, the referee – he complained to the FA about the
assaults on his 'keeper. Mr Howell had had a calming word with George
Kirby after an early foul. He felt he had learned how to handle the enigmatic
Kirby, 'a perfect gentleman off the pitch and a wonderful chap to talk to,
[who] on the field, was like a demon possessed'.

George is minded to claim the 'own goal' that has been attributed to the
Forest goalkeeper – 'Grummitt's not going to knock the ball in his own net,
is he?' – but the referee's view accords with John Arlott's: 'I can see Grummitt
now, thinking "Where's George Kirby?" and, as he took his eye of the ball
and looked for Kirby, the ball hit him and went in the net. Kirby had got to
him and I was accused of not protecting the goalkeeper. Well, you can't
protect goalkeepers who take their eye off the ball'. He suspects that the FA
would have 'consulted' informally the famous international referee who was
there: George Reader – whom we met, in that capacity, in Chapter 8 – had
joined the Southampton Board in 1952 and would become its Chairman
later in 1963.

Whether the FA took such soundings or not, it goes without saying that
it endorsed Denis Howell's interpretation of Kirby v. Grummitt and that
Andy Beattie duly received the usual 'Stand by Our Man' rebuff from
Lancaster Gate. Mr Howell would be in charge of the third game, thank you
very much.

The FA would have done well to check their man's prior engagements.
In his day job, as MP for Birmingham Small Heath, Mr Howell would be
on a parliamentary delegation to Germany. Jack Taylor would have to referee
the decider. So Forest got their change of referee. And a lot of good it did
them. Denis Howell was 'quite amused'. As Stuart Williams wickedly puts it,
even if Forest had wanted to complain, they would surely 'have been
speechless after watching us play the way we did'.

The removal of Forest set up a semi-final against Manchester United.
Busby's side had been having an iffy season – they would finish just three
points and two places clear of their relegated Maine Road neighbours – and
they wanted to avoid playing either Leicester City or Liverpool. It was 'a
piece of luck', in Denis Law's book, to get Southampton and United were
consequently 'brimming over with confidence', according to their captain,
Noel Cantwell. The bookmakers were unmoved by the Saints' quarter-final
performance: they remained the 25-1 outsiders for the Cup. The favourites
were Leicester City at 2-1, with United and Liverpool paired at 9-4.

If these last two sides were all the same to the bookies, the Southampton
players would have preferred to face Liverpool. Having won four of those
five games in 1960-61-62, before Liverpool went up, they would have

savoured another crack at them. David Burnside, who'd arrived since those Liverpool games, shared the general view that the team to avoid was Manchester United – 'because they had all the best players, really … Although they weren't having an outstanding season in the League – for whatever reason – they had individuals that could have beaten anyone in Europe *on the day*'. And to orchestrate those individuals, the Laws and the Charltons, Matt Busby had recently signed Pat Crerand from Celtic.

As George O'Brien saw it, United 'were starting to come half-decent'. He was one of the players who travelled with Ted Bates, after the quarter-final, to watch United lose a League game at Leicester. He was especially 'impressed with Crerand' and the way 'he got everything from the goalkeeper'. Ted discussed how they might stop that particular supply line. It sounds like a job made for Harry Penk, but you didn't shuffle your pack to match the opposition in 1963. If his thoughts on blocking Matthews in 1959 are anything to go by, it wasn't worth asking Sydenham to oblige. Even so, O'Brien feels that John should have been given the assignment and lays at Ted's door the blame for Crerand's freedom to dominate at Villa Park. David Burnside blames David Burnside: if Crerand did the damage, it was because Burnside, his immediate opponent, was 'hopeless: you could have taken me off and the team could have been no different. I was just non-existent. I just blew it altogether and it's probably because I wanted it so much'. David wanted it so much because his two ambitions were 'to play in the Cup Final and to play for England – in that order!'

The Club's idea of preparing for their biggest Cup game for 36 years was to take refuge in a Droitwich hotel. There was a Golf Club across the road from the hotel, but golf was banned after Wednesday. This ban 'was written in the rules', Terry Paine explains: 'Ted believed it made you heavy-legged. He was probably absolutely right, but such was our love of the game of golf and the boredom of sitting around in a hotel: what are you going to do – play a bit of snooker or something?' Paine's answer was to sneak off for nine holes with O'Brien and to hide (unsuccessfully) in a bunker when Ted came looking for them. The less deviant stayed in the hotel. Stuart Williams may have found it 'nice and relaxing' but others were bored. They were stuck for 'too long', Huxford complains, 'in the middle of nowhere'. It was so *'boring'*. Consequently, 'the *tension* grew as the days went by', Burnside recalls. 'It may have been better if we had stayed at home and gone through the normal routine. But the semi-final was a big day. It seemed to be the right thing to do and I can understand why. And we all thought it was right'.

The match itself doesn't merit a whole lot of description. 'It never happened', Huxford says. 'It went so quick, I couldn't believe it'. Denis Law thought it 'one of the scrappiest' matches he had ever played in and didn't exempt from that description his single goal that won the game: it was 'a sloppy affair, although some people said at the time that it showed the versatility of Denis Law'. Having failed to 'connect properly' with a cross, Law 'fell on the floor [and] the ball got caught under my leg. I was lying on my back in the goal-mouth when I managed to get a second stab at it and scoop it out of Ron Reynolds['s] reach into the corner of the net'.

Reynolds confesses that he 'should have swallowed' the cross. Law should not have been allowed the one stab at it let alone two. 'It's one that I should have come for. And I just didn't. He headed down ... I should have had it. It was a bad goal'. While accepting that Ron should have claimed the ball, Terry Paine nevertheless admires how 'Denis Law – probably one of the greatest players I've ever seen – jumped up and stuck it away, in typical Jack-in-the-box fashion'.

An unnamed reporter, quoted in Noel Cantwell's autobiography, agreed with Burnside's self-assessment and found O'Brien disappointing, too:

> Given an efficient pair of inside-forwards, Southampton must have been more troublesome to United's perennially doubtful defence. Paine and Sydenham, on the wings, are quick, intelligent, decisive forwards, while the tall, lean Kirby is excellent in the air, no beginner when the ball is on the ground.
>
> But O'Brien and Burnside were erratic when they weren't lethargic and the sole constructive Southampton player of any quality was Wimshurst – in the first half.

Among the other notable features of this dreadful football match, this writer picked out the 'all-round efficiency' of Crerand, as already acknowledged, plus 'Knapp's resolution, Reynolds's durability, Gaskell's quickness'. With both forward lines disappointing, it is interesting to find both goalkeepers earning recognition. Harry Gregg, the experienced United 'keeper who would apply to be Ted Bates's assistant five years later, had lost his place to David Gaskell, who had kept goal in that famous Youth Cup tie six seasons before. Tony Godfrey, the Saints' 'keeper from that night at Old Trafford, had been dropped early in the season, as we saw at the start of this chapter. Since the quarter-final, though, he'd come in for the injured Reynolds. And, after playing one of his 'best games ever' at Norwich, the Saturday before the semi-final, and getting 'a good write-up', he was hopeful of keeping his place. But Reynolds was restored for Swansea's visit to The Dell on the Monday, even though 'he couldn't kick the ball' and played when 'he wasn't really fit', in Godfrey's opinion, in the big game at Villa Park. Just as for the Blackpool cup-tie in 1959, the experienced 'keeper had it. A 'peeved' Godfrey stood in the tunnel with a 'cheesed-off' Gregg. And, as Cantwell records, a very nervous Gregg.

Gaskell gave Gregg something to be nervous about in the dying minutes when, as Law recalls, he was 'caught off his line and lobbed' by George O'Brien. But the young 'keeper recovered to make 'a helluva good save', in Stuart Williams's estimation, and United were on their way to Wembley. If that late chance for O'Brien is the one they all talk about, Kirby is still haunted by his failure to attack a second-half cross. It's an incident he has had occasion to relive with Bill Foulkes, who had been at school with George's wife and who was marking him that afternoon at Villa Park:

> He once said to me, many years afterwards, 'Can you remember the ball going past the far post in the second half? I thought, at the time, "there's a goal here!" And, for some unknown reason, you didn't run in'. I said 'I know'. I've thought about it many times and I've thought 'Why didn't I go in there?' That would have made the whole difference. For some inexplicable reason, I didn't go in.

If you want to get footballers agonizing, get them to talk about 1-0 defeats – the missed chances, the half-chances that might have been made into chances and all the other might-have-beens. For George O'Brien, the game might have been a lot different – and a lot better to watch – had the two sides not been 'frightened of each other … I think we should have done *our* thing – they were a bit wary of us'. As we have heard from Wimshurst, the free-flowing side had got this far by playing the only way they 'understood how to play'. By the same token, David Burnside had enjoyed his first season in a side that 'was about creating and scoring':

> It always seemed to me that if we conceded two, we could score three. And we didn't worry too much if we got beat sometimes. The mood was 'It's been a bloody good team to beat us, anyway'. That was generally the lovely attitude that was allowed to prevail amongst the team … But, on the most important day of that year, none of us produced what we'd been about all year. If somebody could only have said – and Ted didn't say it that day – 'this day is no different to any other day and you just go and do all the things that we've done all year, then you've got a very good chance of winning. If you get beaten, it won't be because you haven't done all the things that you've done all year'. Now, if only we'd said that to each other – or somebody had said that or we'd have got that collective thing right – then probably Manchester United wouldn't have won that day – because they were full of apprehension and fear as much as we were, I think.

And, even if their opponents hadn't succumbed, the Saints would have at least gone down entertaining. John Arlott could have coped with that: 'the defeat had not even shown the side playing the sweeping attacking football that is its essential character. If they had done that and lost, the blow would not have been so hard'.

Maybe not, but there were a lot of us there to suffer the disappointment, a lot of us who had never seen Southampton in a semi-final before. This time, my father and I were part of the motor cavalcade, merging into the procession of Saints' favours as we reached the Oxford by-pass from Camberley. Yet so many went by rail: 15 special trains – to United's six – came into Birmingham from Southampton. The Saints' fans had needed only three such trains for the Sixth Round tie at Nottingham, but this day was really *special*.

Extra Special
One of the 15 'special' trains that took Saints' supporters to Birmingham for the Semi-Final.
This one needed two engines for the climb through Old Hill Station.

Sadly, they wouldn't need to marshall any trains from Southampton to Wembley. Many of the mortified fans would have the compensation of going there with the Saints 13 seasons later, of course. But Ted Bates had got that one step further, than he had as a player in 1948, to suffer the special disappointment of a semi-final defeat.

There was nothing left to play for in the League, although there were plenty of fixtures yet to be fulfilled in a season extended to catch up from the freeze. The Saints played eight games in May, culminating in a gala night at The Dell on the 22nd. Their opponents, Stoke City, arrived as Champions. Matthews didn't play – a disappointment for the Saints' historian, Duncan Holley, whose first game this was – but he was applauded onto the pitch – Matthews, not Holley – as Footballer of the Year, an honour he had previously won 15 years before. It was a triple celebration: Southampton won the *Sunday Mirror* 'Giant Killers of the Year' award.

Footballer of the Year
Stanley Matthews let Tommy Traynor off, by not playing in the final game of 1962-63
when Stoke City came to The Dell as Champions of Division II.
Matthews is greeted by Ted Bates, to applause from Knapp (left), Burnside and Kirby

And so a funny old season was over. Wimshurst never did get that England call-up. But Terry Paine did. Mike Connolly of Doncaster Rovers may have got the nod to play alongside Jimmy Greaves at Youth level but is was Terry Paine of Southampton who stepped out against the Czechs, in Bratislava on 29 May 1963, partnering Greaves in the first of his 19 appearances for England.

Bashful Giant-Killers

As captain Knapp (No.5) prepares to receive the Giant-Killing trophy, his team-mates cannot bear to
look at him, while trainer Gallagher monitors O'Brien's exercises:
(Left to right): Reynolds, Paine, Wimshurst, Traynor (hidden), Sydenham (half-hidden), Kirby,
Burnside, Huxford, Williams, O'Brien, Gallagher, Ted Bates

Plenty to Celebrate

Last seen as a referee in Chapter 8, George Reader (centre) was now a Southampton director.
He entertains Stanley Matthews (right), the Footballer of the Year, and Bill Ellerington,
at a joint dinner for Champions Stoke and the giant-killing Saints.

Chapter 18
Loyally Paine

There are many who will tell you that Terry Paine should have received a lot more than 19 caps. Terry Paine is not among them: 'Blimey! That's 19 more times than I ever thought'.

Fourteen of the 19 games were in partnership with Greaves. Terry enjoyed that: 'Jim was a *dream*. He used to drift into areas. And the beauty about Jim was you knew that if you gave him it and it was in that certain area, it was in the back of the net'. It seems reasonable to infer that Paine put the ball into 'that certain area' more regularly than Greaves's other right-wing partners. Much has been made of Jimmy's international strike-rate of 44 goals in 57 games. So why do we not hear more about the fact that he scored 17 of the 44 in 14 games alongside Paine? Perhaps because Greaves himself consistently picks out Bryan Douglas as his favourite England partner? Never mind: Terry Paine fans – and I declare a *huge* interest in this regard – will have noticed that he was the outside-right of his era who was selected, in 1998, for the Football League's 100 all-time greats.

We could leave it at that. After all, Paine is not in that much-rehearsed cast of performing artists who could/would/should have won more caps if only England had had a manager who appreciated creativity, flair and all the other hallmarks of genius attributed to that list of overlooked talents from Bowles to Le Tissier. Yet the question of how many more caps Paine might have won is one to get his team-mates going. And it gets them going about matters pertaining to a player's unique relationship with a Club and its manager. It is not just that Terry played 804 games for Southampton. *He played 778 of them for Ted Bates.*

There are those who attribute the alleged shortfall of caps to Terry's attitude to training. He should have trained harder. Cliff Huxford emerges as the principal spokesman for this view. In Alf Ramsey's system, Cliff argues, 'the wide player had to work up and down'.

And Terry didn't work for us. He hardly trained. He was there, but he went through the motions. If he was really fit, he could have been in the England team for a long, long time – I'm sure of that. When you play for England, you can't, all of a sudden, start going up and down like a train … Terry could only do it for half-an-hour or an hour. You can't just switch on like that if it's not in you … A football brain. Two good feet. Brilliant! He could have been better. That's what niggles me.

DELL DIAMOND

Cliff blames both Ted and Terry for Paine's indifferent training. Yet Ron Davies, the full-back, wonders how much fitter Terry could have been: 'He was as fit as any of us'. Tommy Mulgrew agrees: Terry never had weight problems and, however he slopped about in training, 'on the pitch he was transformed – he was fantastic!' Ian White takes a similar stance but broadens out the argument: 'Lots of great players are never good trainers. There's also the theory that you can leave it all on the running track'. And Paine himself takes it even further:

> *Listen, I was never the greatest trainer. But I think there's a difference between training without the ball and training with the ball. And I think it's been proved, over the years, that you get most out of players when you train with the ball. But, in those days, the physical side of the game was looked on to be the basis of your training. You had to run round the field 100 times – that's how it was in those days. But myself and George O'Brien, we always felt you could do as much running with the ball as without the ball. As it's transpired, that's the way the game's gone.*
>
> *I used to love the ball-work. Practice matches – I used to love all that. I didn't take very kindly to lapping and doing what I call 'mindless' running. I realised you had to put in pre-season training, but I hated pre-season – mornings, afternoons, running up hills and down dales.*

Shades, then, of what Peter Vine was saying (in Chapter 13) about the need for a less physical emphasis – for some players, if not others. By Bob McCarthy's reckoning, Paine was able to achieve that ideal of bespoke training simply by being 'his own man'. OK, so he wasn't one of those who 'ran round the pitch, in training, until he dropped', but he did what was required for him to be able 'to turn it on on Saturday and turn full-backs inside-out. If you've got natural ability, all the running round the track is a waste of time. Terry was a *natural*. I don't think if he'd trained harder, he would have been a better player. All the running round the track and sweating won't make flair players better players'. Nicely put, although there are more capricious versions of how the wilful Paine contrived to adapt the training to his needs – most notably by catching a bus or hitching a lift when he was supposed to be cross-country running. It's easy enough when you've heard that story a dozen times to appreciate how Huxford could be 'niggled'.

Yet Paine answers Huxford's concern about his England performances with a tale from the World Cup squad of 1966: Alf Ramsey told him that Bobby Charlton and he 'were the fittest players he'd ever seen'. Terry remembers watching Argentina demonstrate 4-3-3 when they beat Brazil 3-0 in 'The Little World Cup' in São Paulo in 1964. As Ramsey followed suit, in the build-up to the real World Cup, and 'concentrated on the last seven players of his defence', Paine did not mind that the days of 'out-and-out wingers were *numbered*: having played almost 10 years as a wide man, he could readily adjust to another 10 in midfield.

Yes, *twenty* years – and 815 League games. You don't achieve a record like that if you're none too fit. In a *Sunday People* article celebrating Terry's completion, in 1975, of his first 765 appearances, Mike Langley mentioned his inability to touch his toes: his hamstrings were too short, Terry told him; but, then, he'd never had a hamstring injury.

No shortage of counter-arguments, then, to Huxford's assertion. And just what was it Paine needed to sharpen, anyhow? 'In a way, he was like Matthews', Ian White reflects. 'It was his skill at putting people off balance – that's why they never caught him, not because he was fast'. And yet, 'if he had been fitter', White concedes at the last, 'he probably would have been *world class*'.

Even so, Ian's solution to Paine's alleged under-achievement lay less in training than in a transfer: 'The guy should have moved to one of the big fishes. *Then* he would have got all the caps going. I think he was held back here'. Jimmy Melia and George O'Brien agree. George concedes that there *could* be something in Huxford's explanation, but he generally subscribes to the Paine-was-a-Natural School of Thought:

> *I always felt that Terry played the game like he was watching from the Stand. You know, when you're playing the game, you're at the same level as [the other players]. When you're sitting in the Stand, it's an easy game, isn't it? I always got the impression that Terry was sitting in the Stand playing the game, from the way he played it to people … I played against Finney and Matthews, Shackleton – all the great players of that time. I think Terry was certainly the most accurate player I ever played with – flighting it.*

DELL DIAMOND

That word 'accurate' crops up again and again in accolades from admiring team-mates. Take some of the strikers who benefited, like O'Brien, from his accuracy of service. If we leave, for the moment, his First Division successes in this respect – let's not get too far ahead of ourselves – it is still possible to heap up appreciations from his first nine seasons in the lower divisions (which is, amazingly, the period during which he won all his caps). Let's start with George Kirby:

> *A lot of my goals for Southampton came from Terry Paine – because I knew what he was going to do. I knew what he was capable of. He'd get the ball out wide, on the right, and he'd come in along the touchline. He'd pull the 'keeper to the nearpost and I'd be on the back stick. I was deadly from a yard when Painie crossed the ball.*

That makes it sound easy, but George gives credit to Ted for passing on that lesson he had learned from Jimmy Easson, back in the early 1950s (and Chapter 10): 'The reason I was getting so many goals from Painie was because Ted said to me "You must be out to go in"'.

But suppose Kirby – or any other tall No.9 – was unavailable at the back stick? Then Terry's ability to look up and pick out an alternative came into play: as David Burnside explains, it didn't take him 'long to realise that, if I put myself in certain parts of the field, I'd score – because Terry Paine would make sure the ball got there. I knew the ball would arrive in one of two spots. So, if I were there, then it would be down to me to make sure I didn't miss it'. So, once he'd worked out that Kirby was going to be at the farpost, Burnside decided that he needed to be at what he calls 'position three', as he 'knew that the ball would arrive there at certain times and it would be down to me'.

In this regard, Burnside delivered more than Ted had expected: 'He probably got caught up in the team', Ted reasons: with the service on offer, Burnside could go up a gear as a goal-scorer. By way of illustrating how he found space and opportunities to benefit from Paine, Burnside cites how he took up 'position three' to score that historic late equalizer against Forest, which John Arlott described in the previous chapter:

> *There must be minutes to go as Terry comes into the box again. I think 'Well, this is going to be my position' – because George O'Brien is on the front post and I think George Kirby is at the back somewhere, so I'll be in the middle: I'll cover the third part and if the ball comes to me, it's down to me. I don't know whether a shot's gone in and come out or whether it's come straight to me, but it comes to me about eight yards from the goal and in the middle of*

the goal. There are a lot of bodies there – I always remember a lot of bodies – and the ball's arriving to me and it sat there ... I concentrated so hard that I struck it right down the middle. Grummitt must have gone to the near post, so he wasn't there, and I remember it just disappearing through one or two players and into the net.

For this 'third man' ploy to work best, it needed a winger with Paine's exceptional capacity for keeping the ball long enough to suck the 'keeper to his near post and with his unerring ability to discern which of the three positions was 'on'. Norman Dean marvels at that latter aptitude: 'He didn't just hit it. He looked up first'. But how, you have to wonder, did he have the *time* to look up?

He made himself time, didn't he? I think Terry knew, before he got to the by-line, roughly where you were. Then he'd have just one little glance to make sure and his delivery of the ball was excellent, wasn't it? ... He used to lay the ball on a plate for you. You still had to put it in the net but it was nearly done for you.

A tribute, in no uncertain terms, to Terry's *vision*. That's another recurrent word in the accolades. 'His vision was just unbelievable', Jimmy Melia reckons. 'He'd chip a ball anywhere you wanted it'. And he had it so *young*. 'They say you don't get the vision and know the game', John Page claims, 'for two or three years – perhaps more – but he had it all at 17. A natural. He could pick people out. Great vision'. It was that 'great vision', in turn, that the developing Mick Channon felt he learned and benefited from: 'He was a great passer of the ball. He was a great crosser. He was very quick-minded'. As Ted Bates himself put it, Terry Paine could have 'seen a train coming out of the tunnel before it had gone in the other end'.

What was it like, though, for right-backs – and right-halves for that matter – who had to play behind this visionary and maybe go on an overlap or two? 'You'd go on the outside of him', Ron Davies says, laughing at his own misfortune, 'and nine times out of ten you wouldn't get it'. Likewise, Brian Clifton, coming through from right-half to link up with Paine, 'running all over the place – all round him', as Terry holds on, waiting for an opening. 'And *then* he'd lose it. You've just run forward about 30-40 yards. He'd lose it and stand there and you had to run back (laughs). You didn't like that!' (laughs again)

So, if they didn't like it, why did they put up with it? And laugh about it, even? Because, says Davies, 'you couldn't say nothing against *him*. He was too good – brilliant!' Because, says Clifton, 'he had great talent – a wonderful player!' Two young full-backs, coming in later in the 1960s, are just as accepting. It was 'part of my game', says Tommy Hare, to scurry back if an overlap broke down. He didn't mind being exploited, even though he'd have liked Paine to track back a bit. For Bob McCarthy, being left stranded by Terry became 'a standard joke'. Bob would 'go down the line to receive an overlap. Terry would sort of make out he was going to give it to you, then switch the ball to the other side. So you had to get all the way back to cover'. McCarthy accepts that these runs could sometimes serve as a decoy and laughs at the 'standard joke'. And why not? Wasn't this man 'one of the best wingers' he – or any of us – had ever seen? 'He had so much skill on the ball. He could pass a ball tremendously. His vision was unbelievable'. And so on. You willingly paid a price for playing with such a 'wonderful' footballer.

John Sydenham volunteers that same adjective about a player who started out as his peer and who was so often referred to as part of a pair with him. And yet you have to wonder whether, ultimately, Sydenham might have felt overshadowed by Paine – perhaps unfairly so? John denies any such feelings:

> I certainly don't feel I was unfairly overshadowed by Terry Paine because I considered him to be the greatest player that Southampton ever produced. I always had the greatest admiration for him. He was a wonderful player, he had abilities I didn't have and it was often said that, if he had had my pace, he would have done even better than he did … We were with each other as kids, from 17. I know that he worked hard to get where he was, so I never ever had any feelings that I was unfairly overshadowed, because I just thought he was a wonderful player.

I guess most of us would settle for being thought 'wonderful' by our workmates. If Terry Paine had few friends in the Southampton dressing room, it was bursting with his admirers. Which is why they forgave him other shortcomings – most especially his lack of effort, on occasion, away from home and his excessive sarcasm.

~

'There was nobody better than Painie *at home*', Ron Reynolds feels, but 'whenever we went away, we knew we were playing with 10 men: Terry was *gone!* He just didn't want to know. I could throw a ball out to him and he'd be in a dream'. Tony Godfrey says the same. The trouble was that Terry – 'a great player, without a doubt' – felt too secure: 'he was never ever dropped'. As Paul Bennett puts it, 'Painie didn't get chosen. He was just *there*'. That was fine by Bennett – 'Painie stood supreme. That's what it was about' –

but Godfrey was concerned that the team was liable to pay for the unwritten no-dropping clause in Terry's contract with Ted: 'He knew he was admired so much by Ted that sometimes, away from home, if things went bad, he used to drift out of the game'.

Ken Jones, who arrived for the 1965-66 promotion season, believes that this guarantee of a place would sometimes cost others theirs. The logic is simple enough: 'It didn't matter how bad Terry played': he could be 'a waste of space, but he knew he'd be picked the next week. We used to call him "The Rubber Stamp". He was stamped up 42 games a season'. Defeat demanded changes, however, so there would have to be 'a little shuffle' somewhere else in the team. It might be in attack – Thompson would make way for Sydenham, or *vice versa* – but full-backs Jones and Hollywood were another pair who might expect to be swapped when Ted felt that he had to be 'seen to make a shuffle'.

A principal reason for Paine's going into hiding, Jones argues, was the need to avoid the left-backs and other opponents who were 'after him'. The list of would-be avengers is considerable, with the majority of the Leeds team and Portsmouth's Roy Lunniss the most talked about. Terry Cooper feels that Paine, 'a right dirty so-and-so', was 'too shrewd' and 'too crafty' to be caught by most left-backs, himself included.

From time to time, referees would catch up with him, though. Denis Howell was not among them: 'I never had any trouble with him in any matches that I refereed. The only trouble I had with Terry Paine was that he became a Conservative councillor'. To be fair, the former Labour Minister for Sport adds that he was 'pleased to see he went into politics – I think sportspeople should be in politics'. Let's not be tempted down that fork. Let's ponder the consequences, *for the team,* of Terry's antics.

The trouble, his team-mates reckon, was that he could antagonize Cooper's colleagues, *en masse,* and one or more of those team-mates would then become victims of Revie's assassins. Likewise, if Lunniss failed to catch Paine – they called him 'Pogo', John McGrath recalls, for his ability to jump out of lunges – then Wimshurst went in fear of being the sacrifice. He cites the 5-2 win at Fratton Park in the promotion surge of 1966. The 'nasty kick on the ankle' that the *Echo* reported was what Ken had come to expect when Pompey defenders decided it was repayment time.

There is an alternative view. Paul Bennett *enjoyed* the spectacle of Paine 'hyping up' opponents and 'throwing the fuse in'. But, if you marry Wimshurst's assessment to that of Jones, it seems that Paine's team-mates often paid quite a price for his illegitimate niggling of opponents. Then there was the sarcasm.

The idea of footballers objecting to sarcasm may seem ridiculous – but remember the misgivings, in Chapter 7, about aspects of the hyper-acidity towards Bates the player. It is repeatedly claimed that Paine went too far, especially in collusion with O'Brien, in his disrespectful mickey-taking of Bates the manager. You can almost *feel* Norman Dean's disappointment that any player should have engaged in such 'sarcasm' towards Ted, when he was in and about the dressing room and even in training – it was mainly Terry, but George was another culprit: they were in cahoots'. How could Terry be so 'unkind to Ted', Norman asks, especially with Ted being too much of a 'gentleman' ever to 'get back at him' in front of other players?

It may be that Ted the manager didn't hear or comprehend a lot of the dressing-room ribaldry any more than he had as a player – not even when George O'Brien was doing his regular impersonation of the manager's walk. If the way you carry an old knee injury is so obviously manifested in your gait, then you don't tell a group of footballers to 'walk this way' without having somebody enact the obvious pun. George Kirby thinks that Ted 'knew' what O'Brien was doing, but so *what?* To let it pass him by was the hallmark of 'a clever man and a good psychologist', who 'used his psychology and nature to the maximum' and remained 'affable'.

Maybe so, but younger players were more vulnerable to mickey-taking that could become spiteful, even. Of course, Paine was cruel to the novices, says Paul Bennett, who always cites the humiliation, in the gym, of goalkeeper Middleton as an example. So? 'In football, you have to grow up, don't you? You don't complain. You have to grow up very, very quickly'. If surviving the dressing room sarcasm is part of your initiation, that means you have to withstand even the sharp wit of your Paines and O'Briens. And yet Ken Jones talks of older players intervening to stop Terry tormenting yet another of the youngsters.

In fact, Ken sees this kind of cruelty as another manifestation of the nasty streak that provoked all those opposing full-backs and he suggests that it was *this* that cost Terry an abundance of caps:

If he'd been owt like what I call a half-decent person, he'd have made more appearances for England than anybody. To me, he should have played for England for years and years and years. But he weren't liked as you went up and down the country.

Loyally Paine

Tony Godfrey makes a telling qualification, though, of all these criticisms, when he distinguishes between the public and the private – the group and the one-to-one – faces of his less than popular team-mate: 'Terry Paine was always OK when he was on his own', Tony found. 'I could get on very well with him on his own. But, when he was with other people, he used to show off at times'.

That need to be seen to be somebody in the group manifested itself also – if we take John Sydenham's point – in Terry's attitude to authority: 'Painie was a nightmare for discipline. You tell him to run round the pitch one way, he'd deliberately go round the other. He was always trying people out – to the *limits*. It was "I'm Terry Paine. What are you going to do about it?"'. We shall see the problems this created as new staff came to The Dell – starting with John Mortimore in 1968 – charged with improving discipline. Until then, though, to criticise Terry in this regard was to criticise Ted or at least to question whether Terry had been allowed to assume too much authority of his own.

Certainly, more than one player coming to the Club was surprised by the degree of inequality in the dressing room. Arriving from Filbert Street before Paine won his first cap, Ian White had 'never been used to one player dominating' the way Terry did: 'at Leicester, all the lads were the *same*' – even Gordon Banks. It was the same, four years later, for David Thompson coming from Molineux, where he'd been 'treated just the same' as stars like Ron Flowers and Peter Broadbent. Thompson was taken aback by the 'influence' that Paine and Chivers appeared to have: he's 'not saying they were tret any different but they had some sort of say in what went on, I think'. It can cause problems, he feels, when 'players who aren't in the side resent the influence on the manager' that one or two stars have. This is redolent of what Ken Jones said about the selection problem that David and he both faced: so was this an issue for Thompson? 'Not really. I respect players who are good at the job. And I always felt that Ted were a fair bloke'.

Unequal treatment? Undue influence? Serious charges. Charges that are repeatedly put, but which then tend to be half-withdrawn as being what *others* felt. And then, in so far as these charges are pressed, it keeps coming back, it seems, to this – those who got less than their deserts put up with it most of the time, partly because Terry Paine was exceptional and partly because Ted Bates was essentially a fair-minded person.

～

Amid all the talk of unequal treatment and the 'influence' of Terry Paine, I have tried to avoid referring to his 'power' in the dressing room. That's because of the various qualifications that have been put to me. Take Don Taylor, the physiotherapist, who feels that Terry 'really didn't have any power in the dressing room. *As a person,* they'll *suss you out* as quick as anything in the dressing room. I don't know whether he'd survive very long, nowadays, in the dressing room. I think he'd be one of those characters who would move around clubs an awful lot'.

This analysis puts the solution first into the hands of the players and then into the manager's lap. One simple strategy for his team-mates was expressed by Eric Martin: Terry Paine may have 'had a lot to say', but many a time the rest of them 'weren't really listening: they just let him talk'. And, as for the manager, moving him along was not on the agenda. Far from it. Whenever Terry talked of a move, Ted would dissuade him:

Ted Bates! I couldn't win an argument with him if I tried. He was such a nice, persuasive, gentle, kind man. I felt I was letting him down – that's how he made you feel! He made you feel so blooming humble. You felt 'How can you want to leave this club with Ted Bates here?' It was a simple as that, really.

'Simple'? There doesn't seem to be anything remotely simple about the relationship between Ted Bates and Terry Paine and the effect it had on the dressing room. On the one hand, they queue up to tell you that Terry was Ted's favourite, who could train indifferently, play badly away from home and never be dropped. And then they complain that Terry disrespected his manager.

To the extent, of course, that Ted condoned Terry's shortcomings, then it could be argued that he must take some of the responsibility for their consequences. But, then, the very essence of Ted's managerial philosophy was that you tolerated player's weaknesses and played to their strengths. You may recall, from the previous chapter, how moved David Burnside was – literally, from The Hawthorns to The Dell – by Ted's exposition of that theory. It comes up repeatedly in tributes to his style, but Ted puts it as succinctly as anybody:

You take a player's strengths and let the team overcome his weaknesses. That gives the team strength.

If you want a stark example of how a team kept implementing whole-heartedly its manager's philosophy, then you have it, surely, in the way that Terry Paine's team-mates put up with his irritating ways – and worked hard, what's more, to offset some of them – in return for all the benefits of playing with a wonderful footballer, who should have played many, many more times for England.

Chapter 19

A Shame of Two Halves

Terry Paine of England was in fine form for his club in 1963-64, finishing as joint-top scorer as the side had another of those 10:7 seasons – 100 goals scored and 70-odd conceded. A repeat, then, of 1957-58 and 1959-60, but achieved in four games fewer.

The home fans had a treat, as the free-scoring Saints ran up at least six at The Dell on as many as five occasions – both opening the season (v. Charlton) and ending it (v. Rotherham) with a 6-1 win. That final six made it 20 goals in the last four games to bring up the 100. Paine got five of them. O'Brien got seven. But, after three consecutive seasons as top-scorer, it was not George who shared the top spot with his right-wing partner.

That honour went to Martin Chivers, who had kept George O'Brien out for a while, as Ted Bates rang the changes on two from three: Kirby, Chivers and O'Brien. Yet the season had hardly begun before Newcastle were pursuing O'Brien. When the Saints drew 2-2 at Newcastle on 11 September, George scored both goals. In the return, a week later, he scored again in a 2-0 win – his sixth goal in the first eight games. At the Board meeting the following day, though, the manager suggested that any offer 'be seriously considered', as the Club 'had had the best' from O'Brien whose arthritic knee was a cause for concern.

Ted admitted that he had no replacement in mind but hoped that Chivers might be ready 'to take over'. This local teenager had come in briefly, you may recall, at the start of the previous season. The arrival of Kirby had limited him to just one more outing in that exciting campaign – in a 4-1 defeat at Newcastle, when Kirby was resting between the two Forest replays. Although Martin scored the Saints' goal, he 'realised then that I was going to have to get a little bit more strength about me before I had my next chance: I had a big frame, but I wasn't, necessarily, strong'. Some of the increased strength came naturally – 'that was growth spurt: I filled out a bit and put some weight on' – but the 18 year-old was also prospering from a professional regime: 'When you're training every day of the week and you're eating and sleeping football, you're bound to fill out'.

So now the manager was able to think the unthinkable – a phenomenal goalscorer, who'd got 30 goals in 52 games the previous season, could make

DELL DIAMOND

way for Chivers to play alongside Kirby. It happened on 2 November. With exactly a third of the season gone, Chivers came in for 29 games and 22 goals. Nine of these came in the last four games – by which time he had switched to No.9, when Kirby left for Coventry, and O'Brien had resumed at inside-right. Kirby, who had started the season with a hat-trick inside 15 minutes and finished that opening game against Charlton with four, had scored 15 goals in 30 League games when Ted let him go. A ratio of 50 per cent is not at all bad for a No.9 whose robust style created space and opportunities for others. As George O'Brien gleefully puts it, Kirby would 'go in and there'd be bodies lying everywhere and the ball would just be there and I'd whack it in'.

That coming and going at the front was only one of four changes, though, from the giant-killing side of 1962-63. In September, Ron Reynolds experienced a terminal dislocation at Portsmouth. Tony Godfrey had yet another chance. The midfield duo of Wimshurst and Burnside had very few games together. Ian White had spells in each of their positions, inter-changing with a new midfielder, John McGuigan, who'd been playing for Scunthorpe when the Saints went out of the League Cup to them the previous season. And playing very well according to Denis Hollywood, who had been making his Saints debut, at right-half, and marking him. A right-footed wing-half, Denis was persuaded by Ted Bates to become a left-back.

Given Ted's strong views (see Chapter 27) that you need 'a good, natural left foot' on your left flank, this says a lot about his faith in Denis's ability to do the business with his weaker foot. But he was thinking ahead – to the need to replace Tommy Traynor.

In January 1964, though, the 30 year-old Traynor was still in possession and playing, unforgettably, in a dramatic Third Round cup-tie at The Dell. Both White and McGuigan were in – Wimshurst had broken his jaw at Sunderland in November – and Williams had a rare absence as the Saints lined up: Godfrey; Davies, Traynor; McGuigan, Knapp, Huxford; Paine, Chivers, Kirby, White and Sydenham. Their opponents were Manchester United – the earliest possible chance to avenge that disappointment at Villa Park nine months before.

On the Saturday before Christmas, United's Assistant Manager, Jimmy Murphy, came to The Dell to spy on the Saints playing Grimsby. On a frozen surface, Chivers and Sydenham skated freely and each scored twice in a 6-0 win. While that gave Murphy something to think about, the Southampton manager was plotting a preparatory week at the seaside before

SOUTHAMPTON FOOTBALL CLUB *Founded 1885*

MANCHESTER UNITED

Sat. January 4 1964

Match No 12

F.A. CUP — 3rd Round

OFFICIAL PROGRAM

SATURDAY JANUARY 4 1964
Kick-off 3.0 p.m.

SOUTHAMPTON v. MANCHESTER U.

F.A. CUP 3rd ROUND

SOUTHAMPTON
Colours : Old Gold Shirts—Black Shorts

GODFREY 1

WILLIAMS 2

McGUIGAN 4   KNAPP (Capt.) 5   TRAYNOR 3

PAINE 7   CHIVERS 8   KIRBY 9   HUXFORD 6

WHITE 10   SYDENHAM 11

Referee
Mr. CLEMENTS
of West Bromwich

Linesmen
Mr. R. W. Kates
(Red Flag)
Mr. M. V. Sinclair
(Yellow Flag)

BEST 11   HERD 10   CHARLTON 9   MOORE 8   QUIXALL 7

SETTERS 6   FOULKES 5   CRERAND 4

CANTWELL 3   DUNNE 2

GASKELL 1

MANCHESTER UNITED
Colours: White Shirts—White Shorts

the cup-tie on 4 January. This time around, he would make sure that his lads would not be bored. He booked them into a Butlin's hotel at Rottingdean.

This was a mistake. And Ted knew it as soon as they got there. This was not a suitable setting in which to prepare for a football match. Different players have their different versions of how the prospect of relocation was mooted and of how they voted to stay for revelries that would take in New Year's Eve celebrations. But they all seemed to agree that it was a draining week in more ways than one.

'It was a *ball* from start to finish', we're told. 'Birds in the rooms – it was absolute chaos!' You don't ask *which* rooms: it goes without saying that the sexual behaviour of footballers away from home is a private matter – much as it used to be for American Presidents. Suffice it to accept the invitation, from one witness, to 'imagine' what it was like 'with all the Redcoats'. And you didn't have to participate in the revelries to be affected. Martin Chivers – agog, as an 18 year-old, at what some of his elders were up to as Jimmy Gallagher 'worked overtime' to get them early, and unaccompanied, to bed – recalls Ted approaching him, around 11 o'clock on New Year's Eve, to advise him that it was 'probably time for bed, boy'. Martin was going anyhow, he says, but to little avail: there was so much *noise* and, as Tony Godfrey complains, 'the walls were paper thin'.

There was, of course, another indulgence. An indulgence where there is no players' code of silence. Hence we're assured that the drink flowed freely and that it flowed disproportionately into Tommy Traynor. If they didn't write best-sellers about their drinking habits in the 1960s, the players felt free to joke about any drinkers in the squad. In this side, the joke was on Traynor: if he struggled to get to training in mid-week, then Jimmy Gallagher would chuckle, according to George Kirby, that he was laid low with 'ginitis'. But, George is quick to add, Tommy would be fine by Friday – 'no problem'.

No problem, that is, by virtue of a professional code, shared by managers and players alike. Recited to me repeatedly, it states that drinkers and gallivanters may do as they wish during the week – up until Wednesday or Thursday, anyhow – so long as they 'do it on the park on Saturday afternoon'. Or words to that effect. There is, of course, a private appendix or two to that code, which says that some players will feel able to drink as late as Friday – and honourably so. 'We'd have half a Guinness each and that would be it', explains Ron Davies, confessing to the occasional Friday evening outing with Tommy Traynor and Tommy Mulgrew: none of them would drink any more on a Friday, because 'that was our life'. You'd set your own limits and all would be well, so long as you could still 'do it' the next day.

There's the rub. More than one survivor of that visit to Butlin's will explain United's comeback – to win 3-2 from being 2-0 down at half-time – in terms of the ravages of that week away. A flagging second-half performance by the home side is perhaps symbolised in that moment, captured in the video of the Saints' history, where Tommy Traynor collapses in a heap on the goal-line and helps the ball across it for United's second goal. If everybody makes Tommy the Butlin's drinker-of-the-week, nobody makes him the sole victim, come Saturday, of the Rottingdean revels. Tommy was just unfortunate to have been found out so spectacularly on camera. He will tell you how he slipped as he tried to clear and the ball caught the back of his heel. As George Kirby remembers the moment, though, Tommy 'didn't have the strength to kick the ball. He was knackered. He'd had too much of a good time'.

It is significant that Kirby should be so explicit. It would be hard to find an ex-player more scrupulous than George in his reluctance to criticise fellow-professionals, however innocuously, on the record. The fact that he could talk so freely about this incident reinforces my impression of the comparatively relaxed code that players have towards drinking – *even if* it occasionally means that a team-mate or two go so far as to bring into question their ability to 'do it on the park'. Tony Godfrey, another one for taking great care on the record, is generally critical – in a very gentle way – of the debauchery at Butlin's. As a 'fanatic' when it came to pre-match discipline, he felt that some of the players 'did tire a bit after being away and not having a rest'. As Martin Chivers likes to joke, on the after-dinner circuit, 'Butlin's caught up with us in the second half'.

A Shame of Two Halves

It's all very nice for them to joke about it. But weren't we entitled, as paying customers, to expect Godfrey's professional attitude to run right through the team? How can any of them *laugh* about this episode? Even if it was half-a-lifetime ago, how can they laugh at having surrendered a 2-0 lead over Manchester United? 'Bah!', says Terry Paine, 'At the time, you don't think it's going to make any difference to you. It's human nature in many ways'. *Not* a very re-assuring answer for those of us who expect professional athletes to resist the damaging effects of 'human nature'. 'Maybe', says Terry, going onto the defensive, 'we were well beat, on the day, by a better side, second-half. Then again, you could say what went on, that week, contributed to that – sure!'

My own memory of that second half – *before* I saw any video evidence – is of Traynor being run ragged by a teenager on the visitors' right-wing. Willie Anderson was making his FA Cup debut. And so was United's outside-left. George Best had a quiet game against Davies – 'It didn't seem to be any different from Sydenham. He could run, but so could I in those days' – but Anderson had plenty of room on the right.

There are those who blame that not so much on his hapless marker as on the failure to stem the feed. As at Villa Park, Crerand was getting too much room in the second half. Davies blames this on a change of tactics at half-time: Ted should not have decided to have both White and McGuigan withdrawn, to sit on the lead. 'That wasn't our game. Our game was out-and-out attack'.

Crerand now found himself with the kind of space that Forest had ceded to Wimshurst the season before at White Hart Lane. And he used it well, crowning his freedom with the winning goal that is Best's main memory of the game: Crerand 'never scored goals'.

And, not for the first time, I felt that Tony Godfrey's lack of height let him down when he unsuccessfully came out to punch and the ball went loose for Herd to score that second goal through Traynor's legs. Godfrey blames the floodlights. As he explained in Chapter 15, you didn't have to be wearing Ron Reynolds's ashtray-sized lenses to lose the ball in the lights of The Dell.

You can pool the explanations and take your choice, but you just can't avoid giving this cup-tie that hackneyed label: a game of two halves. The first belonged to the Saints, storming towards the Milton Road end. A surge from Martin Chivers, leaving Maurice Setters for dead, to blast an unstoppable shot that asked 'Who needs O'Brien?' And, on the stroke of half-time, Terry Paine heading in a Sydenham cross. The second half was all – for whatever reasons – United, with three goals to set them on their way to another semi-final.

DELL DIAMOND

The Saints were set for nothing more than a goal-scoring rampage – 50 goals in the remaining 19 games – to finish fifth, 16 points behind Leeds United. Don Revie's rebuilding was going fine – he'd assembled a side that would not only win Division Two but would get to Wembley the following season – but there was work still to be done by Ted Bates.

The goalkeeper remained a problem. From his debut in December 1958 to his departure in December 1965, Tony Godfrey would manage to play every season without ever making the jersey his own. His appearance record (in League and Cups) says a lot about the Club's unsuccessful quest for a settled goalkeeper:

58-59	18 games (v. Christie 31)	62-63	6 games (v. Reynolds 46)
59-60	11 games (v. Charles 34; Reynolds 11)	63-64	33 games (v. Reynolds 11)
60-61	8 games (v. Reynolds 41; Charles 2)	64-65	12 games (v. Hollowbread 34)
61-62	45 games (v. Reynolds 1)	65-66	16 games (v. Forsyth 23; Hollowbread 6)

In the month of their FA Cup exit, the club doctor confirmed that Reynolds would not play again. Within the fortnight, Ted was reporting on the first setback in what was to be a two-year search for a Scottish goalkeeper. An inferior scouting report, he told the Board, had ended his interest in Dunfermline's James Herriott.

This report came from his Chief Scout, who had taken up office on the first day of the season. Aged 65 on appointment, he was none other than Tom Parker. It seems that the Saints' former full-back and manager may have got it wrong in the case of Herriott. At the end of the next season, he would join Birmingham City, with whom he would win eight Scottish caps. James Herriott would acquire more vicarious fame, of course, when his name was adopted as a pseudonym by a Sunderland-supporting vet who was branching out as a novelist.

Godfrey saw out an anti-climactic season. In contrast with the settled team that had finished 1962-63, only Cliff Huxford was ever-present in 1963-64. True, Williams, Sydenham and Paine each missed only one League game. Paine was on international duty at Hampden Park on 11 April, the only game of the season for the patient David Chadwick and the only goalless game of a campaign that produced 173 League goals. That's just over four goals a game.

～

When Paine played at Hampden, the Club paid him £200 *not* to play for them. This was one of the outcomes of the financial manoeuvring that had followed the giant-killing success of 1963. As ever, Ted Bates's demands for himself were modest enough. He accepted the new three-year contract, at

£2500, that the Board offered but asked them to replace his three year-old car that had become 'shabby'. And, just as typically, he asked that his four scouts – Kirkman, Wheatley, Billington and Booth – be recognised, in the sum of £50 each, and that Bill Rochford be sent 'a similar amount' for finding Ken Wimshurst.

Ted succeeded on all of those counts. His proposals for the players' wages were remarkably egalitarian: the top six earners should remain on the same *basic* wage, while all of the others, bar one, would receive a small increase. He was concerned, though, that appearance money differed so much between players.

When the Directors held a special Sunday morning meeting, at the Chairman's home on 19 May, to consider the manager's suggested terms for 1963-64, they agreed that five members of the giant-killing XI – Burnside, Knapp, O'Brien, Paine and Williams – should each receive £10 an appearance, while the other first-teamers would get only £5 a match. At first, the only objection to the new terms came from Terry Paine, one of three players on the club's top basic of £32 a week. At another special meeting, with Paine's wages constituting the agenda, the Board adopted a general policy of paying a bonus of £200 to any player selected for a full England or Scotland cap and £100 if it were Wales or either Irish team. Hedging his bets, Paine negotiated a rider with the manager, in the form of a guaranteed £500 minimum for the 1963-64 season. The club had entered new financial territory, whereby the weekly wage could be supplemented with a fee-for-cap bonus for its international stars.

With that policy settled, the appearance money bubble soon burst. Five of the giant-killers who were on the lower rate of £5 objected and the Board agreed, at its meeting of 20 June, to extend the £10 bonus to these five and four others – this despite the concern of the Board to be able 'always to meet current expenditure from normal revenue'. Having affirmed that prudential policy, the Board was minded to

> re-emphasise the principle that money received in donations from the Supporters' Pools [abnormal revenue, so to speak] must be used only for ground improvements and the purchase of other capital items, i.e. houses or Players.

This policy statement on its capital assets is an interesting comment on the times. The efforts of Jimmy Hill and George Eastham may have ended forever the feudal imposition of a maximum wage, but it was still possible for a football club's directors to consider, as inter-changeable assets, its holdings in land and labour.

DELL DIAMOND

It also serves to remind us that the Board had so much of its capital still tied up in housing that it would let out, at low rents, to its players. More and more players would be asking, in the 1960s, to buy their house from the club, but most of this property remained, for the moment, both a way of attracting players *and* a form of competition with them, in that money spent on houses was not available for the higher wages that the emancipated players were demanding.

Requests for minor repairs to players' houses would continue to come to the Board – although, in that 1963 close season, its main landlord-tenant problem was a dispute between two of its tenants.

George Kirby could not tolerate the 'obnoxious' smell from the chickens kept by his neighbour, Cliff Huxford. The Board met Kirby's demands for a 6ft. fence between the two gardens. It is not clear how this would solve the matter for Kirby – out of sight, out of smell? – but it is illustrative of the niggles you have to spend time and money on, when you are landlord to your employees, especially if their tenancy agreements permit chickens in the garden.

If that sounds a trifle unsophisticated, the Club would sign a teenager, during that 1963-64 season, who would later be the subject of so many stories about reporting for training in dung-covered wellies.

⁓

It was in the spring of 1964 that this young man's fancy turned to Southampton. Yet it was so very nearly Swindon. The signing of a 15 year-old Wiltshire schoolboy on 1 March 1964 has become part of the Saints' folklore and, in the way of folklore, there is more than one version of what happened. What follows is an attempt to reconcile the accounts of the young signatory himself and the five adults involved – the Saints' scout, the competing managers and the boy's parents – aided by a substantial report, in the *Salisbury Times,* of how Southampton won the signature, from under Swindon's nose, of Michael Roger Channon.

Although still at school in Amesbury, Mick Channon was already playing for Shrewton United, just down the road from his home in the village of Orcheston, pretty well equi-distant between Swindon and Southampton. Bill Ellerington went to Andover's Walled Meadow to watch a midweek encounter between Hampshire Schoolboys – featuring several Saints' youths, including McCarthy and Ellard at full-back – and Wiltshire. Hampshire won 5-3 but it was the visiting inside-forwards who caught Bill's eye: 'A young lad called Binstead played inside-left for them, not very big but broad. And they had a big, *gangling* inside-right – you know, all arms and legs, floundering all over the place. But he liked to take people on. He wasn't afraid to have a go at them with the ball'. Mick Channon, aged 15.

Bert Head, the Swindon manager, was also watching. And he fancied the same two players. He was especially surprised by the sight of Channon, because he thought he already 'knew every player the [Wilts] Schools had'. He had an advantage over Ellerington, in that he could wander into the away dressing room and make enquiries of the manager: 'Why haven't *I* seen this boy before? What's his background?' He was filled in, he spoke to the lad himself and was referred to Jack Channon, who was there watching his son get two of Wiltshire's goals. Bert Head had no forms on him, but was confident that he would sign young Michael the following Monday.

He was thwarted by 'Snowy' Day of Shrewton, who alerted Ted Bates. After further consultation with Bill Ellerington, Ted dashed up to Shrewton on the Sunday, taking Tom Parker with him, to see Mr Day. He, in turn, delivered the Saints' manager and Chief Scout to the home of Mr and Mrs

ND SOUTH WILTS GAZETTE — FRIDAY, MARCH 6, 1964

SWINDON 24 HOURS TOO LATE AS TED BATES SNAPS UP MIKE CHANNON

Channon — four clubs interested

Michael Channon, the 15-year-old Shrewton inside-forward who has been getting "rave" reports all season, has been snapped up by Southampton. Manager Ted Bates and chief scout Tom Parker drove to the youngster's home at Orcheston at the week-end, discussed terms with his parents and agreed to sign him on a three-year apprentice engagement.

Less than 24 hours after the deal was completed Swindon's chief scout was on the doorstep and manager Bert Head was put off from visiting Michael on Monday evening.

Southampton became the fourth club interested in his future. Arsenal had arranged a trial for him at Highbury at Easter and Devizes Town, of the Wilts Premier League, were also making enquiries.

Michael's week of excitement, culminating in the visit of Ted Bates, started the previous Wednesday when he netted two goals and narrowly missed a hat-trick while playing for Wiltshire Schools against Hampshire Schools at Walled Meadow, Andover.

After the game his father was seen by a Swindon representative. No firm arrangements were made and Southampton, who had been interested in Channon for a long time, quickly stepped in. Tom Parker took the youngster out to lunch on Monday and he is now looking forward to May when he leaves Amesbury Secondary Modern School for his new full-time career at the Dell.

'Outstanding' sportsman

Before he goes, he told the "Salisbury Times" this week, he would like to help his school and the Salisbury and District Schools team in their league and cup fixtures. He will be 16 in November and is described by his sports master Mr. J. Copeland, as "an outstanding all-round sportsman." For his age he is a brilliant ball player and can shoot equally well with both feet.

Said a Shrewton official: "Scouts from several teams have approached him in the correct and normal manner. We are not surprised to see him go. This will be a great

Snapper Up!

The local newspaper reports on how 15 year-old Michael Channon was bought by Southampton on a Sunday – with Tom Parker returning on Monday (to create a false trail?)

(c) Registration Irregularities

Professional Registration Forms signed on a Sunday are not valid, and it is an offence for a Club to induce a player to sign on that day.

The signing of a second registration form before the Council have declared the first form invalid, is also an offence.

FA Rule 26(c), which frightened Ted Bates into believing that he couldn't sign Channon on a Sunday

Channon. Tom Parker took along his cup-winning medals to impress their son. But, to his mother's lasting embarrassment, the 15 year-old was not at all in awe of the proud history being put on show for his benefit: 'I was only interested in playing football. It didn't really matter' for whom.

The folklore generally has it that the Saints won his signature because Mick and his Dad had been going to The Dell – you may have noticed a couple of Mick's games as a supporter being reported in previous chapters – but the clinching factor appears to have been one of *timing*. Once Ted Bates was in the house, he 'wasn't going to leave', says Mick, 'until he had a signature, was he?' Bert Head would arrive on the Monday to find that the deal had been struck on the Sunday.

That Ted Bates signed Mick Channon on a Sunday is well-known. Ted admits as much in his Foreword to *The Alphabet of the Saints*. What he doesn't say, there, is that he then forged the form to make it appear that Channon had been signed on the Monday. The reason for this was a belief that the FA Rules prohibited Sunday signings. If Channon had been signed illegally, then Ted had to cover his tracks.

At first sight, it appears that such a cover-up was necessary. Rule 26(c), as then in force, states categorically that 'registration forms signed on a Sunday are not valid and it is an offence for a Club to induce a player to sign on that day'. But Rule 26 applies to *professional registrations only*. And, as Rule 26(b) prohibits such registration before the signatory's 17th birthday, Mick Channon had to be signed on amateur forms. These are governed by Rule 25 and there is nothing in this rule, that I can find, to prohibit signing on the Sabbath.

I venture to suggest, then, that Ted Bates could have been going around since 1964 thinking that he'd cheated on the FA and being ribbed to that effect whenever he met Bert Head – who's never let Ted forget it, but admits that he 'would probably have done the same' – when, all the time, there was no Never-On-A-Sunday ban of relevance to his trading in Orcheston.

As far as Jack and Betty Channon were concerned, they had entrusted their son to a most caring man. They were impressed by the way he kept in touch with them: he was 'simply the best' in Mrs Channon's book. Norman Dean tells a similar story: 'Ted was excellent with my Mum and Dad whenever they wanted to know anything'. So Ted Bates, whose mother had worried so about him going off as a teenager, to digs in Norwich, was sensitive to the needs of parents whose young sons he had enticed from their care. If you imagine it follows that he was equally concerned about the boys themselves, then Mick Channon will brusquely disabuse you: 'Ted couldn't give a shit as long as you turned up for football and played football. He was only interested in one thing – football. We were thrown into digs. Tom

Parker took us up, introduced us to Mrs Pfeiffer [the landlady] and I was on my own'.

But, then, the teenage Channon was able to focus on football, himself, so much so that he was playing for the Reserves – and scoring at Southend – come September 1964. He was 15 years and 282 days old, its being a leap year, thus breaking Chadwick's record (as charted in Chapter 16).

~

The first team, meanwhile, was in a rather featureless, transitional season. If 1963-64 had been an anti-climax to the excitement of 1962-63, then nothing much was happening in 1964-65, as Ted Bates sought the ingredients for promotion.

If it was notable for anything, it must be the resurrection of George O'Brien. Playing at No.8 with Chivers at No.9, O'Brien scored 37 goals in 45 League and Cup games, as the Saints finished fourth in the League and went out of both Cups to Crystal Palace. After the cup-tie against United the previous season, Ted had advised the Board that the condition of O'Brien's knee was 'deteriorating' and it was agreed that any bidder for his services be advised of this 'weakness'. But there were to be no more bids recorded for O'Brien – or, indeed, for any other members of this in-and-out side.

On the other hand, Ted Bates was buying. In the 1964 close season, on the recommendation of Ron Reynolds, he'd gone back to White Hart Lane to sign another Spurs' reserve, John Hollowbread, who kept Godfrey out for most of 1964-65. The quest for a Scottish 'keeper was on hold, then. And a young Scottish midfielder was refusing to succumb to a Ted Bates tour of the New Forest. Ted's old friend, Joe Mercer, having left Bramall Lane for Villa Park in 1958, was now leaving Aston Villa and 19 year-old George Graham was available from Villa for £6,000. The first 'serious approach' came from Southampton, Graham recalls in his autobiography, and he was soon being taken by Ted on one of his celebrated tours – 'of the club, the town and the countryside. An out-and-out gentleman, he was selling me Hampshire as well as the Saints'. Ted even offered him enough money, which Graham was 'all set to accept' when Tommy Docherty came in with a better deal. George Graham was lost to Chelsea.

Before the season was half gone, though, Ted had a new midfielder, as David Burnside made way for Jimmy Melia. Despite Ted's high hopes for Burnside and his being pleased that he had exceeded them in front of goal, he was disappointed with his contribution when the side was struggling: 'If he picked up the ball, he could do things with it; but, if you didn't get him into the game, you were a little bit short … He was not that sort of fellow that could work hard – he just wanted to work with the ball. It was as simple as that'.

DELL DIAMOND

Jimmy Melia was a deeper-lying schemer, who would manage only a dozen goals in his 152 appearances for the Saints. Since those games against them for Liverpool in 1960-61-62, the twice-capped Melia had moved on to Molineux. But not happily so: 'They used to play a lot of long stuff'. Ted Bates arrived to offer him some short stuff. First, though, he had to convince Melia that it was possible to have a life so far south. Jimmy will 'never forget' how Ted persuaded him to 'come down and have a look':

All the way down in the car he was so nice, so enthusiastic, so full of soccer. He knew everything about me. I couldn't believe it. He knew how many games I'd played, how many goals I'd scored, when I'd first started with Liverpool – Schoolboys. Everything! He kept chatting away and – gosh! – I've been with some bad drivers in my life, but he must be the worst.

Ted's celebrated sales technique served him better in December, then, than it had in July. Melia signed – for a new club record of £30,000. So the side that played most of 1964-65 showed three changes from the giant-killing team of two seasons earlier. Hollowbread (or Godfrey) was in for Reynolds. Hollywood was seldom giving Traynor a look-in and Melia had replaced Burnside. The attacking right-side formation of Williams, Wimshurst, Paine and O'Brien hardly missed a game, but there was an improvement of sorts in the defensive record – only 63 goals conceded. Good enough, as I say, to finish fourth as the strike-force of O'Brien (32) and Chivers (18) rattled in 50 of the team's 83 League goals.

So, if this was still not a promotion side, what remained to be done?

Chapter 20

Up the Saints – At Last!

The key to promotion lay, ironically, not in stability.

Whereas the Championship-winning side of 1960 had four ever-presents and another five players who missed four games or fewer, the squad that would at last get the Saints out of Division Two would have no ever-presents, although four of the forwards – Paine, Chivers, Melia and Sydenham – would manage from 38 to 41 games each.

The sad note – and, if you talk to the man himself, a very bitter note – is the absence from that forward count of George O'Brien. After playing in 16 of the first 18 games, and scoring 11 goals, George never played again for the Club. This time, it wasn't a question of his being dropped. He went down with hepatitis and Ted Bates struggled to replace him. Ken Wimshurst was thrust up front on a couple of occasions, but it was otherwise a matter of shuffling, experimentally, four youngsters.

Two of these would survive to play for the Club in the First Division – Fred Kemp for two seasons and Mick Channon for two spells of superstar proportions. The other two would be promotion fodder at No.9 – Tommy Spencer with three games around Easter, as the Saints took five points, despite his not scoring; and Norman Dean having 18 games for his 11 goals.

Kemp was another graduate from that Molineux academy that had already released young players like Walker and Wimshurst to The Dell. He was still only 19 when he made his debut in November 1965. As we saw in the previous chapter, Channon was only 15 when he signed for the Saints in 1964. By now 17, he made the first of his 591 starts for them on Easter Monday 1966. Dean's arrival at the Club was hinted at in Chapter 1. He was spotted in his native Corby by one of Ted Bates's Midlands scouts – Carvel White. His twin brother and he had come to The Dell in 1938, as part of Tom Parker's ploy of recruiting from Kimbolton School.

Ted's Scottish scout, Sammy Booth, had found him a young wing-half who was converted to right-back for 13 mid-season games. Like Spencer and Dean – and David Chadwick, who had four games on the wing that season – Tommy Hare would not play in Division One for the promoted side. Nor would Tommy Traynor, whose one game that season was the last of his 480 for the Club, or Stuart Williams, who was there, for 35 of those promotion-chasing games, in one full-back position or the other. The reason for their demise was the arrival, in early March from Leyton Orient, of David Webb – with a bitter George O'Brien moving in an exchange deal.

DELL DIAMOND

The other major signing during the season had been completed in December when Campbell Forsyth, a 'keeper with four Scottish caps, arrived from Kilmarnock. Ted's search for a Scot to replace the faithful Godfrey had ended – although he had to wait until Kilmarnock, the 1965 Scottish Champions, went out of the European Cup to Real Madrid.

He had arranged to intercept Forsyth at Heathrow, as the defeated Scots changed planes on the way home from Spain, but was thwarted by the conditions that delayed the first leg of their homeward journey. And there was another potential hazard: George O'Brien. He was sitting at home with his hepatitis, wishing he'd never left Scotland and generally feeling aggrieved that his career had been blown by a manager who couldn't sign defenders.

So the last thing Ted wanted, Campbell Forsyth reckons, was for him to talk to his disillusioned compatriot. 'I must have seen the New Forest about 42 times', Campbell says, as Ted had Tom Parker drive him around – all to keep him away from O'Brien: 'I wasn't allowed to speak to him. I couldn't even 'phone him in case you got hepatitis over the telephone'. As Forsyth recalls, he didn't go to meet, and train with, his new team-mates at all. At last, though, Ted had his man and, this time, Godfrey gave up and went – to Aldershot.

John Hollowbread had started the season in goal. But, in only the sixth game, he had gone the way of Ron Reynolds: he was injured against Coventry and never played again. When Huxford went in goal in that Coventry game, Wimshurst came on as substitute, the first ever to be used by Southampton. This was first season in which the 'twelfth man' was allowed to replace a team-mate during the game. Wimshurst had only 20 starts that season, thanks not so much to White as to David Walker. During the close season, the manager had gone up to Burnley and, literally, knocked on Walker's door and asked (with permission from Turf Moor, of course) if he'd like to play for Southampton. The 23 year-old Walker had been in and out of that impressive Burnley side of the early 1960s. A defensive wing-half, he would be in a few times for Huxford – Cliff actually missed the last three games of this historic season – but would more often be at No.4. Knapp was solid at No.5, until the versatile Webb had a few games there in the run-in.

And that, as they say, completes your line-up – 24 players used in a side that chopped and changed: after fielding the same XI for the first four games, the Saints did not put out an unchanged side again until 18 December. And they did so only once after that until they played the last three games unchanged. If a squad of 24 would be modest enough for today's 14-a-side game, it was a lot for a promotion-seeking side in 1966. Substitutes came on seven times.

~

So how did they do it? By a distinct improvement once they had signed Campbell Forsyth is one way of putting it. He arrived in a side with a record of W10 D3 L7. In the remaining 22 games, the record was W12 D7 L3. Alternatively, you could say that they won six of the first nine games, lost none of the last 12 and managed not to cede too much ground as they lost five times in a spell of nine games between late September and late November.

Those five autumnal setbacks included 1-0 home defeats by promotion aspirants, Manchester City and Huddersfield Town. A young City side was being re-fashioned by Ted's old friend, Joe Mercer. Having had a year away from football since leaving Aston Villa, Mercer had arrived at Maine Road, in July 1965, to revive an ailing City. Supported by another, younger Lilleshall enthusiast, Malcolm Allison, Mercer did so well that Southampton were competing, at the last, with Coventry and Huddersfield, for second place to Manchester City, the pull-away Champions.

The Saints had set off as if intent on winning the thing. A good 3-0 start at Derby – I can still see George O'Brien's flying header – was followed

Still smiling
Despite a poor autumn, Ted Bates was still looking forward to promotion

by three points at home and a first defeat at Carlisle, the only game to which I've ever taken a tent. Southampton then saw off Coventry at The Dell in a run of three wins but were 5-1 victims, in the return at Highfield Road, of the 'Sky Blue Revolution', being effected by Allison's Lilleshall contemporary, Jimmy Hill (who had long since sold on the itinerant Kirby). The next game, by comparison, saw the Saints pretty well end the managerial career of Andy Beattie. Whereas it had taken them three games to put nine goals past his Forest side in that 1963 Cup epic, it took the Saints but an hour to run up nine against Wolves, when Beattie brought them to The Dell in September 1965. He had had an unhappy spell at Molineux, taking over after the brutal dismissal (that had upset Jimmy Melia) of Stan Cullis in September 1964. He had brought Wolves back down to Division Two, the Division they had won in 1932. This was their first visit to The Dell since then.

The story of their 9-3 defeat that finished Andy Beattie as a team manager (although the illness of his wife also contributed, we're told, to his decision) has, of necessity, to be rehearsed here. Knapp opened the scoring for the visitors when he headed past Godfrey after only 35 seconds: even in epic stories, certain basics don't change. But his rampant team-mates rattled five past Dave MacLaren before half-time, with the Wolves getting one back. So 5-2 at half-time. And, before the game was an hour old, it was 9-3. The Saints, who have never managed nine in peace-time games before or since, could not satisfy the chants of 'We want Ten', as Paine and Sydenham each hit the woodwork.

'Argus' enthused, in the *Echo*, about the success of switching Jimmy Melia to a deep-lying role in the No.9 shirt. But this was not a managerial attempt to emulate either the 'Revie Plan', that Manchester City had developed in the 1950s from the Hungarian blueprint, or the Ipswich variant that we encountered in Chapter 16. The explanation was considerably more prosaic and pragmatic than that. Although he had started the season at No.9 – with four goals in six games – Chivers had moved to No.8 for two games when, with O'Brien out, Dean had come in at centre-forward. Now, with George ready to return, Martin announced that he did not want to wear the No.9 shirt. So Ted asked Jimmy if he'd mind doing so.

Melia is amused at the chaos this caused his former team-mates. In a man-marking defence, Dave Woodfield found Jimmy a hard act to follow. This created space for his fellow forwards, all four of whom scored. The Saints were top of the Division and nobody, 'Argus' contended, could 'deny that it is their rightful place'. But then, as I say, came that Autumn anti-climax. It wasn't that they were leaking goals – four of their five defeats in that run were by a 1-0 margin. They came out of it at the end of November with a 5-2 home win against Preston. That was game 19. After a draw at The Valley, the following Saturday, they were down in seventh place, five points adrift of Huddersfield, the leaders, and a point behind Wolves.

Their season, from that game against Preston until the end, had two distinct periods. In the first, a run of 11 games, Chivers scored 18 goals and

Dean eight. They shared the goals when the Saints won 5-2 at Fratton Park on 5 February. Norman Dean scored what 'Observer' described as 'the hat-trick of an opportunist'. This *Echo* reporter was impressed by the side's scoring ability away from home – they had only recently got five at Ninian Park – and suggested that 'while they can do that sort of thing they must be taken seriously for the top places'.

The bubble burst in a 1-0 home defeat by Birmingham. Wimshurst and Hare lost their places. Twelve more games to go. And they didn't lose any of them. New arrival David Webb announced himself with an overhead kick that was the only goal at Molineux and played in every game of this run-in. A bizarre feature of it was that Chivers didn't score. Having got 30 goals in the first 29 games, he had dried up. His back was troubling him, but he kept going – with the help of manipulation and cortisone from a London specialist – missing three and a bit games in a busy April schedule.

It was a strangely low-scoring run-in. Those 12 undefeated games included three 1-0 wins, four 1-1 draws and a 0-0 climax. The crunch came at Easter with two games against high-riding Bristol City. Had City won both of them, they would have gone up in second place. But an own goal handed the Saints a 1-0 win at Ashton Gate on Good Friday and the sides drew 2-2 at The Dell on Easter Monday. With Chivers's back having succumbed and with Dean also injured, Southampton fielded a young strike force that day. Tommy Spencer played his third and last game at No.9. Mick Channon made his debut at No.8 and scored the first of his 185 League goals for the Club.

Denis Hollywood chose a good moment to score his first – in a 3-2 win at Plymouth. This was the first of the three away games with which the Saints finished their season. Their final home game against Charlton was won by a Terry Paine goal from a Martin Chivers cross. A cross that ended a run from the Saints' half along the East Stand touchline. Those huge strides of Chivers gave his pursuer, a young Billy Bonds, no hope of catching him even though he appeared to be travelling so much faster. As Martin crossed and the 'keeper advanced, the ball hit Paine – Terry makes no claim to have been pro-active in this matter – and went in. A goal fit for heroes. In fact, with Chivers retired from the scoresheet, Paine got his name on it nine times in that run-in.

The last time was at Brisbane Road on Monday 9 May. Orient, who were already down, hadn't won at home since November. This was reflected in their home gates, which had dropped to under 3,000 by April. Their last three home matches, though, were against the top three sides. Coventry City and Manchester City each attracted around 6,000. But there were 19,839 there to watch the Saints. Where had they all come from? As for

Spot the Scorer
Easter Monday 1966: Debutant Mick Channon (left) scores his first goal against Bristol City.
David Webb (No.2) admires the jocular jump by Jimmy Melia, pretending to head the goal.

that quarter-final at White Hart Lane three seasons earlier, Southampton had emptied into the far side of London.

George O'Brien, who had had seven starts for Orient without scoring, was sidelined as the home side, despite their record, went ahead. Terry Paine remembers how he came to score the 52nd minute equaliser:

A fluke I think. It was a punt from Campbell Forsyth. And, as it's coming, I read it – everybody might miss it. I've got on my bike early and it's bounced. It's bounced over the top of them and I just head it and stick it in the back of the net'

Just like that. The 1-1 draw was enough for us Saints' fans to run on to the pitch. I lost my red-and-white crêpe sombrero in that jubilant mêlée. But, even as the champagne corks popped in the away dressing room, Ted Bates was telling his side that jubilation was premature. They still had to avoid a six-goal defeat at Maine Road the following Monday if they were, at the very least, to pip Coventry on goal average.

Hence Ted's declaration, as recalled by Terry Paine: 'I'm drinking champagne, but I'm not celebrating'. You can understand his caution after what he had suffered in 1949. Terry Paine was well aware of that hang-up:

when they'd played at Gigg Lane in the February, Ted had reminisced about that game at Bury in April 1949. To save you referring back to Chapter 9, Terry can recite the vital details: 'Ted had a goal disallowed. They went straight down the other end and scored'. If Terry remembers correctly, he had provoked Ted, on that occasion, by reminding him of an explanation for the demise of 1949: *they didn't want to go up.* If you've watched the video of the Saints' history, you may remember that, when Ted was interviewed after the Leyton Orient game, he was still referring to that folklore of '49.

Terry admired Ted's caution – it was so 'professional', but the town was not joining in. With 'everybody celebrating around the town', John Sydenham found it a 'weird sort of time … Everywhere you're going, everyone wanted to give you a drink and celebrate, but you had this nagging thought in the back of your mind that, if you got beat 6-0, it would be all over'. Some of the triumphant Manchester City players added to the tension by hanging around, at Maine Road, to greet their visitors: 'All these guys were standing in the corridor and they were having a laugh and a joke with us about this 6-0 thing'.

But, as the game went on, 'it didn't look' to Sydenham 'as if any team was going to score any goals … It was a great feeling – it was obvious we weren't going to be beaten by 6-0, anyway. The last half hour of that game, everybody's got a smile on their face'. A goalless draw against Mercer's champions meant that the Saints finished second, a point clear of Coventry.

Ted Bates was in the First Division – an experience his father had had before he was born and which had been snatched from Ted himself in that woeful run-in of 1949.

Terry signs off
Terry Paine scores his last Second Division goal for Southampton at Leyton Orient.

TEAMS AND OFFICIALS FOR THIS MATCH

FOOTBALL LEAGUE DIVISION 1

SATURDAY 20 AUGUST 1966

SOUTHAMPTON v. MANCHESTER C.

Red and White Striped Shirts, Black Shorts		Sky Blue Shirts and Shorts
CAMPBELL FORSYTH S	1	HARRY DOWD
DAVID WEBB	2	TONY BOOK
DENIS HOLLYWOOD	3	BOBBY KENNEDY S
IAN WHITE	4	GLYN PARDOE
TONY KNAPP Capt.	5	GEORGE HESLOP
DAVID WALKER	6	ALAN OAKES
TERRY PAINE E	7	MICHAEL SUMMERBEE
MARTIN CHIVERS	8	COLIN BELL
RON DAVIES W	9	JIMMY MURRAY
JIMMY MELIA E	10	JOHN CROSSAN I
JOHN SYDENHAM	11	NEIL YOUNG
Cliff Huxford	substitute	David Connor

OFFICIALS

Referee: Mr. P. BYE (Bedford)

Linesmen: Mr. K. G. G. Gollop (Red Flag)
Mr. G. F. Keep (Yellow Flag)

GOALSCORERS

			(4)
	(1)		(5)
(1)	(4)	(2)	(6)
(2)	(5)	(3)
(3)	(6)		Full-Time Score

Half-Time Score

NEXT HOME MATCHES

Wednesday 24th August 1966, Kick-off 6.15 p.m. Football Combination

PETERBOROUGH

Wednesday 31st August 1966, Kick-off 7.30 p.m. League Division 1

SUNDERLAND

3

Terry signs on
Terry Paine scores his first
First Division goal for
Southampton against
Manchester City.

Chapter 21

Headcase

The Saints started their first season at the top as they had finished the previous one: by playing Manchester City.

Terry Paine also started as he had left off. Having headed in the Saints' last goal in Division II, he scored their first-ever goal in the First Division when the Saints drew 1-1, at The Dell, with their promotion companions.

In the meantime, he'd played for England in the World Cup Finals. Not the final itself, of course: having given Connelly, Paine and Callaghan a game each in the group matches, Alf Ramsey went wingless for the subsequent rounds.

In fact, Terry's England career was over. No more partnering Jimmy Greaves as a prolific goalscoring pair. And he'd have no George O'Brien to 'assist', either, as the Saints kicked off in Division I. But he had a new target to aim at in the six-yard box. And how!

During the summer, Ted Bates had been looking for a new striker to get on the end of Paine's crosses. He cut it fine. On 1 August, he told the Board that Chelsea were asking £80,000 for Bobby Tambling. Still only 24, Tambling had been scoring freely in the First Division and had England caps to his name. At the same Board meeting, though, Ted reported that he had a cheaper alternative in mind – a Second Division centre-forward, of the same age, for whom he had offered £50,000.

When the Board met again on 11 August, it heard that Ted Bates had had to go to £55,000 to bring Ron Davies from Norwich City. Davies had already won five Welsh caps. In 1964-65, his first season at Carrow Road, he had been, according to *The People,* 'Soccer's most wanted man' but Norwich weren't selling. By the middle of 1965-66, however, they were ready to deal. A move to a First Division club looked on the cards – Davies had no preference, provided he could step up a flight – which meant, of course, that Ted Bates could not enter the ring until he'd won promotion.

The Norwich fans were understandably unhappy to be losing their leading goalscorer. Among the writers to the local 'paper, a Mr V.H. Wright from Ted's home town of Thetford, predicted an 'avalanche of criticism', but wished 'Good Luck to Ron Davies' on his step up. Ted, for his part, was predicting that Davies would 'fit in well with our present set-up'. He told the *Echo* that Davies was 'particularly good in the air'. If that was so, he'd noticed something that some of his players had missed. Terry Paine says he can't remember Davies doing anything at all when the Saints played

Norwich four times in 1964-65-66. In fact, he'd scored twice, but Ken Wimshurst's recall is of a player who dropped so deep that he found himself marking him.

There is a degree of truth in the Wimshurst recall. Ron Davies fancied himself more as a centre-forward who dropped back to feed his line, *to lead* his line, than as the far post header for which he was to win such renown at The Dell. Indeed, when fans and team-mates rave about his heading, Ron takes it as back-handed compliment. He was good on the ground, too, and liked to have the ball played up to his feet for him to hold and spray – in the manner we associate more with Osgood or Worthington, say.

Ted Bates and Terry Paine soon made it clear, though, that they wanted less of that. Terry gives 'great credit' to Ted for having foreseen how Davies would fit in: 'He knew what he wanted. He knew how he wanted his teams to play. And when he bought him, that was a stroke of genius'.

~

If you never saw Ron Davies soaring to head home a Paine cross, you may wonder if Terry is exaggerating. So listen to Alec Stock on the matter: 'Ted – a great *buyer!* I envy him the Davies buy. How do you buy a striker like that? You say "Well played, mate!" You think "Where did he get him from?"'

There are, in fact, two stages to Alec Stock's test of a 'great buyer' and Ted Bates can surely be said to have succeeded brilliantly at both of them. First, he had learned his stuff, in Division III, buying on nothing. Bill Ellerington remembers how 'each month a thing comes round, from the Football League or the FA, people who can be bought and for how much. We used to go straight to the back of the book – people to be picked up on a free transfer: "*He* might be good" – and off we'd go and look and bring our reports back'.

That's the kind of basement bargaining to which Alec Stock is referring when he reflects, in his autobiography, that 'being poor makes you choosy': without money, you have to rely on 'a mixture of judgment, luck and bargains'. It seems to be widely acknowledged that Ted's 'luck' in this regard included being able to rely upon the 'judgment' of Bill Ellerington. Terry Paine held it in very high regard: 'Bill Ellerington was the *best* judge of a player there's ever been on the managerial staff' – which is why, when he went to Hereford as player-coach, he called upon that knowledge: 'Bill Ellerington was brilliant!'

We have already seen, in Chapter 14, how Bill's assessment of George O'Brien prepared the way for Ted to satisfy Alec Stock's second criterion: how to buy a player who performs better in your system than he had hitherto. The blossoming of Ron Davies would *prove* the point, as Stock generously acknowledges:

That's the point! There are managers – Cloughie was one – who take players and improve them. Davies couldn't do so badly between those two wingers, could he? Paine just taking them down and crossing them … You see, you are supposed to improve players, aren't you?

The 'improvement' of Ron Davies required him to know his place – at the far stick. Paine would supply the crosses. And so, Davies is quick to stress, would Sydenham. All it needed was for Ron to discover just what a 'leaping ability' he had. Ted Bates had found a centre-forward to suit his wingers, but Davies acknowledges, in turn, his good fortune, to have found a system that suited the ability he never knew he had:

I was very lucky. A lot of players go to clubs that don't suit … The system suited me. I never even thought I was so good in the air. It just developed – blossomed – cos we had two great wingers … I had John Sydenham on the left and Painie on the right. Painie was the best crosser of the ball – the best winger – I've ever played with in my life. All the goals I scored, I give to him – because of his ability.

The admiration was mutual. Paine is unequivocal: 'He's the best I've ever seen in the air. You can take your Tommy Lawtons – you can take whoever you want. I mean, the height that he could get!' And Sydenham, a less accurate crosser of the ball than Paine, found Davies the perfect target. Not only was he 'the greatest header of the ball The Dell's ever seen – the greatest centre-forward in Europe', even – but 'one of the great things with Ron Davies was that, even when maybe you weren't 100 per cent accurate, Ron had the great ability to make your crosses into good ones'. That knack of timing his run and leap, and twisting his neck to convert a miscued cross into a goal-scoring opportunity, was appreciated even by the more precise Paine: 'You could lay the ball into areas and know that he was going to contest the ball. That was the beauty about Ron. You didn't have to pick him out'.

It took a few games for the three of them to get the hang of it – literally so in Ron's case, of course. Then, when he opened his account in the third game – a 3-2 win at Bloomfield Road – it was with a lob over Tony Waiters: 'The keeper came off his line – way out of the box. I was 35 yards out and I couldn't believe it. I just knocked it over his head'. In the next game against Sunderland, he scored his first home goal – 'a very memorable goal' for 'Observer' – following a solo run. Roy Peskett, another of its admirers, issued an early warning: Chivers and Davies may not yet have 'clicked together. But it will come, and goalkeepers had better take out extra insurance!'

It is timely to mention Martin Chivers here. It is easy, when analysing how Davies functioned between two wingers, to leave Chivers – to say nothing of Melia – out of the equation. Martin found himself learning to become 'more of a near post merchant, because Ron was dynamic on the farpost. He was the perfect foil for me. He would knock the ball down to me. They were frightened out of their life of Ron Davies. They couldn't mark both of us. It gave me a lot of space'. Davies reciprocates: 'It was good because Martin could control a ball well. He could play one-twos with me and we were good decoys for each other'. It was that capacity for one-twos that led Ron to prefer partnering Chivers to Channon. Martin can appreciate why Ron felt this: 'I think probably I would put him in more than Mike would. Channon probably held onto the ball longer than I did. I complemented Ron as much as he complemented me'.

We can return – in Chapter 23, with Channon in full flow – to the question of the way Ted required Davies to play with him. It was a way that would have Channon outscoring Davies, whereas the method in 1966-67 would produce 43 goals for Davies and 18 for Chivers – Martin's lowest total since he had won a regular place. However you look at it, his scoring potential had been sacrificed a little for the sake of 'complementing' Davies. But an aggregate of 61 for two strikers is some total for newcomers to Division I. It underlines what Chivers says about the importance of a scoring 'partnership' – which he would later repeat, at White Hart Lane, with Alan Gilzean.

It's a different picture of Martin's contribution to the team than the one painted by George O'Brien. 'If we scored, say, four and he didn't score, he'd be first in the bath. He wasn't too happy. If you got beat 4-3 and Chivers scored three, he'd be delighted'. If that sounds like a bitter exaggeration from the cynical O'Brien, Martin's good friend, Norman Dean, can see a grain of truth in it, in so far as Martin 'did actually feel, I think, that if he didn't score, he didn't have a good game'. And remember what Chivers said on the video of the Saints' history: 'All I wanted to do was to score goals'. Ask him today how selfish he was and he'll tell you that 'all goalscorers *are*'.

All of which speaks volumes for how Chivers adjusted to being a 'foil' to Ron Davies and becoming 'a nearpost merchant'. And there was nobody to take up David Burnside's scoring 'position three' that he described at length in Chapter 18. Jimmy Melia was 'a linker', Terry Paine explains, who didn't get into the penalty area as often as Burnside had. In place of the traditional inside-forward role that Burnside had performed – hit a 30-yard ball to your winger and get yourself into a scoring position – 'Jim was a 10-yard merchant: give it, get it back; give it; get it back'. But, then, it hardly mattered if you had a strike force capable of scoring 61 goals.

Ron Davies didn't let Roy Peskett down. After the Saints failed to score at all against Chelsea – the *only* side that kept Davies goalless all season – Ron's was the only goal at Villa Park. The first ever by a Southampton player on that ground, it was again with the boot. His feet were now leading his head 3-0. In the next game, at Filbert Street, he put his first headed goal for the Saints past Gordon Banks. The *Echo* claimed that 'Ted Bates was particularly pleased because one of the factors which influenced him in signing Davies was the knowledge that he was a specially useful header of the ball'.

Ron was now on a roll. With the goal at Villa Park on 5 September, he started a run of scoring in 10 consecutive League games. And, for good measure, he threw in a hat-trick against Plymouth in the League Cup. The *Echo* rejoiced in the two from 'really class headers', one of them coming from one of 'many examples of Paine's deadly accuracy in placing the ball'. So *this* was what Ted Bates had had in mind?

Ron had a chance to remind everybody of his versatility – he could *still* come deep and do the business – when he played for Wales in November. Wyn Davies had recently signed for Newcastle, who'd led the bidding for Ron before Ted Bates snatched him from Norwich. He played in front of Ron in Wales's 5-1 defeat by England – telling proof for Roger Malone, in the *Daily Telegraph,* of Ron's 'range of ability – frontal spearhead for his club, raider more from behind for his country'. When Southampton entertained Newcastle at The Dell a few weeks later, there were inevitable references to 'the battle of the Davieses'. Ron won – with the *Daily Telegraph* and the *Echo* giving due credit to Tony Knapp's role in the suppression of Wyn. It was 3 December and Ron had now scored in every League game bar one – the 4-1 defeat at Burnley after his 10-match run – since 5 September.

Apart from a barren six-week spell in February and March – assuming you don't count scoring in a friendly at Portsmouth – Davies kept on getting goals. They included three hat-tricks in the New Year, starting with one past Gordon Banks in a 4-4 draw with Leicester in January. In April, the Saints took revenge on Burnley with a 4-0 win at The Dell. Ron's first goal was headed in from a right-wing cross by Denis Hollywood, who was making a rare appearance at right-back and who added the second goal himself. Ralph Hadley said that 'great [was] the only word' for this header.

Really? Henry Blofeld told *his* readers that it was 'glorious' and that the hat-trick merited the freedom of the city. Ron's other two goals also came from right-wing crosses, despite the appearance, at left-back for the visitors, of Dave Merrington. But, then, Merrington feels it unfair that Burnley had to come to The Dell at a warm time of the year. Brian O'Neil, who was missing after a Fairs Cup injury in Frankfurt, makes a similar point: 'every time Burnley played at The Dell, it was always red hot. It was *so* different, weather-wise, from up north'.

And it was even worse, it seems, when Aston Villa came to The Dell for Ron to round off with a four-goal finale in his side's 6-2 win. Lew Chatterley, at right-half for the visitors that May afternoon, remembers how they walked up from the station in the sweltering sunshine to find the heating on and the windows shut in the away dressing room – a warm-up, literally, for the drubbing that awaited them. Ron went into that last game with 39 League and Cup goals – with his head now leading his feet by 20:19. All four against Villa came from his right foot, including a penalty.

LEADING SCORERS

Leading League and Cup goalscorers:
DIVISION 1

| | | | | FA | Lg. | |
			L	Cp	Cp	T
Davies (Southampton)	....		37	3	3	43
Hurst (West Ham)	....		29	3	9	41
Greaves (Tottenham)	......		25	6	0	31
Clarke (Fulham)	....		24	3	2	29
Clark (West Bromwich)	....		19	1	8	28
Tambling (Chelsea)	....		21	5	1	27
Law (Manchester Utd.)	....		23	2	0	25
Martin (Sunderland)	....		19	6	0	25
Chivers (Southampton)	....		22	2	2	24

So that meant a win for the boot, contrary to our image of the soaring Davies, by 23 goals to 20. No matter – it meant a total of 43. Ron was the top-scorer in the Division – and, indeed, the entire Football League – with 37 from 41 games in the First Division, plus another six in as many cup-ties.

～

Aston Villa went down. So did Blackpool – although they did rather better than Villa when they came to The Dell on New Year's Eve, recording their only away win of the season by the resounding margin of 5-1. Fans writing into the *Echo* blamed the manager's experiment with man-for-man marking. So does Ron Davies: 'We were all over the place – like a circus'. Hugh Fisher, the visitors' ring-master in that game, would not go down with them. Ted Bates signed him two months later. 'I was like that', Ted explains:

> *Most of the players I got were people that I'd seen that we'd played against. You look at them and you think 'Yeah! He'd fit into my team'. I used to like to* feel *they'd fit into my team – not get them and* hope *they would. Who was it didn't do enough for me? Not many!*

Preston North End helped Ted to make up his mind that he wanted to buy Fisher from their neighbours. In the week after that Blackpool game, he told the Board that he would like to get Howard Kendall from Second Division Preston. It was when Preston turned down an offer of £75,000 –

some measure of the coup in acquiring Davies for £55,000 – that Ted turned his attention to Fisher. He got him for only £28,500.

Hughie would make the right-half spot his – give or take a cartilage injury, Fred Kemp and a broken leg. Bye bye, Wimshurst – give or take one more appearance as sub' the following season. Ian White was already out of the frame. So Fisher, another Glaswegian, arrived in a first team squad that had just one outfield Scot – Denis Hollywood – but three Scottish 'keepers. Ted actually fielded all three of them in this first season at the top.

Campbell Forsyth started the campaign in possession but he broke his leg – or, to be more accurate, Hollywood broke it for him – in the eighth game, against Liverpool at The Dell. Ted had a young reserve – in fact, he would give the 20 year-old Gerry Gurr his debut later that season – but he felt the need for experience. The nationals speculated that he would turn to White Hart Lane again – for Bill Brown – or to Old Trafford where there was suddenly a surfeit of 'keepers: having made his debut for Chelsea at The Dell, two weeks earlier, Alex Stepney had promptly joined Manchester United. Ted confounded the speculators, however, by swooping, once more, on Molineux to buy another Scot.

Welcome back, Dave MacLaren! Never mind what Jimmy Greaves might have said on the subject of playing three Scottish 'keepers in one season, what price buying one who'd let in nine against you a year earlier? An obvious joke, even if it's at odds with the facts. According to 'Argus', the Saints had put nine past Wolves, *despite* 'several superb saves' by MacLaren, who was 'magnificent in defeat'. He was magnificent, too, on 29 October when the Saints went to Elland Road, where the *Echo* acclaimed him as 'the hero of the match'. As Revie's formidable side warmed up, we were told over the PA that it was Norman Hunter's birthday. MacLaren must have thought it was his.

Two team-mates who especially appreciated his performance were returning to their Yorkshire roots. Ken Jones – who had an 'excellent match' himself, according to 'Observer' – had come to The Dell from Bradford Park Avenue in the 1965 close season. He had had only eight games, in four spells, during the promotion campaign. Able to play either right- or left-back, he was in for his First Division baptism in place of Hollywood: 'I only lived seven miles from Elland Road and to go back up there and win 1-0! But, in all honesty, a fair result would have been 10-1. No matter what MacLaren did, he did right. It hit his arms, legs, crossbar, post … It was unbelievable. We just absolutely got annihilated and how we ever won 1-0!'

David Thompson, playing his second game on the left-wing, agrees. When David Chadwick had been let go at last, in the 1966 close season to Middlesbrough, Ted Bates had raided the Molineux academy, yet again, for

Otley-born Thompson: 'It were a great day for me, to come up to Leeds – all my family were there – and to beat Leeds … Dave didn't know what was happening that day, did he? He'd dive one way and it would hit his legs and that. We should have been about 10-0 down in that game'.

It was a Thompson corner that produced the only goal. Ron Davies salmoned up, way above Jack Charlton, to head it home. As Jim Lawton memorably put it for his readers, 'Ted Bates's men lifted piracy to the level of respectable entertainment'. And Ted unashamedly ran onto the pitch at the end to congratulate his 'keeper. He did the same again when his side got their next away win in March. But this time, the object of his praise was Eric Martin, a 20 year-old 'keeper, signed from Dunfermline in time to make his debut, along with Fisher, in a 1-0 win.

Everton also fielded a new wing-half that afternoon. Howard Kendall had been released by Preston, after all, for £85,000. Harry Catterick, the Everton manager, was willing, in turn, to sell Jimmy Gabriel. Ted Bates had flown to Liverpool that week in a bid to sign him but told the *Echo* that the Scottish international was unwilling to 'move as far south as Hampshire'.

Fisher, nursing an ankle injury, had had a couple of weeks to settle in but Martin was rather rushed into action. On 9 March, only nine days before the Everton game, the Board was receiving the manager's report by 'phone: he was in Dundee, hoping to sign United's goalkeeper, Sandy Davie. Ted would eventually secure Davie's signature, but not until May 1970. In March 1967, he missed him and switched his attention to Martin, who flew down to Southampton on 16 March. If he were to play at Goodison Park two days later, then the manager needed to put him through his paces that Thursday afternoon. Eric thought this might take five or ten minutes, but Ted was more thorough than that:

> *Phew! The guy was nuts! He had me out there for an hour and a half, diving around – with no long pants. There was no grass on the field. I was all cut and everything. He just kept knocking these balls. I guess he just wanted to see whether I was fit or not … Phew! An hour and a half!*

Eric passed that test and went on to impress 'Observer', on the Saturday, with 'about the best display of goalkeeping' he had 'seen in the Saints' side for quite a long time'. And Brian Stanley, having likened his 'firmness and poise' to that of Frank Swift, awarded Martin 10 out of 10.

That's four points more than Everton's Alex Young, the Scottish international inside-forward who was a 'hero' of Martin's. Ted Bates had deputed his outside-left to 'stop him playing'. David Thompson considered himself 'a natural right-winger'. But where have we heard that before? With

Eric Day and then Terry Paine monopolising the No.7 shirt for the best part of 30 years, a succession of understudies had to be prepared to wear the No.11 shirt if they wanted the occasional game. And, in Thompson's case, he was expected to wear it 'to do a job', tracking back in the fashion of Harry Penk – especially away from home – to curb the likes of Alex Young. David didn't mind the role. 'I was pretty mobile … The easiest job in football, if you're fairly fit, is to mark a player out of the game'.

~

Martin Chivers got the only goal at Goodison Park – his 100th for the Club. After three defeats on the trot, it was a win on the way to safety – just. Which meant the Saints could keep Ron Davies, who was being endlessly cited, during the last few weeks of the season, as saying that he'd leave if the side went down. Ron allegedly told Ralph Hadley of *The People* that he'd 'jump over the moon [to] join a top First Division club', while his Chester-born wife, Sylvia, was quoted as saying that she wanted to return north: 'I wish Ron were playing for a Lancashire club'. How fortunate for Manchester United who were 'hunting everywhere' to replace David Herd, who had just broken a leg.

"WHEN DID MR. BATES REALISE YOU WERE A JOURNALIST ?"

The Club retaliated by formally complaining to Hadley's editor about his 'unethical conduct and breach of facilities granted' to him and by withdrawing those facilities forthwith. And Ted Bates used his regular *Echo* column to launch an attack on football reporting in the national press, the 'virulent' nature of which he distinguished from that of a 'fair and factual' local media:

> *The National reporter is usually looking for scandal and sensation. Some are unethical and abuse the Press privileges they receive from clubs, setting up statements of transfer requests, waiting about in passages, gaining conversational interviews with players, who are in various frames of mind after a game, distorting the facts and remarks to suit themselves. This is done blatantly. They will quote players and managers on words they are supposed to have said. I often wonder whether their object is rather to destroy the image of the game in the public eye, than lift it up.*

That didn't stop him recommending that Davies be disciplined and the Board fined him £10. It wouldn't be the last time, alas: 'They used to fine me for everything', Ron says, even though he was 'pretty good: I was never late for training. I was pretty disciplined'. Part of his problem was that he 'used to go golfing with the press' and would make the mistake of trusting them. Ron would say things like 'I'm just out to improve myself. I want to play for the best club in the land and if I have a chance to, I'll go'. All very matter of fact, but 'you know what it is talking to press people: they'll change your words and make you look like the biggest liar in the world'.

But the question of whether Ron Davies was willing to return to the Second Division was on hold – thanks to those last 11 games with Eric Martin in goal. Taking 11 points from that run-in, the Saints finished 19th. They scored, remarkably, 74 goals – only 10 fewer than Manchester United who won the Championship and 10 *more than* Nottingham Forest, the runners-up.

The trouble was the 92 goals conceded – easily the worst deficit in the Division. Something would have to be done about that defence.

Chapter 22

A New Order

So, the Saints were still in the First Division. Ron Davies was still their centre-forward in that 1967-68 season. And Ron Davies was still the top-scorer in the Division.

True, he had to settle for a mere 28 goals and share the honour with George Best. He'd started well enough, with nine in the first five games, including four in a 6-2 win at Stamford Bridge. Chelsea may have been alone in stemming his flow the previous season, but this time Ron pooped Pete's party. Returning from a broken leg, Peter Osgood scored both Chelsea goals, including a solo effort that took him through the entire Saints defence and around Campbell Forsyth. His manager, Tommy Docherty, had never 'seen a better goal', but Davies still grabbed the headlines. Osgood has no argument with that. 'Great player, wasn't he?', he asks rhetorically, as he enthuses about Ron's ability 'just to hang in the air, there. He'd get up there about five minutes before the ball was coming and say "Just stick it there and I'll knock it in for you". Unbelievable!'

Ron hung in the air – how the photographers must have loved him! – to head two of his four that afternoon. As you can see *(right)*, Peter Bonetti didn't want to hang out with him: 'He stayed on his line. Thanks, Bonetti! Whoosh!' Davies got another two when Chelsea came to The Dell in January – although Chelsea had the last laugh with a 5-3 win. Two eight-goal games against the same opponents: shades of Sheffield United in 1952-53 – although the Saints weren't being relegated this time.

And yet they scored fewer goals – 66 – than in that relegation season, fewer, in fact, than in any season since 1951-52. Conversely, though, their defensive record improved slightly – from 92 goals conceded in 1967 to 83 in 1968. This shift was achieved, in part, by sacrificing the left-winger. If you were paying scrupulous attention in Chapter 16, you will remember how Ted Bates had compromised slightly with his trust in two out-and-out wingers when he bought Harry Penk, who would tackle back in earnest. That change was forced upon Ted, though, by the need to replace

Sydenham, while he did his National Service. You may further recollect, from the previous chapter, that David Thompson had now been charged with a Penk-like role, again at the expense of Sydenham.

Thompson had been in digs with Jimmy Melia at Wolverhampton and believes that 'Jimmy put a word in' when he realised that Ted was 'looking for that sort of player'. Indeed he was. But it didn't work out. Thompson got a few runs in 1966-67 – with a part to play, you may remember, in the wins at Leeds and Everton – but he feels his belief in his ability to fulfil Ted Bates's expectations would have been boosted by scoring: 'probably if I'd got a goal early on, it would have given me a bit of confidence'.

David never did score for the Saints, though, in his four seasons at The Dell. He played only 21 League games and a cup-tie or two. This was only partly because Sydenham kept bouncing back – in fact, Thompson outlasted him – and owed more to Ted's later ploy of dispensing with a left-winger entirely and playing an extra midfielder, 'patrolling' in front of the back four. That's the word that David Walker uses for it today. When he was performing that role, they told him he was 'marauding'. I can remember my feeling of *loss,* surrender almost, when I first saw him wearing the No.11 shirt. That must have been at Stoke in October 1968 – but, in the initial 1967-68 experiment, the defender at No.11 would be Jimmy Gabriel.

The versatile Gabriel had decided to come south, after all, in the 1967 close season. Although he didn't feel he 'had an earthly with him', Ted had persevered. Still only 26, Jimmy had played over 250 times for Everton and had won two Scottish caps. Having appeared a similar number of times for Southampton, Tony Knapp moved on to Coventry. Gabriel started the 1967-68 season at centre-half – until he had that experimental flurry at No.11, when David Webb moved to No.5. Gabriel's stay at centre-half ended dramatically when Leicester City won 5-1 at The Dell in October.

It's a game that led Jimmy Martin of the *Leicester Mercury* to applaud an act of considerable sportsmanship by Terry Paine. When Richie Norman, the Leicester left-back, was pulled up by referee Gow for a foul on Paine, he made as if to book him. Terry pleaded 'it was an accident' and Mr Gow put his book away. Had nobody told this reporter (or the referee, for that matter) that Paine's reputation depended upon nobody being able to do him *deliberately?* It is, of course, Campbell Forsyth's reputation that suffered most, though, from this game. Peter Shilton scored Leicester's fifth goal with a clearance from his own penalty area.

Reminiscing for the video of the Saints' history, Shilton attributes this 'complete fluke' to the wind. So do reporters generally, but Forsyth blames Len Stansbridge. Since we last encountered Len, as a goalkeeper in the early chapters, he had become the groundsman at The Dell in 1962. And a perfectionist, Campbell claims, who 'had to *paint* the lines: we had the best lines in the First Division'. Len's hand-painted lines were hard lines – not only literally but, in the case of the Shilton goal, metaphorically for Forsyth. According to Campbell, the ball hit one of Stansbridge's 'hard-baked, painted lines and it *shot*'. Nice try, Campbell, but the video evidence appears to be against you. Watch the Saints' video again and try convincing me that the ball bounces anywhere near any line. A case of wind assistance, I'd say.

Whatever the reason, the goal didn't help a 'keeper who was trying to regain his confidence after that broken leg the season before. His 'confidence was shattered'. Ted and 'the rest of the guys' were sympathetic, but Forsyth would have only eight more games. His last match was that 5-3 home defeat by Chelsea in January.

~

This was also the end for Martin Chivers, who was leaving for Spurs. He had had 'itchy feet' for some time and had asked for a transfer just before the final promotion game. But then he got into the new format with Davies and wondered whether he really wanted to leave: 'It's not an easy thing to do when you're a local boy. I had all my family there'. And Terry Paine had, after all, played all those games for England while he had remained at Southampton. It was playing for the Football League in Dublin in November – when he scored a hat-trick in a 7-2 win – that extended his ambition, he says. Jimmy Greaves, who had to settle for just the one goal on that occasion, talked to him about Tottenham's needs and reporters weighed in with their thoughts that 'Spurs desperately need a player like you'.

His departure was bad news for Ron Davies, whose enjoyment of their one-twos was conveyed in the previous chapter: 'If Chivers had stayed, I think I would have scored a lot more goals'. Support for that view comes from an admiring opponent. For Manchester City's Mike Summerbee, that Davies-Chivers partnership was 'as good as anything you could come across':

Davies was superb. Very under-rated on the ground. When Martin went to Tottenham, I don't think he was as good as when he was working alongside Davies. They had that rapport. When he played alongside Gilzean, it worked sometimes but you'd have a helluva job to find a strike-force like [Chivers and Davies], because they could both play on the ground. It wasn't solely air-power – they had good control and you had the service from the two wingers coming in. You try and value those players today!

This assessment raises two points that need to be addressed. First, Davies *could* do it on the ground. John Sydenham was a convert to that belief. Unlike Paine and Wimshurst, he had thought of Ron as mainly a header of goals and 'useless on the ground'. And that had been the general view, as he recalls, when the news of the Davies signing reached the team on their tour of Holland and Germany. But John came to appreciate Ron as 'one of the greatest players as a *target* man. He just used to come back; lay it off; studs flying up the back of him. His control was good'.

Secondly, what of Summerbee's comparison of Chivers's two partners? Martin won't be drawn. But, regardless of whether he functioned better with Gilzean or with Davies, so many of Martin's team-mates contend that, rather like Alf Ramsey, Martin flourished *with* Spurs – and had 24 caps for England to show for the improvement in his game. That development would confound his critics at The Dell who felt that he especially needed to use his weight more and put himself about a bit.

Terry Paine was puzzled that a player of such 'magnificent' physique 'always left you that doubt whether he really wanted it enough'. Norman Dean, who was like a 'brother' to him, Martin claims, told him 'many a time' – when they were rooming together at the home of Martin's parents and discussing the next day's opponents – that he should 'get stuck in'. Norman especially remembers when Coventry were due at The Dell and Martin was apprehensive about the attentions of George Curtis: 'They used to call him "The Pig" ... I say to him "You're big enough. Get in there". That's what we used to say: "Never mind the centre-halves: you're just as big as them". But he didn't put himself about. He was a bit timid, maybe'.

Ted Bates 'used to get onto him about it' and urged Martin to 'become more aggressive'. Chivers had taken him too seriously and got sent off at Selhurst Park, in the promotion season. 'Alan Stephenson was kicking lumps out of me from the kick-off', he recalls, 'so I whacked him round the ankles from behind and, sure enough, the linesman saw it and off I went. I learned, from that, that I can't be discreet in tackling anyone'.

What Martin didn't learn was how to be more robust: 'You can't put that nasty streak into anyone', he says. As recently as September 1998, Norman Hunter was telling a pre-match gathering at White Hart Lane how 'great' a player Chivers would have been for Spurs, if only he had acquired 'a mean streak'.

If Tottenham couldn't inject that 'devil', it seems to be agreed that Bill Nicholson got him to do more than many of his Southampton team-mates would have expected. But not immediately. Paine can remember Nicholson asking him 'How do you get this fellow to run towards his opponents' goal?' Yet, if Spurs had initially 'found a problem with him', Paine reflects that Chivers 'went on and made a success of the Tottenham move, played for England and scored some great goals. He may have just found that little missing link when he went there, I don't know'.

And who does? And *could* Ted Bates have helped Martin to find it at The Dell? Ted feels Martin did acquire more aggression with Spurs and has 'the greatest admiration' for the way he did so and 'became a really terrific player: if he'd had the aggression when he finished up with me, he wouldn't have left Southampton, I tell you – because he was the only *good* player I ever let go'.

When Chivers was placed on the transfer list in December 1967, Len Shipman, the Football League President was quoted, in the *Daily Telegraph,* as finding the fee of £125,000 to be 'too ridiculous for words'. But that paper's Donald Saunders approved of 'the shrewdest observation' on the subject, coming from Ted Bates, that 'you pay not for ability, but for the shortage of ability'. Strikers were at a premium. Tony Hateley, Mick Jones and Alan Birchenall had each fetched £100,000 of late and Saunders rated Chivers superior to any of them.

Ted Bates used his *Echo* column to re-inforce his point that 'every player has his price, so too has every club, whose responsibility it is to decide on a particular player's football value to the team'. He also took a swing, though, at players who made transfer requests 'through the national press … in an unprofessional way' and regretted that 'loyalty is a fast-receding quality in life. Football is no exception'.

Sad words from a manager on the verge of a unique setback – by his own reckoning – of selling one of his 'good' players. But which clubs had, in Ted's terms, a 'shortage of ability' upfront and a sufficiency of money to fill it with Chivers? The nationals made Stoke City, Arsenal and Spurs the front-runners. Reporters universally speculated that Southampton would get £80,000 and at least one player in part-exchange. Ted Bates was said to have asked Stoke for Gordon Banks, while Bertie Mee was allegedly willing to offload Ian Ure. And Southampton could seemingly take their pick from a hacks' *smörgasbord,* at White Hart Lane, of Terry Venables, Cliff Jones, Alan Gilzean, Phil Beal and Frank Saul. As it narrowed down to Beal or Saul, much was made of Ted Bates flying back from a Scottish scouting trip – the New Year matches were something of a market day for managers from the Football League – with the Spurs manager. But Ted had regularly met Bill Nicholson and Arsenal's Bertie Mee on expeditions to Scotland and Nicholson 'had been on about Martin' for some time.

FRANK SAUL

Eventually, then, it was Tottenham. And it was Frank Saul – and £80,000 – who came to The Dell. Ted says he had Channon coming through and 'there was no way' he could have played both Channon and Chivers alongside Davies. So why on earth accept, in part-exchange, an inside-forward whom he describes as 'really a bit make-weight'? Wasn't there a greater need for a defender? It wasn't that simple for Ted Bates:

> *I thought Frank might do a job for me. Remember Michael was sort of feeling his way, then … I was sure that, if I wanted it, Michael would do it. He was the one I wanted to go in with Davies. Frank had to be part of the deal if I wanted it to go through. But Frank wasn't quite good enough, was he? He was a decent lad. He plodded around a bit.*

What's more, Channon himself can see the sense of Ted's caution: 'Because I was a little bit of a hothead, he wanted a bit of stability as well. He was always worried about my inexperience. He was a cautious man and liked to be a little bit solid'.

In fact, Ted came up with a formation that accommodated both Channon and Saul in a front three, with Frank effectively replacing either Melia or Sydenham. Whatever else this may have achieved, it wasn't League goals from Saul: he managed only two in 49 starts. Yet, as befits a man who had scored in the 1967 FA Cup Final, his 14 cup-ties for the Saints produced 10 goals.

David Webb very soon followed Chivers to London. He'd been alternating between right-back and centre-half and Ted Bates wanted to swap him for Marvin Hinton, who had played the same dual role for Chelsea. When that deal fell through, Ted moved to replace Webb in both positions. He not only got a different Chelsea No.2, Joe Kirkup, in part-exchange, but persuaded John McGrath to come down from Newcastle.

Kirkup had moved south from Newcastle long before, joining West Ham as a 17 year-old. Three Under-23 caps had come his way, the last one in the game against Turkey, at The Dell, in which Burnside had won his only cap. Marvin Hinton was at centre-half in that game: it seems to have been a young side that made quite an impression on Ted Bates. He had in fact pursued Kirkup as early as 1964, but Ron Greenwood did not wish him to leave West Ham. Joe had moved on to Chelsea, though, in 1966. Now Ted Bates had succeeded in prising him from Dave Sexton, who had recently taken over from Tommy Docherty. He made his debut at home to Everton in February 1968. And so did John McGrath. Only Hollywood survived from the previous season's back four as McGrath was paired at centre-back with Gabriel.

John had played for Newcastle on the opening day of the season when they beat Southampton 3-0 at St James' Park. The *Echo* considered that

'Ron Davies was well marked by John McGrath' and Wyn Davies was nationally acclaimed the winner of 'the Battle of the Welsh dragons'. Ron generously concedes victory to his namesake:

> *He was very good in the air – better than me; he was stronger than me – but he didn't have the touch on the ground. And he used to knock them down in the box – he didn't know how to stick them in the net. There's the difference.*

Ron could lay it off, if need be, especially to Jimmy Gabriel, who used to 'read' his knock-downs so well at corners, while John McGrath played the 'disturber' who incommoded the goalkeeper.

If the media enjoyed the occasional notion of a 'battle' between the Davieses, two of Ron's Southampton team-mates like to tell you how Ron won the *war*. Campbell Forsyth is adamant that Ron was '*far, far* superior to Wyn Davies: he was the best I've *ever* seen – and I've seen quite a few'. And for Forsyth, who had to compete with these guys in the air (Ron only in practice games, of course) Ron's superiority included his aerial power: 'Wonderful with his head!' John McGrath was perhaps in better position than anyone to compare the two men: 'Ron was *streets* ahead. The "Golden Eagle" we used to call him because he could get up and fly. Having said that, he wasn't bad on the ground either'.

But, then, McGrath wasn't so bad himself. Like Kirkup, he had won Under-23 honours, twice playing in the same side as Paine at the end of the 1960-61 season. John was to win a reputation as an uncompromising tackler. Peter Vine had had the misfortune to be hit by him on his one appearance for the Saints against Bury: 'I thought I'd run into a brick wall'. Yet there are those who will tell you that, like the young Martin Chivers, the fledgling McGrath needed to put himself about more. Charlie Mitten, who bought him from Bury for Newcastle, found him 'a different type of centre-half: gentle, educated – like Neil Franklin. A good football player. He wasn't hard enough for Newcastle'. Ted Bates also recalls McGrath as 'neat and dainty' – until Joe Harvey took over at Newcastle and 'got him more aggressive'. Goodbye, Franklin. Hello, Frankenstein.

Seeking to tighten a defence that had conceded 92 goals in its first season at the top, Ted knew what he wanted from McGrath: 'his *aggression!*' So,

JOHN McGRATH

when he ascertained that Harvey was prepared to release Mitten's acquisition, he hurried to Newcastle to meet McGrath. Afraid of being beaten to his signature, he asked John to sign an unorthodox promissory note. McGrath recalls how he 'signed for Southampton on a cigarette packet':

We went into this room and had this chat and I said 'Yeah, OK, I'll sign but I'll have to have a word with the missus' ... I couldn't have gone any further – than from Newcastle down to Southampton. And, to be fair, I didn't really fancy going down south. But he's the best talker I've ever met. He was brilliant. He talked my socks down – and I can talk. I said 'Look! I will'. I said 'That's my heart' (points). 'That's my hand'. And I shook hands with him. He went 'just a minute' and he went all round this room and he found this cigarette packet. He tore it in half and he wrote on it John McGrath says he will sign for me tomorrow if his wife says OK. He said 'Will you sign it?' I said 'Ted, I'll tell you now: I'll do it this time, but never ever again. If I give my word, it's straight'. So I signed the cigarette packet and he was OK.

The most nerve-wracking part still faced McGrath, though. He had to come to The Dell to have a medical and sign a more official piece of paper. He took the train to London, where Jimmy Gallagher was waiting to drive him to The Dell. John consequently arrived for his medical unfit to be examined:

He was the worst driver in the world – worse than Ted ... I walk into this medical and I was shaking like a leaf. The doctor said 'How're you doing?' I said 'I'm not too good, actually. There's no way I'll get through this medical. Mr Gallagher's just driven me from London'. He said 'Oh! You'll probably need a whisky'.

John McGrath didn't drink shorts at the time, but accepted a medicinal whisky, passed the test and signed officially. His debut, along with Kirkup, marked a watershed in the Saints' season. They had not won for three months, Davies had been struggling against a succession of minor injuries, they were short of width – Paine was having his first concerted spell at No.10 while Melia recovered from a cartilage operation – and they were in the bottom two. A 3-2 win against Everton lifted them three places up the table – to 18th.

And it lifted dressing room morale: 'I thought we'd won the Cup', Kirkup recalls, 'when we came in the dressing room that night'. An unfortunate choice of phrase – his new team-mates had gone out of the Cup only five days before, losing 3-2 to West Brom in a Fourth Round replay at The Dell and so missing out on Fifth Round tie at Fratton Park.

But the win against Everton was the start of a final 14-game flourish in which the side won six and lost only three. This included a holiday double over Arsenal. Mick Judd made his debut in a 3-0 win at Highbury. A 19 year-old local, Mick had been scoring goals at inside-right for the Reserves. But he could play on either wing – 'I was a bit fast. Bill Ellerington used to say I could catch pigeons' – and had been at outside-right in the previous season's friendly at Portsmouth.

With the squad depleted by injuries received in the Saturday's 2-2 draw with Manchester United, Judd knew over the weekend that he was travelling to Highbury. The manager waited until they were at Waterloo to tell him he'd be playing – still time to ring his family and get them up to London: 'I thought the boss would throw me the 11 shirt – "Keep out wide, run up and down and look pretty"'.

But Ted 'threw' him the No.9 shirt. It was Channon, who'd scored on his own Easter Monday debut two years earlier, who knocked one backed for Judd to do the same. And Joe Kirkup chalked up his first Southampton goal, when an intended cross looped over Bob Wilson and into the net. It was, Joe admits, 'a pure fluke' and some of the Arsenal players said as much as they left the field (though 'pure' wasn't the adjective they selected, apparently). Hugh Fisher rubbed it in: 'What do you mean? We've been practising it all week'. Wilson was still 'mumbling about it'.

But, then, the Arsenal 'keeper had good cause to be disgruntled. He'd just got back into the side with an assurance from Bertie Mee that he had at least six games in which to prove himself. This was game seven. He hadn't kept a clean sheet yet and here was Southampton getting five over Easter, and with a goal like that.

Kirkup wasn't to know that, but he'd enjoyed embarrassing Wilson. Goalkeepers were by now – five years after the protection racket in the case of Kirby v. Grummitt – enjoying more cotton-wool treatment than Joe felt they needed. Wilson was 'a whinger' who would ask referees – 'hands up!' – for more. Joe's misgivings about the Arsenal 'keeper would not be helped by an incident four seasons later – of which more in Chapter 24.

⌒

Their other trip to north London, in that 1968 run-in, was less successful. Spurs won 6-1, watched by the man who was about to start work as Southampton's first Assistant Manager. At a Special Meeting on Sunday 25 February, the Directors had 'decided to relieve the Manager of some of the pressures of work' by appointing an Assistant Manager/Coach. At its next regular meeting, the Board had recorded Ted's agreement that such an appointee 'would be beneficial to the Club to take charge of the coaching, training and discipline of the players'.

DELL DIAMOND

The *Echo* reported three dozen applicants for this new position. Jimmy Scoular was among the eight shortlisted, even though he was in his fourth season as manager of Cardiff City, then enjoying a run in the European Cup Winners' Cup: they would reach the semi-final with Norman Dean scoring in each of their last three games. The Board noted that Scoular 'would be a very strict disciplinarian', but its unanimous choice was John Mortimore.

Born and raised in Hampshire – albeit at the far, Farnborough, end of the county – John remembers coming to The Dell with his father in those early postwar seasons. He was there as a 14 year-old for that famous four-pointer against West Brom in 1949. An amateur international centre-half in his Woking days, while he earned his living as a schoolteacher, he had 279 games for Chelsea – including those encounters with George Kirby in Chapter 17 – and 10 for QPR before becoming Sunderland's player-coach in 1966.

By accepting the appointment at The Dell, John was leaving Sunderland just as Alan Brown was arriving, as manager, from Sheffield Wednesday. More than one of Brown's protegés would come to The Dell, over the next several years, to join the managerial/coaching staff. On this occasion, one of his Hillsborough coaches applied and made an impact: Lawrie McMenemy. Mortimore and he travelled back to London together after the interviews. As the Waterloo train passed through Farnborough, John pointed out that this was home. The move to Southampton was going to be a 'very good' one for him.

When he went to watch that 6-1 defeat at White Hart Lane, John sat next to Sid Owen, the Leeds United coach, who wished him 'Good Luck' in a you're-going-to-need-it kind of way. Mortimore certainly needed something more than his considerable First Division experience – a missing ingredient within Ted's staff that the Board had said they were looking for – if he was going to make the desired impact on a cynical dressing room. It didn't matter that his prominent nose made him an obvious target for Ron Davies's caricatures – everybody, John included, could have a good laugh at that – but he also had to live down his past as a teacher. Terry Paine scoffs at the very idea of putting 'a schoolteacher among seasoned professionals!' Remind Terry how many First Division appearances this teacher had to his name and it makes no difference: 'I know it came over that he was a schoolteacher. And when he walked out! He said (mock posh teacher's voice) "Lads! When I blow my whistle, I want you all to run in towards me". He got off to the worst possible start'. That first impression seems not to have been helped, either, by John's dress and deportment. As Eric Martin puts it, 'John looked like a ballet dancer when he came':

That's what he reminded me of … Tight pants on. I thought 'Man, this guy is different'. But he did his job. The first day I saw him – with his tight pants on and on his tip-toes – I thought 'This guy's in the wrong business'. But he did his job. He was good.

Unlike Paine, then, Martin was prepared to let the evidence of experience contradict his initial prejudice. He could adjust from a regime of 'sit-ups and a medicine ball' to one of 'dance around the track' and other 'new training techniques – a sort of European thing'. John Sydenham never did take, though, to the introduction of 'a clip-board man' and, what's more, 'he didn't have a lot of respect'. John Mortimore's failure to gain 'respect' comes up too often: he seems not to have commanded the kind of authority the Directors were looking for. Ron Davies regrets that 'he had no control – no control whatsoever. John Mortimore was a very nice man. I liked John but he had no discipline. John was too much of a nice guy. I don't think he got the respect from the players that he wanted'.

Hang on! It surely wasn't a case of what a new assistant *wanted*. It was the directors who had decided that discipline needed to be improved and that the solution lay in bringing in a young man to complement the approach of a 50 year-old manager, whose particular style of discipline didn't need fixin' as far as many of the players were concerned. So, anybody accepting this post was on a hiding to nothing and likely to be blamed for disturbing the *status quo*. The last thing that they wanted in the dressing room was *change*. And any agent of change was going to be blamed for doing the Board's bidding.

For Mick Channon – still only 19 when all of this was going on – it was a case of the directors jumping on the Ramsey bandwagon, whose approach to discipline with the national team was suddenly all the rage. Channon was a particular problem.

In the last away game of the 1967-68 season, the side was at Craven Cottage with Mortimore in charge. Fulham, already relegated, took an interval lead of 1-0. Trevor Williamson of the *Daily Telegraph* suggested that a 'half-time talk by assistant manager John Mortimore [had] instilled some fire into Southampton and Channon, a player with a bright future, put them level'. Speculation, obviously – and what he couldn't have known

Rebel without a Pause
Mick Channon, seen at the end of the 1967-68 season, when he was giving offence to the new Assistant Manager.

269

was that Mortimore had, in fact, ordered Mick to change his boots to suit the wet surface. Channon had refused: 'Nobody tells me what boots to wear!' And then, when he scored, he made 'an offensive gesture' (as the Minutes delicately put it) to the bench. Other nationals joined in the acclaim for Channon's performance – Bill Meredith gave him Southampton's top score of eight points – and he was their 'most prominent' forward in the estimation of 'Observer'. None of that mattered to the Board. It fined the young tearaway £20. That wouldn't do much good, as Channon explains:

> It was a change of things – trying to discipline us with curfews and things like that … Blow a whistle and you had to run 100 yards and stand to attention. That didn't happen: 'Hold on! I'm a grown man'. Say 'Come in, lads. I want to have a chat' and I'll do it. I always remember rebelling against that.

Rebellion came not only easy but cheap: 'We still had player power in those days … Fine us a tenner – bad luck! It wasn't going to change our lives that much, was it?' And yet, for Mick Channon, like Eric Martin, this new approach to discipline was a process that all parties could work through: 'It was unheard of, you know. But we got through it. I survived. John Mortimore survived … I think John's a good bloke, but you don't change things overnight'.

Mick suggests that clubs were generally 'trying to break down player power', in the late 1960s, probably stimulated, as just noted, by Alf Ramsey's approach to discipline. And this authoritarian tendency in football was clashing head-on, in Channon's view, with the growing willingness of people, even of his tender age, to question authority generally:

> Everyone was starting to ask things … Everything was being questioned. The police were questioned. The doctors were questioned. So grown-ups and football managers were questioned. So, if a football manager told you to do something, you'd say 'Well, no! I don't think it should be done that way'.

That wasn't quite how young Channon questioned his manager at a well-remembered team meeting early the next season. This time the whole squad was in trouble. Arriving in Harrogate for a weekend break between defeats at Sunderland and Burnley, none of the 13 players respected an 11 o'clock curfew. It was a concerted effort to break it, to the extent that even low-frequency drinkers like Paine and Melia joined in. So it must have surprised George Horsfall, when a 'paralytic' Jimmy was spun through the revolving doors by his team-mates to land at the trainer's feet. It is clear, from Ted

Bates's report to the Board, that *he* had imposed this curfew. Mick Channon – with a Davies-like tendency generally to blame John Mortimore, rather than the directors, for the new order – attributes it to the Assistant Manager.

At the next morning's inquest, Mick naturally sought to exercise his right to question authority. He confesses, in his *Man on the Run* account, that he 'fumbled' his intervention and 'just got more and more tongue-tied'. According to his team-mates, his tongue was tied irremovably to one particular word. They may have been amply accustomed to effing and blinding in the dressing room but they were not used to such a high F-word quotient at a managerial dressing-down. They could not stop laughing. Ted was not so amused. His request for fines all round was, however, rejected by the Board.

Two months later, another curfew was broken, this time between two wins – at Carrow Road in the League Cup and Old Trafford in the League. Nine players found sufficient to celebrate in the 4-0 win over Norwich to keep them out until after midnight. Four of them – Davies, Gabriel, McGrath and Saul – were out until 2.00 a.m. and incurred a fine of £25 each. Frank Saul had a couple of goals to drink to that evening, while the capers of the other three stop-outs – each of whom was having a useful season – provide both a reminder of the question raised in Chapter 19 and a trailer for the next chapter: what does your manner of relaxing matter if it doesn't impair your performance on the park?

～

McGrath and Gabriel had forged a tough partnership at centre-back, with Walker 'marauding' in front of them. It was an especially good season for McGrath. Ever-present in 50 League and Cup games, he played for the Football League at Hampden in March and for Old England v. Young England on Cup Final Eve. Upfront, Davies was rampant with 20 League goals, but alone in reaching double figures.

This all added up to a final aggregate in 1968-69 of 57-48. Hardly in the best tradition of Southampton's free-flowing football. But it made for a variation on the Davies transfer speculation. By February, Alan Hoby had decided, in the *Sunday Express,* that Southampton had now graduated from being 'First Division nobodies' and Ron Davies was being quoted on the virtues of their 'more consistent, far tighter' defence. Some credit to John Mortimore here, then? Off-the-field discipline problems notwithstanding, their tightness on the field took them, that season, to a new height – seventh in the First Division – and to somewhere they had never trodden competitively before.

The Saints were in Europe.

Chapter 23

Only One Team in Europe

The Saints went into Europe because they were the only team in town.

Southampton were in the European Fairs Cup, thanks to the competition's origins in the Inter-City Fairs Cup. This meant that no city could have more than one representative. So Spurs and Chelsea, who had finished above the Saints, had to stand aside as Arsenal went off to Europe.

Southampton went off, on 16 September, to Trondheim to play Rosenborg, coached by Ted Bates's old team-mate and coaching companion, George Curtis. Their BEA Viscount was 'dry'. Free alcoholic beverages would normally have been served, but the *Echo* found 'ample stocks of fruit juice and milk', supplied at the Club's request. The players appeared to need a stiff drink on the night, though, when the *Echo* thought them anxious and 'apprehensive' about possible non-British interpretations of the rules.

Entry into Europe
Ted Bates (left) leads Southampton's first party to play in Europe.
Seen leaving Southampton for Trondheim are (in descending order) Kemp, Sydenham, Gurr, Mortimore, Jones, Stokes, Kirkup, Walker, Fisher, Davies, Channon, Saul, Hollywood, Gabriel, Byrne, Gallagher, Martin,

272

This Euroscepticism was justified when the only goal of the match came from a raised foot to block a clearance by Eric Martin. Ted told the *Echo* that the decision to condone such behaviour was 'diabolical, … but this is something we have to contend with in Europe'.

They contended well enough to win the second leg 2-0 at The Dell and then to beat Vitoria Guimaraes of Portugal 8-4 on aggregate. Next stop Newcastle. Ninth place had been good enough for Newcastle United to qualify. And a 0-0 draw at St James' Park looked good enough for the Saints to do the business at The Dell. But a 1-1 draw took Newcastle through on away goals. They went all the way and won the thing.

The away leg at St James' Park was the second game for a new left-winger. Tom Jenkins had arrived from Reading. Ted Bates was now replacing Sydenham not with a tackler-back of the Penk or Thompson variety but with a mazy dribbler – a 'weaver', as Ted puts it.

Thompson was still in the squad of 17 that assembled for the game at The Dell, but was the odd man out when the manager named his five substitutes. So he walked out during the team-talk and went home – to Otley. They talked on the 'phone and Thompson returned: 'Any other manager would probably have kicked me up the backside'. If he appreciated Ted's approach on this occasion, what David never got at The Dell was confidence. You may recall, from the previous chapter, his feeling that scoring would have helped in this regard. And so would 'a longer run in the team', he reckons. With Jenkins settling in on the left, though, Thompson would have but two more starts.

'I think, sometimes, I shouldn't have been left out', he says, reminding us of what Ken Jones said (in Chapter 18) about the nature of a Ted Bates 'shuffle'. But if he was a victim of such manoeuvres, Thompson is not bitter about it:

> *I probably didn't think he did fair by me sometimes, but that's natural … In his job, you do things which you think are right. You make decisions and you're not going to please everybody all the time. And I don't think, for a minute, that Ted would do anything vindictive.*

If the team needed a confident player at No.11, they certainly began the season in the right way. Mick Judd had worn that shirt for the last 10 games of the previous season, although he felt his 'natural side' was on the right. He had done well there, he reckons, when he switched to that flank during a home win against QPR in the April and had grabbed a couple of goals in the remaining four games of that season. He started 1969-70 in possession and considered himself ready to play on either wing:

DELL DIAMOND

I never felt out of my league. John Sydenham knew that I would take his place. People like David Thompson knew that I had more skills. Frankie Saul said 'You're there!' So that a lot of them knew that one had the ability to carry on and have a go and use it … It was no question that I was going to take Terry Paine's place. That was the way Ted was thinking … All my development was for No. 7.

But his 14th appearance in the second game at Molineux would prove to be his last in the first team. Two months later, a third knee injury in the Reserves would end his career.

He wasn't surprised to be dropped – that's what happens to the younger players when the side loses its first two games. The other youngster to suffer, on this occasion, was Bobby Stokes, a Portsmouth-born Portsmouth reject who had come in for the last four games of 1968-69 – the third player in four seasons, following Channon in 1966 and Judd in 1968, to score on an Easter Monday debut. Now he had to make way for Saul and Judd for Sydenham – away to Manchester United.

John can 'remember overhearing – I think it was John Mortimore and Ted' – discussing whether they dare play an attacking formation at Old Trafford: 'It was "What do we do? Let's give it a go" – like they didn't really want to do that'. It was a gamble that paid off, with Sydenham playing a most memorable part in a 4-1 rout of United. Ron Davies scored all four. Three of them came from Sydenham crosses. Pat Crerand, who played in that game – 'Well, I was on the pitch' – recalls how the Saints' left-winger did the damage less by stripping Shay Brennan than by early crosses. United had known what to expect of Davies, but had not been anticipating such an early service from Sydenham: 'That must have been a ploy', Crerand concludes, by the manager.

Yet there was no need, according to Sydenham, to plot this variation, especially for the occasion. 'Ted deserves credit', John feels, for working on ways of giving his wingers alternative positions to cross to: 'If a winger is getting to the by-line, there's three or four different options' for crossing. Moreover, Davies's 'ability to put them in the net' was such that, sometimes, 'you really didn't need to take it any further' down the line. Such modesty: if Sydenham's crosses worked from the by-line, Ted got the credit; and if they succeeded when hit early, you could thank Ron. Davies is having none of that: Sydenham was hitting his crosses to perfection that afternoon. Billy Foulkes and David Sadler certainly couldn't cut them out and Jimmy Rimmer didn't come for them: 'I couldn't believe it: the 'keeper didn't even challenge me. He stayed on his line and I just stuck them away'. Like Bonetti two seasons earlier, Rimmer left Davies, in vain, to the centre-backs.

Ron remains 'sad' that his free-scoring afternoon spelled the end for Bill Foulkes: Wilf McGuinness, who had just succeeded Matt Busby, promptly bought Ian Ure from Arsenal. Foulkes told Davies, after the game, that he wished they had Ron on their side. Ron told him that that was his 'dream'. He may have been ready and willing to move to any First Division club in 1966, but he would have left The Dell for Old Trafford 'at a heart-beat'. The press would continue to remind Ted Bates and the Southampton Board of United's desire to make Ron's dream come true.

Yet it was a season in which Davies was deposed as the Saints' top scorer. Netting only eight more times in the next 26 League games, he finished with but 12 League goals. Mick Channon led the list with 15. This would remain the way of things for the next two seasons, too. There were two good tactical reasons for this. First, Channon's speed had become a principal weapon, sometimes – and increasingly – more than Davies's head. To make the most of Channon's counter-attacking potential, Ted Bates needed to 'push him up a little bit on his own, so that Ron Davies could get him in early' (see Chapter 27). This gave Davies a chance to prove his ability on the ground, but 'Mick didn't like that', Ted remembers, 'and he used to say so'. Ron wasn't too keen either. As you'll have gathered from the last chapter, he'd preferred playing with Chivers – a 'more intelligent player', who could hold the ball and play one-twos, whereas the 'quicker, sharper' Channon was hovering, in Ted's plan, for Ron's flick-ons.

And secondly, even when he wasn't wearing the No.10 – as he had done, you may remember, during Melia's surgery in 1967-68 – Terry Paine was 'tucking in', more and more, to a midfield role that included hitting Channon on the run. It was so different from the way he had fed O'Brien at the nearpost, but required a similar 'telepathy': 'I *knew* that there were areas where I could hit the ball and I knew that he'd be on his bike. He *knew* when I was going to release it and he knew when to run'.

This role suited Terry – 'luckily for me, I had the ability to read it from those angles as well' – as he lost 'that half a yard'. And, if he could no longer get to the by-line so often, he was now in awe of Channon's ability to do so – 'the *pace!*' For the last two games of that 1969-70 campaign, Terry again took the No.10 shirt. His No.7 shirt – the one Judd had been waiting for – passed to a young Scotsman who had now been earmarked to inherit it. Terry was 30 and Campbell Forsyth understood Ted to be looking for 'somebody in that *mould*'. He thought he had found him at Clydebank in the form of a part-timer called Gerry O'Brien. Ted Bates went to watch him, 'walked round the track' with Forsyth and promptly signed his discovery. He told the Board that, once he was training full-time, O'Brien 'could become a younger edition of Paine'.

But it wouldn't work out that way. Terry Paine would play the whole of the next season at No.7, with another newcomer ever-present at No.10. Brian O'Neil had arrived from Burnley in time to join the team's Asian tour, which culminated in four games in Japan. Denis Hollywood had always wanted to go to Japan and was devastated when Ted Bates left him out of the party. He '*pleaded*' with Ted, who said he would 'abuse' himself. He could stay at home and keep his weight down. And if he didn't report for daily training and weighing, he could expect to be fined. Denis tells this story, heavily laced with lasting regret but with considerable respect for the man who took this tough line: 'He was obviously right – it probably wouldn't have done me any good [to tour]. And I did come in every day and train and have my weight taken. I always thought he was very fair. I don't think he was soft at all … It would have been a nice tour to go on'.

～

With his weight more under control, Hollywood was regular enough the next season, even if he was not one of the four ever-presents – Kirkup, Fisher, Channon and O'Neil – in a settled side. Channon was, as I say, top-scorer with 18 to Davies's 17, although Ron was the principal scorer in a Cup run that ended in the Fifth Round at Anfield. That was the second time the Saints progressed that far in Ron's seven seasons at The Dell. One of his beefs about remaining with Southampton was that he'd have liked 'a chance to get to a Cup Final, or even a semi-final, or *something!* Win something!'

The only thing he won, in 1970-71, was an accolade for his self-restraint. Ron had become, he reckons, 'the most-marked man on the field: as a world-class striker, you get nailed all the time'. A writer for *Inside Football* took, as an example, the opening game of that 1970-71 season, when Manchester City came to The Dell and impeded Ron 'at four consecutive corners. The opposition were obviously petrified of his heading ability and were determined to stop him jumping. A sharp nudge or push at the right time worked wonders and all four corners could have brought his side a penalty kick'.

But no penalty was awarded by a referee who 'left a very frustrated forward fuming about the injustices of the game. In Ron's case, there's no sign of "temperament". He just gets on with the game determined to get revenge in the best possible way – by scoring. In the match in question he scored with his head so in a way justice was done'. Ron offers a similar explanation for receiving only one caution, ever: 'To get my own back, I'd climb up in the air, stick the ball in the net, tap the guy marking me on the arse and say "Get the ball, it's your kick-off"'.

If only it had been that simple! Davies and Channon would have to settle, in 1970-71, for 35 goals between them in a League total of 56. With

44 conceded, that was enough to get the Saints into seventh position, 19 points behind Arsenal's double-winning team. Bertie Mee's side dropped only three points at Highbury that season. One of them was on Boxing Day, when the Saints played out a goalless draw in the snow. The home side had won their previous five games but Eric Martin had a 'blinder' – according to an admiring Bob Wilson, a frozen spectator at the other end.

When the Arsenal came to The Dell for the Easter Saturday return, they were again on a five-win streak. But the Saints had not lost a League game at home since October. The visitors' record prevailed. They won 2-1, although the Arsenal's *Official History* records that 'Mick Channon led a late rally [in] which … the Saints might well have had a penalty when Simpson seemed to grab Davies as he set himself for a header'. The crowd of 30,231 was the Saints' biggest of the season, overtaking the 30,202 who had watched them beat Manchester United 1-0 in November. Their next home game, a fortnight after the Arsenal visit, would attract the third 30,000-plus gate of the season. The visitors were Leeds, the only other contenders for the Championship.

The Saints lost 3-0 to complete Leeds's double over them. The first game, in September, is memorable for the spectacle of Jimmy Gabriel being carried off on a stretcher, as the referee remonstrated with Ted Bates that he could not bring on substitute Tony Byrne: Gabriel was being *sent* off horizontally for having laid out Allan Clarke. It was one of those days when a niggling home side merited George Best's quip that the dirtiest player he ever played against was Leeds United. Clarke was especially irksome and Gabriel eventually wrought his revenge. When he realised that the linesman had seen him, Jimmy went to the floor in a piece of acting that his fellow-defenders still laugh about. And he even persuaded the FA that he should not be suspended. Denis Hollywood, who was appearing at Lancaster Gate the same day, couldn't believe the dossier that Gabriel had with him: there was *no way* Jimmy could get off. But he did.

~

If it was the nasty streak in Gabriel, Hollywood and Paine that was taking Ted Bates too often to FA hearings, it was a challenge by John McGrath, that season, that stimulated the invention of another Shanklyism.

When the Saints beat Liverpool 1-0 at The Dell on 26 September, thanks to an Alec Lindsay own goal, Bill Shankly complained that Lindsay had been pushed. He couldn't leave it at that, though. McGrath had caught Alun Evans so heavily, in a clash of heads, that Evans was knocked out and swallowed his tongue. Southampton, Shankly famously declared, were an 'Ale House' side. McGrath puts his hand up for the incident – 'I nearly killed him, to be fair. I hit him that hard, he hit his head on the ground' –

but his team-mates seem generally to feel that this was another example of Shankly, the terrible loser, over-reacting.

One of the difficulties in assessing the fairness or otherwise of this *soubriquet* is its ambiguity: did the great master of the one-liner mean that the Saints had more than its share of heavy drinkers or that they had too many brawlers?

The origin of the line would suggest the latter. But, in his *Man on the Run* chapter on 'The Ale House Lads', Mick Channon accepts the label on the former grounds, while dismissing the incident that brought it about. As he sees it, Southampton had 'a lot of good players who could score goals', but Ted had to add a few who could 'scratch, bollock and bite … players who could handle themselves. We had to *get* the ball to let Painie play, to get me in or to knock a cross in for Ron to score. It was all *there*'. Eric Martin is another who pleads guilty to the drinking charge. Several of the team were 'running around and partying so much':

> We were still a good team, but the life-style was crazy … Some days, after practice, we'd just go hang out at a bar, throw some darts, that kind of stuff. Then night-time come and off you go! … Just go down and hang around dockland – the bars down there … Quite often, we got more exercise in our night-life than what we did in training.

Compared with the lack of 'night-life' in his Scottish upbringing, Martin found Southampton 'so *alive* – I guess Shankly heard about it'. Like Channon, though, Eric feels that the Liverpool manager over-reacted to the McGrath incident: 'he just didn't like losing'. Or, as John McGrath (who 'got on well with Bill Shankly') puts it, to beat Liverpool was 'the cardinal sin'. And what did their drinking habits matter, anyhow?

> We all were drinkers. But we could play. We worked very hard. None of the staff would referee the five-a-sides in the gym on a Friday morning. Ted always said that, if we played anyone in the gym on a Friday morning, we'd win the European Cup. I saw Denis Hollywood put Ron Davies through the fire-doors [in the gym]. We worked very hard and we trained very hard … We had a great team-spirit.

If that sounds a trifle self-congratulatory, let's call a couple of witnesses from among opponents of the day: Dave Merrington, then at Burnley; and Manchester City's Mike Summerbee. Both adopt a 'so what?' attitude to drinking and echo the 'worked hard' line. No matter that some of these Southampton players may sometimes have 'had one too many', they were, for Merrington, some 'good pros and I think they battled hard for Ted'. And Summerbee, taking an uncannily similar stance to that of McGrath, likens the Southampton night-life to that at Maine Road:

> *All footballers drink. People don't realise how hard they work during the week. Just because a shirt comes out of the top of the shorts [Channon?] or a pair of socks drops to the ground [O'Neil?], it doesn't mean they're like a pub side. They've all got a professional attitude.*
>
> *They weren't Ale House Lads. They worked hard, trained hard and played hard. They did the business. We were the same [at Manchester City]. We were physically a very strong side and physically fit – but we used to enjoy ourselves. I know Bill Shankly was a great manager but he was also a great person at saying things – clichés.*

Ron Davies felt he belonged to 'a *sociable* group' and regretted that it was more than another cliché for Shankly – it was another example of his 'grudge against Southampton':

> *We had some tough games against them and he couldn't accept defeat – cos we were one of the teams he expected to crunch … With the press, nothing could be said against Liverpool and what Shankly says is God's Word, right? He says that [about Ale House Lads] to the press and it's all over the place. And then you're labelled forever after that.*

As the manager of the labelled team, Ted Bates believes that Bill Shankly was entitled to his comment: 'If he thought that, that was his opinion … I didn't ever tend to make any remarks about other people's teams: I used to stick to my own. Shanks probably got a bit upset'. Mick Channon puts his finger on another aspect of Shankly, the grudging loser. It wasn't just that you dare not beat them, 'if you knew Bill Shankly, there was only one team that was ever on a football pitch and that was Liverpool'. Ted had difficulties with this monomania:

> *Every time I spoke to him, I got cheesed off because all I used to hear about was Liverpool. He was like that with his enthusiasm, but it was all one way – Liverpool! … I'd talk about the pitch at The Dell: 'Naw, not as good as ours' … He had this almost – not insane – passion. You could see it coming out of his eyes. A football person – that was him.*

A case of an unduly-focussed pot calling the one-track kettle black? Maybe – in Chris Nicholl's estimation, both men suffered, along with Joe Mercer, from what he calls 'football madness: it's like a kind of "mad professor" look, only it's a "football look". It's as if they don't have any other life'. But Ted's obsession is, surely, with the *game* of football, *not* with blinkered hyping of his club. He may have ranked the game where Shankly famously put it, relative to matters of life and death, but you can't imagine Ted quipping that there were two top-rate teams on the Solent: Southampton and Southampton Reserves. He was no more into boasting about his own team than he was into denigrating other people's.

Not even if they had finished seventh again and were back in Europe.

Chapter 24

Auld Lang Signs

Before they could venture onto the Continent, the side had lost its Assistant Manager to Europe.

John Mortimore had not allotted himself a particular time-span for his apprenticeship at The Dell. But he was invited to coach in Greece. Ted's old team-mate, Joe Mallett, had gone out to Panionios in Athens in 1970 and the Greeks were looking for more British coaches. Mortimore felt that the time was 'right' to go, although he 'wasn't keen to leave'.

That's not because he had any notion of stepping into Ted's shoes, although he feels that the Chairman, George Reader, may have been nurturing him for that eventual role, not least in the way he required him to attend Board meetings.

This was to be the first of several overseas appointments for Mortimore, interspersed with another two spells at The Dell and one at Portsmouth. Working with Ted had equipped him well, he feels for this continental journey:

Working with him for three years was a great experience. I felt I could go anywhere – and I did go. Spain, Benfica. I could go anywhere after working three years with Ted, because I learned as much about the game with Ted as I learned from anybody – coaching courses or anything else.

To illustrate the extent of that debt, John says that Ted taught him even more than his other two great mentors: Ted Drake, at Chelsea; and Alec Stock at QPR. These three men were like 'peas out of pod' to Mortimore:

They were all very similar. They were what I call real gentlemen. Good pros, who would kick you up the backside if you needed it as a player. Great knowledge of the game – great understanding of the game – and, in their own different ways, good man-managers.

Whatever you're managing, you've got to get that respect of the people you're working with. And here were three men that got the respect of players, because they were First Class chaps, they were knowledgeable about what they did and they could handle players and men. They could pass that on to other people. They were as much teachers as they were managers and coaches and they gained this respect from players they dealt with; from staff they worked with; and throughout football.

DELL DIAMOND

John Mortimore is bringing us back, here, to the point that Walter Winterbottom was making (in Chapter 9): you need not only a knowledge of the game but an ability to *impart* it. John stresses that aspect of working with, and learning from, Ted. But, then, 'you *had* to learn about football with Ted, because he didn't talk about anything else'.

You will have noticed how John Mortimore stresses *respect* as a hallmark of his three mentors. I suggested, in the previous chapter, that it was difficult for him – as a young assistant lumbered with a disciplinary role – to win that kind of respect. For some of the players, that came in time, but Mortimore's successor seems to have left without having worked his way through the resistance to change – or to the idea that anyone other than Ted was giving certain kinds of order.

Stuart Williams was at an immediate disadvantage with Ron Davies, who hadn't got on with him when they played together for Wales. Having later qualified as a coach in the USA, Ron generally despairs of the coaching he received in England, but is especially critical of his former Welsh team-mate, who commanded 'no respect whatsoever'. That word again. On the other hand, it doesn't appear to have helped Williams that he had been at the Club and had won so much respect, there, as a player (as we saw in Chapter 17). Take John Sydenham who liked Stuart 'as a person', but who considered his recruitment to be 'a strange move … Stuart definitely wouldn't have been the person that I would have appointed as coach'. And why not? Again, it's about *respect*. 'Stuart just didn't *have* it', Terry Paine concludes: He didn't really have the respect of the players – I think that's what it boiled down to'.

～

Ron Davies was a spectator as the season started – sidelined by a pre-season injury. He returned for the home leg, against Bilbao, in the First Round of what was now the UEFA Cup. A 2-1 win was cancelled out, a fortnight later, by a 2-0 defeat in the away leg. Eric Martin remembers whistling for a taxi in Spain and says it was that – not just his hair-style – that led Hugh Fisher to christen him 'Harpo'.

It was a week that ended badly for Fisher. He broke his leg in a collision with Bob Wilson at The Dell. Terry Paine is prepared to take the blame for the angle at which he 'knocked the ball' forward for Fisher, running towards the Archers Road penalty box: 'Wilson broke his leg, but if I'd given him a better ball, poor Hughie wouldn't have been blind to him coming out … I'm not saying he's gone to break his leg. It may have been his *technique*'. Indeed, it was, according to Wilson, who likens it to the 'direct' approach of his 'boyhood idol', Bert Trautmann. 'You never, ever protect your head' – remember the 1956 Cup Final and Trautmann's famous broken neck – you just take 'the straightest route to the ball', hoping to seize that 'moment' when the oncoming opponent has 'lost control fractionally' and suddenly finds you, 'head-first, at their feet'.

If the opponent's control is close enough – George Best is Wilson's prime example – he may be able to beat the 'keeper's lunge. If not, he will hope to avoid being hit by it. But not if he can't *see* him: Terry Paine's over-hit pass had left Fisher 'blind', he says, to the advancing 'keeper. Terry was less rational about it on the day. Arriving early on the scene – 'it's flapping about in the wind, his leg' – he took issue with the Arsenal 'keeper. Wilson blames that reaction for the stick he received from the Archers End.

Standing under the East Stand – close enough to hear the crack – I have no recall of anyone blaming Wilson, who says the fans along the sides were generally kinder to him than those behind his goal. Fisher never heard the crack himself, though 'everybody keeps telling' him that they did. 'It was probably the first time, that season', that he'd made it into the opponents' box, hoping to beat the Arsenal back four as they came out. He agrees with Paine's evaluation of the pass:

It was a little bit long and a bit wide. So I couldn't see Wilson. I just remember him clattering into me … I think his whole body just came underneath me. I can only assume that he threw himself at me a bit higher than the body probably should have been. But goalkeepers do that: it's part of their game … I'm not blaming anybody. It just happened.

Some of his team-mates are less forgiving. Wilson may have developed the head-first technique of his 'idol', but John McGrath remembers his challenge, on the day, as the 'feet-first' approach of a 'coward'. Joe Kirkup, you may recall from Chapter 22, was no fan of Bob Wilson's, either: 'He never used to like anyone touching him, but he went out with two feet to Hughie and he did him, left right and centre. I don't know whether it was one of those things. I wouldn't have thought he was like that normally, only he certainly sorted Hughie out that day'.

To some of the Ale House Lads, then, Wilson was another ungracious loser, whose whinging irritated them as much as Shankly's sour grapes. This doesn't explain why Wilson got so many knocks – he seems to have been 'crazy' enough, in the words of his book, to fling himself in where the feet were flying. And head-first – not feet-first, as his Dell critics claim. Bill Shankly had remarked, the previous season (after a Liverpool win when he could afford to be generous), that what made Wilson 'outstanding' was his 'courage. He'll dive at players' feet and make quick decisions'. But rationality is not, of course, a recommended ingredient when you're creating folk-devils. And Bob Wilson has certainly become one among Fisher's less forgiving team-mates.

That's a pity, for Wilson liked playing at The Dell. Notwithstanding the reception by the Archers End that afternoon in October 1971, he enjoyed having the crowd close to him: 'I liked people breathing down my neck. It put me under pressure'. In fact, Bertie Mee feels that the relationship between the Saints and Arsenal was especially good. He could meet up with Ted again, while his Chairman, Denis Hill-Wood, was a good friend of the Southampton Chairman, George Reader – so much so that he would come to games at The Dell, when his commitments to Arsenal allowed it.

～

The loss of Fisher for the rest of the season demanded four solutions from Ted Bates. The No.4 shirt would end the campaign in the possession of Jim Steele. 'Ted said he wanted a left-sided player who was hard', Campbell Forsyth recalls. 'They don't come any harder than Steelie. I thought he had a wonderful ability'. Even so, Ted's Scottish scout sought a second opinion: Jock Stein strongly recommended the 21 year-old, who'd played in the Dundee side that had just gone out of the UEFA Cup to AC Milan.

It came as a surprise to Steele to be whisked off by Ted Bates: 'All he talked about [on the 'plane south] was football, football. I was bored to death. It was murder'. Jim had thought he was going to Leeds United, who were looking in Scotland for a successor to Jack Charlton (and would take Gordon McQueen south, later that year). Not that Steele was yet ready to be a centre-back at The Dell. He came straight into the side, on 29 January, at wing-half.

In the meantime, Ted had tried David Walker, Bobby Stokes and Graham Lovett. Walker was nearing the end of his Southampton career, while Stokes was having his first full season. Following his debut in 1969, his appearances, over the next two seasons, had been patchy. Now he was in his versatile element, wearing six different shirts in the course of 41 League games.

Lovett arrived on what was to be a short-term loan from West Bromwich. But his three games included what I think of as a 'forgotten' game. A rare win against Leeds United, who would be runners-up for the third consecutive season. I remember that 2-1 victory in November for a glorious run by Channon who seemed to go right *through* Jack Charlton as he flowed from halfway to score the Saints' first goal. For some reason, though, video-makers rather dwell on the return game, in March, when Leeds won 7-0. Jim Steele had an experimental run-out at centre-back that day – not the way he had been expecting, only recently, to play in that position at Elland Road: 'Horrendous. The worst day of my life, I think'.

An exaggeration, surely – but why do we need to keep seeing that sequence in which Leeds players pass the ball to each other umpteen times? So what? They weren't going anywhere.

So what did it matter? Unless, of course, you were one of those chasing the ball in vain. Terry Paine was not among them. He readily admits that he'd gone 'wittering' to the bench: 'Take me off!' But he still feels the humiliation when he sees it on television. It's an indignity that has followed Ron Davies to the United States. When they show that over-exposed footage there, Americans come up to him: 'I saw you Ron. I saw you chasing around'. Eric Martin thinks it unfair that Terry Paine managed to 'sneak off: we should probably all have come off, that day, and just given up'. The blame was less evenly distributed than that, though. The two young local lads at full-back, Bob McCarthy and Roger Fry, carried the can.

We first met McCarthy, in Chapter 19, playing in the County game from which Channon emerged. He'd made his debut in 1967 but had managed only half-a-dozen games in four seasons. He had more than doubled that total with the run that ended at Elland Road. He felt that he 'did reasonably well in that game, because we all took a thumping, but none of the goals actually came from my side. They were all on the other side'. Fry's side. Roger had been in for most of the season, at the expense of Denis Hollywood, but this was to be his last game for the Club. Hollywood returned to play out the season and bring his total to 266 appearances.

If there's one good thing to be said about the repeated showing of that passing sequence at Elland Road – even when we get to see the seven goals as well – it's that we've been pretty well allowed to forget an even bigger defeat, that season, by Everton. The week after that home win against Leeds in November, the side went with only one change – O'Neil had been injured and substituted at The Dell – to Goodison Park and lost 8-0. Terry Paine led the singing of *Auld Lang Syne* on the train home: 'We *knew* that was the end of that team. It was going to be broken up'.

In fact, Ted Bates kept the same team for the next game – a 5-2 drubbing by Manchester United at The Dell, when George Best ran riot and had a hat-trick to show for it, before he limped off after 70 minutes. 'If there's a better player in the world', Ted Bates told Brian Hayward of the *Echo,* 'I don't know who he is'. Complimenting Davies, who'd been troubled by an ankle injury, on a 'sharp' performance, Hayward suggested that 'he would probably have had a hatfull of goals had he been on the other side'.

Given Ron's long-held wish to play for United, that was surely a case of adding insult, literally, to his injury. But does Hayward's supposition hold up, anyhow? 'Maybe I wouldn't have done so well', Davies himself reflects, 'because I think Painie was a better player than Willie Morgan', who was at No.7 for United in that 5-2 game. And on the left flank, Ron adds, he had Sydenham. His crosses may have been unpredictable, but he got the ball to him a lot more often than Best would when Davies and he played together in the USA. Moving on early to United would probably have got Ron a coveted medal or two, but it may well have suited his style – or, at least, his acquired style – less.

After that United defeat, Ted did make a couple of changes – it was the last of Lovett's three games – but the only serious casualty of that season was Jimmy Gabriel. He kept his place until April, when, ironically, his old club came to The Dell. Everton completed the double. It was Gabriel's last start for Southampton.

The next season – 1972-73 – began with Fisher back in possession at No.4, McGrath at No.5 and Steele at No.6. When deputising for Fisher in midfield, Steele had been, for Terry Paine, 'a carthorse' – a youngster thrown in out of position, 'when he wasn't quite ready'. But now he settled into the position he would grace, three seasons later, at Wembley. McGrath would not last long, though, at No.5. He gave way, in October and for the rest of the season, to Paul Bennett.

That meant that McGrath just missed another Southampton performance to upset Bill Shankly. After Liverpool had drawn 1-1 at The Dell, Steve Curry reported, in the *Express,* that the Liverpool manager had objected to Southampton playing 4-4-2 at home. Curry agreed with Ted Bates that the Saints had done enough attacking to win and had 'provided the game with its star player in the seemingly ageless Terry Paine'. The trouble was, Curry hinted, that 'Shankly rarely has a good word for the Saints'. Now, where have we heard that before?

Paul Bennett had had a couple of games at the end of the previous season, including a debut at home to Spurs. This had brought him up against Martin Chivers, who had been at Taunton's School a few years ahead of him. As coincidence-collectors Holley and Chalk point out, in *The Alphabet of the Saints,* Ron Davies was being marked in that same game by Mike England, who'd been at his school – Basingwerk Secondary Modern – in North Wales. Bennett was succinctly briefed for his school reunion: 'Ted was great. It was a case of "Don't worry. We know Martin. This is what we do. This is how you sort him out. We know what his weaknesses are. Go and kick him. He doesn't like being kicked"'. But hadn't Chivers overcome what Ted had considered to be his weakness: wasn't he now kicking back? 'No', says Paul. 'Martin wasn't a rough player. But he was a very skilful player. He didn't need to be rough'.

School Reunion
Paul Bennett (left) makes his debut against fellow-Old Tauntonian, Martin Chivers.

The other casualties of the eviction orders Paine had predicted were Hollywood and Jenkins. Early in the close season, Denis learned that he'd been given a free transfer. He feels he deserved better notice from Ted:

He should have told me halfway through the season, because he'd obviously made up his mind – or at least two months before the end of the season. He deliberately didn't tell me, because he thought he wouldn't get 120 per cent out of me when he brought me and Big John [McGrath] back to help them stay up ... I'd spent 13 seasons at The Dell and Ted knew I'd run through a brick wall for him ... If you're told when you're playing in the first team, you can put feelers out and perhaps end up with a few clubs looking at you ... I'm not moaning. I'm just telling you the story as I can remember it. I'm not at all bitter or anything like that.

Ever willing to see the funny side, Denis laughs at the notion of being replaced by such a crock as Francis Burns from Manchester United: 'Doc Ramsay [the Club doctor] said his knees were worse than mine!' Burns had three spells, interspersed with injury breaks. The word from the dressing room, though, is that it was not so much his dodgy knees that restricted him to the one season at The Dell as having to live next-door to Brian O'Neil. It's said they 'filled a skip' with the fish and chip papers that Brian had tossed onto the garage roof of his hapless neighbour.

The No.3 shirt, in which Burns made 23 appearances, was passed around that season. When the music stopped, it was being worn by 19 year-old Steve Mills. This Portsmouth-born full-back made his League debut at Stamford Bridge on Easter Saturday. If his was another story of a career unfulfilled – a rapid rise to Under-23 recognition and predictions of a full cap being dashed by a career-ending car crash in 1975 – few will need reminding of how it was to be overtaken, sadly, by the tragedy of his early death from leukaemia in 1988.

There was a certain stability, though, about a defence in which Martin was ever-present. This was the era of what Mick Channon describes as Ted's 9-1 formation, with Channon the solitary one for much of it. Although this meant a reduction in goals scored, from 52 to 47, the side moved up six places, thanks to conceding only 52, compared with 80 in that leaky season of 1971-72. While claiming some of the credit for getting a tighter system, Stuart Williams praises Channon, in the demanding role of 'a loner', and Paine: so often the sole 'outlet' for the defence, he had to hit Channon in his stride (in the way Terry himself described in the previous chapter). 'It was a bit monotonous', Stuart admits. 'People hated playing against us and we were not attractive to watch, obviously'.

Invariably attractive but so often frustrating, Tom Jenkins survived the first five games of the season, before moving on to Swindon. He had flattered so often to deceive. John Sydenham is less disappointed to have been replaced by Jenkins than he is to to have seen how Tom worked out: 'I thought he would become a much better player than he did. When I first saw him, I thought he had great skill – on either foot, inside or out'. As Davies had famously illustrated at Old Trafford, though, he could make good use of an early cross: 'Get it over to him quickly and he would do the rest. But Tom was always wanting to turn people inside-outside. He was a very good player but he didn't need to over-elaborate. He could just have slung balls across ... Tom would turn full-backs inside and out and Ron would get very frustrated in the middle'.

Jenkins's effective replacement at No.11 was Bobby Stokes. Like Jim Steele, Bobby had at last found the shirt he was to wear with distinction at

Wembley. But with a much different style of No.9, of course, than Ron Davies. For the moment, Ron gave way to Paul Gilchrist, who'd arrived from Doncaster Rovers. Sadly, he went out with a whimper – a mere 10 goals in 28 starts.

He could manage only one goal in the three games it took to remove his first club, Chester, from the League Cup. Ron's recall of the away game was one of 'skinning' opponents on the ground. So it's ironic that the game at The Dell afforded one of the most beautiful shots *(below)* of Ron's jumping prowess.

Surviving all of these changes was Terry Paine, the leader of the *Auld Lang Syne* chorus, himself. His nemesis was about to arrive at The Dell, though, as Stuart Williams made way for Lawrie McMenemy.

Hang Up
In his final season for the Saints, Ron Davies was still climbing high against his first club

Taking over

Team Manager Designate, Lawrie McMenemy, shares an idea with Ted Bates.

Chapter 25

Up with Ted, Out with Terry

When Assistant Manager Stuart Williams resigned 'for personal reasons' in April 1973, the Board decided to advertise, in the *Daily Express,* for an 'Assistant to the Manager/Team Manager Designate'.

It is not clear where the second part of this new title came from: it was somehow dreamed up – as Keith Honey, by then the Club Secretary, recalls – to express the Chairman's intent: 'George Reader said he didn't want to commit the Club to saying "Right! You're Team Manager", straightaway'. What was clear was that the Board expected Ted Bates to be around for a while yet: at the same meeting, it granted him a contract of employment until 31 July 1977.

The Directors were very soon contemplating a shortlist to be interviewed by a committee of five. The Manager would join four of the Directors: Chairman Reader; Vice-Chairman Chaplin; and two Chairmen-in-waiting, Alan Woodford and Guy Askham. But neither of the front runners applied. Rather than rely on *Express*-readers coming forward, the Board was courting two of the leading candidates from the 1968 shortlist for the initial Assistant Managership.

John Mortimore, the man who got the job that time around, was ready to return from Greece and was discussing the new vacancy with Chairman Reader: 'he wanted me to come back and I was keen to come back'. But he was also being wooed by the Portsmouth Chairman, John Deacon, to go to Fratton Park as Manager. The incumbent, Ron Tindall, a longstanding friend of Mortimore's, would become General Manager. 'It was a toss-up'. Each job had its attractions: 'Had Southampton said "Team Manager", I think I would have come … I'd had three years as Assistant Manager and Coach and I'd done my apprenticeship. Did I have to come in for another two or three years to be "Team Manager Designate"?'

When John Mortimore accepted the post of 'Team Manager' at Portsmouth, this cleared the decks for one of the runners-up of 1968 – Lawrie McMenemy.

Lawrie had moved on from his coaching position at Sheffield Wednesday, in the middle of the 1968-69 season, to manage Doncaster Rovers. They lost only two more League games that season and, with an undefeated run of 21 games, won the Fourth Division Championship. Two seasons later, though, Doncaster were relegated and McMenemy was sacked. He hadn't long to wait for a call from Grimsby and, in 1972, Lawrie McMenemy was winning – again at the first attempt – another Fourth Division Championship. He had a season with Grimsby in the Third Division before the call came from The Dell.

The statistics of his Fourth Division successes apart, Southampton had three main sources of information about McMenemy. He had been interviewed five years earlier. He knew Ted from Lilleshall. And – not least, it seems – there was Don Revie. As a longstanding friend of Jack Charlton, McMenemy had become a frequent visitor to Elland Road and had become fairly well-known to Revie, from whom Southampton sought an update. The Vice-Chairman was one of the king-makers who spoke to Revie, but Ted Bates seems to have been the principal fixer. Revie 'spoke very well of him' and, by the time McMenemy met Ted and the rest of the Selection Committee, there seemed to be only two questions to settle: the title and the financial terms.

First, would a man who had managed two clubs to championships agree to be a manager-in-waiting? Keith Honey feels that Lawrie 'turned his nose' up at the 'designate' appendage and Mick Channon uses a similar phrase in *Man on the Run*. But the candidate himself says it 'wasn't that big a problem – but it would have been a problem if I hadn't been able to run it in my own way'. He'd 'never heard of that sort of title before'. But, then, he accepted that this was 'a unique situation' in that the outgoing manager had been there so long: when Matt Busby retired in 1969 – momentarily, as we shall see in moment – Ted had become the longest-serving manager still in office. And when a manager voluntarily steps aside, as Busby had and Ted was now doing, it's different from when the manager is fired and the Board is looking for a totally fresh start.

Moreover, his interview in 1968 had given him 'an idea of what sort of people the directors were'.

So I wasn't so surprised as some people might have been as to why they wanted that title. They were people who didn't want too much change, obviously, and I think they were giving themselves an 'out' if things didn't work out.

With a self-belief born of winning two championships, he felt able to accept this unusual title. Those successes may have been in the Fourth Division, but Lawrie had acquired a sense of his financial worth somewhat in excess of Ted's. A failure, on Ted's part, to 'make waves' and demand an annual pay rise for himself and his staff had left the latter on 'a mere pittance'. By accepting Lawrie's view of a wage structure, the Board needed to raise several staff salaries considerably. Yet this re-structuring still resulted in Ted Bates being paid less than his successor-in-waiting.

~

At its meeting on 21 June, the Board appointed Lawrie McMenemy to be Team Manager Designate, 'provisionally agreed to review the title at Christmas' and thanked Ted Bates 'for his unselfish co-operation in these negotiations'. In fact, the Board couldn't wait for Christmas.

On 15 November 1973, Lawrie McMenemy was made Team Manager and Ted Bates became Chief Executive.

Mick Channon assumes that Lawrie had 'put a gun to their heads' and persuaded the Directors to bring forward their review. That was 'the impression we were getting as players', Paul Bennett recalls, 'that he was saying "either you make me manager or I'm on my way"'. Lawrie – who says he 'certainly wouldn't, after a few months, have been knocking' on the Chairman's door – has a different explanation. The press were linking his name with the managerial vacancy at Nottingham Forest. Messrs Reader and Askham met with him and promptly recommended to the full Board, on 15 November, that he be 'appointed Manager forthwith'. A couple of their fellow-directors were disinclined to hurry; but, by a majority of 6:2, the appointment was agreed. The Saints were then lying ninth in the First Division. Yet they were, of course, relegated.

Make way for another piece of Dell folklore. Ted Bates is perceived to have taken the club into fifth place – remember that they had never finished higher than seventh (in 1969 and again in 1971) – before handing over to a raw successor who promptly took them down. There are two misconceptions here. First, it was *after* McMenemy took over in November that the team climbed (over the next four weeks) to its peak of fifth. More important, though, that recall of events crucially under-states McMenemy's role between July and November. From the moment when Ted Bates introduced him to the players – a 'ceremonial handing-over in the dressing room' – Lawrie McMenemy assumed most of the managerial functions.

Judging by what the Board recorded, he was especially active in overhauling the Club's scouting arrangements. Two days before the season began, he presented an outline of his ideas and announced his plans to meet some of Ted's old pals who had been the stalwarts of the Club's scouting network. By October, Lawrie had replaced one of them in a big way. The Club's North East scout, Bill Rochford, would step down in favour of Jack Hixon, whose 'emoluments', inclusive of expenses, would come to £2760 a year for the services of himself and his 'two Associates'. Hixon's role in bringing Tyneside talent, notably Alan Shearer, to The Dell has been well-documented. You don't have to have read the detailed account, in Jason Tomas's biography of Shearer, to appreciate what an important 'signing' Hixon himself was. But it may help you to evaluate what an investment the Board was agreeing to if you consider that the Club's Chief Scout was on £350. Tom Parker still had this honour – but only because Fred Scott had declined to come from Sheffield Wednesday to take on that role.

There were other matters – training, trials, injuries and 'irresponsible actions on the field of play' – on which Bates and McMenemy reported jointly to the Board and some aspects of players' progress on which Ted continued to report alone. 'It was down to Ted as much as anything', Lawrie feels, 'that I effectively became the team manager from Day One: I'd take the team, I did the team-talks, I did the training. Ted was still called "Manager", but Ted didn't do the press conferences – didn't do anything. I did all of that'.

That comes across from the *Echo* report on Lawrie's first morning. Although a track-suited Ted Bates appears in photos of the training schedules on 26 July 1973, it was the team manager designate who gave the *Echo* his view of the morning's session. 'That was it!', Channon recalls. 'He took it all. Ted was gone'. Eric Martin, was reluctant, as when Mortimore arrived five years earlier, to judge the new man at first sight: 'The first thing I saw, the guy was so *big*. Booming voice. I thought "Let's wait and see what he does"'. Terry Paine, on the other hand, blurted out his instant reaction to the size of the man:

> *I made the most stupid remark I've ever made in my life. He walked into the dressing room with Ted, to be introduced to the players, and I've never seen a bigger head on a guy in my life. It was huge – or appeared to be at the time. I said 'Christ! We'll call him "Elephant Head"' … It just, physically, looked like a big head. I look at it now and he's such a big man, it's normal.*

The fact that 'E-Head' became a new Dell nickname may be not be a huge deal, but it's another example of Paine's hasty judgments of newcomers. It would have mattered even less, of course, if Lawrie had turned out to be a transient assistant like Mortimore and Williams. Was he, Eric Martin wondered, 'just another one coming and going'? If the players had grounds to be cautious, Martin feels that they soon had reasons enough to welcome the new broom:

> *The [new] things were all his ideas … I don't know whether it was because it was something new or whether he just got the players fired up more. I think that's what he did more than anything else – with players thinking they could*

do better than what they could do. Ted never took them to that level [of self-belief]. Lawrie took them up there. Lawrie was a good talker – a motivator – the sort of guy who would push people. Ted was good but Lawrie was a lot better than that.

He may have 'lacked' Ted's capacity to 'talk about the game', but Eric wishes Lawrie's ability to motivate and to discipline could have been available sooner: 'If he'd come earlier, he'd have helped me. He'd have probably helped Steelie'. So, impressionable young men who came down from Scotland should not have been allowed to run wild, then? Martin doesn't exactly discount the stories of McMenemy being 'anti-Scottish' and concerned to get to grips with the 'bunch of wild ones' he'd inherited. But when he tells the story of how the Scots 'went missing' on a northern trip, it is with the remorse of a wild one who needed taming: 'I was sent home from that trip, if I remember … I think if Lawrie had come earlier, it would have changed me. He'd have probably straightened me out a little bit'.

When Mortimore arrived, Mick Channon hadn't taken too kindly, you may recall, to anybody trying to straighten *him* out. If he didn't need McMenemy's discipline, he nevertheless gives 'a lot of the credit to Lawrie for a great start to the season'. By which he means that they went the first four games undefeated. So what if they did lose the next four? They wouldn't be beaten again until the end of November – by which time, as we have seen, they would be riding high, with Lawrie in full control.

Far from taking over a team on a predecessor's high, Lawrie McMenemy had played a major role in steering them there. The 'designate' label had been not so much a way of having a prospective manager serve the indefinite 'apprenticeship' that John Mortimore had envisaged, as having him undergo a probationary period, in which the Board had the 'out' that Lawrie had perceived: if the new man didn't get on, full control could revert to the longstanding servant who was still the 'Manager'.

That would be a far less messy way of replacing an established manager than Manchester United had achieved. When Matt Busby retired, in 1969, after 24 years' service, Wilf McGuinness proved what an impossible act his was to follow. You won't need reminding of how Ron Davies's four goals got McGuinness off to an embarrassing start and, halfway through the next season, Sir Matt resumed control. Pat Crerand dismisses, as 'garbage', the stories of Busby meddling in McGuinness's management. As he sees it, Ted was likely to be less vulnerable, in this regard, than Sir Matt for the simple reason that the media were more interested in who was doing what at Old Trafford. And, even if a Busby is 'only too willing to help' only when asked, can an ex-manager avoid being a 'brooding presence'?

DELL DIAMOND

I borrow that phrase from the FA Chairman, Keith Wiseman, a former Southampton Vice-Chairman who has given a lot of thought to relationships between directors, managers and ex-managers with titles ranging from 'Chief Executive' to 'Director of Football'. But, as he joined Southampton's Board long after it had had to manage Ted Bates's exit, the question as to whether and how Ted Bates could avoid getting in Lawrie McMenemy's way was one that needed to be put to Guy Askham, the sole survivor of the Board that oversaw this major change. His answer is succinct. It was never going to be a problem 'cos Ted's Ted' and Ted had agreed with the decision that 'the time had come to relinquish the role of Team Manager':

> *He understood that the next man in had to come in and do it his way …*
> *That meant it was a relatively easy transition … He allowed Lawrie to do*
> *the front and the leadership and he was always there if Lawrie said 'Go and*
> *look at somebody with me this evening' or 'What do you think about that?'*
> *or 'Are our tactics right?' Then he'd give that opinion. I always gained the*
> *impression: if Lawrie didn't ask him, he didn't give it.*

It suited the Board to have Ted keep 'a bit of a watching brief', as Keith Honey puts it, on its behalf. And it initially suited Lawrie, Mick Channon reckons, to have Ted as go-between to the Board: 'Lawrie's no mug: he kept Ted pretty close to his side because, in Ted, he had a bloody good ally in the sense that Ted would have the ear of the Board, that's for sure'. There may have been the occasional tension, to which some of the directors were capable of contributing. So, somebody like Sir George Meyrick, who 'always had a lot of respect' for Ted, 'football-wise', could ask him in front of Lawrie at a Board meeting, what he would have done in a particular situation. There was 'no way' that Ted was going to answer that question and 'make it more difficult for Lawrie than it was'. Equally, though, there was no way he would have told Sir George that his question was out of order.

That would, of course, have been more like Lawrie's style – the 'upfront' approach which was part of his attraction to Ted when he brokered his appointment. But, then, Lawrie had a different notion of what he would have liked Ted, 'in a perfect world', to have said:

> *I would have liked Ted to say 'I don't know what's happening down there [in*
> *the dressing room]. Whatever Lawrie's doing, I'm sure he's right'. But Ted's*
> *way – his old-fashioned way – was 'If in doubt, say nowt'. My way was*
> *different. My way was 'If in doubt, ask what the hell they're on about: let's get*

it out, now'. That was youthfulness against experience. I would be in with an
over-the-top tackle, whereas Ted would tend to jockey and wait.

You may deduce from this that the problem of adjustment lay less between
the two men – the 'upfront' young manager and his predecessor who could
have been a 'brooding presence' – than with the directors. It was they who
were having to adjust from a longstanding, deferential servant – Busby-
trained in the matter of dealing with his Board (see Chapter 13) – to a
brash young man who was more capable of saying what he thought.
Alluding, in his *Diary of a Season,* to such problems of change, McMenemy
records that Ted and he 'weathered it'.

So what went wrong? That's a question that provokes more agnosticism
than accusation. Hugh Fisher, for instance, 'would love to have an answer: I
honestly don't know what went wrong'. How could the team that Lawrie
had been steering into a strong position go tumbling down the table, taking
only one point from their next twelve away games? They had so far to fall
that they didn't get into the bottom three until the last week of the season.
And this was the first season that three were relegated. The Saints went
down with 36 points, well clear of the other relegated teams, Manchester
United (32) and Norwich City (29), and with more points than teams
usually got in 20th place. In three of their previous seven seasons in the
First Division, Southampton had finished 19th, with totals between 29 and
34 points.

So one answer is bad luck: you didn't go down with 36 points. Another
is that some players were as complacent about staying up as some of Ted
Bates's team-mates had been about going up 25 years earlier. You can't
believe what could happen and you don't adjust to prevent it. This was
especially problematic for the sliding Saints, since their last four home
games were against fellow-strugglers: Birmingham City (0-2), Chelsea (0-0),
West Ham (1-1) and Manchester United (1-1). The first three of those
teams each finished one point above the Saints, so it seems natural to
ponder 'what might have been'. The defeat by Birmingham on 23 March
began a run of seven games without a win, so that a last day win at Everton
was too late. Losing to Birmingham – six points below them before the
game – was a sickener. Lawrie McMenemy had watched the Blues lose at
bottom-placed Norwich in midweek but warned his side not to
underestimate them.

Hugh Fisher says that that wasn't the problem. By the time they faced
Birmingham, 'the pressure was on'. And the loyal support of the fans didn't
serve to lift that pressure:

DELL DIAMOND

'When you're struggling – and you're out there and things aren't going well for you as a team in general – you can feel the pressure coming from the terraces ... When you're out there, you know the importance of the match. The Club's status in the First Division's at stake, so that does put you a little bit on edge and I suppose you sometimes don't end up playing your natural game – you do things that are probably different from what you would normally do. You might get rid of the ball quicker. Consequently, we were scrappy that day. Birmingham – Burns and Trevor Francis – were no great shakes, but we weren't very good that day, either. I think it was purely pressure ... It's easier said than done, but if you try to play your own game – if you're a natural get-the-ball-down-and-pass-it type of player – rather than try to be constructive, sometimes you just hoof it forward because of the pressure of the game. And it becomes a mess.

By that token, it might have helped if all these games against teams at the bottom were away from home. So how come West Ham beat them 4-1 at Upton Park on Good Friday – and then rubbed it in by drawing at The Dell on Easter Monday?

None of this addresses any of the points raised in the McMenemy *Diary* about the nature of the dressing room he inherited, with 'so many gangsters that Al Capone would have struggled to get a game'. In this regard, he distinguishes between 'rascals' – the likes of Jim Steele – with whom he could get along, and with 'villains' who had to go. It seems generally to be accepted that Lawrie needed to impose himself and to make changes of personnel. The only blame that any of the players seems inclined to attach to him is for being in too much of a hurry. As Channon puts it, 'he was very impatient to get his hands on everything and change things'. Having 'done well' as Team Manager Designate, he now 'wanted to change too much too quick'. Guy Askham agrees: 'he chose, as many managers do, to change the personnel around and we got caught out'.

That view is endorsed, ironically, by his first signing, David Peach, who made his full debut at Ipswich on 2 February, a 7-0 defeat that has joined the Leeds debacle of 1972 in Danny Baker's horror video of *Right Hammerings*. Peach feels that 'Lawrie tried to change the side too quickly. And you can't do that'. But there weren't that many new players coming in, surely?

That's right, but it was the way we played and [the difference] between his attitude to the game and what Ted's were. And those lads were Ted through-and-through. It's very difficult because we've all got our own ideas. He could have let it settle down – he could have just let it go until the end of the season – and establish himself in the Club; and we wouldn't have been relegated.

298

Yet McMenemy took his time over the Peach signing. Even though he had been after him while he was at Grimsby, he still dispatched Ted Bates to watch him – 'on numerous occasions', David believes. Haste was not, then, a problem in itself. For Paul Bennett, who felt that the defence – himself included – was too young and inexperienced, letting Kirkup go in February was a mistake and Peach 'was not what we wanted: David didn't have the experience either'. But, then, you can buy the wrong kind of experience – in the form of Peter Osgood from Chelsea, say? Bennett was most impressed that 'a world-class player' could come into the Southampton dressing room and treat everyone, including him, as an equal:

JOE KIRKUP

One of the nicest guys I've known in football, who treated me very, very well. He used to let me borrow his car – when I was a young kid [of 22]. An absolutely lovely guy, he really was – but, at that particular time, it was not what we wanted. It's easy to say it now, but I'd have been content to come out of the side – if he'd bought an experienced player, it probably would have been me or one of the other, younger players – but what the defence was crying out for – and what it had up to the start of that year [before Joe Kirkup was let go] – was the blend that Ted built of good, experienced players and very keen and enthusiastic young players, which was working.

If the new manager was unlikely to consult his young players about the type of experience he should buy, he did ask the Club Secretary for an opinion: how did he think Ted and the Board would feel about investing in the Chelsea super-star? Keith Honey was dubious: 'We were losing by silly scores. It was obvious we wanted somebody in defence'. Indeed, here was a side that would end up with the worst defensive record in the Division, conceding 20 goals more than Manchester United, who finished four points below them. So 'we didn't want – what seemed to me at the time, in my ignorance – a fancy Dan, like Peter Osgood for a quarter of a million'. But Ted backed Lawrie's judgment: 'It was a lot of money, but I encouraged them to let him get on with it. If you have a manager, you've got to back him up'. It grieved Keith Honey to think of money that 'Ted had spent years accumulating gradually, without throwing away anything, going to get a flash signing that would look good in the Press'.

Osgood arrived, of course, to look good in red-and-white stripes. But not immediately. There would be widespread agreement with David Peach's assessment that Osgood made a 'helluva' contribution over the following two seasons. But his ten games that season did little for the cause. Peach suggests two reasons for this. For a start, Peter had been in dispute with Chelsea since being dropped on New Year's Day and – no matter that Channon admires Osgood's attitude to training – there was perhaps a question mark over his fitness during that onerous run-in. Secondly, 'it was "All Change" again', as Peach puts it. 'We had to change the way we played to accommodate him. Peter was more of a ball-player. All this was happening and we were slipping down the League'. Indeed, Osgood's only goal in that 10-match spell came in the futile last day win at Goodison Park.

That was also the second game for another acquisition, Lew Chatterley from Aston Villa. Having been with Lawrie at Grimsby, Lew followed him to the Dell. Although only 29, he was expecting only a coaching role: it 'never entered my head that I'd get a game'. So how did this appear to the dressing room? Did they trust McMenemy's acolyte? 'They were quite good. But there was always that air. Channon did once suggest that I was "Lawrie's Man" – which implied that I could have been planted in the dressing room'. It wasn't malicious, Chatterley feels – 'just a throwaway, a flippant kind of remark. But it's stuck in my mind, to this day, that I was "Lawrie's Man". You think "Did he mean that?"'. Shades of Joe Mallett's concern (in Chapter 7) that intentional digs against a team-mate might sometimes be disguised as dressing room banter.

McMenemy's decision to play Chatterley – twice that season and five times the next – would not aid his credibility with the fans. Yet the crowd was patient. Lawrie recalled, in his *Diary,* that the crowd 'jeered, booed and hissed' him. But these protests lacked the 'intensity' of those Keith Honey recalls from the early years in the First Division, when BATES MUST GO was chalked on walls. 'People were much more patient' with McMenemy, Guy Askham feels, than they would be with Ian Branfoot: 'Their expectations weren't perhaps quite so great; television wasn't around [so much]; the world was different'.

Even so, the fans' forbearance would be tested, the following Christmas, when Chatterley was 'fetched off', as he recalls, in what proved to be his last game, at home to Sheffield Wednesday: 'Lawrie got tremendous stick and I got tremendous stick'. McMenemy feels that 'there was no excuse for what the crowd did that day': he had made a mistake, but 'they targeted one player'. For his part, Lew accepted that 'Lawrie had enough problems without having a problem with me' and moved to Torquay as player-coach.

The crowd's unrest was witnessed by Wednesday's Peter Rodrigues, who'd heard McMenemy 'was sort of interested' in him. As the team bus left The Dell, he told his team-mates that he 'wouldn't sign for them if they were the last club in the Football League'. Well not yet, anyway.

Up with Ted, Out with Terry

If this Wednesday game is much talked about, McMenemy was generally given time – both by the fans and the Board – to regroup and go back up. In the immediate aftermath of relegation, directors like Guy Askham, a particular champion of the McMenemy appointment, were able to keep their nerve: 'We thought he was the man for the job'. But some of the Board wondered whether Ted Bates might wish to make a Busby-like return. There was never any question of this being put to the vote, since Lawrie had no stronger champion than Ted himself:

There's no doubt that I could have come back if I had wanted. I could have got back easily. But you don't do that! Lawrie couldn't understand that I was so loyal to him. I was responsible for him getting the job and there was no way, when he was struggling, I was going to get back again. As far as I was concerned, when I was finished, I was finished. If somebody's struggling, manager-wise, then you've got to help him. Then, if you find he's too weak to do the job, well, of course, he has to go then. Half the time, they sack them before they've even got started … To become a successful manager, you need three years with a club. Now that is a long time for directors to wait if things are not going well. If they take the easy way and get rid of him, then they've got to get somebody else and start all over again.

McMenemy had a free hand, then, to continue his rebuilding during the 1974 close season. Exit Terry Paine. It was a disappointing end to a record-breaking run of 804 appearances for the Club. Terry was substituted in the penultimate game at Turf Moor, where he left the field so grudgingly that he failed to shake hands with Nick Holmes. Another local boy, who'd come to The Dell in his St Mary's school blazer to sign for Ted Bates in 1970, Nick had made his debut at left-back in April 1974 and would gradually ease his way in the following season, sharing left-flank duties with David Peach in a manner that would serve the side so well at Wembley.

Holmes still remembers that first time he came off the bench to replace an ungracious Paine. When the side was doing well in the autumn, Brian O'Neil had told *Goal* that Terry had been 'playing almost better than I can ever remember him doing'. But the substitution at Burnley was his sixth of the season. Was it now time for him, at 35, to step down a division or two? Hugh Fisher thinks it was: 'He was still a great passer of the ball; but I think, with hindsight, probably "Yes"'. Yet Paul Bennett cannot see why: Terry was still 'doing it on the field'.

For most of Terry's team-mates, though, this wasn't the main issue. It was more a question of whether Lawrie needed to remove his undue influence from the dressing room. As a younger member of the squad who valued experience, Paul Bennett felt 'there was no need to rock the boat: if you have a Fourth Division manager coming in to take a First Division club', he surely needs to hang on to experienced players like Paine, who 'knew more about football than he ever did', and Kirkup. But Eric Martin is sympathetic, in this regard, to the new broom: Terry Paine had 'been there so long, he was part of the community. I'm sure it was hard for Lawrie to come in with Terry being there, because he was so loyal to Ted. And Ted was so loyal to Terry. I'm sure it was difficult'.

We must be wary, though, of labelling Paine, or anybody else, 'a Ted Bates man'. Channon used this phrase about himself in his first autobiography, *Home and Away,* but is keen to emphasise that his commitment to Ted Bates did not inhibit a commitment to Lawrie McMenemy: 'I thought I performed for Lawrie. I *know* I did. I got on very well with Lawrie'. The point is, surely, that loyalty to Ted, whether it was Paine's or Channon's or whosoever's, was only one problem for the new manager. There was also the question of credibility: however many championships McMenemy might have won in football's basement, how could he hack it with the internationals in the Southampton dressing room?

Lew Chatterley contrasts the control Lawrie had had at Grimsby, where 'the players were just grateful to be in the side' with the 'struggle' he had at The Dell to handle the likes of Paine and Channon and even some of the

lesser stars: 'Terry Paine was Top Man. He'd always been Top Man. He liked his way. Channon was an up-and-coming superstar and he liked *his* way. Lawrie'd got to come in and "Lawrie Who?" was the word. He'd then got to instil his way of doing this and doing that. Lawrie had to prove to them that he

Toppled Man
Paine's team-mates are divided as to whether the 'Top Man' should have remained, in some capacity, at The Dell.

could manage *them*'. And that power struggle could be easier if Paine's influence were removed. As Channon put it, in *Man on the Run,* here were two 'dominating personalities and both wanted to be top man': Terry was 'Mr Southampton and if [Lawrie] wanted that title he'd have to get rid of him'. Hugh Fisher comes to the same conclusion: 'Lawrie was a strong character. He obviously wanted to be his own man. I think one of the quickest ways was to break up the Paine-Bates relationship'.

So is Hugh saying that Ted was still associating, at this stage, with Terry? 'No. The guy now had the stripe on his sleeves and that was it: Ted was up behind the scenes'. Terry confirms this – although Ted made an exception when he left the field, that last time, at Turf Moor: 'Ted said something to me afterwards, one of the few times: "Don't worry, son"'. There was no question, though, of Ted making 'any comment on either side – on my side or on Lawrie's side. As far as I know, he gave Lawrie McMenemy 120 per cent in support. I would have thought, knowing the man as I do'.

But there's still a further question: if a new manager needed to remove Paine's influence, *as a player,* might he have used him on the coaching staff? Terry had hoped to 'get a job there' once he stopped playing:

> *But, obviously, it wasn't to be … He wanted to sweep clean: there was no doubt about that. It was the Old Guard that was going to be swept away – the likes of me. He wanted me out. I still think he saw me as a danger to his position. He could see that I had such popularity at the Club – on the terraces and I always got on well with the Board. He needed to nip it.*

And more than one of the younger players saw Terry as the heir apparent. Paul Bennett had expected him 'to go onto the coaching staff and eventually finish up as manager. And he would have done it. He would have been brilliant at it'. Bob McCarthy had likewise assumed that Terry would become 'Ted's Second-in Command' and 'take over' when Ted retired. So it was a 'surprise' to Bob when Lawrie released the crown prince: 'He could have contributed a lot more to the Club by staying'. But, then, if 'Lawrie feared for his job', McCarthy can see why he would want to be rid of someone who had become so 'strong at The Dell … Lawrie probably wanted a clean sweep – bring his own coaching staff in. So Terry was obviously the first one to go'.

Indeed, by the time he released Paine, Lawrie had already begun to build his new coaching team. In addition to Chatterley, he had brought Jim Clunie from Grimsby to take over from Bill Ellerington, who had agreed to switch to scouting duties. And, after being substituted in his first game of

DELL DIAMOND

1973-74, John McGrath hung up his boots – to be more correct, Lawrie told him to throw them in the bucket as he left the field at Coventry – and took over the Youth team. John was another associate, from his Newcastle days, of Lawrie's. Ted's old team-mate, Bill Stroud, would be his bucket-and-sponge man, but McGrath's appointment added to Terry Paine's sense of a Northern invasion, in which there was, he regretted, no place for him.

But, then, there was hardly a job there for Ted himself. He might be the 'Chief Executive', with a contract running into the 1977 close season, but that didn't mean that his successor knew 'what to do with him: there wasn't a position for Ted, really'.

Chapter 26

Keeping the Chief out of Mischief

It seems to be clear that Ted Bates was neither a 'chief' nor an 'executive'.

Lawrie McMenemy soon assumed comprehensive control of the Club's operations. As he puts it himself, he 'was running the place like a house: I was always very aware of costs and balance sheets and budgets'. Others will insist, more graphically, that he even counted the toilet rolls.

Whatever Lawrie did or didn't do, there were no executive tasks for Ted. He could help, for a while, as a go-between with the Board – witness the discussion about the Osgood signing – but otherwise he seems to have had three roles: to be a therapeutic companion for Lawrie; to look after the administration of Schoolboy signings; and to contribute to two kinds of scouting – reporting on upcoming opponents and checking out possible signings.

The principal form of therapy came on a Friday afternoon, if they weren't travelling away:

Ted used to love coming in on a Friday afternoon. We'd take a ball in the gym and we'd stay there for half an hour, an hour, just kicking the ball to each other. If I was really uptight, I'd kick the ball as hard as I could. He'd stay there all day and he knew it was me getting rid of my frustrations. He knew the signs – he'd been through it. We liked each other, but I think the biggest common denominator was that we'd both sat in The Chair. You get people in this game who are in there 20/30/40 years: they're assistants or they're trainers or they're number twos or whatever – they mebbees have a little spell, filling in, but they're not managers and they can't do it.

And Ted was 'good company' for Lawrie away from The Dell, including overseas tours, which Ted *'deserved'* to be on: 'The Club owed him that. He'd *earned* the right. Ted loved the patter and loved being one of the [coaching/managerial] lads'.

Ted's performance in the second role – looking after the Schoolboy signings – showed that he had lost none of his penny-pinching ways. When a parent wanted his son to be released by the Club, the FA revealed that he had never been registered. It emerged that Ted had been getting the forms properly signed but had then stuffed them in a drawer: why send the FA £2.50 a form, or whatever the sum was, when there was no real need?

Such office tasks had never, of course, been Ted's forte. He was very well suited, though, to spying missions. He enjoyed scrawling out his cryptic thoughts on players and still talks about players in pen-pictures: clipped descriptions in which verbs are rare (as you can see in the next chapter). And it was a good way for a young manager to make use of an older colleague: let him go out and do the research; then you get to interpret it to the lads. A case, as Peter Rodrigues saw it, of 'picking the brain of the older man and then coming in [to the team-meeting] and expressing it in his way. It's all right having Ted there, but you have to impose your own authority and your own style'.

The FA Cup run of 1976 gave Ted the chance to watch six opponents, including Manchester United before the Final – half-a-dozen times,

Homework Boy at Wembley
Ted Bates done brilliant at his 'homework', according to Mick Channon, here seen trying to act upon it, despite Martin Buchan's obstruction

according to McMenemy: 'It was brilliant. He played as big a part as anyone … His reports were excellent. He knew what to look for. He'd look at set-pieces – did they mark up or were they sloppy? Was there any particular pattern?'. Ted did his 'homework', Channon feels: 'Everything he said – they were enthusiastic; they were busy – but you could stop them. If you could stick out the first 20 minutes, you had a chance'. Hugh Fisher and Peter Rodrigues both remember a focus on the United wingers – 'stop them playing, basically'.

If that seems vague, it could be that McMenemy's psychology is largely to blame. Lawrie was wont to make dramatic use, Nick Holmes recalls, of reconnaissance reports on opponents. Nick felt especially sorry, in this regard, for John Mortimore, when he returned to The Dell in 1979:

Keeping the Chief Out of Mischief

John would come back with the most lovely, detailed report – page upon page of what the opposition did – and the number of times that Lawrie would come in and he'd show you – "Right! This is what we've got" – and he'd throw it in the bin. He'd say "It's what we do – not what they do". That was Lawrie. He made you believe that you were going to beat them doing what you're good at.

To be fair, this act of collective motivation would often be complemented by a one-to-one chat about an opponent. If there was 'no game-plan' that Nick can recall for the Final, Lawrie 'would secretly take you aside and have words'. Ironically, given the efforts of the Board since 1968, Ted still became involved in a matter of discipline during the Cup run. Rodrigues can't be sure, but thinks it was when they'd gone away to prepare for the semi-final. They had broken the curfew: 'We had our little half-a-lager and – I don't know how he found out about it but – we came across the road and Ted Bates was there. He gave us a right bollocking – as did Lawrie'. Rodrigues respected Ted's intervention: 'He was there. He was still part of that club. You respect people like that. If he wanders up and says something, you take it the way it's meant. You say "Yeah, you've been in the game 20/30 years [40 would have been nearer the mark]: I'll accept that"'.

Rodrigues did have prior reason to esteem Ted Bates: he'd heard, 'through the grapevine somewhere', that Ted had been interested in him while he was still at Leicester. That's true. He was on Ted's shopping list in May 1970 – a list of five that also included Wolverhampton's Jim McCalliog. But Ted subsequently explained to the Board that 'the risk of obtaining his transfer was too great owing to Achilles trouble'. Is that right? And Asa Hartford had a dodgy heart, I suppose.

His Achilles held up for Peter to play Gordon Hill off the park – literally – and to climb those Wembley steps to collect the FA Cup. An unbelievable postscript to his career. For Paul Bennett, that Wembley moment was proof that Lawrie McMenemy had learned from his initial mistakes: 'He brought in experience. He won the FA Cup. He *did* it!' But Jim Steele felt that this great occasion in the Club's history was somehow diminished because Ted was not a big enough part of it: 'Ted Bates should have been in charge when we won the Cup. He'd got the nucleus of the team. It's a shame we won the Cup and he wasn't in charge'.

It depends how you define 'nucleus', but that description of the 12 that walked out at Wembley is surely less than fair to McMenemy. Six of them – Turner, Rodrigues, Peach, Blyth, Osgood and McCalliog – had been signed by him. The other six – Steele, Channon, Stokes, Fisher, Holmes and Gilchrist – had signed for Ted Bates. The first four of these had established their places in the team under him. Holmes had been given his break by

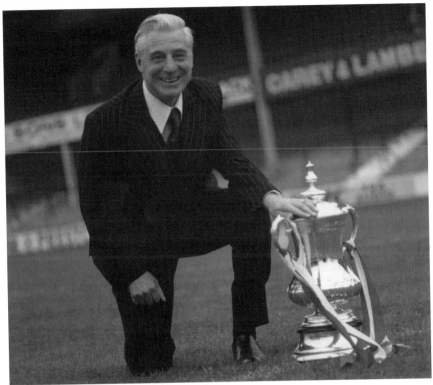

Hands on the Cup
Having failed to make it as a player in 1948 and as a manager in 1963, Ted Bates at last lays claim to Southampton's FA Cup

McMenemy, who had converted Gilchrist to midfield. He took the place of the injured Fisher for the semi-final, scored a goal (if you ignore Mick Channon's mischievous contention that Paul's long shot flicked his sock) and was in the Final line-up, with Fisher as the unused substitute.

That can surely be said to represent a team in evolution, from the side that Lawrie took over from Ted in November 1973. In fact, this side would play together again only in the Charity Shield defeat by Liverpool. When McMenemy brought Fisher on as sub', that August afternoon, that was the end of his Cup-winning side and he was rebuilding for promotion.

~

Ted would be part of the rebuilding team. Even after he became a director in 1978, he would continue to watch potential signings.

To celebrate promotion back to the First Division in 1978, the Club went to Barbados – as they had done in 1976, upon winning the Cup. As Lawrie walked on the beach with Ted, he shared some of his plans for the future, proposals he would put to the Directors. These included Ted's joining the Board.

Keeping the Chief Out of Mischief

It seems not to have occurred to this loyal servant of the Club that he could ever be any more than that: how could he possibly be a Director of 'a Gentlemen's Club', as Lawrie puts it? 'It was always "Upstairs, Downstairs" in Ted's view. They were real gentlemen, landowners, knights of the realm and things like that. And, I never forget, Ted said "Boy, even you couldn't get me on this Board" – because he'd come up in the old, touch-the-forelock kind of thing, pleased to be alive'. And anyway, Ted asked, whatever would he *do* as a director? Simple, said Lawrie, all you have to do is put your hand up when I kick your ankle under the table. The seating arrangements soon scuppered that condition of appointment, but John Mortimore likes to tell the same story.

Going to Portsmouth had proved 'a big mistake' for Mortimore and he had duly left for Portugal. Now he was back for a second stint as Assistant Manager and doing conscientious reconnaissance work. Ted continued to be part of that operation. Not necessarily alone – maybe as second, or even a third, opinion. John Mortimore especially recalls Ted's thoughtful contribution when the two of them went with Lawrie, in 1981, to watch David Armstrong.

In April 1977, towards the end of his stint as Chief Executive and as Lawrie was getting nearer to turning a side that had won the Cup into a side that could play its way out of the Second Division, Ted and one of the coaches went to watch a prospective centre-back. Aston Villa were playing at Highbury. But Lawrie's target wasn't. Chris Nicholl was out of the Villa side. Meeting them in 'one of Arsenal's top rooms' and having no idea why this pair from Southampton was there, Nicholl became involved in the first of many football debates with a man who 'knows more about football than anybody else I've ever spoken to – and can communicate it … His knowledge, and his feeling for football and football people, was absolutely outstanding'.

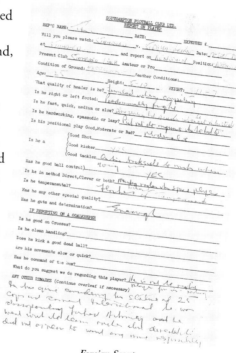

Foreign Scout
Director, Ted Bates, 'continued to be part of the reconnaissance operation' and here files his report on Renquin, the Standard Liège No.5, in September 1980

309

DELL DIAMOND

When he signed for the Saints three months later, Nicholl had the prescience to have a special bonus clause inserted in his contract: 'I was so sure I could get promotion with Southampton, I wouldn't sign until Lawrie put me on double the bonus for promotion'. A good bet for a player who had immediately gained promotion with each of his previous clubs (Halifax, Luton and Villa). But, given the one-to-one nature of contractual dealings, Chris cannot be sure, of course, that he was on twice the bonus of his team-mates: 'Maybe he just told me I was. He had Alan Ball, Peter Osgood, Channon. I said to him "All these players haven't got you promotion. But I will". These are the kinds of things you say when you're negotiating a contract'.

It worked. Nicholl was paired with another new signing, Mick Pickering from Barnsley, in a defence that took Southampton back to the First Division with a most uncharacteristic aggregate of 70:39 – compared with 72:67 the previous season.

If he immediately helped to get Southampton promoted, it took Chris Nicholl a little longer to work his alternative oracle: he'd developed a habit of getting to League Cup Finals. Villa had beaten Norwich at Wembley in 1975 and Everton at Old Trafford – in a second replay – in 1977. Do you remember that Nicholl goal – with his left foot from way out on the right – floating into the Everton goal? David Jones can. His goalkeeper looked as though he was 'putting his arm out for the No.99 bus'. That's how Southampton's 1997 manager recalls that goal by the 1985 manager.

Nicholl got to his third final with Southampton, OK. And he expected a third winners' medal, at the expense of Nottingham Forest in 1979:

We were playing well, going well. I was very confident there – much too confident, obviously. I cost us a goal – certainly one of them. It came into the near post. I read it properly and stopped the ball. And all I'd done was stop the ball for Birtles to stick it in. My job wasn't to control balls. My job was to kick 'em out. It's the kind of thing you do when you're confident. You take liberties.

Lawrie McMenemy also made a misjudgment at Wembley that day – not by taking liberties but by being too cautious:

I've never told anybody at all about this. I intended, on the League Cup Final day, to get Ted to lead the team out. But I didn't want to tell him – because I knew he wouldn't do it. I kept waiting for the right time and I mucked it up ... I intended to get him down to the dressing room and let him lead them out. I was going to stand there – and then run away. I didn't tell anybody, because if he had got wind of it, he wouldn't have come in. But I couldn't engineer getting him down from where he was – it's such a long, long way at Wembley – and it all went awry. What made it worse for me was that, unknown to me, Brian Clough had got Peter Taylor to lead Forest out.

It would have been a wonderful sight, for Southampton fans, to see Ted Bates walking out at Wembley towards the end of his 42nd season at the Club. The new director was still coming into The Dell regularly to jog around the track, have a shower and talk football to whomsoever was around. McMenemy and Chatterley both laugh about the day when Ted asked Lew for some new kit, thereby setting up a head-on clash between Lawrie's legendary tight housekeeping – 'I wouldn't let anybody have too much gear' – and Ted's legendary tight-fistedness. 'Ted didn't give a damn what he wore', Lawrie reckons: 'he'd come dressed like a tramp. Lew said "I've *got* to give him some new shoes". I said, "Are you, buggery? Get him to buy some". He said "I'm going to have to. He's running round in two left shoes"'.

Although Ted's chats, on these occasions, were mainly with the coaching staff, Chris Nicholl was able, often enough, to carry on talking to the man who had so impressed him at Highbury:

I found it much easier to talk to Ted Bates than Lawrie McMenemy … I wasn't on the same wavelength as Lawrie, but Ted Bates – yeah! I came with ideas of going into coaching and management. I just found, in Ted, an instant football communication … I could always talk football with him and he was a willing talker. It was just there, straightaway – right from the start. All the time: anywhere, in hotels; travelling; on pre-season breaks – or mid-season or after-season … Always!

So it was appropriate that Ted should track him down to a hotel, during Grimsby's pre-season in 1985. Lawrie McMenemy had left – that made it two managers at The Dell spanning just under 30 years – and the Board was again using Ted as king-maker.

If the Board wanted to appoint one of their own who was doing well, as a managerial apprentice elsewhere, then Chris Nicholl had less going for him than Ian Branfoot. Ian had played for Lawrie at Doncaster and had spent five years in his coaching team at The Dell before going to manage Reading, initially as an Assistant Manager, becoming Manager during their 1983-84 promotion season. He wasn't interested – when the possibility was mooted – in succeeding his mentor at The Dell, so the door was open for the less-experienced Nicholl, who had had two seasons at Grimsby as player-assistant manager.

He had not long retired from the player part of that title when he took a call from Ted at the team's pre-season hotel: would he be interested, Ted wondered, in becoming Southampton's manager? He was. But, with so little managerial experience behind him, he was very reliant on Ted for advice:

Ted's influence – although it was very subtle and never ever led to any awkward moments – was huge. The Board was always guided by him. I was a brand new manager and needed great *help. Ted Bates was that help – and that anchor. And he was so strong in his knowledge and feeling for the Club; the Directors knew his judgment was sound – on every aspect of running the Club … In the Board meetings, and in my dealings with the Board and the rest of the Club, Ted was a huge influence.*

He was always around and he was always available. Ted was involved in just about everything – in all decisions. Not officially and not publicly – but privately. He was always *instrumental in my thoughts on football … I'd have been* lost *– absolutely lost – but for Ted Bates. He always kept a balance, without taking my side particularly, on everything.*

That kind of support for Chris Nicholl extended to the coaching staff, as Dennis Rofe explains. Although Dennis usually sat with Nicholl on the team coach, they both liked to reflect with Ted on the game from which they were returning: 'We'd just talk about how he saw the game. There is a *type* of director that likes to give his opinion, but Ted was never one of those: he wouldn't come and force his opinion, but if he was asked, he would give you his opinion'. And then there were the moments after Ted's jog:

I often wondered what was going through Ted's mind as he jogged round there, because there must have been a whole host of memories. After he'd gone out and religiously done his 10 or 15 laps, very often he would come into the staff room.

Or, sometimes when we'd get back from 'A' team games – Ted made a point of going to watch Youth team games, Reserve team games – he would come in while we were putting the kit away and the physio would be sorting out the injured players. We'd just have five or 10 minutes sometimes in there. Ask Ted what he thought about the game and he would be very honest – but very constructive; never de-structive.

He usually saw the good points in people – or he let the good points override the bad points. When you go to watch players who you may be interested in, you can either see what they're good at or you can come back and say what they can't *do. Ted would usually go and look at them and tell you what they could* do.

Keeping the Chief Out of Mischief

Go and look at players? Yes, Chris Nicholl occasionally used Ted in this capacity – 'not officially, but he wanted to do it', Chris says – until John Mortimore took over that side of the operations.

Chris Nicholl lasted six seasons – the survival rate was dropping arithmetically from 18 to 12 to six – but that seems like a life sentence by subsequent standards. Nicholl's successors have had rather less need to turn to the ex-manager in their midst. Indeed, during the Ball-Merrington-Souness sequence of managers, when Lawrie McMenemy was available as the Director of Football, I wouldn't have expected the manager to be using Ted as a sounding board at all. And yet a description of Ted Bates's role at the Club, in the 1990s, may surprise you as much as it did me. Managers, from Branfoot to Jones, have talked about their exploitation of Ted's knowledge. So, even, have the players I spoke to. And new directors joining the Board have used Ted for an informal induction to their role.

The rest of this closing chapter takes, in turn, those three kinds of listener to the Saints' sage.

~

First, the managers. When Chris Nicholl went in 1991, Ian Branfoot was interviewed by Guy Askham and Ted Bates. In 1985-86, while Nicholl had been establishing himself at The Dell, Branfoot had been winning the Third Division with Reading. And, following their relegation and his dismissal, he had had a couple of seasons as Steve Coppell's assistant at Crystal Palace.

Any account of Branfoot's difficult time as Southampton's manager is likely to focus more on his style of play – especially when Paul Moody was being preferred to Matthew Le Tissier – rather than on the obligation to sell off some of the young players who had blossomed under Nicholl. 'I *had* to sell all my best players', Branfoot explains:

> There were no ifs and buts: I was told that Shearer had to go. I didn't want to sell him ... I went to every Finance meeting, every Executive meeting, every Board meeting and, because of that, I knew everything about the Club, I knew the financial situation at the Club and, when they said to me he had to be sold, he had to be sold.

If it didn't seem such a bad idea with a 'phenomenal' three million on the table – 'it was absolutely, totally unheard of to take that kind of money in one hit' – it got worse, of course. Ruddock and Flowers '*had* to go: at a club like Southampton, you can't compete with the wages'. But it was surely the spending of that income and the unattractive style of football that led to his being 'crucified', as he puts it, by supporters. As somebody who admired Branfoot's dignified response to some of the more virulent criticism, I confess that I nevertheless stood at the Milton Road end, before the Port Vale cup-tie in January 1994, holding up a red card to signal my belief that he must go.

Much of his difficulty in reacting to the fans lay in the need, as he saw it, 'to protect the Board. I couldn't say "It's nowt to do with me what's happening. I've been told to sell these players. I can't give them the wages"'. He was supported, in turn, by the Board, including Ted, being faithful to his belief – as cited in the previous chapter – that any manager deserves three years to establish himself: 'Ted never, ever wavered. He was always available. He realised the problems that there are – there are always problems if you sell your best players, but you've got to get on and get through. Ted was always supportive – never anything else. Most of the Board were'.

The red-card protests of the fans coincided with a another threat to Ian Branfoot: the return of Lawrie McMenemy. While he 'will always be grateful to Lawrie for the opportunity to come to Southampton, I knew I would never go it [as manager] with Lawrie'.

Enter Alan Ball, to work with the first Director of Football at The Dell. With McMenemy available to him, I'd not expected Ball to have much need, as I say, of Ted. He roundly disabused me:

> When I was the manager, he came to every single game away from home. Many is the time, coming back from a game, I found myself sitting with him – whether he came to sit with me or I went to sit with him. He put marvellous things into my head – about games and how things had gone, and what he liked and what he didn't like, and what he saw and what he thought. I found him fascinating to listen to. He's absolutely besotted with the game. In my 18 months as the manager, he was marvellous to me – absolutely brilliant.

If Dave Merrington had a tough time in his season – 1995-96 – as successor to Alan Ball, it was a very different experience from that of Ian Branfoot: 'The fans were absolutely fantastic', he reckons, but 'mebbees I should have had better support from behind the scenes when the crunch-time came'.

Like Branfoot, Merrington had answered the call from McMenemy to come and look after the juniors. With so much being written about Alan Shearer, attention has been properly paid to Merrington's role in his development. One such writer, David Conn, describes Dave, in *The Football Business,* as 'one of football's most distinguished and best youth developers'. Matthew Le Tissier's endorsement of that view was demonstrated in his presentation of his first England shirt to his Youth team mentor. 'Dave was the biggest influence on my career from the age of 16 to 19', Matt contends. 'It's a shame things didn't work out for him as the first team manager. He wanted to have a go at the Number One job. He'd earned the *right* to have a go. But Dave's personality was more suited to being the Youth team manager'.

Merrington's most ardent supporters – and, as I have intimated, there were plenty of those – would probably agree with Matthew's assessment about the variations in 'personality' required in handling different tiers of teams within a football club: shades of Bill Ellerington's concern about Sid Cann way back when in Chapter 10. And yet those supporters would probably still ask the question we were all asking during the one season of his contractual three that he was allowed to serve: was he being helped or hindered by having a Director of Football?

~

'The jury is still out', Keith Wiseman suggests, on 'the concept' of a Director of Football. And we do not require a verdict to be returned. But, if you were looking for an 'ideally equipped' candidate for the position, Dennis Rofe would have nominated Lawrie McMenemy. In *practice,* though, Rofe felt that McMenemy 'couldn't quite cut the reins of management. He couldn't quite come to terms with the fact that he wasn't manager. Ted had done that superbly'.

Keith Wiseman makes a similar point: 'Some people find it much more difficult than others to release authority or release power. I don't think Ted ever had any difficulty in slipping from one role to the other without being a threat to anyone who'd taken his job. He was very good like that'. In Dave Merrington's book, McMenemy lacked a crucial ingredient for the Director of Football position: *humility.*

Much as he believes that 'there's a need for that type of position', the introduction of a third party into the traditional link between Chairman and Manager will 'work', in Merrington's view, 'only if you have a guy who's employed to do the football job and a guy who's humble enough to recognise what his role is'.

Which is why Merrington feels that Ted Bates could have been a Director of Football:

Ted was a man who I felt was humble enough to keep his distance and say 'I'm here if you need me' and he'd give you the support without forcing anything upon you. I think Ted would probably have been the ideal *one to do that because he was a man who only gave you* help. *If you wanted any guidelines, he would only give you them when you asked him for them'.*

DELL DIAMOND

A beautifully composed comment on what Ted might have been able to do for a manager when he was in the first flush of retirement. But fanciful. The reality is that he has continued to perform – as and when asked – his informal, advisory role. David Jones arrived in 1997, without any Director of Football – McMenemy had gone and he didn't feel the need to have him back. While he imagines that 'there was quite a lot of talk' about how he might work with Lawrie McMenemy, he 'didn't actually want that':

> I just felt that I didn't know him and I needed a fresh challenge and a fresh start. I think – no disrespect to Lawrie – that he would have had his own ways. And the one thing people don't like, in any industry, is change. I think I would have been at loggerheads with Lawrie. I think it needed me to find my own way within the game and there's people here I can draw upon.

Those people include his entourage of assistants and Ted Bates: 'I've sat with him, on overnight trips, to many games … Whatever he says always seems to be good for me, because it's a learning process for me and he has an abundance of knowledge that I draw on. Listening to him and what he's got to say, he's probably the *best* at one-liners I've ever heard'.

As that final tribute comes from a Liverpudlian who learned, in his younger days, from Bill Shankly, an explanation may be required. When Ted's admirers talk, as they invariably do, of his way with 'one-liners', they are referring not to quips in the Shankly mode but to a capacity to make his point with a maxim of a markedly gentler nature. Keith Wiseman has a fine stock of these, as picked up from Ted's half-time summaries, starting with the example of a new signing, 'who shall remain nameless', in the mid-nineties:

> Ted sat there, solemnly looking at the play, and at half-time he said to Guy Askham, 'Didn't pay too much for him, did we?' He could see the chap wasn't quite up to it, but he had such a kind and gentle way of making his point. Another example: again, a nameless player was having enormous difficulty in bringing the ball down and controlling it in less than a 15ft turning circle. Ted watched this effort going on and finally baulked. 'I think I'd rather have the space', he said.

More of Ted's conversations with directors in a moment. Before that, I wanted to see how Saints' players of the 1990s perceived him.

What could footballers of this generation possibly have to talk about to Ted Bates? Kevin Moore, who'd come to The Dell as a 29 year-old in 1987, had the advantage of being able to discuss men who'd played with his father,

Norman Moore, and with Ted. But what did it entail, I wondered, for his generation to talk of 'respect' for the likes of Ted? Simple – 'He'd been there and done it'.

There is something very non-ageist about the way in which young footballers value the experience of their elders. As Moore's contemporary, Micky Adams, assured me, 'the players of today want to learn. And if somebody has a quiet word with you, it can help'. Maybe so. But was it possible, I wondered, for Ted to impart the benefit of that experience with a 'quiet word', here and there, without interfering? For Adams, 'it wasn't interfering at all: it was basically the players asking *him* questions, more than him coming to you – because he's done it all'. Really? 'Done it all?' He had never played in the First Division. That didn't matter to Adams: just having been a manager guarantees you respect and 'Ted has an *abundance* of respect from everybody'.

That extended, I was to learn, to younger players – if those I spoke to are representative. Francis Benali, Jason Dodd and Matthew Le Tissier each learned the ropes in Dave Merrington's Youth set-up and made his debut for Chris Nicholl in the late '80s. They talk just like their elders: 'Everybody knows what Mr Bates has done for the Club', Le Tissier suggests, 'and he has the total respect of everybody here. It is nice to see that he is still interested. Just by his sheer presence – being on the coach'.

The only difference, here, is that it comes natural to these three young men to talk, respectfully, of 'Mr Bates', even though 'he enjoys it', Dodd says, 'when you call him "Ted" – "Hello, Ted!" and all that sort of thing. "Hello, Jason!" – on the team coach and at meals when you're at away games'. Benali also likes to talk to 'Mr Bates' on his travels and 'can sit and listen to him for ages – whether it's on the bus or in a hotel restaurant'.

As if determined to extract an ageist sentiment somehow – why should footballers be an exception to the vogue? – I asked about Ted jogging round The Dell while they were apprentices doing their afternoon routines: were there no 'look at Grandad' jibes? Far from it, Frannie insists: 'Even then [in the mid-1980s], he must have been a fair age and to be coming out and running round the pitch was a kind of inspiration. You think "Blimey! Surely we should be able to do this running work, if Mr Bates is running round at the age he is"'.

Frannie's memory goes back, in fact, to when Ted ran round with George Horsfall, six years Ted's junior, who died in 1992. When you think back to them running around Botafogo's stadium together in 1948 – remember the photo' in Chapter 8? – it becomes easier to believe that, even in the sarcastic world of football, these two old men, and later Ted on his own, really were admired for coming in for a run. 'We used to look at him',

Jogging – the Memory
To imagine George Horsfall running around
The Dell with Ted Bates, in the late 1980s,
refer to the photo' of them in Brazil (page 98)

Benali recalls, and say '"Look! Superb!" I'd love to be doing that at his age'. Dodd agrees:

You wouldn't joke about it because it was Ted. It was Mr Bates, wasn't it? Some other old fellow pottering round, you'd probably have a little giggle, but not when you see Mr Bates, because of what Mr Bates is.

And you know, from the way he says it, that he's referring not to Ted's formal status at the Club but to what he stands for, having 'done it all'.

But could he have 'done it' as a manager today? That's a question which Ian Gordon has often debated with Keith Wiseman and Brian Hunt. Keith Wiseman, Vice-Chairman of the Club until he became the FA Chairman, was introduced in the previous chapter and has already had a word or two in this one. His successor as Vice-Chairman, Brian Hunt, was on the books, in Sid Cann's day, as a teenager. Ian Gordon came a different route to the boardroom. Family tradition – he reminisces about his grandfather going to the Cup Final with the Saints at the turn of the century – dictated that he be a Saints' supporter. That used to be 'the Number One criterion', he says, for membership of the Board: 'You had to be a Southampton fan, through and through'.

Ian Gordon considers Ted to be 'a marvellous man-manager and I think he would continue to be successful as far as that is concerned. I think – and he would admit this – that he would have struggled as far as the financial side is concerned'. Ask how Ian Gordon can possibly judge Ted's man-management skills and he'll tell you to observe the way he talks to current players and encourages them.

Brian Hunt's judgment relies a lot on Ted's shrewdness:

I think Ted is a lot shrewder – football-wise – than a lot of people give him credit for. You've got to take like for like, of course: if Ted had managed today, he wouldn't be 80 years old. If he were 45 to 50, he would have been able. Yes! I think he would. If you think about the difference, Ted's football and football today, the difference is pace.

Keeping the Chief Out of Mischief

Thanks!

Keith Wiseman (right) thanks Ted, on his Dell Diamond Day (3 May 1997), for his 'enormous help'

But neither of those assessments addresses the issue of discipline, a matter that worried the Board when Ted was 50.

Brian Hunt 'wouldn't say Ted was the best disciplinarian in the world. Ted did things in his own way, I will say that. I think that, where Ted was clever, he got the best out of players when he wanted the best out of players. Provided they did it for Ted when he wanted them to, that was good enough for Ted'.

And Ian Gordon fears that that 'own way' of Ted's may not have worked today: 'He would have had great difficulty in disciplining players today. I think he would have had terrible problems'.

Finally, these three directors enthuse, like the managers and players above, about lessons they have learned from Ted. Keith Wiseman has found him an 'enormous help' – not least in after-the-match inquests:

> He's very good at helping you to keep your feet on the ground. He's always said 'Never decide anything at five o'clock on a Saturday – because you're just too wound-up, and into it, and you'll get it wrong'. That kind of advice has certainly been very true. It's amazing how different things seem, even on the following Thursday morning – at a Board meeting or something – than they did on the previous Saturday night. He's been so wise in that sort of way and really very helpful to people coming on to the Board, as younger directors.

Brian Hunt and Ian Gordon each likes to get Ted, one way or another, for the journey to an away game and both try to sit next to him on arrival (Ted sits with Mary and their daughter, Jo, at home games). Brian Hunt spent his first year as a director, 'on the coach of a Friday, talking about past players and where they are and does he see them?' Having been a teenager on the books, as I say, he and Ted have former team-mates in common.

Ian Gordon, on the other hand, has had to take the 'huge step from being a fan to being a director. You see a totally different perspective'. While his 'passion for the Club' helped him, he needed an induction from Ted.

His main chance of getting that is when there's an away game in London or thereabouts and Ted doesn't fancy going on the coach and staying overnight. In that case, Ian Gordon and his wife – he married a 'fanatic' – chauffeur Ted: 'Just sit in the car and let him talk. I love doing it!' If he has a monopoly on that privilege, he has to compete, as I've implied, to sit next to Ted at an away game. 'There's always an argument', Rupert Lowe says, as to who's going to have that seat.

The recently-arrived Chairman found himself, at the beginning of 1998, with a prestigious vacancy to fill. The Club President, John Corbett, who had come to The Dell as a director in 1936 – even before the young Eddie Bates arrived – died on 5 January. His death meant that Ted – who had been the Vice-President since 1993 – became the longest-standing member of this 'family club' and that Mary became the senior member in the Directors' Box, where she has had a seat since she came to the Club in 1945.

It also meant that the Board determined, on 29 January 1998, to elect Ted Bates to be Club President. Rupert Lowe is pleased with that decision:

It's very fitting that Ted's now the President after what he's done for the Club. He's clearly still a very good judge of a footballer. He's a very good judge of a team and the balance within a team. He's the sort of person who – correctly – can be President, hopefully, when we build the new stadium and, hopefully, take the Club forward even further.

Not bad for an errand boy who providentially swapped counties, thereby starting a journey that brought him to The Dell more than 60 seasons ago.

```
MINUTES of Board Meeting held at The Dell, Southampton,
        on Thursday 29 January 1998 at 2.00 p.m.

Present:          Mr R.J.G. Lowe (Chairman)

                  Mr A.E. Cowen, Mr I.L. Gordon, Mr B.H.D. Hunt
                  Mr M.R. Richards, Mr K. St.J. Wiseman.

In attendance:    Mr B.P. Truscott (Secretary)
                  Mr D.A. Jones    (Group Financial Director)
                  Mr J. O'Sullivan (Commercial Manager)
                  Mr D.R. Jones    (Team Manager)

CLUB PRESIDENT:   Following the recent death of John Corbett, it was
    1/98          unanimously agreed that his successor in the
                  position of Club President should be Ted Bates.

TEAM MANAGER:     A report detailing match results and the injury
    2/98          situation was circulated.
```

Mutual Exchange

This postscript to Ted's
first 60 seasons or so originally
consisted of two chapters:
his select Saints XI for that period
(which originally appeared in the
programme for 3 May 1997, his
DELL DIAMOND DAY);
and an appraisal of him.

This commemorative
paperback edition has an
additional chapter – an
attempt to capture the
five years between the
publication of the book
in November 1998
and his death in
November 2003.

TED BATES.

Chapter 27
My Team – by Ted

FOOTBALL SUPPORTERS are basically football managers at heart.

The fascinating thing about football is that we all see the same game differently. So when I was invited to select my best Southampton side through the past 60 years, I knew that I'd be inviting you to compare my selection with yours.

I want my team to be attacking and entertaining, so I've gone for a 4-2-4 formation. And to be considered for my team, you'd have to have played 100 first team games. That ruled out stars in the making like Shearer and stars in transit like Keegan. But that still left me with a large pool for each position. We have had so many great players over the 60 years that I have been here.

It is easy to select a team for any one era. For instance, if you asked me the best team I ever played in, I would name the side that came so close to promotion under 'Daddy Dodgin' – Black; Ellerington, Rochford; Wilkins, Webber, Mallett; Day, Curtis, Wayman, Bates and Grant. Perhaps you would want Ramsey at full-back – although, because his war-time appearances don't count in the 'official' statistics, Alf actually went to Spurs before he'd played 100 times for the Saints. But, then, the reason he went was that Ellerington was keeping him out of the team. So it follows, for me, that Bill should be preferred anyhow.

It's so much harder, though, to imagine how players of quite different eras would mesh together in the modern game. In fact, it is an impossibility. And yet I'm sure that, all things being equal, if they'd grown up today, the 11 players I've chosen (with five substitutes, of course) would have more than held their own in the Premiership and – more important – would have given our supporters a sense of pleasure from watching them.

Peter Shilton would be in goal. Solid, reliable and single-minded and so positive in one-on-one situations. I bought Eric Martin when we were struggling and he proved steady and solid enough. Enough to be my sub.

My full-backs would *be* full-backs. I'm not keen on wing-backs. **Bill Ellerington** gets my vote at right-back not only over Ramsey but – fan that I am of Jason Dodd – over anybody since. Very strong. Accurate right foot. A good positional sense. Read the game well. My left-back would have a strong left foot. I like players that are strong on their natural side. I'd rather have somebody with a good, natural left foot than somebody who's more two-footed but not quite as good. David Peach did so much for us in the Cup Final and scored a few useful goals, but I chose **Tommy Traynor**, so strong in the tackle and such a good all-round competitor. You knew what he was going to do and he could do it well.

I bought some good centre-backs. Knapp, McGrath, Gabriel and Steele. But I've chosen **Mark Wright** and **Chris Nicholl,** good defenders who each used the ball well. Mark, quick and alert, likes to come away with the ball. Chris, tight and very solid, gave nothing away in five very good years for us. Jim Steele, good left foot and competitive and another good user of the ball, would be on the bench.

Alan Ball, such a good one-touch player. Everything he played was early. And he got on with it – so busy and purposeful, so competitive and constructive. What's more, he was a leader on the field, always helping other players. Sadly, that means no place for Steve Williams, so reliable and so composed on the ball. As I say, my other midfielder would have to be left-footed. Nick Holmes, such a solid grafter for the team, just loses out to **David Armstrong,** so mobile and hard-working and a good finisher.

And so to my front four. **Terry Paine.** Such control and such vision. An immaculate crosser of the ball, he could get to the by-line and he could score goals, too. And he could look after himself physically against full-backs. **Mick Channon,** strong, skilful and direct, such good control and such a good finisher. Very quick on the counter-attack. That was one of his great strengths for me, so I used to push him up a little bit on his own, so that Ron Davies could get him in the game early and he'd get behind defenders. Mick didn't like that and he used to say so. He was a very strong-minded individual. As a manager, I liked players who could stand up to me and have a 'chat' like that.

Paine and Channon must be two of the best Southampton players ever. Mick was so good that I could afford to let Martin Chivers go – a good player who scored a lot of goals. In my time, even at our club, I could keep players I wanted to keep. It would hurt me if I was managing today – when players expect to move more often – and somebody I'd brought through from a youth wanted to go when I wanted him to stay.

Ron Davies was so outstanding in the air and so good at getting on the end of crosses that he probably got less credit than he deserved for his finishing on the ground and for holding the line together so well. That line would be completed by **Matthew Le Tissier,** with his good control and composure on the ball, his accurate passing and his dead-ball strikes from outside the box. Matthew has that something about him. He doesn't run about enough for some people but you have to take Matthew's strengths. *I've always said that, in a team, you take a player's strengths and let the team overcome his weaknesses. That gives the team strength.*

DELL DIAMOND

You will agree that mine is a strong team. It would be entertaining. And it has 11 winners.

That doesn't mean I'd expect you to pick the same team. Whether you've been a Saints' fan for sixty years or six months, one thing is certain. You will say

'Why did he pick him? '

SHILTON

ELLERINGTON   TRAYNOR

WRIGHT   NICHOLL

BALL   ARMSTRONG

PAINE   Le TISSIER

CHANNON   DAVIES

SUBSTITUTES
Martin, Steele, Williams, Holmes, Chivers

Chapter 28

On Ted – by acclaim

So has the lad done brilliant?

A lot depends on what and how you're counting. As to *what* we should count, see Ted's appearance record (kindly compiled by Gary Chalk) below. We've already had enough qualitative evaluations of Ted the player and there's no need to try and *rank* him: let's just say that we didn't expect to see him in the Football League's Top 100, along with Terry Paine.

| | FIRST TEAM | | | | | | | RESERVES | | | | | |
| | DIV 2 | | FA Cup | | Total | | | L Comb | | LC Cup | | Total | |
Season	A	G	A	G	A	G		A	G	A	G	A	G
1937-1938	15	1	1	0	16	1		22	4			22	4
1938-1939	14	2	0	0	14	2		21	4			21	4
1939-1940*	1	0			1	0		1	0			1	0
1945-1946			4	1	4	1							
1946-1947	22	4	0	0	22	4		9	4	2	0	11	4
1947-1948	22	10	4	0	26	10		12	4	1	0	13	4
1948-1949	34	11	1	0	35	11		7	5			7	5
1949-1950	33	16	2	0	35	16		3	1			3	1
1950-1951	29	10	2	0	31	10				5	1	5	1
1951-1952	18	8	0	0	18	8		13	0			13	0
1952-1953	15	3	0	0	15	3		2	1			2	1
Total	**203**	**65**	**14**	**1**	**217**	**66**		**90**	**23**	**8**	**1**	**98**	**24**

War Years	South B		War Cup		Total	
1939-1940	12	8	2	1	14	9
	South C					
1939-1940	14	5			14	5
	SR Lge		War Cup		Total	
1940-1941	12	3	0	0	12	3
	FL South		War Cup		Total	
1942-1943	23	12	6	2	29	14
1943-1944	29	7	6	1	35	8
1944-1945	30	9	6	4	36	13
1945-1946	41	14			41	14
Total	**161**	**58**	**20**	**8**	**181**	**66**

KEY

*The abandoned season of 1939-40 is not part of most 'official' records

A	Appearances	**L Comb**	London Combination	**SR League**	Southern Regional League
G	Goals	**LC Cup**	London Combination Cup	**FL South**	Football League South

But should we try to rank Ted *the manager?* This is where the question of *how* you're counting comes in. In the invaluable *Breedon Book of Football Managers,* the authors allot points, based on competitions won, to managers since 1888. Ted Bates is nowhere – compared with his old rivals like Alec Stock (25th=) and Alf Ramsey (67th=). Lawrie McMenemy is joint 28th.

But *how,* I wondered, might those who had played under him score Ted? To test that, I developed 10 questions based on Johnny Rogan's 1989 book, *The Football Managers.* Rogan sums up the qualities of 'the perfect football manager – if such a creature exists'. Most of those qualities entailed a balance between one attribute and a near opposite. Clever stuff as a list of 'qualities', but not ideal, I soon realised, for a questionnaire to which respondents can attach scores. Notwithstanding, I persevered with my invitation to players to score each question out of 10, so that a 'perfect' performance by Ted Bates would have earned him 100 points.

The responses, from 35 players, hardly purport to be scientific but they cover a seemingly representative timespan. You won't be surprised to see that Ted's highest score – of 8 out of 10 – was for where he trained the spotlight. It had not occurred to me, however, that even-handedness would be Ted's lowest ranking. Yet 21 out of 35 scored him lowest on this criterion.

1	Took decisions based on experience and experiment, yet he used intuition, too	7.6
2	Cautious with money, yet willing to spend big if and when a player was worth it and the Board had the money	8.1
3	Street-wise, but never intellectually intimidating	7.7
4	Even-handed man-manager, who had no favourites in the dressing room	6.3
5	Professionally remote, yet close enough to the directors to get what he needed from them	7.7
6	Sensitive to his players' problems, yet capable of giving them a right roasting	7.0
7	Animated yet reflective - both in victory and defeat	7.4
8	A skilful negotiator and keen listener	7.4
9	Ever loyal to individual players yet ever willing to sacrifice them for the ultimate good of the club	8.0
10	An approach to PR that trained the spotlight on the club rather than himself	8.3
	AVERAGE	*7.6*

Ted's favouritism was clearly quite an issue. But, then, as I suggested at the end of Chapter 18, it was something for which players tended to forgive both Ted and the principal beneficiary. They had reason to do so: *results!* The footballers I have met in this project have convinced me that they'll generally overlook all manner of frailty so long as an errant team-mate delivers. And the same goes, it seems, for this manager.

What I'm saying, then, is that scoring a football manager, criterion by criterion, is interesting up to a point, but may not tell us a whole lot. Might it have been more helpful to invite *qualitative* answers? How did my respondents feel about the total person: how did Ted Bates deliver professionally, weaknesses notwithstanding?

On Ted – by acclaim

I *did* ask that question. Here are a few of the answers – representing phases of his 60 seasons and perspectives from different parts of the game, while avoiding undue repetition of the many accolades in the main text:

From his best-man, when he married Mary in 1940:

A good bloke, Ted was. He was a good player and all. He used to give everything when he went out on the pitch, old 'Bullet Head'. He'd head any ball, no matter how heavy it was. He loved the game. I'm not surprised he's stayed there all these years, cos he was a good servant.

JACK BRADLEY

From his manager in the late 1940s:

A nice lad. Quiet. Too quiet. Not as confident as he could have been. A good club man. He let you talk to him. He didn't take over like some lads do. He would stand back. He was loyal to the manager.

BILL DODGIN

From his centre-forward in that side:

We worked nicely together. He was a good passer of a ball, Ted. Great footballer and I'd fit in with him great. I could read him, know where he was going to put the ball.

CHARLIE WAYMAN

From the man they swapped for Charlie Wayman:

Ted did not have all the ability in the world, but his plusses outweighed his minusses. Although there is an adage in football that there is no substitute for ability – this is very, very true – but ability must always be allied to supreme, physical effort. As far as Southampton was concerned, there was never a bigger heart than Ted Bates. I should like to pay some credit to Mary Bates. What a good job she did at Southampton when it was not fashionable to have lady Secretaries! **The Bateses are the Club.**

EDDY BROWN

327

DELL DIAMOND

From the man who awarded him his FA Coaching Certificate:

First of all, he was a great coach. When I say 'great coach', he was above what I call average standard and he was at that level where you could say he was a Staff Coach [at Lilleshall sessions]. That means he was good at that job. Now, how he applied himself was in his own character. Ted was a very conscientious person – conscientious about anything he did. If you mention Ted Bates to me, I can almost see him smiling. A likeable man. An industrious fellow – I had some good coaches who were very lackadaisical: they wouldn't start on time and that sort of thing. Ted would be down-to-earth and get on with the job – straightaway! To me, that stamped the man.

SIR WALTER WINTERBOTTOM

From the team-mate who stimulated Ted to coach:

Ted is one of the best coaches I've ever run into, in my football career – in his way. I have great admiration for Ted Bates. I would say that – like many other things in life – perfection is a long, long way away. If there was a League of all those people trying to qualify to get perfection, then I would have to put Ted Bates at the top. When you're in his company, it's never a difficulty. His human behaviour is in the Premier Division.

GEORGE CURTIS

From a longstanding team-mate, who later played under him, coached the youth team and scouted:

With his head – near post – Ted was dynamite. I must say I was surprised when he was appointed manager. But he grew in stature. What I admired was he wasn't too proud to ask anybody about football. He built a team from a rag-bag side – which it was when I was there – to a good, polished diamond. His appointment was one of the best things that ever happened to the club.

BILL ELLERINGTON

On Ted – by acclaim

A backroom view from a physiotherapist who shared Ellerington's surprise:

Ted fooled me. I never thought Ted had the depth and the knowledge and the intellect to do what he did with the Saints. I was very surprised when he got the managerial job. He was a good, second team trainer: I thought that was about the limit of his abilities. But he blossomed out. I had a feeling that Mary had a lot to do with it, that Mary was a very strong supporter and that she gave him confidence in himself, because he didn't look managerial class.

DON FEATHERSTONE

From the captain of his first promotion side in 1960:

A football fanatic. I've never come across anybody so single-minded. He could not switch off. He'd say 'How's the family?', then football, football, football. In all aspects of the game put together, he's top of the list to my mind. He took Southampton from the Third to First on a shoestring. He achieved the maximum for the Club.

CLIFF HUXFORD

From the captain of his second promotion side in 1966:

Ted Bates is unique in English football. Honesty, integrity, ambition, hard-working. He's the most honest manager I ever worked under. Maybe he could have been harder but I've never met a more hard-working manager. How Mary stood it I don't know.

TONY KNAPP

From the perspective of being his 'other' winger – the one who played only 397 times for him:

The Club will never, ever have anyone like him. There never was, and there never will be, anyone like him again. I just feel a lot of respect for him. I certainly didn't agree with him over the years: we had loads and loads of disagreements. But, at the end of the day, I believe we ended up with mutual respect for one another. And I think he was a very shrewd man with regards to signing players and building teams.

JOHN SYDENHAM

DELL DIAMOND

From the referee in the 1963 FA Cup saga with Nottingham Forest:

He's such a genuine man. A man of tremendous integrity. A lot of referees fear talking to some managers who will try to use the situation to their benefit. You didn't fear talking with Ted Bates. There was nothing like that about Ted Bates at all. A friend of mine who had a lot of admiration for Ted Bates was Joe Mercer. They were both whole-hearted football men, with high principles about the game and about their conduct.

DENIS HOWELL

From one of Joe Mercer's stars, who enjoyed coming to The Dell:

I always put Mr Bates in a position with the Busbys and the Shanklys and the Mercers and the Nicholsons, because he was a very respected man. You knew when he came into the room, he was there. When you went to the club, the directors were all country gentlemen. They weren't like lots of the directors of football clubs, who are spivs, in different versions, today. That's what it was about, Southampton. And the man who epitomised it, in every way, is a gentleman, respected in the game of football not only by the Southampton players but by all the players of my era. Everybody, in that particular era, respects him. And when they think about Southampton, they always think of Mr Bates. He epitomises what Southampton has always been about – a clean, entertaining, nice place to go and play football.

MIKE SUMMERBEE

From the perspective of a player he used as 'a catalyst' and who was 'surprised' to be sold on so soon:

He's a gentleman, first and foremost. He's a very good psychologist and he's got a hidden, ruthless streak. If he's got to chop somebody, he'll chop them – no problem! He's not soft. He might look it, but he's not soft. And he's a very good tactician, football-wise.

GEORGE KIRBY

From the standpoint of being a perpetual reserve:

He was one of the nicest fellows I've ever met – as a gentleman. I probably didn't think that he did fair by me sometimes, but that's natural. But, if everybody were like Ted Bates, it would be a lot better world … He's a Yorkshireman, anyhow, isn't he – basically?

DAVID THOMPSON

330

On Ted – by acclaim

From one of the three Scottish goalkeepers Ted fielded in his 1966 promotion side, who finds parallels with three great Scottish managers:

> *Ted Bates had the charisma and the charm of a gentleman like Matt Busby. He had the dedication and enthusiasm – and the involvement – of Bill Shankly. And he certainly was as astute and as aware as Jock Stein.*
>
> CAMPBELL FORSYTH

From two managerial contemporaries:

> *Ted was a real good, conscientious player and a manager. As a manager, he was fairly tight: he got every ounce he could out of a player and did it well. He deserves to be with a team for 60 years, because he's such a likeable guy. He was so conscientious that nothing passed by without he knew a bit about it. He was a bit unlucky that – like me at Swindon – he didn't have millions of pounds to play with. I think that's a true judgment of a manager – somebody who can see one in the raw as a schoolboy, or a youth and bring him up to be a star name.*
>
> *Any fool can sign six young players. You've got to start from there, after you've signed them and work hard to get them to be household names. It's a long, long drive.*
>
> BERT HEAD

> *One of the things about that period, management was so good. Management was so bloody honest. There was Ted, Ted Drake, Bill Nicholson. They all worked their guts out for their side. They weren't going to get rich. They had a job of work ... Ted – a great buyer! I envy him the Davies buy: how do you buy a striker like that?*
>
> ALEC STOCK

DELL DIAMOND

Upon serving an apprenticeship under him, as his Assistant Manager:

A real gentleman. A good pro. He handled men superbly. A terrific knowledge of the game. He knew it inside out and could pass that onto others. That gained respect from players he dealt with, from staff he worked with and throughout football. Working with him for three years was a great experience. I felt, after being with Ted, I could go anywhere to work – to Benfica, Spain, Greece, anywhere. I learned as much about the game from Ted as I learned from anybody – from coaching courses or anywhere else. He does impart knowledge. You just learned about football from Ted. You had to learn about football because he didn't talk about anything else. A football man. A Southampton man. Incredible man.

JOHN MORTIMORE

From his managerial successors :

Ted, as a bloke, is a one-off. He never sought fame and fortune, yet his achievements demanded both. He wasn't bothered about being on the television. Ted and Bill Nicholson, and people like that, didn't want to go in the press-room, even. Those lads were famous for saying nowt.

The word 'legend' is misused a lot, but I think in Ted's case, it's the apt word. I think Ted deserves everything, and more, for the work he did in the early days. I just like to think that I built on the groundwork he had done. The foundations were right.

LAWRIE McMENEMY

He knows more about football than anybody else I've ever spoken to – and can communicate it. And can enlighten you, can give you know-how, can give you knowledge. He just knows everything and it seeps through his bones. It's in his blood. He's still like that. When I talk to him, he's still talking football. He's still kicking a ball, in his mind.

I still see him, today, when we're walking our dogs. Ted still looks like a footballer. It's his bandy legs and a certain way of movement. He is a footballer and that little white dog could be the ball'.

CHRIS NICHOLL

On Ted – by acclaim

From the Club Captain:

A fantastic man! He's always very cheerful and happy to have a chat with you, around the Club – no matter where you are or what you're doing. He has such an amount of information, and he's experienced so many things through his life and career, that you can't help but be interested when you sit down and talk to him.

FRANCIS BENALI

From the current Vice-Chairman, who was on the books, as a teenager, when Ted Bates was a player:

Ted Bates is synonymous, above everyone else, with this Club. What Ted has done for this Club! The way that he's done it, the manner in which he's carried it out – and he's been through every job, from playing right through to President. And each one has been an honour for the Club and I think the Club have been honoured to have him.

I think he stands for everything that is good about Southampton Football Club and for everything that is good about professional football – I REALLY DO.

BRIAN HUNT

About the next chapter...

The background to the new chapter that follows overleaf is outlined in the preface to this paperback edition at page (xviii), where I have thanked those who have helped in its assembly.

I am grateful, for photos used with permission in this chapter at the pages indicated, to the following:

Southampton FC, for photos by Mike Atkelsky (as kindly retrieved for me by Mark Bratcher and Nikki Saunders at Cedar or by Jo Dalton and Jon Evans at the club) – page 335 right, 336, 339 top and bottom two, 342, 346, 348; Mary Bates – 337 both, 338 left, 339 middle, 340; *Southern Daily Echo* (as kindly retrieved by Jez Gale and Paul Green) – 335 left, 338 right, 347 all three.

Chapter 29

The Final Chapter

On 3 May 1997, Ted Bates stepped out onto the Dell pitch – a moment captured in the photographs on page 319 and the back cover – to mark the 60th anniversary, to the very day, of his arrival at the Club.

I was impressed, as intimated in the Preface, by the warmth of his reception. Having embarked on his biography two years earlier, impressed by the length of his loyal service but otherwise knowing very little about him, I had amassed ample evidence of his popularity among the ex-players I had interviewed; but this was for me the first indicator that a man who had stepped aside as manager a generation ago, in 1973, was such an esteemed figure among the fans, so many of whom would not have known him as a manager and so few of whom would have been able to remember him as a player.

The next six years would present several opportunities to confirm the respect and affection in which Ted was held and this new chapter is, as much as anything, a testimony to that. It is a quite remarkable story of a man who had celebrated his 80th birthday in May 1998 and who would, within the year, be suffering from short-term memory loss – in addition to the impaired hearing that had long handicapped him – yet whose high-profile life would include an invitation to Buckingham Palace and several other public appearances: a paradox, in other words, of an octogenarian gradually disengaging from an active routine, yet being often accorded celebrity status.

I first saw Ted publicly fêted by an assembly composed both of fans and ex-players, in November 1998. The occasion – a triumph for its organiser, former centre-half Paul Bennett – was both a launch of *Dell Diamond* and a celebration, a year late, of Ted's 'diamond' anniversary. Paul wanted it to be open to the fans – people like his Mum. There were two ways of achieving that ambition. First, it could be a day of two halves: an inexpensive afternoon; and an evening that consisted of a sit-down dinner with the usual speeches. And by finding sponsors, Paul ensured that the fans would not have to pay over the odds.

The highlight of the afternoon was an unscripted variation on *This is Your Life,* in which former Saints took turns, chronologically from Doug McGibbon on, to pay tributes to Ted and tell such yarns as spontaneously grabbed them. The younger men patiently waited their turn and then self-edited so effectively as to avoid repetition. Consequently, their tales were pleasingly original, ranging from the sober and reflective, with Johnny Walker so emotionally overcome by the nostalgia that he couldn't talk at all, to stand-up comedy, starring Eddy Brown. It over-ran substantially, but the fans revelled in 30-odd former Saints taking them through 40 seasons of Ted's 60 at The Dell.

The climax to a stirring day was a presentation, by Ron Davies, of a signed blow-up of his brilliant caricature of Ted that appears as a frontispiece to this book. Both Ron and Ted were back in town, the next day, now accompanied by Terry Paine, to sign copies of *Dell Diamond* at the Saints Bargate Store. Davies and Paine were obviously a big draw – *too* big in so far as the shop had to send out for more books and the *Echo* reported frustrated fans complaining that it was like 'a pub with no beer'. Within days, the book had sold out, but it was soon reprinted for more signings in Southampton, Eastleigh and Basingstoke, where it became clear that Ted was an attraction in his own right.

It was when he was signing in Eastleigh, though, that I noticed how suspect his short-term memory had become: goodness knows how many times he asked me what I was doing for Christmas. But for the moment his long-term recall remained fairly sharp – sharp enough for him to make some useful recordings over the next two years, anyhow. Thus, in the summer of 1999, he recorded his memories of management for the club's official *Millennium Video*. If you have a copy, it's a performance worth re-viewing. You see Ted enthusing, in that gentle but infectious way of his, about such events as his signing of Davies and how he had foreseen him

Ted is joined by Ron Davies (left) and Terry Paine for the first book signing at the Saints Bargate store.

The local branch of Saints Supporters – here represented by Sheila Barton – helped to organise the Basingstoke signing.

thriving on the service of Paine and Sydenham. We returned to the Paine theme in the autumn when Ted reminisced, on the record, for my forthcoming biography of Terry.

And come the next summer, he relived games, going back to 1949, for what became his foreword, in November 2000, to *Match of the Millennium*. Then out he came, accompanied this time by Matthew Le Tissier, to sign copies of that book (see the line-up on the inside back-cover).

～

At about this time, Ted was notified of his next public appearance – in the New Year's Honours list. He had been appointed MBE. With 1 January 2001 being a Monday, it meant that the list could be published in the press on Saturday 30 December and so Ted Bates MBE could come out and take a bow – well, to give us a wave *(right)* – before that afternoon's game against Derby County.

This was not the first attempt to get an award for Ted. Director Ian Gordon recalls a previous occasion, maybe 10 years before, when the Board liaised with local MPs to that end. He wishes Ted could have been honoured sooner, when he could have enjoyed it more – and when he deserved it: as Vice-Chairman Brian Hunt puts it, 'Ted should have had it 20-30 years ago. *No*-one could have been a better ambassador for *any*-thing than Ted Bates'. It can probably be safely asserted that this latest, successful recommendation took off at the *Dell Diamond* dinner. In the course of his speech, Terry Paine suggested that, if his own loyalty to Southampton FC had helped to secure his MBE, then it was about time Ted was similarly honoured.

It seemed that some fans were looking to us at Hagiology Publishing to follow-up Terry's nudge. But when we approached the club, we were advised that Dr Alan Whitehead MP had already submitted a recommendation and that we should request that any submission by us be added to his. And so we did. Drafting that recommendation was a pleasingly straightforward task: a few of the tributes from the Great and the Good were reproduced from Chapter 28 to demonstrate both the *respect* in which Ted was held across the game – extending to the FA's first head of coaching, Sir Walter Winterbottom, and a leading referee, Lord (Denis) Howell – and his *standing* in the game, as summed up by Campbell Forsyth's ranking him with the likes of Bill Shankly, Jock Stein CBE and Sir Matt Busby CBE.

In so far as there is a *pro forma*, recommendations should include, we were told, a note of the nominee's *contribution to the community*. I cited two aspects of my post-publication experience: of witnessing his reception at signings, where I could eavesdrop on expressions of gratitude for what he had done for this admirer or for his or her family; and of fans approaching me with accounts of this man who'd come to their humble patch to hold a coaching session or to present a trophy.

The letters after his name brought a new challenge. Upon this book's third printing in August 2001, I found Ted signing himself 'Ted Bates MBE'. Sadly, though, he could not be guaranteed to remember those three letters in the right order. One fan has a collectors' item: a copy attributed to him with the appendage 'BEM'. As I say, sad, but you had to see the funny side – it was pretty much a case of having to laugh or you'd cry. Ted had always preached that we should not dwell on a player's weaknesses but play to his strengths. And so it was with his dementia. You had to ignore the limitations of the present and help him live in the past. True, he had told the *Echo,* most unsentimentally back in the spring, that he would not shed a tear upon leaving The Dell – 'I like to look forward, not back' – but as far as conversation with him was concerned, it by now paid you to stick with the past. But, then, what a comprehensive past Ted had to share with you!

That's if he could hear what you were saying. According to Brendon Batson – the former West Brom full-back, now of the FA – who was next in line to be presented to the Queen, Ted was having trouble, in the wings, hearing and following the directions on how to approach her. As you can see from the photograph *(right),* he had to cock his head, in his characteristic way, in the hope of catching the Royal drift.

Mary and Ted at Buckingham Palace

DELL DIAMOND

He was much in demand in 2001. In April, he was made a Freeman of the City of Southampton. Then, on a June evening, he took his grandson Steven with him to The Dell, to shut the gates.

With the mayor of Southampton, Cllr. Peter Wakeford, on the occasion of being made a Freeman of the City of Southampton.

Ted is joined by grandson Steven to shut the gates at The Dell, after 103 years, for the last 64 of which he had served the Club.

And, in August, he opened the Friends Provident St Mary's Stadium. 'It was entirely fitting', Rupert Lowe felt, 'that Ted should be there to open the new stadium which, but for the foundations he'd put in, I suspect would never have happened'.

Having unveiled a commemorative plaque and then cut the ribbon at the pitch-end of the tunnel, Ted came out with Matthew Le Tissier to perform the opening ceremony - the man whose managerial skills had rehabilitated the club in the 1950s and 1960s, accompanied by the man whose playing skills had kept Southampton in the Premiership and made a new stadium both a necessity and a possibility.

Matthew and I agreed, towards the end of that season, that I would approach Ted for a foreword to his testimonial programme that I was editing. He had a few pearls – for a foreword typical of his shrewd appreciation of talent and demeanour. The makers of a documentary on Alf Ramsey found it more difficult to get Ted elucidating before a camera. When their programme was shown in June 2002, we had but a sentence from him and it was left to the ever-lucid Bill Ellerington to recount Ramsey's Southampton years.

338

The President opens the new stadium

Clockwise from above:
He has unveiled a plaque
with Chairman Rupert Lowe.

Mary (right) and daughter Jo join him
at the entrance to the tunnel.

He cuts the ribbon.

He is joined by Matthew Le Tissier,
co-star of the opening ceremony.

DELL DIAMOND

During the previous 12 months, Bill had started to call on Ted and Mary. He had learned that their dog had died, in June 2001, and that Ted was no longer getting out of the house to walk Pepé – the white poodle featured with him at page 332. It takes a leap of imagination to see Bill Ellerington, now 80 but still standing straight and tall, as poodle-replacement therapy, but Ted and he were able to relive events – and, even moreso, recall personalities – of 50 years ago. True, he had to withstand Ted's repeatedly commenting on his figure – 'You were always lucky with your weight, weren't you, Bill?' – and he found that the man famed for conversing only on football could now talk *family*. Ted could still talk football, though:

Bill Ellerington stands straight and tall behind Ted at the retirement party, in May 2002, of physio Don Taylor.

> *He would bring up different players and he'd go back quite a while, to when he first took over. He spoke a fair bit about Mr Henwood [see page 159] and we talked about how fortunate we were with the young players we got because they were mostly handy: Terry Paine; and Martin Chivers, who lived just up the road; Sydenham; Mick Channon… Things like that – and who we got and who we didn't get. What* isn't *interesting, talking about football?*

To say that Ted 'struggled on' would be to resort to cliché. The struggle was for those around him – principally his family – to adjust to his 'deterioration', as Mary puts it. If no longer walking Pepé was a landmark, not renewing his driving licence, and then getting rid of his car in December 2002, was another. His daughters had become increasingly worried about his capacity at the wheel. But, then, as Mary has pointedly reminded me – jocularly recalling passengers' stories like that of Jimmy Melia (at page 240) – 'everybody pulled his driving to pieces all his life. That was nothing new – he couldn't deteriorate much further'.

He had by now stopped going to away games, even in the car of Ian Gordon, who had been taking him (see page 320) to matches in London and maybe Birmingham. He was now limited to home games. The club ensured that he would get to them by arranging for a taxi to collect him and Mary - accompanied as ever by their older daughter, Jo – and to take them home after tea in the boardroom. As far as the refreshment rituals were concerned, it was business as usual on a matchday. But the President was no longer holding court. Before lunch, 'he would sit over in the window area', Mary recalls, 'and everybody would come over – "Hello, Ted! How are you?" "I'm fine, thank you". There wasn't any follow-up conversation from Ted… Afterwards, we would sit and have tea and sandwiches… Others would get up and walk about but he'd sit with us. He'd talk about the game – though not a lot, really'. It reminded Brian Hunt of the last two years of meeting Bob Paisley at Anfield:

He used to sit in the chair and just smile at you: he didn't speak. It was just the same with Ted, but it's a great credit to him that he still came to football. He was obviously enjoying it - he was obviously very content in his own mind, obviously very content with watching the football. He was not a demonstrative person when it came to watching football matches.

I experienced this matchday withdrawal for myself in October 2002. I had been charged with minding a distinguished visitor to the game against Manchester City: Ivan Golac. He had always enjoyed joking with Ted, who wondered whether he would ever see him head a ball, and asked to see him. Ivan is pleased to have had 'a nice chat, but he looked a bit tired' – though, in truth, most of the chatting was left to Mary. To paraphrase Brian Hunt, Ted was by now only there for the football.

Shortly after that, he was diagnosed with Alzheimer's Disease. But the taxi continued to bring him to the stadium – right up to the FA Cup Sixth Round tie with Wolves. He had a fortnight in hospital and couldn't get to the semi-final. When I gate-crashed his 85th birthday party three weeks later, he was sufficiently perky to encourage hopes that he'd be fit for the Final. The Board was keen to get him to Cardiff, so much so that there was talk of chartering a helicopter. But Mary was not holding her breath: 'I knew it would be too much for him: the spirit may be willing – and the heart – but the poor old legs wouldn't carry him'.

Two days after the Final, he had his last public outing, a final visit to St Mary's - to the Terry Paine Suite, where Terry, watched by John Sydenham, was presenting his first England cap to the Club. How apt that the two players who had been with him all the way from the youth team to Europe should be with him for his swansong.

~

Now that he had stopped going to home games, Ted would have another visitor to his home: John Mortimore, his first Assistant Manager who had retired in the summer of 2002 and had duly been appointed Vice-President (a position that had been vacant ever since Ted succeeded to the Presidency

Ted's last outing was to accept Terry Paine's first England cap for display in the Terry Paine Suite.

in January 1998). Like me, John would constantly be told that he was 'looking well':

> *That was no hardship – it was just good to see him... When he was able to go to the new stadium for matches, then, of course, we saw him; but when that stopped, then I made a point of trying to see him... Towards the end, he couldn't hold a conversation of any sort. Mary put me off a couple of times because Ted just wasn't getting up and doing anything. That was very sad: you felt you wanted to see him, but it was of no benefit to him.*

Indeed. I was not among his summer visitors. As we strove to put the latest Hagiology book, *In That Number,* to bed, I had occasion to speak on the 'phone to Mary and to learn that Ted now needed nursing care at home. Yet that did not prepare me for the news when I next rang on Saturday 22 November to ask if I might stop by to present a copy of that book, just published, to Ted. He was too ill to receive me, so Mary and I agreed that I'd try again soon. Come Tuesday, though, Ted was admitted to a nursing home where, in the early hours of the next day, Wednesday 26 November, he died. He never did see this book that charts Saints' 57 post-war seasons, in each of which he had had a role. As Frank Keating commented, in the *Guardian,* 'the only sadness' about this comprehensive chronicle was that 'Southampton's most saintly eminence... did not live to relish and savour every one of its 628 pages'.

The Final Chapter

Other tributes in the broadsheets followed suit. Ivan Ponting, in the *Independent,* acknowledged Ted to be 'the Father of the Saints', while the anonymous *Times* obituarist captured him more prosaically as 'a kind of gaffer… who was less interested in appearing on television advertisements than waking up at 5am to make sure all the players' kit was clean and that all the bulbs in the team bus were working'.

All good stuff, if slightly diminished by the inaccuracies that seemed to beset these obituaries, notably that Ted's father (Leeds City, 1907-09) had managed to play for Leeds United (formed 1919) and – perpetuating the myth addressed at page 293 – that Ted had made way for McMenemy a month later (and four places higher) than he in fact did. And there were other mistakes: Ponting had Ted serving in the Army *during* the War, whereas we know he joined up after it (see page 59), while the *Times* had Ron Davies signed in time to contribute to promotion in 1966. So did the *Guardian*'s Brian Glanville, who was confused also as to the sequence of Ted's war. And he should have avoided contextual details if he could not get them right. If his inaccurate reporting both of Alf Ramsey's position on arrival and of the extent of Charlie Wayman's unavailability in April 1949 were comparatively minor irritants, his account of Mary Bates's position was not merely careless but utterly bizarre and potentially offensive: according to Glanville, after becoming manager in 1955, Ted appointed Mary Secretary. Even if we ignore the fact that she never attained the post of Secretary – an easy enough mistake, perhaps – and overlook the silliness of suggesting that the club's manager would have appointed its Secretary, any half-decent research would have revealed that Mary had already been the club's Assistant Secretary for 10 years when her husband became manager. It is sad that the family of a man who had endured lazy London-based reporters 'distorting the facts' (see page 257) should be treated in this cavalier fashion after his death.

Fortunately, the club was on the ball: Graham Hiley compiled a centre-spread for the next programme (for the Carling Cup-tie with Portsmouth on 2 December), paying tribute to the man who was known, 'to Saints fans everywhere,' he suggested,

as Mr Southampton… He was effectively the father of this football club, laying all the foundations not just for the current success but for its whole philosophy… his qualities of decency and honour shine as a hallmark throughout the club. The word legend is often over-used in football but Ted Bates fully lived up to that tag in everyone's opinion but his own… He was genuinely surprised that what he considered to be a privilege should be deemed worthy of an MBE.

DELL DIAMOND

I hope that excerpt does justice to a nicely-crafted eulogy. Among those whose tributes Hiley assembled for his spread were Ted's two most loyal sons who had been with him, as just noted, for his last public appearance six months before: Terry Paine and John Sydenham, phoning in from South Africa and Australia, respectively. Sydenham concluded with 'condolences to Mary and the family. Nobody could have given more support than you over all those years.'

Just so – and because Eddy Brown had paid tribute to Mary when I was eliciting comments on Ted (see pages 327-333 above), I reproduced his accolade – trumpeting that 'the Bateses *are* the Club' – in the space afforded me at the end of the spread. If you look back at those tributes and note their sheer *range,* you will appreciate my difficulty in selecting but six of them, including Brown's call to 'give some credit to Mary'. My choice echoed, by and large, the selection cited in the recommendation for the MBE: Winterbottom on a 'conscientious' and 'industrious' coach; Howell on the 'tremendous integrity', so respected from a referee's perspective; Knapp on the 'unique' attributes of his 'most honest manager'; Nicholl on the man who 'knew more about football than anybody else I've ever spoken to'; and Forsyth's exquisite assessment of him against the triple-yardstick of Busby, Shankly and Stein.

～

In a footnote to the spread, the club made a plea: it hoped that Ted's 'gentlemanly nature' would 'be reflected' during the one minute's silence that would precede the game and was 'confident the Pompey supporters will pay their respects as solemnly as the Southampton fans did when Aaron Flahavan [Portsmouth's Southampton-born goalkeeper] was killed in a car crash'. The Portsmouth Chairman Milan Mandaric gave notice, elsewhere in the programme, that he 'would find it very difficult to believe and accept if any of our fans did not give proper respect but I am confident they will behave with the correct dignity'.

I confess that I shared their confidence: however 'fierce' the rivalry to which the Chairmen referred in the programme's joint message, were there really people incapable of suspending it for a minute? To have acknowledged that possibility and to have bowed to it would have meant being 'knocked off course', Rupert Lowe felt, by a 'lunatic fringe' – so there would be a minute's silence at what he considered to be 'the appropriate game'

But silence there was not. When a small minority of Pompey fans acted in the manner feared, a few home fans at that same (Northam) end arrogated to themselves the right to hush the nuisances. The din became worse, whereupon a few folk at the Chapel End unhelpfully decided to boo and referee Poll blew his whistle to bring this appalling episode to a close.

The Final Chapter

When the sides re-assembled for a League game on 21 December –
a bit like the proverbial buses, two games between the Solent 'rivals' had
suddenly come along at once – a page of the programme was given over to
a sample of the 'silent majority' of Portsmouth supporters deploring the
behaviour – variously described as 'disgraceful', 'disgusting', 'despicable',
'mindless', and 'moronic' – of the vocal few. The Chairman felt that home
supporters could use a second chance, five days later, to pay their respects.
The one minute's silence was therefore repeated – and impeccably observed
– at the Charlton game on 7 December.

~

Two days later, Ted's funeral was held at St Mary's Church. His 15 year-old
grandson, Steven, read Kipling's *If* which, he told us, had been granddad's
favourite poem: he had had a framed copy on the wall of his office at
The Dell. Why didn't I know that? Well, somehow it had never occurred
to me to ask Ted about his taste in poetry and he was, of course, renowned
for not volunteering information that had not been asked of him. But then,
as Steven read Kipling's words of advice, it could have been a manager
enjoining his Youth team to take heed:

> *If you can keep your head when all about you*
> *Are losing theirs and blaming it on you;*
> *If you can trust yourself when all men doubt you,*
> *But make allowance for their doubting too;*
> *If you can wait and not be tired by waiting,…*

And so on, climaxing in the pay-off for the young player who follows the
advice and matures to professional status:

> *Yours is the Earth and everything that's in it;*
> *And – which is more - you'll be a Man, my son!*

There are words in the interim, of course, for established players and
managers, too, not least in the second verse:

> *If you can meet with triumph and disaster*
> *And treat those two imposters just the same.*

Mary jokes that the reference to 'triumph and disaster' was especially apt for
a manager of Southampton – there has not been 'much in between; it was
either one or t'other' – but this is not a bad motto, surely, for any manager's
post-match interview. As Lawrie McMenemy has reminded us (at page 332),

DELL DIAMOND

Ted's generation did not do too many of those, but some lines from the first two verses speak to Ted's way of dealing with the media's 'distortions':

Or, being lied about, don't deal in lies,
Or, being hated, don't give way to hating…

…If you can bear to hear the truth you've spoken
Twisted by knaves to make a trap for fools

Those words might equally be applied to his habit of keeping his own counsel when his players were abused by another manager (see page 279). As Brian Hunt puts it, 'Ted would always see the good side: if he didn't like you, you never knew'. And *I* never knew that Kipling had written a guide to temperament for footballers and managers, with special reference to the values that Ted Bates brought to the game. Following Steven to the lectern, Rupert Lowe captured those values in a memorable line of his own: 'the position of the game's curator of honesty and decency is now vacant'.

Mike Channon was quoting nobody, except Ted Bates – 'the original ET', he artfully observed. The words – or, rather, utterances – that he quoted had been regularly used, he claimed, by a manager seeking to stall: 'eh? eh? pardon? pardon? what? what?' This reminded me of George Kirby's assessment (at page 226) that Ted was 'a clever man and a good psychologist' who would pretend not to catch on to the mickey-takers in

the dressing room. Like Kirby, Channon (at the lectern, *right*) clearly admired the approach: he had sometimes adopted it in his management of his stables. The Lad Channon had Done Brilliant. Mary's first choice, Terry Paine, had been unable to get a return flight at short notice. But the sub did not let the side down. Mary thought it was 'great'.

Having accepted Mary's invitation to join the family mourners going on to the crematorium, I witnessed what was for me the most moving moment of the day. As the cortege approached the St Mary's Stadium, two of the bearers alighted and proceeded to lead the procession past the ground on foot. As we came alongside the Itchen Stand, there was a rank of staff – perhaps 40 or more – standing in silence, facing the road. There were no cameras present to record this. Not that I needed a camera – that sight will not leave me in a hurry.

Among the mourners
Left: Ted's two visitors in his final years, Bill Ellerington (left) and John Mortimore.

Above: Two members of the current squad, Matt Oakley (left) and James Beattie.

Below: Ted's family. In the front are (from the left) son-in-law Robert with his son Steven, Mary and younger daughter Jackie.

What that bleak forecourt needs now, of course, is a statue of Ted Bates. That is not what the family favours, although Jo acknowledges that 'what the fans want' should perhaps have precedence. On the eve of the funeral, the *Echo* reported a 100 per cent backing, in a telephone poll, for a statue, but mentioned alternative suggestions, by regular letter-writer, Chris Newman, for a bust in reception – 'out of harm's way' – or perhaps an artist's version of Ted with Lawrie McMenemy holding the FA Cup.

The idea of a bust in the foyer, on the model of Herbert Chapman's at Highbury, appeals to Mary Bates. But it would be seen by only a tiny few on match days. This alternative has its charms, but I can't imagine it satisfying the campaigners for a statue. The Board has ruled out neither a statue nor a bust - although the Chairman is concerned that 'there are many Health and Safety

reasons why a statue is not a particularly great idea'. If that would be no obstacle to a bust indoors, the directors are wary of another problem with any memorial of this kind: 'if we give one to Ted, there will be other people who will be upset if they don't have one'.

It is beyond my comprehension that anybody could think his own claim to such recognition matches that of a man who served the club for a continuous 66 years - which is why I would not endorse Chris Newman's idea of a memorial shared with somebody else, whether it be Lawrie McMenemy or George Reader, or any of the players after whom suites at St Mary's have been named. Ted Bates's service to Southampton FC was *special* and a special memorial is warranted.

Meanwhile, the family has approved the introduction of a Ted Bates Trophy, to be contested each year in a match between Saints and foreign opponents – a variation, Brian Hunt points out, on what the Board did in memory of George Reader, in whose name it established a cup, to be competed for by schoolboys. The new trophy was inaugurated with a 1-1 draw against Bayern Munich on 26 January 2004.

The party for the inaugural presentation of the Ted Bates trophy.
(Left to right): Club President John Mortimore; Ted's daughter, Jackie Jarvis; the captains, who had swapped shirts, Michael Ballack and Jason Dodd; and Vice-Chairman Brian Hunt.

If a trophy in his honour pleases Ted's family, that is sufficient for me to applaud its introduction. But there will be few Saints fans, I imagine, who consider it an adequate memorial to a man whose contribution to Southampton FC and, indeed, to British football, far exceeds anything I imagined when I set out on my journey of discovery in 1995. I expressed, in my original prefatory remarks, the thrill of discovering the esteem of Ted Bates – a theme to which I have returned at the start of this new chapter. I brought it up at his funeral with his sister Alice, whom I had not seen since the *Dell Diamond* launch five years before. I reminded her of an exchange we had had that evening, over dinner:

'I never knew my brother was so famous', she had observed.
'Nor did I, Alice', I had replied.

But now I know. And what a unique privilege the learning process has been.

Sources

It will be obvious that the main source of information for this book has been the interviews with those named on the back cover – and, for this edition, by those thanked at page (xviii) – supplemented by players' press cuttings, mostly from the *Echo,* and by the Board Minutes from 1936-78.

You will also have gathered, from the Preface, how utterly dependent this book has been on those two essential sources on the Saints' history: *Saints – a complete record* (Breedon Books, 1987) and *The Alphabet of the Saints* (Polar, 1992).

The other reference books that I needed always to hand were the relevant years of the *News Chronicle Football Annual,* the *News of the World Football Annual* and the *Rothmans Football Yearbook.* Nor would I have got very far without recourse to Barry Hugman's *Rothmans Football League Players Records* (the 1981 edition sufficed) or *The Breedon Book of Football Managers* (1993) by Dennis Turner and Alex White.

It should be apparent, in the text, where I have drawn upon other books and an article or two:

Richard Adamson, *Bogota Bandit - the outlaw life of Charlie Mitten, Manchester United's Penalty King,* Mainstream, 1996.
David Rayvern Allen, *A Word from Arlott,* Pelham Books, 1983.
Gordon Andrews, *The Datasport Book of Wartime Football 1939-46.*
John Arlott, 'A Southampton Football Epic', *Hampshire: the County Magazine,* June 1963 (reproduced in David Rayvern Allen, *Another Word from Arlott,* Pelham Books, 1985).
Walley Barnes, *Captain of Wales,* Stanley Paul, 1953.
Dave Bowler, *Winning Isn't Everything: a biography of Sir Alf Ramsey,* Gollancz, 1998.
Karren Brady, *Brady Plays the Blues: my Diary of the Season,* Pavilion, 1995.
Ron Burgess, *Football: My Life,* Souvenir Press, 1952.
Noel Cantwell, *United We Stand,* Stanley Paul, 1965.
Mick Channon, *Man on the Run,* Arthur Barker, 1986.
Mike Channon, *Home and Away,* Stanley Paul, 1977.
David Conn, *The Football Business,* Mainstream, 1997.
Anne Coddington, *One of the Lads,* HarperCollins, 1997.
Football Association, *Rules of the Association and Laws of the Game: Season 1963-64,* FA, 1963.

DELL DIAMOND

David Frith, *England versus Australia,* Lutterworth Press, 1981.

George Graham, *The Glory and the Grief,* André Deutsch, 1995.

Jimmy Greaves, *My World of Soccer,* Stanley Paul, 1966.

Aidan Hamilton, *An Entirely Different Game,* Mainstream, 1998.

Ron Harris, *Soccer: the Hard Way,* Pelham Books, 1990.

Martin Jarred and Malcolm Macdonald, *Leeds United - a complete record,* Breedon, 1996.

Brian Johnston, *Someone Who Was,* Methuen, 1992.

Harry Johnston, *The Rocky Road to Wembley,* Sportsmans Book Club, 1957.

Dave Juson, 'Boys from Brazil', *Saints Magazine,* September 1995.

Stephen Kelly, *It's More Important than That,* Virgin, 1996.

Bernard Knowles, *Southampton: the English Gateway,* Hutchinson, 1951.

Denis Law, *Denis Law: an autobiography,* Queen Anne Press, 1979

Lawrie McMenemy, *The Diary of a Season,* Arthur Barker, 1979.

Christopher Martin Jenkins, *The Complete Who's Who of Test Cricketers,* Queen Anne Press, rev. edn., 1987.

Stanley Matthews, *The Stanley Matthews Story,* Oldbourne, 1960.

Max Marquis, *Anatomy of a Football Manager,* Arthur Barker, 1970.

Pelé, *My Life and the Beautiful Game,* Doubleday, 1977.

J.B. Priestley, *The English Journey,* Heinemann, 1934.

Alf Ramsey, *Talking Football,* Stanley Paul, 1952.

Bobby Robson, *Time on the Grass: an autobiography,* Arthur Barker, 1982.

Johnny Rogan, *The Football Managers,* Queen Anne Press, 1989.

Jack Rollin, *Soccer at War 1939-45,* Willow Books, 1985.

Alan Rowlands, *Trautmann: the biography,* Breedon Books, 1990.

Ian St John's Book of Soccer Lists, CollinsWillow, 1995.

Phil Soar and Martin Tyler, *Arsenal 1886-1995,* Hamlyn 1995.

Alec Stock, *A Little thing Called Pride,* Pelham Books, 1982.

Jason Tomas, *The Goal Machine,* Mainstream, 1997.

Dennis Turner and Alex White, *Fulham - a complete record,* Breedon, 1987.

Fred Venables, *Terry Venables: son of Fred,* Weidenfeld and Nicolson, 1990.

Terry Venables and Neil Hanson, *Venables: the autobiography,* Michael Joseph, 1994.

Tom Whittaker, *Arsenal Story,* Sportsmans Book Club, 1958.

Andrew Wilson, 'Special Football Supporters' Trains', *Back Track,* Vol.11, No.9, 1997.

Bob Wilson, *You've Got to be Crazy,* Arthur Barker, 1989.

Billy Wright, *The World's my Football Pitch,* Arrow, 1956.

The Saints Millennium Video, Route One Broadcasting, 1999.